Fundamentals of Human Resource Management

Visit the **Fundamentals of Human Resource Management** Companion
Website **at www.pearsoned.co.uk/torrington** to find valuable student
learning material including:

- Multiple choice questions to test your understanding
- Extra case studies and exercises
- Extensive links to valuable resources on the web
- An online glossary to explain key terms

FUNDAMENTALS OF HUMAN RESOURCE MANAGEMENT

MANAGING PEOPLE AT WORK

Derek Torrington

Laura Hall

Stephen Taylor

Carol Atkinson

FT Prentice Hall
FINANCIAL TIMES

An imprint of **Pearson Education**
Harlow, England • London • New York • Boston • San Francisco • Toronto • Sydney • Singapore • Hong Kong
Tokyo • Seoul • Taipei • New Delhi • Cape Town • Madrid • Mexico City • Amsterdam • Munich • Paris • Milan

Pearson Education Limited
Edinburgh Gate
Harlow
Essex CM20 2JE
England

and Associated Companies throughout the world

Visit us on the World Wide Web at:
www.pearsoned.co.uk

First edition published 2009

ISBN: 978-0-273-71306-7

British Library Cataloguing-in-Publication Data
A catalogue record for this book is available from the British Library

Library of Congress Cataloging-in-Publication Data
Fundamentals of human resource management : managing people at work / Derek Torrington . . . [et al.]. — 1st ed.
    p. cm.
    ISBN 978-0-273-71306-7 (pbk.)
    1. Personnel management – Study and teaching. 2. Supervision of employees – Study and teaching. 3. Personnel management – Great Britain. 4. Supervision of employees – Great Britain. I. Torrington, Derek, 1931– II. Title: Managing people at work.

    HF5549.15.F86 2009
    658.3–dc22

                                                                         2008037200

10 9 8 7 6 5 4 3 2 1
13 12 11 10 09

Typeset in 10/12pt Minion by 35
Printed and bound by Rotolito Lombarda, Italy

The publisher's policy is to use paper manufactured from sustainable forests.

Brief Contents

Managing people: fundamental skills   367

Supporting resources

Visit **www.pearsoned.co.uk/torrington** to find valuable online resources

Companion Website for students
- Multiple choice questions to test your understanding
- Extra case studies and exercises
- Extensive links to valuable resources on the web
- An online glossary to explain key terms

For instructors
- An Instructor's Manual containing teaching notes, additional case studies and class activities
- Powerpoint slides that can be downloaded and used for presentations
- Testbank of assessment questions

Also: The Companion Website provides the following features:

- Search tool to help locate specific items of content
- E-mail results and profile tools to send results of quizzes to instructors
- Online help and support to assist with website usage and troubleshooting

For more information please contact your local Pearson Education sales representative or visit **www.pearsoned.co.uk/torrington**

Contents

Contents

7. Reward management   152

8. Employee relations   181

Contents

3. The appraisal interview

4. Coaching

5. The disciplinary interviews

Contents

Guided Tour

Each chapter opens with **Learning Objectives**, which enable you to focus on what you should have learned by the end of the chapter. These are followed by an opening vignette: a short illustration of the importance of the topic, not always from the world of business organisations!

CHAPTER 6

People development

The objectives of this chapter are to:

1. Review the context and importance of learning and development in the UK
2. Identify the value of learning and development to the organisation and the individual
3. Discuss the role of the line manager in learning and development, with special emphasis on coaching
4. Explain the use and value of competencies in learning and development
5. Explore a range of development methods
6. Debate the value of e-learning

Skills shortages?

Which do you believe poses the greater danger to the future of the UK or you personally: global warming or terrorism? Taking the one you have chosen, would you say that it's a bigger threat to the country or you than avian flu? And how do all these three rate against the skills shortage as menaces to our national prosperity?

Yes, that's right – the skills shortage.

What's that? You say you weren't aware there was a skills shortage?

... this is Peter Kingston in the Guardian's Further Education Editor, writing in 2007, and he goes on to say:

125

Chapter 11 Human Resource strategy

Employee relations implications and challenges

Preparing the whole organisation for what will happen and how it will happen and explaining the reasons behind this is important, where time allows. Constant communication and information is critical at this time. There is evidence that employers will experience a breach of trust in the psychological contract, and handling the downsizing in the most humane and procedurally fair manner is important in minimising this. Survivors, in addition to those who leave, are likely to experience this. One of the authors investigated a company where a previously relational psychological contract was transformed into a transactional contract as a result of downsizing.

The line manager as downsizing agent

Those directly involved in putting a downsizing programme into action include the CEO, HR specialists and potentially all levels of managers. In some very large organisations there may be dedicated downsizing agents but in this section we focus on the role of the line/senior manager who will sometimes be supported by an HR specialist. Molinsky and Margolis (2006) suggest that until recently little attention has been paid to the impact on those individuals who carried out the downsizing. Those who take an active part in a downsizing programme may experience emotional distress, physical pain and fatigue, and Clair and colleagues (2006) suggest that this results in their reduced effectiveness both during and after the programme. It is therefore important to address this issue as it creates concerns both for the managers' well-being and for the performance of the organisation.

> **WINDOW ON PRACTICE**
>
> Molinsky and Margolis (2006) describe the case of Apparel Incorporated (a US Fortune 500 company although the name has been changed to preserve anonymity) which carried out a downsizing programme. The company made a real effort to make sure its processes were procedurally fair and offered generous severance pay and outplacement support. They briefed managers on the reasons for the programme so that they could explain these coherently to all employees, and trained them in how to carry out a termination interview in a respectful and compassionate manner using a common script. Managers were given role play opportunities to practise termination interviews. However, in spite of sound policies and procedures both line managers and HR specialists had great difficulty handling the termination interviews and were often unable to carry these out as planned. The authors argued that this was because the emotions of the managers carrying out these interviews were neglected and not prepared for. The managers experienced anxiety, fear, sympathy, guilt and shame, which they had not expected, when required to deliver the message to friends and colleagues.
>
> Source: A. Molinsky and J. Margolis (2006) 'The emotional tightrope of downsizing: Hidden Challenges for Leaders and their Organizations', Organizational Dynamics, Vol. 35, No. 2, pp. 145–59.

268

Two key features recur regularly through all chapters. The **Window on Practice** focuses on specific examples of theory in action in a readily recognisable context. A wide range of **Activities** encourage you to apply key concepts to your own experience, or to examine the issues in more detail.

Key debate: What are the people management implications of downsizing?

Consequently, these three theories do not necessarily represent simple alternatives. It is also likely that some board directors and even HR managers are not familiar with any of these theories. In spite of this, organisations, through their culture, and individuals within organisations operate on the basis of a set of assumptions, and these assumptions are often implicit. Assumptions about the nature and role of human resource strategy, whether explicit or implicit, will have an influence on what organisations and managers actually do. Assumptions will limit what are seen as legitimate choices.

Understanding these theories enables managers, board members, consultants and the like to interpret the current position of HR strategy in the organisation, confront current assumptions and challenge current thinking and potentially open up a new range of possibilities.

So far we have taken a look at the assumptions behind different ways of approaching HR strategy. Now we move to more practical matters. HR strategy in an organisation may be nothing more than a not very precisely-defined sense of direction, such as 'to be an employer of choice'; alternatively it may be detailed. It may be complete, covering all aspects of human resource management, or it may focus on a current critical issue such as downsizing, to which we now turn our attention.

KEY DEBATE: WHAT ARE THE PEOPLE MANAGEMENT IMPLICATIONS OF DOWNSIZING AND WHERE DOES THE LINE MANAGER FIT IN?

The prevalence and nature of downsizing

The last two decades have seen waves of downsizing in response to competitive pressures, often brought about by changing market demands and processes, increasing use of technology and the utilisation of cheap labour in emerging economies and Third World countries. Downsizing is often associated with restructuring, acquisitions and mergers, in addition to other measures to increase efficiency and minimise costs. Downsizing can be allied to efforts to change the skills base of the organisation and the use of outsourcing and offshoring. We explored in Chapter 1 the impact that downsizing may have in the psychological contract.

> **WINDOW ON PRACTICE**
>
> **Prevalence of downsizing**
>
> As this chapter was being written in late June 2007 the media were awash with downsizing stories.
>
> The first was Cadbury Schweppes which on 19 June reported that it was selling off the US beverages business and had adopted a four-year plan to

261

Each chapter closes with a **Key Debate**, which explores an area of contemporary academic or professional contention and encourages you to exercise your critical thinking skills.

At the end of each chapter, **Summary Propositions** recap and reinforce the key points - they're a useful revision tool. These are followed by **General Discussion** topics which may be used in class discussion, or as a basis for projects and assignments.

Further Reading, Weblinks and **References** have all been specially selected as valuable, relevant and up-to-date so that you can pursue your study of each chapter in more depth and detail.

Visit the Companion Website to this text at **www.pearsoned.co.uk/torrington** to test your understanding with **Self-Assessment Questions**.

Preface

Overview and approach

At the time of writing there has been major economic turbulence due to western economies over-reaching themselves at the beginning of the twenty first century at a time when the Russian economy has begun to grow markedly and those of China and India are expanding dramatically. Behind these developments is the world-wide concern about the supply of oil, gas and other natural resources. Western countries teeter on the brink of recession and the economy of Italy is already shrinking.

Managing people in the business always has to be done within the economic and social context of the individual enterprise, but human behaviour and attitudes are much less volatile than economic circumstances, so we bring this book to our readers as a text in which is embedded an awareness of, and sensitivity to, the economic realities of the first quarter of the twenty first century but rooted in the evidence and research findings that already exist.

This book is about managing people and is directed at those who are not HR specialists, either as students or professionals. The rationale is that all managers – indeed everyone who goes to work – have an interest in, experience of, and responsibility for human resource management. All managers need to know about it, and need to develop competence in some aspects, while relying on their HR colleagues for the more specialised elements.

In line with our aim of addressing primarily students on general business and management or related degree programmes, rather than specialist students of HRM, we have first covered all the essential areas that managers need to understand and be able to implement. Secondly, we have written the material from the perspective of people outside the field and role of HRM, whether they be in managerial roles or not. Thirdly we have reviewed especially our understanding of previous periods when economic slowdown or similar changes brought about changes that affected employment practices, like the shift in the west away from manufacturing towards services as the main driver of the economy. All this is built in to the text to ensure that it is absolutely relevant for to-day and to-morrow, no matter what fashionable ideas may come and go.

Structure

Our overall structure is of fifteen chapters. Each chapter deals with the broad topic area of its chapter title, before concluding with an exploration of one particular key and contemporary issue within that topic area. This aims to engage the reader as deeply as possible within this area and focus on the practical considerations for a line manager.

At the end of the book, we include some additional skills-based material that equips students with the necessary competences which are central to managing people in different face-to-face situations.

Learning features

There are several design features to assist readers further in using and learning from the text; these include:

- **Window on Practice boxes** provide a range of illustrative material throughout the text, including examples of real company practice, survey results, anecdotes and quoted material, and court cases.
- **Activity boxes** encourage readers to review and critically apply their understanding at regular intervals throughout the text, either by responding to a question or by undertaking a small practical assignment, individually or as part of a group.
- **Discussion topics**: at the end of each chapter there are two or three short questions intended for general discussion in a tutorial or study group.
- **Web links** are given as appropriate at various points in the text. These are either to the text's companion website, where there is a great deal of further material, or to other websites containing useful information relating to the topics covered.
- **Annotated readings** for each chapter suggest further relevant readings, with guidance on their value.
- **Chapter objectives** to open and **Summary propositions** to conclude: each chapter sets up the readers' expectations and reviews their understanding progressively.
- There are full **references** at the end of each chapter to aid further exploration of the chapter material, as required.
- **Website: www.pearsoned.co.uk/torrington** has more material, including case studies or exercises for each chapter and support for both tutor and student.

Reviewers

This book has gone through an intensive review process to ensure it really meets the needs of non-specialist students in HRM. We would like to thank the reviewers who have read chapters at every stage in the development of this new book and we are very grateful for their insightful comments and recommendations. Our thanks go to:

Dr. David Banner, University of Westminster
Dr. Rory Donnelly, University of Manchester
Dr. Susan Durbin, University of the West of England
Jocelyne Fleming, University of Gloucestershire
Dr. Geraint Harvey, Swansea University
Dr. Lesley Mearns, University of Newcastle
Dr. Kevin Morrell, University of Birmingham
Jeff Newall, University of Derby
Ann Pendleton, University of Bolton
Dr. Linda Perriton, University of York
Dr. Louise Preget, Bournemouth University
Dr. Peter Samuel, University of Nottingham
Dr. Nick Wilton, University of the West of England

Acknowledgements

We are grateful to the following for permission to reproduce copyright material:

Figure 1.2 from *Fairness at Work and the Psychological Contract* (1998) written by D. Guest and N. Conway with the permission of the publisher, the Chartered Institute of Personnel and Development, London (www.cipd.co.uk); Figure 2.1 originally published in *People Management* (1984), and reproduced with permission; Table 3.1 and Figure 4.1 from *Survey Report: Recruitment, Retention and Turnover* (2007) with the permission of the publisher, the Chartered Institute of Personnel and Development, London (www.cipd.co.uk); Table 3.2 source: National Statistics website: www.statistics.gov.uk. Crown copyright material is reproduced with the permission of the Controller Office of Public Sector Information (OPSI); Table 4.1 from *Human Resource Management: A Contemporary Approach*, Pearson Education Ltd. (Beardwell, I., Holden, L. and Claydon, T. 2004); Table 5.2 from 360 degree feedback from another angle in *Human Resource Management*, reprinted with permission of John Wiley & Sons, Inc. (Bracken, D.., Timmreck, C., Fleenor, J. and Summers, L. 2001); Figure 5.3 and Table 5.3 from *Managing Performance: Performance Management in Action* (2005) written by M. Armstrong and A. Baron with the permission of the publisher, the Chartered Institute of Personnel and Development, London (www.cipd.co.uk); Figure 6.1 from *The Competencies Handbook* (1999) written by S. Whiddett and S. Hollyforde with the permission of the publisher, the Chartered Institute of Personnel and Development, London (www.cipd.co.uk); Figure 7.3 from *Strategic Reward*, Kogan Page Limited (Armstrong, M. and Brown, D. 2006); Figure 8.1 from Bach, S. (Ed) *Managing Human Resources: Personnel Management in Transition 4th Ed.*, Oxford: Blackwell (Marchington, M. and Wilkinson, A. 2005); Table 10.1 from Employers move on equal pay in *IDS Report No. 897*, IDS, (2004); Figure 11.1 and Figure 11.2 from *Strategic Human Resource Management*, reprinted with permission of John Wiley & Sons, Inc. (Fombrun, C., Tichy, N..M. and Devanna, M.A. 1984*)*; Table 11.1 from Linking competitive strategies with human resource management practices in *The Academy of Management Executive*, © The Academy of Management Executive, (Schuler, R.S. and Jackson, S.E. 1987); Figure 11.3 from Human Resources and sustained competitive advantage: a resource-based perspective in *International Journal of Human Resource Management*, Taylor and Francis Ltd. (Wright, P., McMahon, G. and McWilliams, A. 1994), reprinted by permission of the publisher (Taylor & Francis Ltd, http://www.tandf.co.uk/journals); Table 12.1 adapted from *The Managerial Grid*, Grid International, Inc. (Blake R.R. and Houston J.S. 1964); Table 12.2 from *Management of Organizational Behavior: Utilizing Human Resources, 5th Edition*, Pearson Education, (Hersey, P. and Blanchard, K.H. 1988); Table 12.3 reprinted by permission of *Harvard Business Review* from Leadership that gets results by D. Goleman, March–April, 2000. Copyright © 2000 by the

Harvard Business School Publishing Corporation, all rights reserved; Table 13.1 from *Survey Report: The changing HR function* (2007) with the permission of the publisher, the Chartered Institute of Personnel and Development, London (www.cipd.co.uk).

MS p. 36 Atkinson C., *Career Development International*, volume 7, issue 1, pp. 14–23 © Emerald Group Publishing Limited all rights reserved.; MS p. 69 Dick P., *Personnel Review*, volume 33, issue 3, pp. 302–321 © Emerald Group Publishing Limited all rights reserved; MS p.138 from O2 hires on Performance in *People Management*, (Philips, L. 2007); MS p. 142 from First-line filter: screening candidates for selection in *Employment Review*, IRS (Suff R. 2005), IRS is part of the XPERTHR Group – www.xperthr.co.uk; MS p.178 from Orange Blossoms in *People Management*, (Johnson, R. 2006); MS p. 189 from This is not a circular in *People Management*, (F. Storr 2000); MS p. 196 from Human Factors International (www.hfi.com); MS p. 207 from Short Changed *in People Management*, (Kingston P. 2007); MS p. 213 adapted from *Change Agenda: Learning and the Line: The role of line managers in training, learning and development* (2007) written by S. Hutchinson and J. Purcell with the permission of the publisher, the Chartered Institute of Personnel and Development, London (www.cipd.co.uk); MS p. 240 from Julie Diligent in *People Management*, (Clarke E. 2006); MS p. 272 from Investing in Excellence at the Crown Prosecution Service in *Employment Review*, IRS (Suff R. 2006), IRS is part of the XPERTHR Group – www.xperthr.co.uk; MS p. 334 from Downloading pornography in *IDS Brief 637*, IDS, (1999); MS p. 354 reprinted by permission of *Harvard Business Review* from Winning the talent war for women: sometimes it takes a revolution by D. McCracken, November–December, 2000. Copyright © 2000 by the Harvard Business School Publishing Corporation, all rights reserved; MS p. 366 adapted from Arriva: dramatic results on diversity in *Equal Opportunities Review* , Michael Rubenstein Publishing (Wolff C. 2007); MS p. 397 from Human resource management strategies under uncertainty in *Cross Cultural Management: An International Journal*, volume 13, No 2 pp. 171–186, SAGE Publications (Fields D., Chan A., Aktar S. and Blum T. 2006); MS p. 439 from In at the deep end in *People Management*, (Smedley T. 2007); MS p. 469 from One step beyond in *People Management*, (Pickard J 2004); MS p. 490 from I*nternational Management, 6*[th] *Edition*, Pearson Education, (Deresky, H. 2008).

We are grateful to the Financial Times Limited for permission to reprint the following material:

Chapter 8 Employees want to hear it 'straight' from the boss's mouth!, © Financial Times, 1 December 2006.

In some instances we have been unable to trace the owners of copyright material, and we would appreciate any information that would enable us to do so.

CHAPTER 1

Introducing human resource management

The objectives of this chapter are to:

1 Explain the different ways in which the term 'human resource management' is used

2 Set out the main objectives of the human resource function

3 Explore the contribution of HRM activity to the achievement of organisational objectives

4 Describe the major contemporary trends in the business environment that are affecting HRM practice

5 Review key current developments in human resource management

6 Debate the state of the psychological contract in UK organisations

In March 2008, twenty-five years after it was first planned, Terminal Five at Heathrow Airport in London finally opened its doors to passengers. The total cost of the building was £4.3 billion. The new terminal was exclusively for the use of British Airways, which had been planning for several years to move all its existing operations from the various other terminals at Heathrow into Terminal Five and had gone as far as to contribute £330 million to its flamboyant interior design. The day before the opening an article in the *Financial Times* reported executives' concerns that the look of the place would raise expectations too high, but that it was 'beyond imagination to contemplate failure' (Blitz, 2008). Yet spectacular failure was what followed.

▶

▶ In the first few days of operation over 300 flights scheduled to depart from Terminal Five were cancelled, very long queues formed at check-in and transfer desks, while some 28,000 passengers found themselves separated from their luggage. The immediate cost to British Airways was £16 million, but the long-term direct costs were authoritatively estimated to be around £150 million (BBC 2008a), quite apart from vast further losses resulting from a deterioration in the airline's already poor brand image.

And why did this debacle happen? It appears that the major reason was simply extaordinarily poor management of people. The major immediate problem arose because the staff were not properly trained to use the equipment at Terminal Five and were unprepared when it came to solving the technical 'glitches' that quickly appeared once the baggage-handling machinery started operating. In addition long delays were caused on the first day as a result of staff being unable to find the staff car park or get through security screening on schedule. Later on, as flights began to arrive, staff simply failed to 'remove luggage quickly enough at the final unloading stage' (BBC 2008b).

Matters were not helped by the persistence over a long period of poor employment relationships at British Airways. Done and Willman (2008) reported that the failure of the airline to solve this fundamental problem was the real underlying cause of the Terminal Five debacle. An unnamed Heathrow executive said that they had all been expecting an outbreak of 'fuck'em disease' as the new Terminal opened and some staff simply decided 'not to work very hard'. British Airways' staff were not committed either to the success of the operation or to their employer. Goodwill was in short supply leading staff to be intransigent and unco-operative when effort, positive enthusiasm and flexibility were what was required.

All organisations have to draw on a range of resources to function and to achieve their objectives. They need access to capital to finance their operations, land and premises to operate from, energy, equipment and raw materials in order to manufacture a product or deliver a service. They also require access to some form of distribution network so that they can publicise, sell or dispense their goods and services. In addition, human resources are required in order to provide organisations with know-how, ideas and manpower. In a competitive market economy the effectiveness and efficiency with which an organisation manages its relationship with the suppliers of all these kinds of resources determines its success. And the scarcer the resource and the more critical it is to a particular organisation's operations, the greater the skill, time and effort needed in order to manage the relationship (Hatch 1997, pp. 78–81).

There was a time when most people employed by organisations were required simply to provide manual labour. Relatively little skill, experience or intelligence was needed to do the jobs. The requisite training was cheap and speedy to provide, and payment methods unsophisticated. Finding people to do the work was rarely a problem and there were no restrictions of significance when it came to firing those who were not satisfactory or who displeased managers in some other way. This remains the situation in some industries and in some parts of the world, but in industrialised countries such as the UK it is now rare. Instead we have a situation in which the great majority of jobs require their holders to have mastered some form of specialised skill, or at the very least to possess attributes which others do not share to the same extent (National Statistics 2006, p. 7). The demand for higher-level skills has grown particularly quickly, there being a need for many more people to fill professional and managerial jobs than was the case twenty years ago. Moreover, almost all informed commentators believe that these established trends will accelerate in the future.

Just as the workforce has changed, so have the methods used to manage its members. The more specialised their roles, the harder it has become to find individuals with the right skills, qualifications, attributes and experience to undertake them. It has also become harder to keep people once they are employed because competitors are always keen to secure the services of the most talented people by offering them a better deal. Employing organisations have had to acquire a capacity for developing people effectively, together with increasingly sophisticated approaches to recruitment, selection, retention, employee relations and performance management. Further sophistication is required thanks to the substantial body of employment regulation that now governs the management of the employment relationship in countries like the UK.

These developments have led to the evolution of an increasingly complex human resource management function, charged with overseeing all aspects of managing the relationship between an organisation and its people in a professional and productive manner. The management of people, however, can never be a responsibility shouldered by specialists alone. It is an area of management activity that all managers must share if it is to be carried out effectively and contribute to the achievement of competitive advantage.

In this chapter we introduce HRM by setting out its purpose and showing how the effective management of people helps organisations to achieve their objectives. We go on to identify the key current environmental trends that are having an impact on HRM in organisations, before considering some of the major general HRM issues which contemporary organisations are having to grapple with. Our 'Key Debate' in this chapter concerns the state of the psychological contract in UK workplaces. Are the expectations of employers and employees as far as their relationship is concerned in the process of changing fundamentally? Or is there in fact more continuity than change in the way we and our managers view the nature of our association?

DEFINING HUMAN RESOURCE MANAGEMENT

The term 'human resource management' is not easy to define. This is because it is commonly used in two different ways. On the one hand it is used generically to describe the body of management activities covered in books such as this. Used in this way HRM is really no more than a more modern and supposedly imposing name for what has long been labelled 'personnel management'. On the other hand, the term is also widely used to denote a particular approach to the management of people which is clearly distinct from 'personnel management'. Used in this way 'HRM' signifies more than an updating of the label; it also suggests a distinctive philosophy towards carrying out people-oriented organisational activities: one which is held to serve the modern business more effectively than 'traditional' personnel management (Guest 1987, Legge 1995). In this book we will use the first of these two definitions.

The role of the human resource function is best explained by identifying the key objectives to be achieved. Four objectives form the foundation of all HR activity. These are: staffing objectives, performance objectives, change-management objectives and administration objectives.

Staffing objectives

Human resource managers are first concerned with ensuring that the business is appropriately staffed and thus able to draw on the human resources it needs. This involves designing organisation structures, identifying under what type of contract different groups of employees (or subcontractors) will work, before recruiting, selecting and developing the people required to fill the roles: the right people, with the right skills to provide their services when needed. There is a need to compete effectively in the employment market by recruiting and retaining the best, affordable workforce that is available. This involves developing employment packages that are sufficiently attractive to maintain the required employee skills levels and, where necessary, disposing of those judged no longer to have a role to play in the organisation. The tighter a key employment market becomes, the harder it is to find and then to hold on to the people an organisation needs in order to compete effectively. In such circumstances increased attention has to be given to developing competitive pay packages, to the provision of valued training and development opportunities and to ensuring that the experience of working in the organisation is, as far as is possible, rewarding and fulfilling.

Performance objectives

Once the required workforce is in place, human resource managers seek to ensure that people are well motivated and committed so as to maximise their performance in their different roles. Training and development has a role to play, as do reward systems to maximise effort and focus attention on performance targets. In many organisations, particularly where trade unions play a significant role, human resource managers negotiate improved performance with the workforce. The achievement of performance objectives also requires HR specialists to assist in disciplining employees effectively and equitably where individual conduct and/or performance standards are unsatisfactory. Welfare functions can also assist performance by providing constructive assistance to people whose performance has fallen short of their potential because of illness or difficult personal circumstances. Last but not least, there is the range of employee involvement initiatives to raise levels of commitment and to engage employees in developing new ideas. It is increasingly recognised that a key determinant of superior competitive performance is a propensity on the part of an organisation's employees to demonstrate **discretionary effort**. Essentially this means that they choose to go further in the service of their employer than is strictly required in their contracts of employment, working longer hours perhaps, working with greater enthusiasm or taking the initiative to improve systems and relationships. Willingness to engage in such behaviour cannot be forced by managers. But they can help to create an environment in which it is more likely to occur (Purcell 1993).

Change-management objectives

A third set of core objectives in nearly every business relates to the role played by the HR function in effectively managing change. Frequently change does not come along in readily defined episodes precipitated by some external factor. Instead it is endemic and well-nigh continuous, generated as much by a continual need to innovate as from definable environmental pressures. Change comes in different forms. Sometimes it is merely structural, requiring reorganisation of activities or the introduction of new people into particular roles. At other times cultural change is sought in order to alter attitudes, philosophies or long-present organisational norms. In any of these scenarios the HR function can play a central role. Key activities include the recruitment and/or development of people with the necessary leadership skills to drive the change process, the employment of change agents to encourage acceptance of change and the construction of reward systems which underpin the change process. Timely and effective employee involvement is also crucial because 'people support what they help to create' (Evans 1994).

Administration objectives

The fourth type of objective is less directly related to achieving competitive advantage, but is focused on underpinning the achievement of the other forms of objective. In part it is simply carried out in order to facilitate an organisation's smooth running. Hence there is a need to maintain accurate and comprehensive data on individual employees, a record of their achievement in terms of performance, their attendance and training records, their terms and conditions of employment and their personal details. However, there is also a legal aspect to much administrative activity, meaning that it is done because the business is required by law to comply. It is particularly important that payment is administered professionally and lawfully, with itemised monthly pay statements being provided for all employees. There is also the need to make arrangements for the deduction of taxation and national insurance, for the payment of pension fund contributions and to be on top of the complexities associated with Statutory Sick Pay and Statutory Maternity Pay, as well as maternity and paternity leave. Additional legal requirements relate to the monitoring of health and safety systems and the issuing of contracts to new employees. Accurate record keeping is central to ensuring compliance with a variety of newer legal obligations such as the National Minimum Wage and the Working Time Regulations. HR professionals often downgrade the significance of effective administration, seeking instead to gain for themselves a more glamorous (and usually more highly paid) role formulating policy and strategy. This is short-sighted. Achieving excellence, professionalism and cost effectiveness in delivering the basic administrative tasks is not only important in itself; it also helps the HR function in an organisation to gain and maintain the credibility and respect that are required in order to influence other managers in the organisation.

Activity 1.1

Each of the four types of HR objective is important and necessary for organisations in different ways. However, at certain times one or more can assume greater importance than the others. Can you identify types of situation in which each could become the most significant or urgent?

Delivering HRM objectives

The larger the organisation, the more scope there is to employ people to specialise in particular areas of HRM. Some, for example, employ employee relations specialists to look after the collective relationship between management and employees. Where there is a strong tradition of collective bargaining, the role is focused on the achievement of satisfactory outcomes from ongoing negotiations. Increasingly, however, employee relations specialists are required to provide advice about legal developments, to manage consultation arrangements and to preside over employee involvement initiatives.

Another common area of specialisation is in the field of training and development. Although much of this is now undertaken by external providers, there is still a role for in-house trainers, particularly in management development. Increasingly the term 'consultant' is used instead of 'officer' or 'manager' to describe the training specialist's role, indicating a shift towards a situation in which line managers determine the training *they* want rather than the training section providing a standardised portfolio of courses. The other major specialist roles are in the fields of recruitment and selection, health, safety and welfare, compensation and benefits, and human resource planning.

In addition to the people who have specialist roles there are many other people who are employed as human resources or personnel generalists. Working alone or in small teams, they carry out the range of HR activities and seek to achieve all the objectives outlined above. In larger businesses generalists either look after all personnel matters in a particular division or are employed at a senior level to develop policy and take responsibility for HR issues across the organisation as a whole. In more junior roles, human resource administrators and assistants undertake many of the administrative tasks mentioned earlier. It is increasingly common for organisations to separate the people responsible for undertaking routine administration and even basic advice from those employed to manage case work, to develop policies and to manage the strategic aspects of the HR role. In some cases the administrative work is outsourced to specialist providers, while in others a **shared services model** has been established whereby a centralised administrative function is distinguished from decentralised teams of HR advisers working as part of management teams in different divisions (*see* Reilly 2000). Figure 1.1 summarises the roles and objectives of HRM.

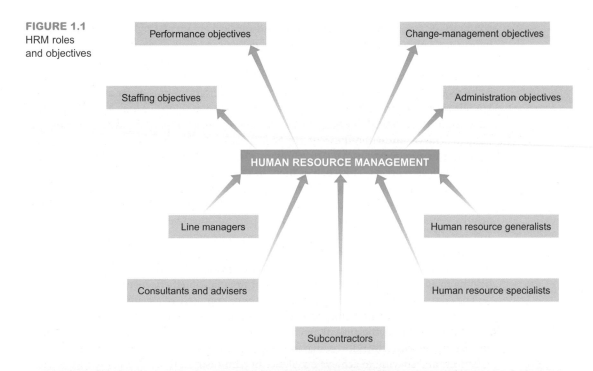

FIGURE 1.1
HRM roles
and objectives

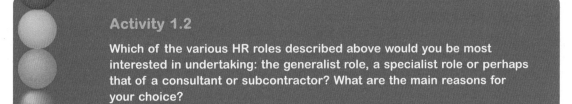

Activity 1.2

Which of the various HR roles described above would you be most interested in undertaking: the generalist role, a specialist role or perhaps that of a consultant or subcontractor? What are the main reasons for your choice?

HRM AND THE ACHIEVEMENT OF ORGANISATIONAL EFFECTIVENESS

For the past decade the theme which has dominated the HR research agenda has been the study of links between HR practices and organisational effectiveness. Throughout the book we make reference to this research in the context of different HR activities, but it is helpful briefly to set out at the start how what happens in the field of HR impacts on an organisation's ability to meet its objectives.

What those objectives are will vary depending on the type of organisation and its situation. For most businesses operating in the private sector the overriding long-term objective is the achievement and maintenance of competitive advantage, by which is meant a sustained period of commercial success vis-à-vis its principal competitors. For others, however, ensuring survival is a more pressing objective. In the public and voluntary sectors notions of competition and survival are increasingly present too, but here organisational effectiveness is primarily defined in terms of meeting a service need as cost efficiently as possible and to the highest achievable standard of quality. Meeting government-set targets is central to the operation of many public sector organisations, as is the requirement to ensure that the expectations of users are met as far as is possible. For all sizeable organisations there is also a need to foster a positive long-term corporate reputation (Roberts and Dowling 2002). Developing such a reputation can take many years to achieve, but without care it can be lost very quickly with very damaging results. In particular, organisations need to maintain a strong reputation for sound management in the financial markets. This enables them to raise money with relative ease when it is needed and also helps to ensure that managers of investment funds and financial advisers see it or its shares as a desirable place to put their clients' money. The maintenance of a positive reputation in the media is also an important objective as this helps to maintain and grow the customer base. In this context corporate ethics and social responsibility are increasingly significant because they are becoming more prominent factors in determining the purchasing decisions of consumers. The HR function should play a significant role in helping to achieve each of these dimensions of organisational effectiveness.

The contribution of the HR function to *gaining* competitive advantage involves achieving the fundamental aims of an organisation in the field of people management more effectively and efficiently than competitor organisations. These aims were discussed above – mobilising a workforce, maximising its performance, managing change effectively and striving to achieve excellence in administration.

The contribution of the HR function to *maintaining* competitive advantage involves recognising the significance of the organisation's people as an effective barrier preventing would-be rivals from expanding their markets into territory that the first organisation holds. The term **human capital** is used more and more often in this context to signify that the combined knowledge and experience of an organisation's staff is a highly significant source of competitive advantage largely because it is difficult for competitors to replicate easily. Attracting, engaging, rewarding, developing and retaining people effectively is thus vital. Failing to do so enables accumulated human capital to leak away into the hands of competitors, reducing the effectiveness of commercial defences and making it harder to maintain competitive advantage.

Fostering a positive reputation among would-be investors, financial advisers and financial journalists is also an aspect of organisational effectiveness to which the HR function makes a significant contribution. Key here is the need to reassure those whose job is to assess the long-term financial viability of the organisation that it is competently managed and is well placed to meet the challenges that lie ahead in both the short and the longer term. The ability to attract and retain a strong management team is central to achieving this aspect of organisational effectiveness as is the ability of the organisation to plan for the future by having in place effective succession planning arrangements and robust systems for the development of the skills and knowledge that will be key in the future. Above all financial markets need to be assured that the organisation is stable and is thus a safe repository for investors' funds. The work of Stevens and his colleagues (2005) is helpful in this context. They conceive of the whole human resource contribution in terms of the management of risk, the aim being to ensure that an organisation 'balances the maximisation of opportunities and the minimisation of risks'.

Finally, the HR function also plays a central role in building an organisation's reputation as an ethically or socially responsible organisation (Pinnington *et al.* 2007). This happens in two distinct ways. The first involves fostering an understanding of and commitment to ethical conduct on the part of managers and staff. It is achieved by paying attention to these objectives in recruitment campaigns, in the criteria adopted for the selection of new employees and the promotion of staff, in the methods used to develop people and in performance management processes. The second relates to the manner in which people are managed. A poor ethical reputation can be gained simply because an organisation becomes known for treating its staff poorly. In recent years well-known brands of fast food chain in the UK have suffered because of their use of zero hours contracts, while several large multinationals have had their reputations stained by stories in the media about the conditions under which their employees in developing countries are required to work.

Activity 1.3

Which organisations in your area have the best reputations as an employer? Which have the worst reputation? Why is this? To what extent do you think it would benefit the poorer employers to improve their reputations and why?

MAJOR TRENDS IN THE HRM BUSINESS ENVIRONMENT

The major trends in our contemporary business environment are well understood, well documented and uncontroversial. People differ, though, in their understanding of the speed of change and of the extent to which all organisations are or will be affected. As far as product markets are concerned the big trend is towards ever more intense competitive pressures, leading some to argue that we are now entering the era of hyper-competition (Sparrow 2003, p. 371). This is being driven by two major developments, the significance of which has increased considerably in recent years.

First, we are witnessing moves towards the globalisation of economic activity on a scale that has not been experienced before in human history. More and more, the markets for the goods and products we sell are international, which means of course that competition for those markets as well as our established ones is also increasingly becoming international. Large organisations that were able to dominate national markets a decade or two ago (many owned and operated by governments) are now mainly privately owned and faced with vastly more competition from similar organisations based all over the world. This has led to consolidation through the construction of global corporations and strategic alliances whose focus in terms of people management is also international.

The second major antecedent of hyper-competition is technology, which moves forward at an ever-accelerating pace year by year. Developments in information technology, energy production, chemical engineering, laser technology, transportation and biotechnology are in the process of revolutionising the way that many industries operate. It is partly the sheer pace of change and the need for organisations to stay ahead of this very fast-moving game which drives increased competition. Being the first to develop and make efficient use of new technologies is the means by which many organisations maintain their competitive position and can thus grow and prosper. But IT, and in particular the growth of e-business, is significant too because it has the potential to increase greatly the number of competitors that any one organisation faces. This is because it makes it much easier for customers and potential customers to compare the price and quality of what your organisation offers with what others can offer.

What does this mean in practical terms from the point of view of the HR manager? First, it means that practices continually have to be developed which have the effect of enhancing an organisation's competitive position. Ways need to be found of improving quality and of bringing to market attractive new products and services, while at the same time ensuring that the organisation remains competitive in terms of its cost base. Secondly, it means that a good deal of volatility is the norm and that change, often of a profound nature, is something that people working in organisations must expect and be ready for. So a capacity for organisational flexibility has become central to the achievement and maintenance of competitive advantage. Thirdly, there are direct practical outcomes. For example, HR managers have to learn how to manage an international workforce effectively and how best to attract, retain, develop and motivate people with those relatively scarce skills that are essential if an organisation is effectively to harness and deploy evolving technologies.

For the HR manager, however, unlike colleagues in other areas of management, responding to product market developments is only part of what is needed. Other major trends are equally important and must also be understood and built into decision making. There are two areas which are particularly important:

- labour market trends
- the evolution of employment regulation

Developments in the labour market are significant partly in terms of the numbers of people and skills available, and partly in terms of attitudes towards work and the workplace. Major developments appear to be occurring in both these areas. Many industries, for example, have found themselves facing skills shortages in recent years (CIPD 2007, p. 4). The impact varies from country to country depending on relative economic prosperity, but most organisations in the UK have seen a tightening of their key labour markets in recent years. Unemployment levels have remained low, while demographic trends have created a situation in which the number of older people retiring is greater than the number of younger people entering the job market. There are all kinds of implications. For a start, employers are having to make themselves more attractive to employees than has been necessary in recent years. No longer can they simply assume that people will seek work with them or seek to remain employed with them. In a tight labour market individuals have more choice about where and when they work, and do not need to put up with a working environment in which they are unhappy. If they do not like their jobs there are more opportunities for them to look elsewhere. So organisations are increasingly required to compete with one another in labour markets as well as in product markets. This has implications for policy in all areas of HRM, but particularly in the areas of reward, employee development and recruitment.

Labour market conditions along with other social trends serve to shape the attitudes of people towards their work. In order to mobilise and motivate a workforce, HR managers must be aware of how these are changing and to respond effectively. One of the most significant trends in recent years, for example, has been a reduced interest on the part of employees in joining trade unions and taking part in their activities. A more individualistic attitude now prevails in the majority of workplaces, people focusing on themselves and their own career development rather than standing in solidarity with fellow workers. Another well-documented trend is the increased desire for employees to achieve a better balance between their home and work lives and their increased willingness to seek out employers who can provide this.

The growth in the extent and complexity of employment regulation is a third area which HR managers are obliged to grasp and the elements of which they must implement in their organisations. Before 1970, with one or two exceptions, there was no statutory regulation of the employment relationship in the UK. An individual's terms and conditions of employment were those that were stated in the contract of employment and in any collective agreements. The law did not intervene beyond providing some basic health and safety protection, the right to modest redundancy payments and a general requirement on employers and employees to honour the contractual terms agreed when the employment began. Since 1970 this situation has wholly changed (Shackleton 2005). The individual contract of employment remains significant and can be enforced in court if necessary, but there has been added to this a whole range of statutory rights which employers are obliged to honour. The most significant are in the fields of health and safety, equal pay, unlawful discrimination and unfair dismissal. Much recent new law such as that on working time, family-friendly rights, consultation and discrimination on grounds of sexual orientation, age and belief has a European origin, and a great deal more can be expected in the years ahead.

Activity 1.4

It is often argued that the impact of current environmental trends is to make HRM harder to carry out effectively. To what extent do you agree with this point of view and why?

MAJOR THEMES IN CONTEMPORARY HRM PRACTICE

As you read this book you will be introduced to a range of debates, some concerning operational issues, some focusing on strategy, some theoretical, some ethical and others which concern the impact on HRM practice of longer-term developments in the business environment. However, it is helpful, before we start to introduce the various areas of HRM activity, to introduce some of the broader underlying issues which are having a significant impact in more general terms.

Skills shortages

The dominant feature of the current HRM environment in the UK is the combination of increasingly competitive product markets with increasingly tight labour markets. On the one hand this means that employers are having to compete harder to recruit and retain the staff they need. At the same time, however, highly competitive markets for goods and services are putting a premium on operational efficiency. The result is that organisations are unable to compete for talent simply by paying people more money. The environment is thus resource constrained at a time when skills shortages are prevalent. There is nothing new about this situation in some industries and organisations. What is new now is that the majority of organisations are affected and the problem is long-term rather than temporary. As a result many of the HRM initiatives that are generating most interest at present are those which serve to improve employees' experience of working life in organisations, but which do not cost a great deal to implement. You will read about many of these later in the book. Good examples are the development of 'total reward' perspectives, employee engagement initiatives and the development of employer branding.

Best practice versus best fit

The debate between best practice and best fit is both interesting and significant and has consequences across the field of HRM. As well as being a managerial issue it concerns one of the most significant academic controversies in the HR field at present. At root it is about whether or not there is an identifiable 'best way' of carrying out HR activities which is universally applicable.

Adherents of a best practice perspective argue that there are certain HR practices and approaches to their operation which will invariably help an organisation in achieving competitive advantage. There is therefore a clear link between HR activity and business performance, but the effect will only be maximised if the 'right' HR policies are pursued. While there are differences of opinion on questions of detail, all strongly suggest that the same basic bundle of human resource practices or that a general human resource management orientation tends to enhance business performance in all organisations irrespective of the particular product market strategy being pursued. The main elements of the 'best practice bundle' that these and other writers identify are those which have long been considered as examples of good practice in the HRM field. They include the use of the more advanced selection methods, a serious commitment to employee involvement, substantial investment in training and development, the use of individualised reward systems and harmonised terms and conditions of employment as between different groups of employees.

The alternative 'best fit' school also identifies a link between human resource management practice and the achievement of competitive advantage. Here, however, there is no belief in the existence of universal solutions. Instead, all is **contingent** on the particular circumstances of each organisation. What is needed is HR policies and practices which 'fit' and are thus appropriate to the situation of individual employers. What is appropriate (or 'best') for one will not necessarily be right for another. Key variables include the size of the establishment, the dominant product market strategy being pursued and the nature of the labour markets in which the organisation competes. It is thus argued that a small organisation which principally achieves competitive advantage through innovation and which competes in very tight labour markets should have in place rather different HR policies than those of a large firm which produces low-cost goods and faces no difficulty in attracting staff. In order to maximise competitive advantage, the first requires informality combined with sophisticated human resource practices, while the latter needs more bureaucratic systems combined with a 'low cost, no frills' set of HR practices.

To a great extent the jury is still out on these questions. Interestingly, however, some fields of HRM practice are dominated by best practice thinking, while others broadly accept best fit assumptions. A good example of the former is employee selection, while reward management provides a good example of a field in which best fit thinking prevails.

Ethics, regulatory compliance and competitive advantage

One element of 'good practice', if not 'best practice', is a commitment on the part of an organisation to manage the relationship with its people ethically and in accordance with the expectations of the law. The trouble is that this can be quite a costly aspiration. First, it tends to reduce flexibility due to the requirement for lengthy procedures to be followed when dismissing, recruiting and managing performance. Secondly, it restricts the ability of managers to take decisions purely in the interests of the organisation. Instead a balance must be struck between this and the legitimate interests of employees.

The dilemma is effectively illustrated with reference to the management of an employee who is not performing adequately – a very common situation. Provided the employee has completed more than a year's service, the expectation of the law is that the employer will act 'reasonably', following the guidance given in the handbook issued by the Advisory, Conciliation and Arbitration Service (ACAS). This requires the employer to hold a formal meeting to discuss the matter, to give a formal warning to the employee concerned and then to put in place measures to help them reach an acceptable standard of performance. The position must then be formally reviewed after sufficient time has passed to permit the employee to demonstrate the required improvement. Failure to do so should result in the issuing of a further warning and a further opportunity to improve. Only after this has failed to produce an adequate standard of performance can the employee be dismissed. It is a long-winded process which can take several months to complete, during which time relationships can become very strained. Compliance with the ACAS procedure is what the law expects and also represents a fair and ethical approach. But it is not necessarily good for a business seeking to maintain high standards in a competitive marketplace.

Alternative approaches are thus always being sought, some of which carry a degree of risk. Sometimes managers will dismiss in the full knowledge that they are acting unlawfully, calculating that the employee will soon find alternative employment and will not choose to pursue the matter to an employment tribunal. Another approach is simply to pay the person concerned a sum of money that is equal to or slightly greater than that they would win in the tribunal, again hoping that no legal action will then follow. The danger is that it might, leading not just to legal bills, but also to negative publicity and the development of a reputation as a poor employer.

The more employment regulation that is introduced, the greater the number of situations in which dilemmas such as this have to be faced and decisions made about how to proceed. The choices are often difficult. Should we do what is most effective and efficient, if somewhat risky? Or should we act ethically and lawfully, even if the short-term interests of the organisation may suffer as a result?

Sustainable flexibility

Another contemporary issue in HRM which has general significance is an apparent clash between two very different organisational imperatives. On the one hand, the fast-changing nature of the competitive environment dictates that organisations must develop a capacity for flexibility if they are to compete effectively. On the other hand, success is also very much determined by an approach to management which engenders high levels of commitment on the part of staff, particularly where their discretionary effort is a key means by which competitive advantage is maintained. The problem is that these two imperatives tend to be incompatible. Flexibility inevitably leads to insecurity because it creates a situation in which organisations are unable to demonstrate high levels of commitment to staff, particularly over the longer term. How, then, can an organisation expect to receive high levels of commitment back from its people? It is a very difficult conundrum to address, but there are examples of organisations which have made progress in doing so. The key, as was pointed out by Reilly (2001), is to focus on 'mutual flexibility' by which is meant initiatives which increase an organisation's capacity to be flexible, but which also benefit employees. Many are currently being developed under the banner of a 'work-life balance' agenda, providing employees with part-time working options, flexible working hours, annual hours contracts and temporary career breaks. Another major area of development is in multiskilling, whereby the content of jobs is far less rigidly prescribed than used to be the case. This increases organisational flexibility, reduces costs and also benefits employees in terms of longer-term career development.

Activity 1.5

Think about organisations you have worked for or with which you are familiar. To what extent are their managers having to grapple with the four issues identified above? How far do you consider their approaches to be successful and why?

KEY DEBATE: THE STATE OF THE PSYCHOLOGICAL CONTRACT

We turn now to consider our key debate in this chapter, the state of the psychological contract in the UK. In order to inform this debate, we first discuss the increase in focus on the psychological contract and briefly review some relevant theory, before exploring in detail the differing arguments on the extent to which the state of the contract has changed.

Growing interest in the psychological contract

The term 'psychological contract' was coined as long ago as the 1960s, yet it is only in the past two decades that there has been significant and sustained interest in it. In this period, it has gained acceptance as a broad explanatory framework for understanding employee-organisation linkages (Rousseau 1989) and has been widely adopted in organisational research when considering the employment relationship. There are two major reasons for this: first, the shift in focus in the employment relationship to an individual rather than a collective level and the associated emergence of human resource management (HRM) as a means of managing the employment relationship and, secondly, the pace of change in product markets globally and the subsequent changes wrought to the employment relationship.

As we note in Chapter 8, trade union influence has diminished to a significant degree since the early 1980s and the proportion of the workers whose terms and conditions are determined by collective bargaining is at an all-time low. Alongside this, HRM has emerged as a mechanism for establishing the relationship between manager and employee at an individual level and it is this individual level focus to which the psychological contract is ideally suited. We do not intend to dwell here on heavy theoretical definitions, noting only that this is a matter of intense academic debate, but rather present a pragmatic definition suitable for the purposes of this discussion of the psychological contract as a set of expectations or obligations between employer and employee which serve to govern the employment relationship. Thus the contract serves to establish what is expected of both the employer and employee, going beyond the legal contract and working at an individual not a collective level and being open to influence by HRM policy and practice, as we shall see in the next section.

We noted earlier the intense forces for change in the past two decades that have impacted on the employment relationship in the UK. Some argue that such change has fundamentally changed the psychological contract and this again has brought the concept to prominence. This is the focus of our key debate which we detail below.

Activity 1.6

What changes have occurred to the employment relationship in an organisation with which you are familiar? What has caused this? What implications does this have?

FIGURE 1.2

Source: This table is taken from Fairness at Work and the Psychological Contract (1998) written by D. Guest and N. Conway with the permission of the publisher, the Chartered Institutue of Personnel and Development, London (www.cipd.co.uk).

What is the psychological contract?

There is a huge array of highly theoretical psychological contract literature but it is not our intention to review this in detail here. Rather, we present an overview of such theory as is relevant to understanding both the significance of HRM in the psychological contract and the debate on the state of the contract. The Chartered Institute of Personnel and Development (CIPD) has engaged in significant research into the psychological contract, publishing annual reports on the subject, and we present in Figure 1.2 a model of the contract that CIPD has refined and developed over a number of years.

The key elements of this model are that individual and organisational, rather than collective, factors influence the psychological contract, together with HR practice. It is suggested that HR practices such as recruitment, training and reward are all highly significant in creating what Guest and Conway (1998) call a 'positive' psychological contract, that is, one where trust is high, fairness prevails and both parties perceive that the other has 'delivered the deal' (fulfilled their expectations and obligations). We noted earlier in the chapter the emphasis within HR on demonstrating a link to organisational performance and the CIPD model contributes to this. Thus a positive contract will lead to outcomes such as commitment, motivation and performance. Conversely, failure to deliver on the deal, termed 'breach' of the contract, will have negative outcomes such as poor motivation and reduced performance. The role of HR in influencing the contract with appropriate policies is apparent, although CIPD research suggests that few organisations do in fact try to manage the psychological contract.

The content of the psychological contract contains 'delivery of the deal' and this requires further explanation in order to understand the debate on the state of the contract. The 'deal' is the obligations and expectations that employer and employee have of each other. A common way of describing the deal is as either transactional or relational, although many suggest that this is an oversimplification. We present in Table 1.1 obligations or expectations that might fall within the two types of contract.

TABLE 1.1 Elements of the 'deal'

Transactional contract might contain	Relational contract might contain
Employer	**Employer**
● Pay	● Job security
● Performance-based pay	● Career prospects
● Having a job	● Training and development
Employer	**Employee**
● Long hours	● Loyalty
● Multiskilled	● Conformity
● Willing to change	

Traditionally, it has been argued that relational contracts are more likely to lead to the positive outcomes discussed above and many UK organisations have developed such contracts. A prime example of this was Marks and Spencer, which was well known at one time for its treatment of employees, including a strong paternalistic element in which they 'looked after' their staff through provision of, for example, onsite canteens and dental treatment.

Activity 1.7

How would you describe the psychological contract in your organisation: transactional or relational? What impact does this have on outcomes such as performance and motivation?

The state of the psychological contract

We come now to the heart of the debate: what is the state of the psychological contract in the UK? Across the 1990s and into this decade, there have been widespread reports of the changing contract or 'deal'. These have been in both newspapers and scholarly journals. The suggestion is that the forces that are driving dramatic economic change, outlined earlier in this chapter, have also driven change in the psychological contract, reducing the extent to which it is relational. Trends such as downsizing and redundancy have radically altered the deal, doing away with the 'old' deal which offered a 'job for life' and career progression, leading to organisations with flatter hierarchies facing continuous change in which career opportunities are difficult to assure. The 'new' deal is argued to be largely transactional, focused on pay and swapping employee loyalty and conformance for long hours and high performance.

The interest in this change has arisen to a large extent as a result of its implications. We discussed above the negative impact of breach of the contract and it has been widely argued that the transition in the contract from old to new has been considered to be a breach of the contract and that the consequences for the employment relationship have been extremely negative. A whole range of studies investigated the psychological contract and indicated that significant organisational change had led to a deterioration in the state of the psychological contract (see, for example, Hallier and James 1997 and Coyle-Shapiro and Kessler 2000). These studies were generally case study based, considering the employment relationship in specific organisations, sometimes in specific populations, yet they stretched across public and private sector organisations. Without exception, they demonstrated significant evidence of breach of contract and outcomes such as poor morale, reduced motivation and increased intention to quit (Doherty *et al.* 1996, Turnley and Feldman 1998, Pate and Malone 2000). Such changes and their associated outcomes were clearly linked to downsizing and restructuring initiatives and demonstrated the negative impact of changing the psychological contract on the broader employment relationship. They provided compelling evidence of a high degree of change. Sparrow's (1996) study in the financial services sector, for example, suggests that nearly all respondents believe that career opportunities were reduced, many anticipate that they will be made compulsorily redundant and hardly any expect that the organisation will fulfil its obligations to them. Similarly, Coyle-Shapiro and Kessler (2000) suggest that most employees perceived breach of contract in respect of the employer fulfilling its obligations to them and Turnley and Feldman (1998) suggest that not only do many employees believe that the organisation has reneged on its obligations to them, a number feel that the organisation has not even entered into any commitments to them and thus there can be no breach. A significant degree of change is identified and negative consequences such as poor morale and job satisfaction are reported.

WINDOW ON PRACTICE

The changing contract at a major high street bank

There have been a number of studies into the psychological contract in high street banks, once stable, hierarchical and paternalistic institutions. The study we report here was longitudinal, covering the period 1993 to 2000, which allowed consideration of changes to the psychological contract over a period of time. External forces had seen the bank attempt to shift from its traditional bureaucratic structures to more flexible, fluid structures and the consequences for the employment relationship were apparent.

The bank had adopted the rhetoric of 'employability rather than employment', suggesting to employees that it was not able to offer job security and that employees were to be responsible for managing their own careers, which were no longer likely to be up hierarchical 'ladders'. The organization thus attempted to define a new psychological contract. Employees were, however, very resistant to this, valuing the job security and career progression that the old contract had offered. The negative perceptions of the contract were made worse by the bank's failure to provide systems to support employees in managing their own careers. In other words, there was a rhetoric of employability but this was not supported in reality with practices that helped employees to develop it and they were left floundering, old career development systems and job security having been removed, and a vacuum left in their place.

The imposition of the new deal meant that it was not accepted by employees, who still sought the job security and traditional career paths offered in the old deal. This meant that perceptions of breach of a formerly relational contract were widespread and led to the creation of a transactional contract in which employees were instrumental, focusing on money, and many changes, including work intensification, led to expressions of demotivation, insecurity and powerlessness. Concerns were also expressed by employees over their own performance and the performance of the organization as a result. The state of the contract at the time of the study was clearly very poor.

Source: Atkinson, C. (2002) 'Career Management and the Changing Psychological Contract', *Career Development International*, Vol. 7, No. 1, pp. 14–23.

The received wisdom was then that the psychological contract had undergone radical change in the UK and that the imposition of the new deal had led to a workforce that was demotivated, demoralized and insecure. Since 1996, however, CIPD has commissioned a series of research reports into issues surrounding the psychological contract. The first of these reports that not as much change as has been suggested has taken place within the contract (Kessler and Undy 1996), a theme continued in subsequent CIPD reports (*see*, for example, Guest and Conway 1997, 1998, 1999). These reports differ from those suggesting that wholesale change has taken place in that, rather than considering case study organisations, they tend to consider general, representative populations. These reports suggest, however, that a traditional psychological contract continues to exist and that the old deal is still very much in evidence. An early survey (Guest *et al.* 1996) identified that up to 20 per cent of the population consider themselves to have a poor psychological contract, although the reasons for these perceptions are not explored in any detail.
The survey thus suggests that for the large majority of their sample, the psychological contract is still founded on job security and stable careers, a finding clearly at odds with those presented above. Later surveys indicate increasingly positive psychological contracts within a stable employment relationship (Guest and Conway 1998, 2001, 2003, CIPD 2005) and seem to confirm the suggestion that the degree of change to the psychological contract has been over-reported. Indeed, a 'survey of surveys' based on a number of sources supports this and reports that British workers are not as greatly dissatisfied as has been widely suggested (Guest and Conway 1999). Statistics drawn from this survey suggest that 88 per cent of employees are fairly or very secure in their jobs, that 64 per cent believe good employee relations exist in their organisations and that over 70 per cent of employees have high levels of job satisfaction. Similarly there is evidence to suggest that traditional careers are still common (Mallon 1998, Guest and McKenzie-Davey 1996), with the hierarchy still used for motivation and progression. However, there is increasing evidence over the past five or so years that professionals, in particular, are moving into self-employment or agency work (*see*, for example, Purcell *et al.* 2005).

Further, it is argued that job security is not reduced by using figures that demonstrate that the average length of job tenure is unchanged since the early 1970s (Overell 2002).

We are then left wondering: what is the state of the contract? Is the old deal still widely to be found, or is the British workforce facing the 'new deal' and suffering its negative consequences? The reasons for the disparity in research findings are very complex. It could be argued that the findings arise from specific contexts, that is, that the large-scale surveys reporting little change consider general populations, in which the traditional psychological contract may not have been present and thus little change has occurred, whereas the case studies focus on specific sectors such as financial services or the former nationalised industries. The latter have perhaps experienced a degree of change not experienced in the population at large, thus explaining the disparity in findings. Certainly the case study organisations were acknowledged as having formerly had a traditional psychological contract which, it could be argued, may not have been as prevalent in other organisations. Contradicting this, however, is that the survey studies suggest that this traditional contract continues to exist in a broad range of organisations (Guest *et al.* 1996), which is certainly not supported by case study findings.

The answer may also be found in the populations under study, in that the large-scale surveys again consider general populations, whereas the case studies tend to focus on managerial or professional populations. It may again be that the changes within these specific populations have been more marked than in the population as a whole, especially given Cavanaugh and Noe's (1999) assertion that the extent to which employees had experienced involuntary job loss, downsizing or restructuring renders more congruent their beliefs about the new psychological contract. Clearly the populations under consideration within the case studies had experience of such issues which may have strongly influenced their views.

Another explanation may be that temporary work and contract work are spread more evenly across different sectors (see, for example, Burke 1998), and have therefore become more visible. Similarly, different groups have different sets of expectations and subjective feelings of job insecurity. Younger workers accept insecurity, almost as the norm (see, for example, Smithson and Lewis 2000), but older workers feel the psychological contract has been violated. Older workers may have the same expectations as before but realise that the employer is no longer going to fulfil their part of the bargain (see, for example, Herriot *et al.* 1997; Thomas and Dunkerley 1999).

We have also argued in our research that research method may influence the outcome of the different studies (Atkinson 2004). This link appears to be striking; survey studies generally reporting a positive psychological contract, case studies a negative one. Kessler and Undy (1996) also report a difference in their findings using case study and survey methods. While this theme is as yet under-explored, it may nevertheless be an important contributor to resolving the debate.

A further fundamental issue is that the psychological contract is perception based (Rousseau 1989) rather than being any concrete tangible entity. Smithson and Lewis (2000) argue that public perceptions of increasing insecurity may have more to do with the characteristics of those whom the insecurity now affects, such as graduates and professional staff, rather than an increase in the phenomenon. So perceptions of insecurity may not be borne out by job tenure figures and the 'new deal' may be reflected in people's expectations rather than their labour market experiences (King 2003), but these perceptions and expectations nevertheless influence the state of the psychological contract.

Our conclusion on the state of the psychological contract is that the 'new' deal, while perhaps not dominant in every organisation, has made significant inroads into the UK employment relationship. The extent to which the new deal exists is debated, but we argue that, for employees as for customers, perceptions are reality. Thus employers need, for example, to tackle perceptions of job insecurity, even if these perceptions are not supported by job tenure figures. Those employers who can manage employee perceptions that a relational contract still exists will, we suggest, be those who are most successful in achieving positive outcomes for both employer and employee, leading to high organisational performance.

Activity 1.8

Do you think that the old deal or the new deal is more common in UK organisations? Outline your reasons for this.

SUMMARY PROPOSITIONS

1.1 Human resource managers are concerned with meeting four distinct sets of organisational objectives: staffing, performance, change management and administration.

1.2 The HRM function contributes to the achievement of different dimensions of organisational effectiveness. Prominent are the gaining and maintaining of competitive advantage, the fostering of a positive standing in financial markets and the development of a reputation for corporate social responsibility.

1.3 Most current debates about human resource management in general focus on the extent and nature of the responses needed in the face of developments in the business environment. The most significant are greater competitive intensity, tighter labour markets and increased regulation.

1.4 Three of the most prominent current debates in HRM focus on the implications of skills shortages, the relative wisdom of the 'best fit' and 'best practice' approaches and the interrelationship between HR practice and corporate ethics.

1.5 In recent years the concept of the psychological contract has come to prominence. The extent to which we have seen fundamental change in the expectations that employers and employees have about their relationship remains a matter of debate.

GENERAL DISCUSSION TOPICS

1 To what extent do you agree with the view that the contract of employment is gradually changing to a contract for performance?

2 The philosophy of HRM set out in this chapter makes no reference to the customer. David Ulrich, a professor at Michigan Business School, believes that it is important to refocus HR activities away from the firm towards the customer so that suppliers, employees and customers are woven together into a value-chain team. What difference do you think that would make?

3 How far do you think it is possible to agree with both the 'best fit' and 'best practice' perspectives on HRM? In what ways are they compatible with each other?

FURTHER READING

Two books of articles by academic writers cover all the major contemporary debates about HRM practice and the impact of environmental change on the way people are managed in the UK. These are:

Bach, S. (ed.) (2005) *Managing Human Resources: Personnel Management in Transition*. Oxford: Blackwell.

Storey, J. (ed.) (2007) *Human Resource Management: A Critical Text*. London: Thomson.
Also valuable is a well-written and well-referenced introduction to evolving research into psychological contracts and their significance:

Conway, N. and Briner, R. (2005) *Understanding psychological contracts at work*. Oxford: Oxford University Press.

REFERENCES

Atkinson, C. (2002) 'Career Management and the Psychological Contract', *Career Development International*, Vol. 7, No. 1, pp. 14–23.

Atkinson, C. (2004) 'Why methods matter: researching the psychological contract', *Human Resources and Employment Review*, Vol. 2, No. 2, pp. 111–16.

Bach, S. (ed.) (2005) *Managing Human Resources: Personnel Management in Transition*, 4th edn. Oxford: Blackwell Publishing.

BBC (2008a) 'BA's terminal losses top £16 million', BBC News website, 3 April.

BBC (2008b) 'What did go wrong at Terminal 5?', BBC News website, 30 March.

Blitz, R. (2008) 'The trouble with great expectations', *Financial Times*, 26 March.

Burke, R. (1998) 'Changing career rules: clinging to the past or accepting the new reality?', *Career Development International*, Vol. 3, No. 1.

Cavanaugh, M.A. and Noe, R.A. (1999) 'Antedents and consequences of relational components of the new psychological contract', *Journal of Organizational Behavior*, Vol. 20, pp. 323–40.

CIPD (2005) *Managing Change: the role of the psychological contract*, London: Chartered Institute of Personnel and Development.

CIPD (2007) *Recruitment, Retention and Turnover*. London: Chartered Institute of Personnel and Development.

Conway, N. and Briner, R. (2005) *Understanding Psychological Contracts at Work: A Critical Evaluation of Theory and Research*. Oxford: Oxford University Press.

Coyle-Shapiro, J. and Kessler, I. (2000) 'Consequences of the psychological contract for the employment relationship: a large scale survey', *Journal of Management Studies*, Vol. 37, No. 7.

Doherty, N., Bank, J. and Vinnicombe, S. (1996) 'Managing the Survivors: the experience of survivors in British Telecom and the British financial services sector', *Journal of Managerial Psychology*, Vol. 11, No. 7, pp. 51–60.

Done, K. and Willman, J. (2008) 'Goodwill of staff is often in short supply', *Financial Times*, 5 April.

Evans, R. (1994) 'The Human Side of Business Process Re-engineering', *Management Development Review*, Vol. 7, No. 6, pp. 10–12.

Guest, D.E. (1987) 'Human resource management and industrial relations', *Journal of Management Studies*, Vol. 24, No. 5.

Guest, D. and Conway, N. (1997) *Employee Motivation and the Psychological Contract*. London: Institute of Personnel and Development.

Guest, D. and Conway, N. (1998) *Fairness at Work and the Psychological Contract*. London: Institute of Personnel and Development.

Guest, D. and Conway, N. (1999) *How Dissatisfied are British Workers? A survey of surveys*. London: Institute of Personnel and Development.

Guest, D. and Conway, N. (2001) *Employer Perceptions of the Psychological Contract*. London: Chartered Institute of Personnel and Development.

Guest, D. and Conway, N. (2003) *Pressure at work and the psychological contract*. London: Chartered Institute of Personnel and Development.

Guest, D. and McKenzie-Davey, K. (1996) 'Don't write off the traditional career', *People Management*, February.

Guest, D., Conway, N., Briner, R. and Dickman, M. (1996) *The State of the Psychological Contract in Employment*. London: Institute of Personnel and Development.

Hallier, J. and James, P. (1997) 'Management enforced job change and employee perceptions of the psychological contract', *Employee Relations*, Vol. 19, No. 3, pp. 222–47.

Hatch, M.J. (1997) *Organization Theory. Modern, symbolic and postmodern perspectives*. Oxford: Oxford University Press.

Herriot, P., Manning, W. and Kidd, J. (1997) 'The content of the psychological contract', *British Journal of Management*, Vol. 8, pp. 151–62.

Kessler, I. and Undy, R. (1996) *The New Employment Relationship: examining the Psychological Contract*. London: Institute of Personnel and Development.

King, Z. (2003) 'New or traditional careers? A study of UK graduates' perceptions', *Human Resource Management Journal*, Vol. 13, No. 1, pp. 5–26.

Legge, K. (1995) *Human Resource Management: Rhetorics and Realities*. London: Macmillan.

Mallon, M. (1998) 'The portfolio career; pushed or pulled to it?', *Personnel Review*, Vol. 27, No. 5.

National Statistics (2006) *Labour Market Review*. Basingstoke: Palgrave Macmillan.

Overell, S. (2002) 'Job theories need a little more work', *Personnel Today*, No. 10, December, p. 14.

Pate, J. and Malone, C. (2000) 'Post-psychological contract violation: the durability and transferability of employee perceptions: the case of TimTec', *Journal of European Industrial Training*, Vol. 24, No. 2, pp. 158–66.

Pinnington, A., Macklin, R. and Campbell, T. (2007) *Human Resource Management: Ethics and Employment*. Oxford: Oxford University Press.

Purcell, J. (2003) *Understanding the people and performance link: unlocking the black box*. London: Chartered Institute of Personnel and Development.

Purcell, J., Purcell, K. and Tailby, S. (2005) 'Temporary Work Agencies: Here today, gone tomorrow?', *British Journal of Industrial Relations*, Vol. 42, No. 4, pp. 705–25.

Reilly, P. (2000) *HR Shared Services and the Realignment of HR*. Brighton: Institute of Employment Studies.

Reilly, P. (2001) *Flexibility at Work*. Aldershot: Gower.

Roberts, P.W. and Dowling, G.R. (2002) 'Corporate reputation and sustained superior financial performance', *Strategic Management Journal*, Vol. 23, No. 12, pp. 1077–93.

Rousseau, D.M. (1989) 'Psychological and implied contracts in organizations', *Employee Responsibilities and Rights Journal*, Vol. 2, No. 2, pp. 121–39.

Shackleton, J.R. (2005) 'Regulating the Labour Market', in P. Booth (ed.) *Towards a Liberal Utopia?* London: Institute of Economic Affairs, pp. 128–43.

Smithson, J. and Lewis, S. (2000) 'Is job insecurity changing the psychological contract?', *Personnel Review*, Vol. 29, No. 6.

Sparrow, P. (1996) 'Transitions on the psychological contract: some evidence from the banking sector', *Human Resource Management Journal*, Vol. 6, No. 4, pp. 75–92.

Sparrow, P.L. (2003) 'The Future of Work?', in D. Holman, T. Wall, C. Clegg, P. Sparrow and A. Howard (eds) *The New Workplace: a guide to the human impact of modern working practices*. Chichester: Wiley.

Stevens, J. (ed.) (2005) *Managing Risk: The Human Resources Contribution*. London: LexisNexis Butterworths.

Storey, J. (ed.) (2007) *Human Resource Management: A Critical Text*, 3rd edn. London: Thomson.

Thomas, R. and Dunkerley, D. (1999) 'Careering downwards? Middle managers' experiences in the downsized organisation', *British Journal of Management*, Vol. 10, pp. 157–69.

Turnley, W.H. and Feldman, D.C. (1998) 'Psychological contract violations during corporate restructuring', *Human Resource Management*, Vol. 37, No. 1, pp. 71–83.

CHAPTER 2

Organising a workforce

The objectives of this chapter are to:

1 Examine the reasons for growth in various forms of organisational flexibility

2 Describe forms of numerical, functional and temporal flexibility and critique such flexibility

3 Examine the reasons for the increased focus on work-life integration (WLI)

4 Describe a range of WLI practices

5 Discuss the rhetoric versus reality of achieving WLI

The traditional nine-to-five working day is in decline thanks to new flexible working rights legislation, the Government has said. But its own annual survey of employee and employer attitudes to flexible working, released yesterday by the Department for Business, Enterprise and Regulatory Reform (BERR), fails to support the assertion.

The survey of more than 1,400 workplaces found fewer people now work from home than in 2000 and that there has been little change in the number of people applying for job-sharing and flexitime working in the last four years. The Government chose to focus on the fact that 92pc of employers said they would now consider a flexible working request from any member of staff, despite the legislation only requiring employers to do so for some employees.

Source: Richard Tyler **www.telegraph.co.uk/money/main.jhtml?xml=/money/2007/12/04/ cnflex104.xml**, 05/12/2007.

The excerpt above is one of many articles in UK newspapers that deal with the issue of working time and work organisation. We hear that businesses are struggling with both skills shortages and ever increasing demands to provide a family-friendly workplace and, somewhat at odds with this, are reports of redundancy and job insecurity being rife, and stress and long working hours being the norm. We consider in this chapter a number of these issues, seeking to separate the rhetoric from the reality of working lives. First we discuss the way the working time of employees is organised, the types of flexibility needed by businesses and the job insecurity that may accompany it. Then we discuss the increasing need to meet employees' demands for flexibility. In our key debate we explore the extent to which work-life integration (WLI) is a reality for many employees and conclude that, for the most part, working lives are dominated by forms of flexibility that meet organisational rather than employee needs.

WORKFORCE ORGANISATION

An increasingly important aspect of organising a workforce is measures to achieve flexibility. We considered in Chapter 1 the main external forces affecting businesses over the past few decades, such as globalisation, technology and an economic base that is increasingly dominated by service industries. Here we consider the implications of these, and other, changes for workforce organisation to meet the need for workforce flexibility, not only by employers but also by employees.

Globalisation of markets has led to ever greater product market competition and an increased need to gain competitive advantage. In striving for this, employers have provided less secure jobs, using 'flexible' workers in order to keep costs down and to retain or increase market share. Developments in technology enable a greater control of workflow, requiring flexible working hours to extend capital utilisation. The changing economic base towards more service industries with an emphasis on knowledge and knowledge workers has also influenced flexibility, as jobs in a knowledge-based economy tend to be more flexible than industrial jobs, with more varied working hours (Bishop 2004). Allied to this has been a perceived need for '24/7' service availability, leading to a dramatic move away from the standard working time model of 9–5 Monday to Friday and to employers demanding a far more flexible approach to work organisation.

The demand for flexibility has not all, however, been from employers. It has coincided with changes that have created a greater supply of labour at non-standard times. One of the primary drivers of this has been the increased labour force participation of women, particularly women in the childbearing years, which has led to an increased requirement for flexible working arrangements in order to accommodate childcare responsibilities (Fagnani et al. 2004). There has also been an increase in single parent families and dual career couples, meaning that a growing proportion of the workforce has to reconcile both work and non-work commitments. This increases the supply of labour at non-standard times, such as nights and weekends. A further demographic influence is the ageing population of western countries, with employees demanding flexibility to deal with both childcare and elder care responsibilities. Pension concerns (see Chapter 7) may also force workers to remain in the workforce longer than previously anticipated and research has shown that older workers frequently aspire to work flexibly in the later stages of their careers (CIPD 2005).

Thus there has been a coincidence of need over recent decades in employers and employees requiring enhanced working time flexibility although, as we see later in this chapter, it is often employer needs that have taken precedence.

Activity 2.1

1 What changes have organisations faced as a result of developing technology?

2 Explain why these have affected workforce organisation.

3 List some examples of this from an organisation with which you are familiar.

Organising for flexibility

Work organisation concerns the design of jobs and working patterns in order to meet both employer and employee need for flexibility. The impact of this is that work organisation is central to the whole employment relationship, and strongly influences organisational performance. Flexibility that responds to employer needs has dominated from the mid-1980s until relatively recently, with many employees experiencing significant change to traditional working patterns. Atkinson (1984), for example, suggested a 'flexible firm' model that explained employer behaviour in terms of work organisation and flexibility. However, tight labour markets in recent years increasingly require employers to accommodate employee demands for flexibility in order to recruit and retain scarce labour.

An emerging body of literature considers forms of employee flexibility that are often described as 'work-life balance' or 'work-life integration'. While demand- and supply-driven flexibility are commonly considered separately, we have argued elsewhere (Atkinson and Hall 2005) that they should both form part of the work organisation and flexibility debate and this is the approach we adopt in this chapter. Indeed, we believe that employee-driven flexibility is emerging as such a critical issue within organisations that we focus our Key Debate on it later in the chapter.

FLEXIBILITY FOR ORGANISATIONAL BENEFIT

It is often argued that employer and employee needs in flexible working practices are complementary and that the practices adopted have benefits for both parties. There are tensions, however, between employer and employee needs, with the employer often dominating. Practices presented as beneficial to employees are, in fact, often detrimental to them (Bishop 2004, Harris 2003). For example, despite meeting the needs of some employees for flexibility, part-time work is often insecure and low paid. Nevertheless, it can be argued that the meeting of employee need is dependent upon whether the employee has access to a contract of choice. We present below flexible working practices that are typically considered to be demand led, adopting Atkinson's (1984) model of the flexible firm.

Model of the 'flexible firm'

Atkinson (1984) describes how firms may develop flexibility in their approach to employment, as shown in Figure 2.1. The model comprises forms of flexibility including numerical, temporal and functional and we consider these below.

Numerical flexibility

Numerical flexibility allows the organisation to respond quickly to the environment in terms of the numbers of people employed. Some traditional full-time, permanent posts are replaced by short-term contract staff, staff with rolling contracts, outworkers, and so on. This enables the organisation to reduce or expand the workforce quickly and cheaply.

FIGURE 2.1
Atkinson's model of the flexible firm

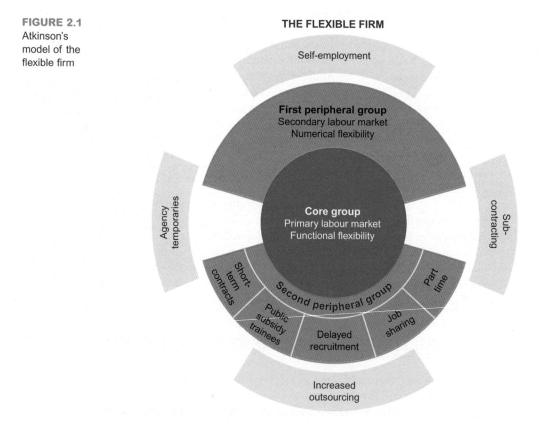

(*Source*: J. Atkinson (1984) Manpower strategies for flexible organisations', *Personnel Management*, August. Used with the permission of the author).

The flexible firm in this analysis has various ways of meeting the need for human resources. First are core employees, who form the primary labour market. They are highly regarded by the employer, well paid and involved in those activities that are unique to the firm or give it a distinctive character. These employees have improved career prospects and offer the type of flexibility to the employer that is so prized in the skilled professional with wide experience and adaptability.

There are then two peripheral groups: first, those who have skills that are needed but not specific to the particular firm, like typing and word processing. The strategy for these posts is to rely on the external labour market to a much greater extent, to specify a narrow range of tasks without career prospects, so that the employee has a job but not a career. Some employees may be able to transfer to core posts, but generally limited scope is likely to maintain a fairly high turnover, so that adjustments to the vagaries of the product market are eased.

The second peripheral group is made up of those enjoying even less security, as they have contracts of employment that are limited, either to a short-term or to a part-time attachment. There may also be a few job sharers, although this is not widely practised. An alternative or additional means towards this flexibility is to contract out the work that has to be done, either by employing temporary personnel from agencies or by outsourcing the entire operation, adjusting the organisation boundary, redefining what is to be done in-house and what is to be contracted out to various suppliers.

Temporal flexibility

Temporal flexibility concerns varying the pattern of hours worked in order to respond to business demands and employee needs. Moves away from the 9–5, five-day week include the use of annual hours contracts, increased use of part-time work, job sharing and flexible working hours. For example, an organisation subject to peaks and troughs of demand, such as an ice cream manufacturer, could use annual hours contracts so that more employee hours are available at peak periods and less are used when business is slow. Flexible hours systems can benefit the employer by providing employee cover outside the 9–5 day and over lunchtimes, and can also provide employee benefits by allowing personal demands to be fitted more easily around work demands.

Research evidence suggests increasing use of temporal flexibility. Longer opening hours in retailing and the growth of the leisure sector means that many more people now work in the evening (17 per cent) and at night (6 per cent) than used to be the case. The proportion of jobs that are part time also continues to rise, albeit at a slower rate than in the 1970s and 1980s, while the length of the working week for higher-paid full-time workers has increased by three hours on average during the past decade. There has also been some growth in the use of annual hours, but these arrangements have not become as widespread as was predicted a decade ago. Only 6 per cent of employers have chosen to adopt this approach for some of their staff (Kersley *et al.* 2006).

Functional flexibility

The term 'functional flexibility' refers to a process in which employees gain the capacity to undertake a variety of tasks rather than specialising in just one area. Advocates of such approaches have been influenced by studies of Japanese employment practices as well as by criticisms of monotonous assembly-line work. Horizontal flexibility involves each individual employee becoming multiskilled so that they can be deployed as and where required at any time. Vertical flexibility entails gaining the capacity to undertake work previously carried out by colleagues higher up or lower down the organisational hierarchy.

Case 2.1 on this book's companion website, **www.pearsoned.co.uk/torrington** explores flexible working strategies further.

WINDOW ON PRACTICE

Pindar Set had been typesetting the *Yellow Pages* directories for eighteen years. Until May 1995, the firm was a one-customer, one-site business, enjoying a highly profitable ten-year contract to design and set advertisements for *Yellow Pages'* customers. The arrangement was very stable and the structure and management of the business was, as the company itself admits, decidedly traditional. All that changed when *Yellow Pages* indicated that it wanted to move to a shorter-term contract with tighter margins and greater responsiveness to customer demand, including new turnaround times and a new emphasis on quality and customer service.

Pindar Set had a mixture of working arrangements with some staff working in large departments where each person handled only a part of the production process, while others worked in smaller teams with a broader range of skills. The company considered whether it was organised in the best way, whether people were skilled and deployed in the right way and whether it was right that one person did only one part of a task. The result was that, from 1997, the company set about training all its unskilled staff to do skilled jobs, phasing out unskilled text-inputting jobs completely. All the unskilled workers upgraded as planned, despite some initial wariness of the new accreditation process that was established to ensure consistent standards across the business. Remedial training was provided where necessary. Employees were also trained to follow a job through from start to finish, reducing the internal 'pipeline' from 80 processes to one.

Multiskilling was part of a wider change programme, including team working and changes in shift patterns, and has delivered real business benefits for Pindar Set. Profit has increased, the company has been able to introduce new services and customer complaints have fallen.

Adapted from: Crabb, S. and Johnson, R. (2000) 'Press for Success', *People Management*, 9 November.

The primary purpose of functional flexibility initiatives is to deploy human resources more efficiently. It should mean that employees are kept busy throughout their working day and that absence is more easily covered than in a workplace with rigidly defined demarcation between jobs. A further efficiency gain comes from employees being more stretched, fulfilled and thus productive than in a workplace with narrowly defined jobs. Despite its potential advantages research suggests that employers in the UK have been less successful than competitors elsewhere in Europe at developing functional flexibility. According to Blyton (1998), this is primarily because of a reluctance to invest in the training necessary to support these new forms of working. By contrast, Reilly (2001) points to employee resistance and the increased likelihood of errors occurring when functional flexibility programmes are introduced. It could also simply be a reflection of increased specialisation as jobs become more technically complex relying to a greater extent on specific expert knowledge. Either way the Workplace Employment Relations Survey (WERS) (2004), shows a decline in formal multiskilling programmes during recent years. In 2004 only 19 per cent of workplaces reported that at least three-fifths of their core employees were trained to do more than one job, compared with 29 per cent in 1998 (Kersley *et al.* 2006, p. 92).

Debates about flexibility

The growth in flexible working arrangements combined with their promotion by governments since the 1990s has led to the development of robust debates about their desirability and usage in practice. As much controversy has centred on the Atkinson model of the flexible firm as on the rather different elements that go to make it up. There has been a continuing debate, for example, about whether the model of core and periphery is a description of trends or a prescription for the future. Two streams of research have flowed from these interpretations. The first concerns the extent to which the model has been adopted in practice, the second focuses on the advantages and disadvantages of the model as a blueprint for the future organisation of work.

Evidence on the first of these questions is patchy. There is no question that rhetoric about flexibility and the language of flexibility is increasingly used. The flexible firm model appears to be something that managers aspire to adopt, but the extent to which they have actually adopted it is questionable. While some evidence suggests that there has been a steady increase in part-time work across Europe, findings from the ESRC funded 'Future of Work Programme' in the UK have challenged the degree of change that has actually occurred. Nolan and Wood (2003) have found that traditional working patterns, premised upon full-time permanent employment, remain dominant. Further, in many organisations the drive for economies of scale means that far from becoming more flexible, organisations are just as likely to introduce bureaucratic systems and standardised practices in response to competitive pressures. And yet we also have seen for a long period now increased use of part-time workers, consultants, subcontractors, agency workers and of moves towards multiskilling. Karen Legge's (1995) conclusion that flexibility is used in a pragmatic and opportunistic way rather than as a strategic HRM initiative thus seems to hold true today.

The desirability of flexibility is debatable. The theoretical advantages for organisations are to deploy employee time and effort more efficiently so that staff are only at work when they need to be and are wholly focused on achieving organisational objectives throughout that time. However, the extent to which this is achieved in practice is not clear. Many writers equate the term 'flexibility' with 'insecurity' and argue that the consequences for organisations in terms of staff commitment and willingness to work beyond contract are damaging, staff turnover is likely to increase and recruiting talented people will be harder too. It is questionable that the flexible firm model, at least as far as the 'peripheral' workforce is concerned, is compatible with best practice approaches to HRM which seek to increase employees' commitment. Another view, however, is that soft HRM adopting high-commitment HRM practices can adopt functional flexibility through practices such as flexible job design, cross-training, use of teams and work groups and job rotation and enlargement. Lepak and Snell (1999) go further in arguing that soft and hard approaches may not be mutually exclusive and that the ability to manage different forms of flexibility may give an organisation sustainable competitive advantage, one that draws on robust HR policies.

Further critiques arise, however, from Sisson and Storey (2000, p. 83) who make the further observation that too much 'hollowing out' can impair organisational learning and lead to the loss of expertise, a loss from which it is difficult to recover. These unintended consequences, it is argued, can worsen rather than improve an organisation's competitive position. Others (*see* Heery and Salmon 2000, Burchell *et al.* 1999) see too much flexibility as having damaging longer-term economic consequences. For example, it can lead to a reduced willingness by employers to invest in training, the absence of which creates skills shortages that hold back economic development. It can also lead to a situation in which managers exploit the vulnerability of peripheral workers by intensifying their work to an unacceptable degree. Finally, it can be argued that in dividing people into 'core' and 'peripheral' groups, flexible firms perpetuate inequality in society more generally and that this leads to poverty, crime, family breakdown and political alienation. Fudge and Owens (2007) label the new types of work 'precarious' and point to the fact that in most cases such work is carried out by women who are much less likely than men to enjoy the benefits associated with long-term, full-time, stable, pensionable employment and with an income which is sufficient to sustain a household.

WINDOW ON PRACTICE

Tuselmann (1996) argues that a high degree of interdependence exists between the different forms of flexibility, that there are costs and benefits of each, and that organisations choose an optimal mix dependent on their market conditions and the country in which they operate. He suggests that a high degree of functional flexibility may be generally inconsistent with a high degree of numerical or financial flexibility. It has been argued that while Britain pursues numerical flexibility, in an unregulated and decentralised labour market, there is a greater emphasis in other parts of Europe on functional flexibility. In particular Germany has successfully followed this route within a highly regulated framework with a high degree of centralisation and industrial relations consensus. Tuselmann notes that this framework also constrains organisations' pursuit of numerical, temporal and financial flexibility, and that as Germany experiences increasing competitive pressures, their model of labour flexibility is at a crossroads.

There are other balances in resourcing strategy that can be addressed, for example the balance between numbers of permanent staff employed and the hours that each employee works. In November 1993 Volkswagen in Germany announced that in their current poor financial situation they were employing too many people. In order to avoid redundancies they agreed with the workforce that hours would be reduced by 20 per cent so that they worked a four-day week, and that wages would be reduced by 10 per cent. There is a good deal of emphasis in Europe on reducing the working week to help reduce redundancies, unemployment and absence levels, and to improve family life.

Activity 2.2

1 What evidence can you find in your organisation to support a more flexible approach to work organisation?

OR

2 What evidence can you find based on your own employment history to support a more flexible approach to work organisation?

3 How have you/employees responded and why?

KEY DEBATE: WORK-LIFE INTEGRATION

In this key debate, we explore the increasing focus on work-life integration, considering mechanisms by which this might be achieved. A number of high-profile organisations now seek to position themselves as 'employers of choice' by adopting such WLI policies and it is increasingly suggested that WLI is high up the agenda of many UK organisations. Certainly the latest WERS (Kersley *et al.* 2006) noted that more flexible working options are available than were found in the previous 1998 survey. However, the fact that practices are available says little about their uptake and does not explore the 'rhetoric versus reality' of WLI in UK organisations.

At this early stage in the twenty-first century for some people the value of work is changing. The notion of 'downshifting', swapping a life of total commitment to work and possible high rewards, for less demanding, or part-time work or self-employment, combined with changes in employee supply outlined earlier in the chapter have served to create an increased employee demand for flexible working opportunities and led to a wide range of legitimate work options under the banner of work-life balance or work-life integration (WLI). Tight labour markets and their associated recruitment and retention difficulties have led employers to seek to meet this demand rendering WLI a key issue in organisations in the UK and across Europe, America and such eastern countries as Japan.

Work-life integration practices

WLI options focus on three different types of work flexibility. First, there is flexibility in terms of the number of hours worked; secondly, the exact timing of those hours; and, thirdly, the location at which the work is carried out. Clearly some options may reflect all three types of flexibility. While UK legislation only addresses the need of parents and other carers (*see* Chapter 9), there is a strong lobby for flexible work options to be potentially available for all employees. There are many possible work-life integration options, and clearly not all of these options are appropriate for all jobs or employees, and employers will need to be convinced of the business benefits of any work-life integration option. In addition work-life integration will mean different things to different people, depending on their age, life circumstances, values, interests, personality and so on. At present flexible options are predominantly taken by women (IRS 2002). Part-time working remains the most available and most popular (*see*, for example, CIPD 2005; Kersley *et al.* 2006), and in some sectors is now so common that it is often not recognised as a flexible approach. In our own research in a variety of functions in the health service (Hall and Atkinson 2006) we found that part-time was rarely identified as flexible work to achieve WLI, even though it was very much in evidence, and informal approaches to work flexibility such as unplanned time off and individual agreements about start and finish times were the most commonly mentioned and used. Table 2.1 lists the main options.

We explain these in more detail in *Human Resource Management* (Torrington *et al.*, 7th edn, 2007, ch. 31).

An interesting contribution is made by Strachan and Burgess (1998) who suggest that, in addition to the commonly accepted practices outlined in Table 2.1, employers should also provide practices to ensure both income and job security. Their argument is that employment that does not generate enough income to support a family cannot be described as 'family friendly' and casual employees, who often remain outside the organisation's internal labour market, may be denied WLI benefits. We return to this argument in the 'rhetoric versus reality' section below, noting for now the problems that may arise for employers providing WLI practices while also seeking other forms of flexibility from employees.

TABLE 2.1 Options for achieving work-life balance

Part-time	Term-time working	Unpaid leave
Flexitime	Job share	Unpaid sabbaticals
Compressed week	Self-rostering	Work from home
Annual hours	Shift swapping	Informal flexibility

Activity 2.3

1 What WLI practices are offered by your organisation?

2 Which type of employees access these practices most?

3 How do WLI practices fit with other forms of working time flexibility?

OR

1 What kind of flexible working practices would benefit you?

2 How easy would it be for organisations to provide these?

Benefits of work-life integration

As we note in Chapter 9, there is limited regulation of WLI in the UK, the government adopting a 'business case' approach to it. This approach suggests that the benefits that flow from adopting WLI practices are greater than the costs associated with them, thus encouraging employers to offer such practices. We consider in this section the benefits that are said to accrue from WLI practices that underpin this 'business case'.

WLI practices have been shown in some instances to raise morale, increase levels of job satisfaction and reduce absence, especially unplanned absence. IDS (2006) reports that organisations in its survey found flexible working had a positive impact on retention, recruitment and absenteeism, and these perceptions were shared by respondents to the CIPD survey (2005) who also report very positive impacts on motivation.

WINDOW ON PRACTICE

Benefits experienced

Scott (2007) reports on the Britannia Buidling Society, which found that absence and employee turnover have both reduced as a result of its flexible working policy. Absence dropped from 3.06 per cent in 2004 to 2.35 per cent in 2006 and turnover from 18.94 per cent in 2004 to 12.6 per cent in 2006. Whilst the society had adopted flexible working before 2004 it was ad hoc and inconsistent so improvements were made by getting board commitment, engaging people across the business in focus groups and including the input of representatives into a new HR policy on flexible working. Britannia also claims that there is a direct link with customer satisfaction.

▶

▶ Phillips (2007) reports on Ellis Fairbank, Recruitment Consultants who state that flexible working for all staff has increased productivity and helped to attract top talent. They also found lower absence, reduced employee turnover and raised morale. The Consultancy used flexible working in their advertising campaign to attract staff.

Such advertising is a surprisingly underused practice. The CIPD (2005) found that only 36 per cent of respondent employers to its survey used flexible working in their recruitment advertising compared with 74 per cent who communicate this information in staff handbooks.

Sources: Summarised from Scott, A. (2007) 'Flexible Working cuts absence', *People Management*, Vol. 13, No. 6, p. 15, 22 March; and Phillips, L. (2007) 'Add muscle with flexible work', *People Management*, Vol. 13, No. 5, p. 10, 8 March.

Increased levels of performance have also been found as employees are less tired and so able to work more effectively. Kodz *et al.* (2002) found that productivity and quality of work had both improved, as had staff retention and the ability to recruit staff. Perry-Smith and Blum (2000) found that bundles of work-life balance policies were related to higher organisational performance. In our own research we found that informal flexibility was highly valued and associated with employee discretionary effort in terms of supporting colleagues, and patients where appropriate, and being available and flexible to cover emergencies. Employees appreciated the flexibility they were given and therefore wanted to give something back, recognising the need for 'give and take'. Some employers have argued that staff on shorter working hours are still producing the same amount of work that they did on full-time hours; however, this was found to be, at least partly, due to the fact that they were working longer than the part-time hours they were being paid for.

In a baseline study covering employers and employees, conducted by the Institute for Employment Research at the University of Warwick and IFF Research Ltd (Hogarth *et al.* 2001), 91 per cent of employers and 96 per cent of employees felt that people work better when they can balance their work with other aspects of their lives. Employers can also find that such policies meet business needs for flexibility and are a way of addressing diversity issues.

WLI: rhetoric versus reality

Having outlined the benefits of WLI for both organizations and employees and the 'business case' that has led to the increasing availability of flexible working options, we now review the current state of WLI.

Barriers to WLI

So far the demand for flexible work options is much greater than the take-up, and this has been referred to as the 'take-up gap'. Hogarth *et al.* (2001) report that 47 per cent of employees not currently using flexitime would like to do so, and 35 per cent would like a compressed week. The desire for working different or more flexible hours is a significant determinant of employees moving jobs either within or between employers (Boheim and Taylor 2004) to achieve the flexibility they desire, and the researchers also point to rigidities in the British labour market which does not offer enough jobs with flexible hours. Some work-life balance strategies cost the organisation money and financial limits are set for such practices to be viable. The AA experienced difficulties in setting up teleworking at home. The productivity of teleworkers was greater than that of site-based staff, but in order to offset the cost of technology and infrastructure such workers had to be more than 1.5 times as productive as site staff. To gain such productivity tight management and measurement of home-based teleworkers is necessary (Bibby 2002).

Policies and some line managers may limit access to work-life balance to certain groups, which is clearly evidenced in the latest WERS (Kersley *et al.* 2006). There is also evidence that some employers do not take a strategic approach to work-life balance, but use it in a fire-fighting manner, to deal with situations when they reach breaking point (for example in a case study of a Further Education college, *see* Glynn *et al.* 2002). Whilst organisations can sometimes easily provide reduced hours work for, say, administrative and sales staff, it is much more difficult to do this with professional staff. Anecdotal evidence suggests that many professionals moving from full- to part-time work find that they are really expected to do a full-time job in part-time hours and with part-time pay. Edwards and Robinson (2004) found that the lack of a strategic approach to reducing hours for nurses resulted in an unsatisfactory situation for both part-timers and full-timers alike, as shown in the Window on practice below.

WINDOW ON PRACTICE

Part-time working for qualified nurses

Edwards and Robinson (2004) researched part-time working for nurses in three NHS trusts and found that flexible working had evolved reactively as a response to requests from full-time nurses wishing to work part time. Senior and middle managers reported that nursing culture did not support part-time working and that some line managers were unenthusiastic. Whilst line managers perceived that part-time working aided retention and to some extent recruitment, they identified disadvantages as communication and information flow; management and supervision, including continuity of service and nurse availability, and work orientation (for example, not wanting responsibility or promotion or taking on new tasks and roles). Nursing staff themselves reported that there was a tendency for management to give part-time staff different and often less central roles. On a range of activities, including acting as a team leader; attending management, practice development and research meetings; shadowing senior staff; and developing clinical guidelines, the researchers found that part-time staff were

▶

▶ always less involved than full-time staff. Part-timers were also less satisfied with their training and career progression than full-time staff. The researchers identified a circle of skills erosion and being limited to a narrow range of tasks for part-timers, which diminishes flexibility for part-timers and does not provide the best return for the employers. Edwards and Robinson identified that problems resulted from the way that part-time working was implemented in that part-timers occupied jobs normally designed for full-timers which were not necessarily suited to or planned for part-timers. Whilst the employers had acquiesced in responding to requests for part-time work they had made minimal additional effort to adjust the systems of work organisation to support part-time working.

Source: Summarised from Edwards, C. and Robinson, O. (2004) 'Evaluating the Business Case for Part-time Working amongst Qualified Nurses', *British Journal of Industrial Relations*, Vol. 42, No. 1, pp. 167–183.

There is evidence in the literature that work-life balance requests for childcare reasons would be dealt with more favourably that requests on any other basis. The association that work-life balance practices have with women bringing up children creates two problems. The first is that work-life balance is 'ghettoised' (*see*, for example, Rana 2002), as something done for women with children who are not interested in real careers. The second is that this causes alienation from the rest of the workforce who are not allowed these special privileges. In particular, working part time has been a popular option in combining work and other commitments, and yet there is considerable evidence that this limits career development (*see*, for example, MacDermid *et al.* 2001).

There is some evidence that the public sector makes much better provision for work-life integration than the private sector. Case 2.2 on this book's companion website, **www.pearsoned.co.uk/torrington**, explores this further.

Activity 2.4

Discuss the following statement. To what extent do you agree or disagree with it, and why?

'Employees should be equally entitled to WLI options, as long as business needs are met. It doesn't matter whether the reason is childcare, the desire to engage in sports activities, do extra gardening, or just loll around on the sofa watching television.'

The take-up of work-life balance options is often equated with lack of commitment to one's career or to the organisation. In the baseline study Hogarth *et al.* (2001) found that two-thirds of male employees felt that their career prospects would be damaged if they worked part time, and CIPD (Rana 2002) found strikingly similar results in its survey of work-life balance.

In addition there are many employees who are committed to full-time hours because financial commitments mean that they require full-time pay, which severely limits the type of flexibility that they feel is appropriate. Heavy workloads may prevent requests for flexible working, and where departments are inadequately staffed flexible options are severely curtailed. High levels of work, combined with pressure from the organisational culture may also have unexpected consequences for those employees opting to reduce their hours to part time from full time. Furthermore in many organisations individuals have to be proactive and suggest flexible solutions which meet business needs and this is difficult when there are few precedents and a lack of understanding of what is available or possible. In our own research (Hall and Atkinson 2006) we found that although the Health Trust was keen to support work-life integration and had an appropriate policy, few employees were aware of what was available or knew how to locate the policy. In their Work Foundation survey Visser and Williams (2006) report that focus group participants felt that work-life balance options were not well communicated to them. In addition the majority of organisations in an IRS survey had no procedure for employees to use to request flexible working (IRS 2002).

The CIPD survey (Rana 2002) reports that 74 per cent of respondents believed that working hours is not an indication of commitment, 84 per cent felt that individuals working part time were not less committed and 77 per cent believed that organisations should allow employees to attend to personal commitments in working time, and then make the time up. However, while these figures demonstrate that there have been some shifts in attitudes, culture remains a major barrier to take-up. Long hours cultures with early and late meetings are hard to shift. It is argued that more middle and senior manager role models of flexible working are needed and that there need to be work-life integration champions.

Managers' role in WLI

Whether or not there is a work-life integration policy in existence, it is often line managers who will be the 'main arbiters of whether work-life balance policies become a reality . . . both by their attitudes and management practices' (Glynn *et al.* 2002, p. 5). The Work Foundation found that managers were the main barrier to introducing and implementing work-life integration policies (CIPD 2003). While it is clear to those at a senior level in the organisation that WLI practices can be of value, it is line managers who have the unenviable task of reconciling both performance and flexibility, especially where flexible working for some may mean higher workloads for others. There is a pressure on line managers to be fair and their decisions about who can work flexibly and in what way are under scrutiny and may result in a backlash. We have said before that there is a general lack of a strategic approach to work-life integration and one of the consequences of this is that when an employee reduces his or her hours the remainder of the work tends to be reallocated to the remaining full-time workers. Murphy (2006) in an IRS survey found that employers appeared not prepared to pick up the costs associated with work-life integration. It is apparent that flexibility presents many challenges for line managers, just one of many HR and other responsibilities that they have, and often they lack training and experience in how to implement WLI practices. That said, our own research in the NHS demonstrates that, in the face of national skills shortages, managers in the Professions Allied to Medicine areas (e.g. Occupational Therapy) were very creative in implementing flexible working to address recruitment and retention difficulties.

WINDOW ON PRACTICE

Managing part-time working in the Police Service

Dick (2004) reports on the impact of part-time working for police officers located in a large metropolitan constabulary in the north of England. There was no human resource strategy which addressed the aims for implementation and management of part-time working. Officers put forward a proposal for part-time working and how their hours should be scheduled. There was a view from the HR department that line managers were resistant to part-time working but Dick found a number of contradictions and difficulties for managers in dealing with this issue. Operational policing is a demand-led activity over 24/7 with unpredictable events. There is a tradition of staying behind at the end of a shift to complete work, to work extra shifts at short notice and be on call over 24 hours. This was a clear issue as part-timers in this case had often opted for reduced hours so that they could be available at specific times to deal with childcare responsibilities. Managers of part-time officers felt they could not force them to work extra hours when needed due to fear of a backlash and an industrial tribunal. Only one part-timer thought the availability culture was a legitimate response to the demands of the job, others felt that a more creative approach was possible, and felt that solutions were available through culture change. Managers often objected to part-time working because of the lack of consistency of supervision that this would entail. In order to meet the demand for part-time working managers often put part-timers in a non-central role, but this brought with it the perspective that part-timers were being marginalised. Dick identified that previously managers were not able to recoup the hours lost when an officer went part time, but a new policy to enable this had just been introduced. Also part-timers were able to negotiate the shifts they desired with the consequence that full-timers got more than their fair share of unpopular shifts, and Dick identifies a possible change to paying part-timers for the specific shifts they actually work, which was not happening at the time.

This is a good example of the way that work is constructed according to a set of rules based on what works for a full-time officer, but which causes serious problems when applied to part-timers.

Source: Summarised from Dick, P. (2004) 'Between a rock and a hard place: The dilemmas of managing part-time working in the police service', *Personnel Review*, Vol. 33, No. 3, pp. 302–31.

Managing workers who are not visible (working at home, for example) is a particular concern for line managers. Felstead *et al.* (2003) report the fear that working at home is a 'slacker's charter', but they also found that homeworkers themselves had fears about not being able easily to demonstrate their honesty, reliability and productivity. Some managed this by working more hours than they should in order to demonstrate greater output. To counteract this fear, managers in Felstead's study introduced new surveillance devices, set output targets and brought management into the home via home visits. Managers also felt that home working represented a potential threat to the integration of teams and the acceptance of corporate culture, and that it impeded the transmission of tacit knowledge. There is also a concern that only some employees have the characteristics to be successful homeworkers, and Felstead *et al.* (2003) develop this idea in some detail. Overall, managing working-time flexibility has emerged as a challenge in the past few years and line managers are likely to need much more support and encouragement in order to do this effectively.

Employee role and WLI

WLI is not available to most employees. Felstead *et al.* (2003) reveal that the option to work at home is usually the privilege of the highly educated and/or people at the top of the organisational hierarchy. People in these jobs, they suggest, have considerably more influence over the work processes they are engaged in. They also report that although more women work at home than men, there are more men who have the choice to work at home. Nolan and Wood (2003) also note that work-life balance is not for the lower paid. They report that 5 per cent of such employees hold more than one job, and usually work in low-paid, low-status jobs in catering and personal services. A similar scene is painted by Polly Toynbee (2003). She also reports that many of these low-paid workers work for agencies and are therefore distanced from the ultimate 'employer'. In these circumstances work-life integration policies are unlikely to be available in any case. Even working only for one employer Toynbee reports a hospital porter saying, 'you can't survive, not with a family, unless you do the long, long hours, unless you both work all the hours there are' (p. 59). Felstead *et al.* (2002) highlight an assumption in the work-life integration literature, which portrays working at home as always a 'good thing'. They argue that what is important is the *option* to work at home, as some people work at home doing low-paid unsatisfying jobs with no choice of work location, such conditions not necessarily being conducive to work-life integration. This reinforces the need outlined by Strachan and Burgess (1998), cited above, for policies of income and employment security to be included with WLI practices if more sophisticated policies are to be considered to be effective.

Rhetoric or reality?

Despite a number of blue chip organisations which actively publicise their WLI practices, we suggest that problems of implementation, line manager resistance and the restriction of such practices to certain groups means that WLI is still an aspiration rather than a reality for many employees. White *et al.* (2003), for example, argue that WLI practices are enjoyed by only a small proportion of the workforce, and in any case have only a small effect on the problem. They argue for more fundamental changes in working practices with safeguards to protect work-life integration, such as giving teams themselves the responsibility for addressing work-life integration issues when setting output targets for themselves. We suggest that work continues to be organised in a way that predominantly meets the needs of employers, the 'business case' for WLI integration often failing to initiate sufficient action to offer genuine WLI to the majority of employees.

Activity 2.5

'Work-life integration is just another fad. In a few years time it will be superseded by another issue.'
To what extent do you agree with this statement and why?

SUMMARY PROPOSITIONS

2.1 There are many types of organisational flexibility, such as those outlined in Atkinson's (1984) model of the flexible firm.

2.2 Critiques of organisational flexibility suggest that it may not be successful in achieving its aims.

2.3 Work-life integration policies generally provide options around how many hours are worked, exactly when these hours are worked and where they are worked.

2.4 When employees are given some control over their work-life integration they are likely to be more satisfied with work, have greater commitment to work, be more productive and stay longer in the organisation.

2.5 Barriers to work-life integration include understaffing, line manager fears, worries about career damage, lack of a strategic approach to reduced hours working and organisational culture.

2.6 The rhetoric of availability of WLI is not matched by the reality: the need for organisational rather than employee forms of flexibility continues to dominate.

GENERAL DISCUSSION TOPICS

1   Discuss the claim that flexible resourcing strategies should be welcomed by the individual as they provide new areas of opportunity rather than a threat.

2   To what extent do you believe that WLI is a realistic aim for the majority of employees?

FURTHER READING

Brown, P., Green, A. and Lauder, H. (2001) *High Skills: globalization, competitiveness and skill formation*. Oxford: Oxford University Press.
The authors draw on the results of a large international study to compare and contrast the different approaches being used around the globe to promote skills acquisition and to create a high-skill labour force. Their analysis focuses in particular on the impact of economic globalisation on skills development.

Pollert, A. (1988) 'The flexible firm: fixation or fact?', *Work, Employment and Society*, Vol. 2, No. 3, pp. 281–316.
Although published some years ago, this article is the best and most coherent critique of Atkinson's model of the flexible firm and the management trends it has influenced for two decades.

CIPD (2005) *Flexible Working: The Implementation Challenge*. London: Chartered Institute of Personnel and Development.

Examples of good practice in both public and private sector organisations, incorporated with some of the results from the CIPD's 2005 flexible working survey.

Kossek, E. and Lambert, S. (eds) (2005) *Work and Life Integration: Organisational, Cultural and Individual Perspectives*. London: Lawrence Erlbaum Associates.
A useful book as a broad, rather than just an individual approach to work-life integration is taken. The book is equally appropriate for practitioners and academic study, as there is a dual focus on theory and practical aspects.

Rabinowitz, S. (2007) 'Book Reviews: Work, family, and life interfaces: a selective book review', *Career Development International*, Vol. 12, No. 2, pp. 1362–1436.
An interesting selection of eight books published in 2005/6 focusing on the work/life interface giving a flavour of developments in thinking and including multicultural and multidisciplinary perspectives.

REFERENCES

Atkinson, C. and Hall, L. (2005) 'Improving Working Lives: the role of gender in flexible working', paper presented to the Gender, Work and Organisation Conference, University of Keele, July 2005.

Atkinson, J. (1984) 'Manpower strategies for flexible organisations', *Personnel Management*, August.

Bibby, A. (2002) 'Home start', *People Management*, Vol. 8, No. 1, 10 January, pp. 36–7.

Bishop, K. (2004) 'Working Time Patterns in UK, France, Denmark and Sweden', **www.statistics.gov.uk/articles/ labour_market_trends_/working_time_patterns.pdf**.

Blyton, P. (1998) 'Flexibility', in Poole, M. and Warner, M. (eds) *The IEBM Handbook of Human Resource Management*. London: Thomson.

Boheim, R. and Taylor, M. (2004) 'Actual and preferred working hours', *British Journal of Industrial Relations*. Vol. 42, No. 1, pp. 149–66.

Burchell, B.J., Day, D., Hudson, M., Ladipo, D., Mankelow, R., Nolan, J., Reed, H., Wichert, I. and Wilkinson, F. (1999) *Job insecurity and work intensification: flexibility and the changing boundaries of work*. London: Joseph Rowntree Foundation.

CIPD (2003) 'Managers obstruct flexibility', *People Management*, Vol. 9, No. 18, p. 9.

CIPD (2005) *Flexible Working: Impact and Implementation: An employer survey*. London: CIPD.

Dick, P. (2004) 'Between a rock and a hard place: The dilemmas of managing part-time working in the police service', *Personnel Review*, Vol. 33, No. 3, pp. 302–31.

Edwards, C. and Robinson, O. (2004) 'Evaluating the Business Case for Part-time Working amongst Qualified Nurses', *British Journal of Industrial Relations*, Vol. 42, No. 1, pp. 167–83.

Fagnani, J. *et al.* (2004) 'Gender, parenthood and the changing European workplace', *Transitions Research Report # 2: Context Mapping Report for the EU Framework 5 funded study*. Printed by Manchester Metropolitan University: Research Institute for Health and Social Change.

Felstead, A., Jewson, N., Phizacklea, A. and Walters, S. (2002) 'The option of working at home: another privilege for the favoured few', *New Technology, Work and Employment*, Vol. 17, No. 3, pp. 204–23.

Felstead, A., Jewson, N. and Walters, S. (2003) 'Managerial control of employees working at home', *British Journal of Industrial Relations*, Vol. 41, No. 2, June, pp. 241–64.

Fudge, J. and Owens, R. (2007) 'Precarious work, Women and the New Economy: the challenge to legal norms', in J. Fudge and R. Owens (eds) *Precarious work, Women and the New Economy*. Oxford: Hart Publishing.

Glynn, C., Steinberg, I. and McCartney, C. (2002) *Work-life balance: The role of the manager*. Horsham: Roffey Park Institute.

Hall, L. and Atkinson, C. (2006) 'Improving Working Lives: Flexible Working and the role of employee control', *Employee Relations*, Vol. 28, No. 4.

Harris, L. (2003) 'Home-based teleworking and the employment relationship', *Personnel Review*, Vol. 32, No. 4, pp. 422–37.

Heery, E. and Salmon, J. (eds) (2000) *The Insecure Workforce*. London: Routledge.

Hogarth, T., Hasluck, C., Pierre, G. with Winterbotham, M. and Vivian, D. (2001) *Work-life Balance 2000: Results from the baseline study*. Research Report 249. London: DfEE.

IDS (2006) *Flexitime Schemes*, IDS Studies No. 822, London: IDS.

Institute of Management (2001) *The Quality of Working Life Report*. London: Institute of Management.

IRS (2002) 'Hanging in the balance', *IRS Employment Review*, No. 766, 30 December, pp. 6–11.

Kersley, B., Alpin, C., Forth, J., Bryson, A., Bewley, H., Dix, G. and Oxenbridge, S. (2006) *Inside the Workplace: Findings from the 2004 Workplace Employment Relations Survey*. London: Routledge.

Kodz, J. (2003) *Working long hours: a review of evidence*, Vol. 1, Employment Relations Research Series, No. 16.

Kodz, J., Harper, H. and Dench, S. (2002) *Work-life Balance: Beyond the Rhetoric*, Institute for Employment Studies Report No. 384. Brighton: Institute for Employment Studies.

Legge, K. (1995) *Human Resource Management: rhetoric and realities*. Basingstoke: Macmillan.

Lepak, D.P. and Snell, S.A. (1999) 'The human resource architect: toward a theory of human capital allocation and development', *Academy of Management Review*, Vol. 24, No. 1, pp. 31–48.

MacDermid, S., Lee, M., Buck, M. and Williams, M. (2001) 'Alternative work arrangements among professionals and managers', *Journal of Management Development*, Vol. 20, No. 4, pp. 305–17.

Murphy, N. (2006) 'Work: Our flexible friend', *IRS Employment Review*, No. 850, pp. 8–15, 7 July.

Nolan, P. and Wood, S. (2003) 'Mapping the future of work', *British Journal of Industrial Relations*, Vol. 41, No. 2, pp. 165–74.

Perry-Smith, J. and Blum, T. (2000) 'Work-family human resource bundles and perceived organizational performance', *Academy of Management Journal*, Vol. 43, pp. 1107–17.

Rana, E. (2002) 'Balancing Act Earns UK respect', in *The Guide to Work-life Balance*. London: CIPD.

Reilly, P. (2001) *Flexibility at Work*. Aldershot: Gower.

Rosendaal, B.W. (2003) 'Dealing with part-time work', *Personnel Review*, Vol. 32, No. 4, pp. 474–91.

Sisson, K. and Storey, J. (2000) *The Realities of Human Resource Management: Managing the Employment Relationship*. Buckingham: Open University Press.

Strachan, G. and Burgess, J. (1998) 'The "family friendly" workplace', *International Journal of Manpower*, Vol. 19, No. 4, pp. 250–65.

Torrington, D.P., Hall, L.A. and Taylor, S. (2007) *Human Resource Management*, 7th edn. Harlow: Pearson Education.

Toynbee, P. (2003) *Hard Work: Life in low-pay Britain*. London: Bloomsbury.

Tuselmann, H.-J. (1996) 'The path towards greater labour flexibility in Germany: hampered by past success?', *Employee Relations*, Vol. 18, No. 6, pp. 26–47.

Visser, F. and Williams, L. (2006) *Work-life Balance: Rhetoric vs Reality*. London: The Work Foundation and Unison.

White, M., Hill, S., McGovern, P., Mills, C. and Smeaton, D. (2003) ' "High performance" management practices, working hours and work-life balance', *British Journal of Industrial Relations*, Vol. 41, No. 2, June, pp. 175–95.

CHAPTER 3

Recruitment and retention

The objectives of this chapter are to:

1 Identify alternative courses of action to take when an employee leaves an organisation

2 Compare and contrast the major alternative recruitment methods

3 Assess developments in recruitment advertising and Internet recruitment

4 Introduce the concept of employer branding

5 Examine recent trends in job tenure and turnover in the UK

6 Outline the main reasons for voluntary resignations

7 Explore some approaches which improve staff retention rates

8 Debate the likely severity of future skills shortages and their impact

Typing in terms such as 'recruitment problems', 'retention difficulties' or 'skills gaps' into Internet search engines brings up thousands of articles attesting to the trouble employers increasingly have finding appropriately qualified staff to fill their available vacancies. The most acute difficulties are faced by those seeking to employ people with higher-level specialised skills, the result being the development of labour markets which are both very tight and increasingly international. Increasing pay can help to ease skills shortages, but the extent to which any organisation is able to increase pay is limited by the need to remain competitive. The other major alternative approach used involves recruiting overseas. But there are sometimes major barriers to taking either of these two routes.

Nowhere is this more true than of the world's armed forces, which are facing major recruitment and retention problems, particularly at senior levels and among specialised groups such as maintenance engineers. In 2008 it was reported that skills shortages in Australia meant that only half of the country's submarine fleet was presently capable of action (Smith 2008). The reason was an inability to recruit, and particularly to retain, sufficient skilled technicians, many of whom have skill sets which are in fierce demand in the mining industry. Chinese mining companies, in particular, are prepared to pay people twice or three times the salaries they receive working for the Australian navy. Representatives of mining companies hover around naval bases on payday, luring technical staff into conversation and offering them improved packages.

The same is true of many industries – in particular IT, engineering, energy supply and in the market for financial services professionals. There are not enough people with the skills required chasing the available jobs. Investing in training new people is an obvious approach to take, but the training often takes five years or more and at the end of it, trainees are free to sell their services to the highest bidder. So there is always a need to recruit more aggressively and work harder and harder at retaining existing people.

The mobilisation of a workforce with the potential to perform effectively is the most fundamental challenge faced by an organisation's human resource function. Unless good people can be recruited and subsequently retained for a reasonable period of time it becomes very difficult to maximise levels of performance and hence to achieve any degree of sustained competitive advantage.

When labour markets are loose, as happens when a country's economy goes into a period of recession, unemployment rises and the skills which employers seek are in plentiful supply. At such times, for most employers, recruiting and retaining people is unproblematic. There is no need to spend a great deal of money on recruitment drives because there are plenty of suitable potential recruits actively seeking work. At the same time, staff retention is less of a problem because existing employees have fewer alternative job opportunities open to them. By contrast, when an economy is growing, and particularly when it is developing in new directions, skills shortages arise. The more severe these become, the harder it is for employers to recruit and retain people with the skills, attributes and experience that are required.

In recent years the UK economy has experienced a strong and sustained period of economic growth leading to the development of relatively tight labour market conditions. As a result, recruitment and retention issues have moved to the top of the HR agenda, underpinning many of the more significant contemporary developments in the field. In addition, more money is being spent on these areas of activity, leading to substantial growth in the recruitment industry. Elsewhere in the world some of the largest economies are experiencing historically unprecedented rates of economic growth which far outpace those being experienced in the UK. The Chinese economy, for example, is currently growing at a rate of 11 per cent a year and the Indian economy by 7 per cent (Winters and Yusuf 2007, p. vii). Here skills shortages have become very severe indeed, recruitment and retention issues rising to the top not only of the HR agenda, but also the agendas of all major companies and government agencies.

In this chapter we start by setting out and explaining the major contemporary developments in the field of recruitment, focusing on the different approaches that can be adopted and the circumstances in which each is most appropriate for organisations to use. We go on to look at how organisations address the need to retain their staff and at the policy prescriptions that are most effective at reducing unwanted turnover. Our key debate in this chapter concerns the extent of skills shortages in the UK, both today and in the future. How serious a problem is our economy facing and what organisational and public policy prescriptions are required to tackle it?

RECRUITING IN A TIGHT LABOUR MARKET

Over three million people are recruited by employers in the UK each year, an increasingly costly and difficult process when skills are in short supply and labour markets are tight. According to the successive annual surveys of recruitment practice undertaken by the Chartered Institute of Personnel and Development, a very substantial majority of respondents report experiencing recruitment difficulties, particularly when it comes to finding appropriate management and professional staff (CIPD 2005, 2006 and 2007). In such circumstances the employer is required to 'sell' its jobs to potential employees so as to ensure that it can generate an adequate pool of applicants. Job opportunities have to be presented in such a way as to make them attractive to people in terms of the rate of pay, the likelihood of career development and the quality of the employment experience in the widest sense. Importantly it is necessary to recognise that the recruitment process is not by any means finished at the point at which a pool of applications has been received. It continues during the shortlisting and interviewing stages and is only complete when an offer is made and accepted. Until that time there is an ongoing need to ensure that a favourable impression of the organisation as an employer is maintained in the minds of those whose services it wishes to secure (Barber 1998).

That said, however tempting it may be to do so, it is also important to avoid overselling a job in a bid to secure the services of talented applicants. Making out that the experience of working in a role is going to be more interesting or exciting than it really will be is an easy trap to fall into, but ultimately it is counterproductive because it raises unrealistic expectations. These then are quickly dashed, leading to unnecessary demotivation and, in many cases, an early resignation. The result is a failed recruitment episode in which money has been spent, but little recouped by way of a return on the investment. So a balance always has to be struck in recruitment between putting over an attractive message to the target labour market and ensuring that people are not misled in any way about what to expect if their applications are accepted and a job offer made.

Sometimes, of course, when a full-time employee resigns or when an organisation expands its activities it is possible to avoid the creation of a vacancy because there are other ways of filling the gap. Recruiting a like-for-like replacement may be the most obvious tactic when a vacancy occurs, but it is not necessarily the most appropriate. Listed below are some of the options:

- reorganise the work
- use overtime
- mechanise the work
- stagger the hours
- make the job part time
- subcontract the work
- use an agency to supply a temporary worker

Activity 3.1

Can you think of further ways of avoiding filling a vacancy by recruiting a new employee? What are the advantages and disadvantages of the methods you have thought of? For what types of job with which you are familiar would each of your methods, and those listed above, be most appropriate?

METHODS OF RECRUITMENT

Internal recruitment

Vacancies are often filled internally. Sometimes organisations advertise all vacancies publicly as a matter of course and consider internal candidates along with anyone from outside the organisation who applies. This approach is generally considered to constitute good practice and is widely used in the UK's public sector. However, many organisations prefer to invite applications from internal candidates *before* they look to their external labour markets for new staff (Newell and Shackleton 2000, pp. 116–17; CIPD 2006, p. 8). There are considerable advantages from the employer's perspective. First it is a great deal less expensive to recruit internally, there being no need to spend money on job advertisements or recruitment agencies. Instead a message can simply be placed in a company newsletter or posted on its intranet or staff noticeboards. Further cost savings and efficiency gains can be made because internal recruits are typically able to take up new posts much more quickly than people being brought in from outside. Even if they have to work some notice in their current positions, they are often able to take on some of their new responsibilities or undergo relevant training at the same time. The other advantage stems from the fact that internal candidates, as a rule, are more knowledgeable than new starters coming in from other organisations about what exactly the job involves. They are also more familiar with the organisation's culture, rules and geography, and so take less time to settle into their new jobs and to begin working at full capacity.

Giving preference to internal recruits, particularly as far as promotions are concerned, has the great advantage of providing existing employees with an incentive to work hard, demonstrate their commitment and stay with the organisation when they might otherwise consider looking for alternative employment. The practice provides a powerful signal from management to show that existing employees are valued and that attractive career development opportunities are available to them. Failing to recruit internally may thus serve to put off good candidates with potential from applying for the more junior positions in an organisation.

The main disadvantage of only advertising posts internally stems from the limited field of candidates that it permits an organisation to consider. While it may mean that someone who 'fits in well' is recruited, it may also very well mean that the best available candidate is not even considered. Over the long term the organisation can thus end up being less well served than it would have been had internal candidates been required to compete with outside people for their posts. For this reason internal recruitment sits uneasily with a commitment to equal opportunities and to the creation of a diverse workforce. Talented candidates from under-represented groups are not appointed because they never get to know about the vacancies that the organisation has.

It is also important to note that the management of internal recruitment practices is difficult to carry out effectively in practice. Research carried out by the Institute of Employment Studies (2002) shows that serious problems often occur when internal candidates fail to be selected. This is because they tend to enter the selection process with higher expectations of being offered the position than is the case with external candidates. Bitterness, antipathy and low morale are thus likely to follow. Moreover, failed internal candidates are considerably more likely to pursue claims of unfair discrimination following a selection process than external candidates. For these reasons it is essential that great care is taken when managing internal recruitment to ensure that the approach taken is both fair and seen to be fair. Giving honest, full, accurate and constructive feedback to failed candidates is an essential part of the process.

External recruitment

Once an employer has decided that external recruitment is necessary, a cost-effective and appropriate method of recruitment must be selected. There are a number of distinct approaches to choose from, each of which is more or less appropriate in different circumstances. As a result most employers use a wide variety of different recruitment methods at different times. In many situations there is also a good case for using different methods in combination when looking to fill the same vacancy. Table 3.1 sets out the usage of different methods reported in a recent survey of 802 UK employers (CIPD 2007).

It is interesting to compare the figures in Table 3.1 with those reported in surveys of how people actually find their jobs in practice. These repeatedly show that informal methods (such as word of mouth and making unsolicited applications) are as common as, if not more common than, formal methods such as recruitment advertising. In 2002, the Labour Force Survey asked over a million people how they had obtained their current job. The results are shown in Table 3.2.

TABLE 3.1 Usage of various methods of recruitment by 905 organisations in 2007

Method	per cent
Advertisements in local press	75
Corporate website	75
Recruitment agencies	73
Specialist journals and trade press	61
Employee referral scheme	47
Word of mouth/speculative applications	44
Jobcentre Plus	43
National newspaper advertisements	45
Apprentices/work placements/secondments	33
Education liaison	32
Search consultants	29
Commercial job-board Internet sites	21
Posters/billboards	11
Radio/TV	6
Other	10

Source: This table is taken from Survey Report: Recruitment, Retention and Turnover (2007) with the permission of the publisher, the Chartered Institutue of Personnel and Development, London (www.cipd.co.uk).

TABLE 3.2 Methods of obtaining a job

	Men (%)	Women (%)
Hearing from someone who worked there	30	25
Reply to an advertisement	25	31
Direct application	14	17
Private employment agency	10	10
Job centre	9	8
Other	12	9

Source: Labour Market Trends (2002), 'Labour market spotlight', *Labour Market Trends*, August.

Informal recruitment is not generally considered to constitute good practice. This is because in using the approach an organisation denies itself the opportunity to select the best possible candidate from a wide pool of applicants. The approach is also strongly criticised on ethical grounds because it has the effect of favouring friends and relatives of existing employees and hence tends to deny opportunity to disadvantaged groups, helping to perpetuate social inequality. However, when seen purely from the perspective of the employer seeking a good worker cheaply and quickly, it is understandable that it is used very extensively. Moreover, there is plenty of research evidence which suggests that informal recruits are often stronger performers than those who are recruited formally and that they are less likely to leave at an early date too (*see* Iles and Robertson 1997 and Barber 1998, pp. 22–32). Why this should be the case is a matter of debate, but it could well be linked to the fact that someone recruited via word of mouth is likely to have a clearer idea about what working for an organisation in a particular role will be like. Moreover, informal recruits are more likely to enjoy the job, simply because they are working alongside people they know, like and trust.

The various methods of formal recruitment have benefits and drawbacks too, and the choice of a method has to be made in relation to the particular vacancy and the type of labour market in which the job falls. A general review of advantages and drawbacks is given in Table 3.3.

Activity 3.2

Think about a job you have done in the past, one you are doing now or one which a member of your family is employed to do. What recruitment method or combination of methods was used? What were the advantages and disadvantages of the approach that was used when seen from the perspective of the employer? Could an alternative approach have been more effective?

Recruitment advertising

In order to assist them in drafting advertisements and placing them in suitable media, many employers deal with a recruitment advertising agency. Such agencies provide expert advice on where to place advertisements and how they should be worded and will design them attractively to achieve maximum impact. Large organisations often subcontract all their advertising work to an agency with which a mutually acceptable service-level agreement has been signed. Recruitment advertising companies (as opposed to headhunters and recruitment consultants) are often inexpensive because the agency derives much of its income from the commission paid by the journals on the value of the advertising space sold, the bigger agencies being able to negotiate substantial discounts because of the amount of business they place with the newspapers and trade journals. A portion of this saving is then passed on to the employer so that it can easily be cheaper *and* a great deal more effective to work with an agent providing this kind of service.

In choosing where to place a recruitment advertisement the aim is to attract as many people as possible with the required skills and qualifications. The employer also wants to reach people who are either actively looking for a new job or thinking about doing so. The need is therefore to place the advertisement where job seekers who are qualified to take on the role are most likely to look. In some situations newspaper readership figures are helpful when deciding where to advertise. An example would be where there are two or more established trade journals or local newspapers competing with one another, both of which carry extensive numbers of recruitment advertisements. Otherwise readership figures are unimportant because people tend to buy different newspapers when job searching than they do the rest of the time. It is often more helpful to look at the share of different recruitment advertising markets achieved by the various publications, as this gives an indication of where particular types of job are mostly advertised.

TABLE 3.3 Advantages and drawbacks of traditional methods of recruitment

Job centres

Advantages: (a) Applicants can be selected from nationwide sources with convenient, local availability of computer-based data.
(b) Socially responsible and secure.
(c) Can produce applicants very quickly.
(d) Free service for employers.

Drawbacks: (a) Registers are mainly of the unemployed rather than of the employed seeking a change.
(b) Produces people for interview who are not genuinely interested in undertaking the job.

Commercial employment agencies and recruitment consultancies

Advantages: (a) Established as the normal method for filling certain vacancies, e.g. secretaries in London.
(b) Little administrative chore for the employer.

Drawbacks: (a) Can produce staff who are likely to stay only a short time.
(b) Widely distrusted by employers.
(c) Can be very expensive.

Management selection consultants

Advantages: (a) Opportunity to elicit applicants anonymously.
(b) Opportunity to use expertise of consultant in an area where employer will not be regularly in the market.

Drawbacks: (a) Internal applicants may feel, or be, excluded.
(b) Cost.

Executive search consultants ('headhunters')

Advantages: (a) Known individuals can be approached directly.
(b) Useful if employer has no previous experience in specialist field.
(c) Recruiting from, or for, an overseas location.

Drawbacks: (a) Cost.
(b) Potential candidates outside the headhunter's network are excluded.
(c) Recruits remain on the consultant's list and can be hunted again.

Visiting universities

Advantages: (a) The main source of new graduates from universities.
(b) Rated by students as the most popular method.

Drawbacks: (a) Need to differentiate presentations from those of other employers.
(b) Time taken to visit a number of universities (i.e. labour intensive).

Schools and the Careers Service

Advantages: (a) Can produce a regular annual flow of interested enquirers.
(b) Very appropriate for the recruitment of school-leavers, who seldom look further than the immediate locality for their first employment.

Drawbacks: (a) Schools and the advisers are more interested in occupations than organisations.
(b) Taps into a limited potential applicant pool.

The decision on what to include in a recruitment advertisement is important because of the high cost of space and the need to attract attention; both factors will encourage the use of the fewest number of words. As a minimum it is necessary to explain the job content, the location from which the job holder will work and to give information about how to apply. Many employers are coy about declaring the salary that will accompany the advertised post. Sometimes this is reasonable as the salary scales are well known and inflexible, as in much public sector employment. Elsewhere the coyness is due either to the fact that the employer has a general secrecy policy about salaries and does not want to publicise the salary of a position to be filled for fear of dissatisfying holders of other posts. All research evidence, however, suggests that a good indication of the salary is essential if the employer is to attract a useful number of appropriate replies (*see* Barber 1998, pp. 42–3). Table 3.4 indicates various advantages and disadvantages of the different methods of job advertising.

E-recruitment

The use of the Internet for recruitment purposes is, along with the substantial recent growth in international recruitment, the most striking recent development in the field, but its practical significance remains a question of debate. When the Internet first became widely used ten to fifteen years ago it was often predicted that it would revolutionise the recruitment industry. In the future, it was argued, most of us would find out about jobs through web searches. It now appears that these predictions greatly overstated the influence that the Internet would have. Incomes Data Services came to the following conclusion having carried out an extensive survey of approaches used by UK organisations:

> **Although the significance of online recruitment is growing, it has to be remembered that the medium is not appropriate for all jobs or for all candidates. There are still some people who are not comfortable using a computer and even 'web savvy' applicants may be deterred by the perceived impersonal nature of online recruitment . . . There is, therefore, still a role for conventional advertising, particularly when recruiting locally or for hard-to-fill jobs. Ultimately, many employers may seek to combine online and traditional approaches to maximise their chances of securing the best candidate. (IDS 2006, p. 2)**

Internet recruitment takes two basic forms. The first is centred on the employer's own website, jobs being advertised alongside information about the products and services offered by the organisation. The second approach makes use of the growing number of cyber-agencies which combine the roles traditionally played by both newspapers and employment agents. They advertise the job and undertake shortlisting before sending on a selection of suitable CVs to the employer.

For employers the principal attraction is the way that the Internet allows jobs to be advertised inexpensively to a potential audience of millions. According to Frankland (2000) the cost of setting up a good website is roughly equivalent to that associated with advertising a single high-profile job in a national newspaper. Huge savings can also

TABLE 3.4 The advantages and drawbacks of various methods of job advertising

Internal advertisement

Advantages:
    (a) Maximum information to all employees, who might then act as recruiters.
    (b) Opportunity for all internal candidates to apply.
    (c) If an internal candidate is appointed, there is a shorter induction period.
    (d) Speed.
    (e) Cost.

Drawbacks:
    (a) Limit to number of applicants.
    (b) Internal candidates not matched against those from outside.
    (c) May be unlawful if indirect discrimination. (*See* Chapter 10.)

Vacancy lists outside premises

Advantage:
    (a) Economical way of advertising, particularly if premises are near a busy thoroughfare.

Drawbacks:
    (a) Vacancy list likely to be seen by few people.
    (b) Usually possible to put only barest information, like the job title, or even just 'Vacancies'.

Advertising in the national press

Advantages:
    (a) Advertisement reaches large numbers.
    (b) Some national newspapers are the accepted medium for search by those seeking particular posts.

Drawbacks:
    (a) Cost.
    (b) Much of the cost 'wasted' in reaching inappropriate people.

Advertising in the local press

Advantages:
    (a) Recruitment advertisements more likely to be read by those seeking local employment.
    (b) Little 'wasted' circulation.

Drawback:
    (a) Local newspapers appear not to be used by professional and technical people seeking vacancies.

Advertising in the technical press

Advantage:
    (a) Reaches a specific population with minimum waste.

Drawbacks:
    (a) Relatively infrequent publication may require advertising copy six weeks before appearance of advertisement.
    (b) Inappropriate when a non-specialist is needed, or where the specialism has a choice of professional publications.

Internet

Advantages:
    (a) Information about a vacancy reaches many people.
    (b) Inexpensive once a website has been constructed.
    (c) Speed with which applications are sent in.
    (d) Facilitates online shortlisting.

Drawbacks:
    (a) Can produce thousands of unsuitable applications.
    (b) Worries about confidentiality may deter good applications.

be made by dispensing with the need to print glossy recruitment brochures and other documents to send to potential candidates. The other big advantage is speed. People can respond within seconds of reading about an opportunity by emailing their CV to the employer. Shortlisting can also be undertaken quickly with the use of CV-matching software or online application forms.

In principle e-recruitment thus has a great deal to offer. In practice, however, there are major problems which may take many more years to iron out. A key drawback is the way that employers advertising jobs tend to be bombarded with hundreds of applications. This occurs because of the large number of people who read the advertisement and because it takes so little effort to email a copy of a pre-prepared CV to the employer concerned. In order to prevent 'spamming' of this kind it is necessary to make use of online shortlisting software which is able to screen out unsuitable applications. Such technologies, however, are not wholly satisfactory. Those which work by looking for key words in CVs inevitably have a 'hit and miss' character and can be criticised for being inherently unfair. The possibility that good candidates may not be considered simply because they have not chosen a particular word or phrase is strong. The same is true of online application systems which include a handful of 'killer' questions designed to sift out unsuitable candidates at a very early stage. The tendency is for people who have a somewhat unconventional career background simply to be disregarded when, in fact, they may have the required talent or potential to do an excellent job.

The fact that there are so many drawbacks alongside the advantages explains why so many employers appear to use the Internet for recruitment while rating it relatively poorly. When asked to rank recruitment methods in terms of their effectiveness very few employers place the Internet at the top of the list (only 7 per cent according to a 2003 CIPD survey). While employers rank the Internet highly vis-à-vis other methods in terms its cost effectiveness, they are much less convinced when asked about the quality of applicants and the ability of web-based advertising to source the right candidates (IRS 2005, p. 45). Established approaches such as newspaper advertising and education liaison are much more highly rated and are thus unlikely to be replaced by e-recruitment in the near future.

Recruiting from overseas

As labour markets have tightened, skills shortages have become more acute and as employers have found it harder to recruit UK-based staff at a salary level that is affordable, they have increasingly been looking overseas as a major source of staff. The accession of ten new countries to the EU in 2004 greatly assisted in this respect, permitting, according to official estimates, over half a million people to come into the UK to work by the end of 2006 (Blanchflower *et al.* 2007).

Running large-scale overseas recruitment campaigns is expensive and it is an activity that has to be planned carefully if it is to yield effective results. Over recent years, as demand for overseas workers has increased, a number of well-run agencies with a high level of knowledge and experience of specific labour markets have become established, and many employers use them. Others, particularly NHS Trusts and larger recruiters of skilled workers, have developed their own competence in this area and recruit directly. IDS (2005) gives the following sound advice:

- Recruit in countries where skills and qualifications are comparable with those in the UK. This reduces the length of time it takes for each new migrant worker to adapt and begin performing at a high level.
- Recruit in countries with relatively high unemployment and relatively low wages vis-à-vis the UK. Elsewhere workers will have a great deal less motivation to move to the UK.
- Meet potential candidates face to face before employing them. Do not rely on telephone interviews or the opinion of an agency. This typically involves flying managers out to an overseas destination to run intensive interview days or assessment centres.
- Ensure that candidates have strong communication skills and a sufficient level of competence in the English language before recruiting them.
- Ensure that appropriate accommodation is provided when the new recruits first arrive in the UK along with support systems so that they feel welcome and become effective quickly.

It is also important to be aware of the various ethical issues associated with overseas recruitment. Care must be taken, for example, to ensure equal treatment with UK nationals so that neither group perceives that the other is being given favourable treatment by their employers. Another major ethical issue relates to the recruitment of 'key workers' such as doctors and nurses in developing countries where they are in short supply. In recent years a number of governments have rightly complained that the NHS is robbing local health providers of the staff they need to help ensure the health of their own people.

Activity 3.3

The extent of overseas recruitment, particularly from Eastern Europe, is often criticised by representatives of UK workers and by bodies that campaign for the rights of disabled people and the long-term unemployed. In recruiting workers from other countries, they argue, wages in the UK are being kept much lower than they otherwise would be, while employers are freed from any requirement to offer career and development opportunities to people living on benefits. What is your opinion on these questions? Should overseas recruitment be limited by government or should employers be free to recruit whom they wish from across the EU, and perhaps, the whole world?

EMPLOYER BRANDING

In recent years considerable interest has developed in the idea that employers have much to gain when competing for staff by borrowing techniques long used in marketing goods and services to potential customers. In particular, many organisations have sought to position themselves as 'employers of choice' in their labour markets with a view to attracting stronger applications from potential employees. Those who have succeeded have often found that their recruitment costs fall as a result because they receive so many more unsolicited applications. Central to these approaches is the development over time of a positive 'brand image' of the organisation as an employer, so that potential employees come to regard working there as highly desirable. Developing a good brand image is an easier task for larger companies with household names than for those which are smaller or highly specialised, but the possibility of developing and sustaining a reputation as a good employer is something from which all organisations stand to benefit.

The key, as when branding consumer products, is to build on any aspect of the working experience that is distinct from that offered by other organisations competing in the same broad applicant pool. It may be relatively high pay or a generous benefits package, it may be flexible working, or a friendly and informal atmosphere, strong career development potential or job security. This is then developed as a 'unique selling proposition' and forms the basis of the employer branding exercise. The best way of finding out what is distinct and positive about working in your organisation is to carry out some form of staff attitude survey. Employer branding exercises simply amount to a waste of time and money when they are not rooted in the actual lived experience of employees because people are attracted to the organisation on false premises. As with claims made for products that do not live up to their billing, the employees gained are not subsequently retained, and resources are wasted recruiting people who resign quickly after starting.

Once the unique selling propositions have been identified they can be used to inform all forms of communication that the organisation engages in with potential and actual applicants. The aim must be to repeat the message again and again in advertisements, in recruitment literature, on Internet sites and at careers fairs. It is also important that existing employees are made aware of their employer's brand proposition too as so much recruitment is carried out informally through word of mouth. Provided the message is accurate and provided it is communicated effectively over time, the result will be a 'leveraging of the brand' as more and more people in the labour market begin to associate the message with the employer.

WINDOW ON PRACTICE

Like many fast food chains, Burger King and McDonalds have found it hard to recruit managers to run their restaurants. Such workplaces have long suffered from a poor image in the labour market and lose out as a result in the recruitment of graduates and junior managerial staff, many of whom would prefer to work pretty well anywhere else. Burger King reversed its fortunes to a great extent during 2002 and 2003 by running a shrewd recruitment advertising campaign rooted in an employer branding exercise. The advertisements were strikingly

designed and printed in colour to at...
featured in one corner, but this was...
working as a Burger King manager...

- the fact that the job was never dul...
- the career development opportunit...
- the relatively attractive salary pack...

In the week after the first advertise...
hundred people phoned for further det...
new managers. The company's equival...
only twenty applicants, none of whom...
McDonalds has also developed a bol...
campaigns, making good use of the em...
itself of the image as a bad employer to ....ganisation in
the fast food market the company has ha... ...uffer the ignominy of seeing the
term 'McJob' being included in the *Oxford English Dictionary* and being defined
as a job which is badly paid, unstimulating and having few prospects. It has,
however, sought to turn this notoriety to its advantage by running recruitment
campaigns which flag up the positive aspects of a career with McDonalds
(flexibility, fast career prospects, etc.) while incorporating the slogan 'Not bad for
a McJob?'. In addition the company has revamped its selection procedures so
that would-be staff at all levels experience a day working in a restaurant before
they are offered a job. This has the twin advantages of ensuring that they know
what to expect and do not accept a job on false premises, while also helping
recruiters to make better-informed judgement about their suitability.
Sources: IRS (2003) and IRS (2006).

STAFF TURNOVER RATES AND TRENDS

In recent years there has been a mismatch between the rhetoric about job tenure and
the reality. Much mileage continues to be made by some consultants, academics and
management gurus out of the claim that 'there are no longer any jobs for life', suggesting
that the length of time we spend working for organisations has fallen substantially in
recent years. In fact this is a misleading claim. All the available evidence strongly suggests
that job tenure has been broadly stable for several decades. OECD statistics show that
average length of time that *permanent employees remain in a job* remained steady at or
around eight years from 1992 until 2002 (Auer *et al.* 2004, p. 3), while Labour Force
Survey data confirms that long periods of job tenure remain the norm for a substantial
portion of the working population (*see* Table 3.5). People tend to move from employer
to employer early on in their careers, often staying in one employment for just a few
months. But once they find a job (or an employer) that they like, the tendency is to

...enure in the UK among permanent employees

...rvice	% of the workforce
...1–2 years	27
...years	24
5–8 years	13
8–12 years	9
Over 12 years	24

Source: Adapted from DTI 2006, p. 4.

remain for several years. 'Jobs for life' have, in truth, always been a relative rarity, but the evidence suggests that long-term tenure remains a reality for many employees. Over a third of UK employees have already been in their current jobs for over eight years.

The overall figures mask substantial differences between tenure and turnover rates in different industries. Studies undertaken annually by the Chartered Institute of Personnel and Development persistently show retailing and catering to be the sectors with the highest turnover levels, with rates averaging over 40 per cent in recent years. By contrast the most stable workforces are to be found in the public services, where reported annual turnover rates are only 13 or 14 per cent (CIPD 2007, p. 29). Rates also vary from region to region and over time, being highest when and where average pay levels are highest and unemployment is low, and between different professions. As a rule, the more highly paid a person is, the less likely they are to switch jobs, but there remain some highly paid professions such as sales where turnover is always high. It is also interesting to observe how much more inclined younger workers are to switch jobs than their older colleagues. Macaulay (2003) calculated what proportion of employees had completed more than a year's service with their employer. For the over-fifties the figure was 86 per cent, for the 18–24 age group it was only 51 per cent.

Activity 3.4

Why do you think staff turnover rates are so much higher in some industries than others? Make a list of the different factors you consider may account for variations.

WINDOW ON PRACTICE

The length of time that employees remain in their jobs, or at least with the same employers, varies considerably from country to country. Auer *et al.* (2006) analysed the proportion of staff who had less than a year's service in the OECD countries and the proportion who had completed more than ten years' service. The country with the most shorter-term employees is the USA, where 24.5 per cent have less than a year's service, while only 26.2 per cent have been with their employers for more than ten years. At the other end of the scale is Greece, where only 9.8 per cent have less than a year's service and as many as 52 per cent have over ten years' service. High rates of job stability are also common in Italy, Belguim and Portugal. By contrast relatively low stability rates are found in the UK, Denmark and Ireland.

There is some debate about the level which staff turnover rates have to reach in order to inflict measurable damage on an employer. The answer varies from organisation to organisation. In some industries it is possible to sustain highly successful businesses with turnover rates that would make it impossible to function in other sectors. Some chains of fast food restaurants, for example, are widely reported as managing with turnover rates in excess of 300 per cent. This means that the average tenure for each employee is only four months (Ritzer 1996, p. 130; Cappelli 2000, p. 106), yet the companies concerned are some of the most successful in the world. By contrast, in a professional services organisation, where the personal relationships established between employees and clients are central to ongoing success, a turnover rate in excess of 10 per cent is likely to cause damage to the business.

People leave jobs for a variety of different reasons, many of which are wholly outside the power of the organisation to influence. In many cases people leave for a mixture of reasons, certain factors weighing more highly in their minds than others. We look briefly at these factors below.

Outside factors

Outside factors relate to situations in which someone leaves for reasons that are largely unrelated to their work. The most common instances involve people moving away when a spouse or partner is relocated and finding it difficult to cope with juggling the needs of work and family. To an extent such turnover is unavoidable, although it is possible to reduce it somewhat through the provision of career breaks, forms of flexible working and/or childcare facilities.

Functional turnover

The functional turnover category includes all resignations which are welcomed by the employer. The major examples are those which stem from an individual's poor work performance or failure to fit in comfortably with an organisational or departmental culture. While such resignations are less damaging than others from an organisation's point of view they should still be regarded as lost opportunities and as an unnecessary cost.

Push factors

With push factors the problem is dissatisfaction with work or the organisation, leading to unwanted turnover. A wide range of issues can be cited to explain such resignations. Insufficient development opportunities, boredom, ineffective supervision, poor levels of employee involvement and straightforward personality clashes are the most common precipitating factors. Organisations can readily address all of these issues. The main reason that so many fail to do so is the absence of mechanisms for picking up signs of dissatisfaction.

Pull factors

The opposite side of the coin is the attraction of rival employers. Salary levels are often a factor here, employees leaving in order to improve their living standards. In addition there are broader notions of career development, the wish to move into new areas of work for which there are better opportunities elsewhere, the chance to work with particular people, and more practical questions such as commuting time. For the employer losing people as a result of such factors there are two main lines of attack. First, there is a need to be aware of what other employers are offering and to ensure that as far as possible this is matched. The second requirement involves trying to ensure that employees appreciate what they are currently being given. The emphasis here is on effective communication of any 'unique selling points' and of the extent to which opportunities comparable to those offered elsewhere are given.

Activity 3.5

Think about jobs that you or members of your family have left in recent years. What were the key factors that led to the decision to leave? Was there one major factor or did several act together in combination?

STAFF RETENTION STRATEGIES

The straightforward answer to the question of how best to retain staff is to provide them with a better deal than they perceive they could get by working for alternative employers. Terms and conditions play a significant role, but other factors are often more important. For example, there is a need to provide jobs which are satisfying, along with career development opportunities, as much autonomy as is practicable and, above all, competent line management.

Pay

There is some debate in the retention literature about the extent to which raising pay levels reduces staff turnover. On the one hand there is evidence to show that, on average, employers who offer the most attractive reward packages have lower attrition rates than those who pay poorly (Gomez-Mejia and Balkin 1992, pp. 292–4), an assumption that leads many organisations to use pay rates as their prime weapon in retaining staff. On the other, there is questionnaire-based evidence that suggests that pay is a good deal less important than other factors in a decision to quit one's job (Bevan *et al.* 1997). The consensus among researchers specialising in retention issues is that pay has a role to play as a satisfier, but that it will not usually have an effect when other factors are pushing an individual towards quitting. Raising pay levels may thus result in greater job satisfaction where people are already happy with their work, but it will not deter unhappy employees from leaving. Sturges and Guest (1999), in their study of leaving decisions in the field of graduate employment, summed up their findings as follows:

> As far as they are concerned, while challenging work will compensate for pay, pay will never compensate for having to do boring, unstimulating work. (Sturges and Guest 1999, p. 19)

Recent research findings thus appear to confirm the views expressed by Herzberg (1966) that pay is a 'hygiene factor' rather than a motivator. This means that it can be a cause of dissatisfaction at work, but not of positive job satisfaction. People may be motivated to leave an employer who is perceived as paying badly, but once they are satisfied with their pay additional increases have little effect.

The other problem with the use of pay increases to retain staff is that it is an approach that is very easily matched by competitors. This is particularly true of 'golden handcuff' arrangements which seek to tie senior staff to an organisation for a number of years by paying substantial bonuses at a defined future date. As Cappelli (2000, p. 106) argues, in a buoyant job market, recruiters simply 'unlock the handcuffs' by offering equivalent signing-on bonuses to people they wish to employ.

It is important that employees do not perceive their employers to be treating them inequitably. Provided pay levels are not considerably lower than those paid by an organisation's labour market competitors, other factors will usually be more important contributors towards high turnover levels. Where the salaries that are paid are already broadly competitive, little purpose is served by increasing them further. The organisation may well make itself more attractive in recruitment terms, but the effect on staff retention will be limited. Moreover, of course, wage costs will increase.

While pay rates and benefit packages may play a relatively marginal role in the retention of good people, reward in the broader sense plays a more significant role. If employees do not find their work to be 'rewarding' they will be much more likely to start looking for alternative jobs. This is a good deal harder for managers to achieve because different people find different aspects of their work to be rewarding. There is thus a need to understand what makes people tick and to manage them as individuals accordingly. Getting this right is difficult, but achieving it is worthwhile from the point of view of retaining people. It is far harder for would-be competitors to imitate the effective motivation of an individual than it is for them to increase the salary that a person is paid.

Activity 3.6

The case for arguing that pay rates have a relatively minor role to play in explaining individual resignations rests partly on the assumption that other elements of the employment relationship are more important. It is argued that people will 'trade in' high pay in order to secure other perceived benefits and that consequently low-paying employers can retain staff effectively.

What other factors do you think employees consider to be more important than pay? What role can the HRM function play in helping to develop these?

Managing expectations

For some years research evidence has strongly suggested that employers benefit from ensuring that potential employees gain a 'realistic job preview' before they take up a job offer. The purpose is to make sure that new staff enter an organisation with their eyes wide open and do not find that the job fails to meet their expectations. A major cause of job dissatisfaction, and hence of high staff turnover, is the experience of having one's high hopes of new employment dashed by the realisation that it is not going to be as enjoyable or stimulating as anticipated. Several researchers have drawn attention to the importance of these processes in reducing high turnover during the early months of employment (e.g. Wanous 1992, pp. 53–87; Hom and Griffeth 1995, pp. 193–203).

Realistic job previews are most important when candidates, for whatever reason, cannot know a great deal about the job for which they are applying. This may be because of limited past experience or it may be because the job is relatively unusual and not based in a type of workplace with which job applicants are familiar. An example quoted by Carroll *et al.* (1999, p. 246) concerns work in nursing homes, which seems to attract people looking to undertake a caring role but who are unfamiliar with the less attractive hours, working conditions and job duties associated with the care assistant's role. The realistic job preview is highly appropriate in such a situation as a means of avoiding recruiting people who subsequently leave within a few weeks.

Induction

Another process often credited with the reduction of turnover early in the employment relationship is the presence of effective and timely induction. It is very easy to overlook in the rush to get people into key posts quickly and it is often carried out badly, but it is essential if avoidable early turnover is to be kept to a minimum. Gregg and Wadsworth (1999, p. 111) showed in their analysis of 870,000 workers starting new jobs in 1992 that as many as 17 per cent had left within three months and 42 per cent within 12 months. No doubt a good number of these departures were due either to poorly managed expectations or to ineffective inductions.

Induction has a number of distinct purposes, all of which are concerned with preparing new employees to work as effectively as possible and as soon as is possible in their new jobs. First, it plays an important part in helping new starters to adjust emotionally to the new workplace. It gives an opportunity to ensure that they understand where things are, who to ask when unsure about what to do and how their role fits into the organisation generally. Secondly, induction provides a forum in which basic information about the organisation can be transmitted. This may include material about the organisation's purpose, its mission statement and the key issues it faces. More generally a corporate induction provides a suitable occasion to talk about health and safety regulations, fire evacuation procedures and organisational policies concerning matters like the use of telephones for private purposes. Thirdly, induction processes can be used to convey to new starters important cultural messages about what the organisation expects and what employees can expect in return. It thus potentially forms an important stage in the establishment of the psychological contract, leaving new employees clear about what they need to do to advance their own prospects in the organisation. All these matters will be picked up by new starters anyway in their first months of employment, but incorporating them into a formal induction programme ensures that they are brought up to speed a good deal more quickly, and that they are less likely to leave at an early date.

WINDOW ON PRACTICE

IRS (2000, p. 11) describes an original approach taken to the induction of staff at a large Novotel Hotel in London. Unusually for the hotel industry the induction programme here lasts for three weeks. It includes some job shadowing of experienced staff, but also consists of several days spent in a training room learning about the hotel's main services and learning how to deal with difficult customers. A variety of training techniques are used including quizzes, games, discussion forums and role play exercises. The management saw their retention rates increase by 12 per cent after the introduction of the new programme.

Family-friendly HR practices

Labour Force Survey statistics show that between 5 per cent and 10 per cent of employees leave their jobs for 'family or personal reasons' (IRS 1999, p. 6), while Hom and Griffeth (1995, p. 252) quote American research indicating that 33 per cent of women quit jobs to devote more time to their families – a response given by only 1 per cent of men. To these figures can be added those quoted by Gregg and Wadsworth (1999, p. 116) which show average job tenure among women with children in the UK to be over a year shorter than that of women without children and almost two years shorter than that of men. These statistics suggest that one of the more significant reasons for voluntary resignations from jobs is the inability to juggle the demands of a job with those of the family. They indicate that there is a good business case, particularly where staff retention is high on the agenda, for considering ways in which employment can be made more family friendly.

Many employers, however, have decided to go a good deal further down this road than is strictly required by law (*see* Chapter 10). The most common example is the provision of more paid maternity leave and the right, where possible, for mothers to return to work on a part-time or job-share basis if they so wish. Crèche provision is common in larger workplaces, while others offer childcare vouchers instead. Career breaks are offered by many public sector employers, allowing people to take a few months off without pay and subsequently to return to a similar job with the same organisation. Flexitime systems such as those described are also useful to people with families and may thus serve as a retention tool in some cases.

Training and development

There are two widely expressed, but wholly opposed, perspectives on the link between training interventions and employee turnover. On the one hand is the argument that training opportunities enhance commitment to an employer on the part of individual employees, making them less likely to leave voluntarily than they would if no training were offered. The alternative view holds that training makes people more employable and hence more likely to leave in order to develop their careers elsewhere. The view is thus put that money spent on training is money wasted because it ultimately benefits other employers.

Green *et al.* (2000, pp. 267–72) report research on the perceptions of 1,539 employees on different kinds of training. They found that the overall effect is neutral, 19 per cent of employees saying that training was 'more likely to make them actively look for another job' and 18 per cent saying it was less likely to do so. However, they also found the type of training and the source of sponsorship to be a significant variable. Training which is paid for by the employer is a good deal less likely to raise job mobility than that paid for by the employee or the government. Firm-specific training is also shown in the study to be associated with lower turnover than training which leads to the acquisition of transferable skills. The point is made, however, that whatever the form of training an employer can develop a workforce that is both 'capable and committed' by combining training interventions with other forms of retention initiative.

The most expensive types of training intervention involve long-term courses of study such as an MBA, CIPD or accountancy qualification. In financing such courses, employers are sending a very clear signal to the employees concerned that their contribution is valued and that they can look forward to substantial career advancement if they opt to stay. The fact that leaving will also mean an end to the funding for the course provides a more direct incentive to remain with the sponsoring employer.

Improving the quality of line management

Many voluntary resignations are explained by dissatisfaction on the part of employees with their line managers. Too often, it appears, people are promoted into supervisory positions without adequate experience or training. Organisations seem to assume that their managers are capable supervisors, without recognising that the role is difficult and does not usually come naturally to people. Hence it is common to find managers who are 'quick to criticise but slow to praise', who are too tied up in their own work to show an interest in their subordinates and who prefer to impose their own solutions without first taking account of their staff's views. The solution is to take action on various fronts to improve the effectiveness of supervisors:

- select people for line management roles following an assessment of their supervisory capabilities
- ensure that all newly appointed line managers are trained in the art of effective supervision
- regularly appraise line managers on their supervisory skills

This really amounts to little more than common sense, but such approaches are the exception to the rule in most UK organisations.

WINDOW ON PRACTICE

In 2007 the Chartered Institute of Personnel and Development's annual survey on recruitment and retention matters asked employers to state what steps they were currently taking to address staff retention. The range of initiatives was extensive and broadly appropriate given what the research evidence tells us are the principal reasons for voluntary resignations. The top ten initiatives were as follows:

10 offering coaching/mentoring/buddy schemes (22 per cent)
 9 improving work-life balance (25 per cent)
 8 improving employee involvement (27 per cent)
 7 removing age-related policies and practices (27 per cent)
 6 improving line management HR skills (30 per cent)
 5 improving benefits (30 per cent)
 4 increasing pay (32 per cent)
 3 improving selection techniques (35 per cent)
 2 improving induction processes (36 per cent)
 1 increasing learning and development opportunities (38 per cent)

KEY DEBATE: THE SIGNIFICANCE OF SKILLS SHORTAGES IN THE UK

If current trends are maintained we can expect to see continued increases, year on year, in the number of jobs being created by British organisations. In 2006 there were 37.1 million people of working age in the UK, of whom 27.6 million were in employment, a further 1.5 million being self-employed (National Statistics 2006). The total number of jobs has grown steadily in recent years at a time when many major industries have seen the introduction of labour-saving technologies and when millions of jobs have effectively been 'exported' to developing countries where labour costs are much cheaper. Major industrial restructuring has occurred, yet the demand for labour over the long term has increased steadily. Provided the economy continues to grow, we can thus expect to see further increased demand for people on the part of employers over the coming decade.

But what sort of skills will employers be looking for? Long-term trends paint a clear picture, but to what extent will these continue in the future? The official method used to classify occupations in the UK was changed in 1999, so it is not possible to make a precise comparison of today's figures with those produced by government statisticians before then. Nonetheless an obvious long-term pattern can be seen in the two sets of statistics presented in Tables 3.6 and 3.7. These show a pronounced switch occurring over a long period of time, and continuing strongly in more recent years, away from skilled, semi-skilled and unskilled manual work towards jobs which require higher-level and more specialised skills. The major growth areas have long been in the professional, technical and managerial occupations, but there has also been a considerable increase in service-sector jobs which require the job holder to deal directly with customers. These changes

TABLE 3.6 Changes in occupations 1951–1999

Occupation	% in 1951	% in 1999
Higher professionals	1.9	6.4
Lower professionals	4.7	14.9
Employers and proprietors	5.0	3.4
Managers and administrators	5.5	15.7
Clerks	10.7	14.9
Foremen, supervisors and inspectors	2.6	3.1
Skilled manual	24.9	12.7
Semi-skilled manual	31.5	23.0
Unskilled manual	13.1	5.9

Source: Labour Force Survey statistics accessed at **www.statistics.gov.uk**.

TABLE 3.7 Changes in occupations 2001–2006

Occupation	% in 2001	% in 2006
Managers and senior officials	12.9	14.7
Professional occupations	11.7	12.7
Associate professional and technical occupations	13.2	14.2
Administrative and secretarial	14.9	13.5
Skilled trades	9.5	8.4
Personal services	7.5	8.3
Sales and customer services	8.6	8.6
Process, plant and machine operatives	8.7	7.4
Elementary occupations	13.2	12.1

Source: Labour Force Survey statistics accessed at **www.statistics.gov.uk**.

reflect the shift that has occurred over recent decades away from an economy with a sizeable manufacturing sector, towards one that is dominated to a far greater degree by the private and public services sectors.

Activity 3.7

Why do you think countries such as the UK have seen so great a transformation in their industrial structure since the 1970s? Why are there so many fewer manufacturing jobs and so many more jobs in the service sector? Why are organisations so much more likely to employ small numbers of people than was the case fifty years ago?

One of the most vigorously contested debates among labour market economists concerns the nature of the skills that employers will be looking for in the future, a debate that has very important implications for government education policy, which, as a result, is itself controversial (*see* Grugulis *et al.* 2004). In recent years a highly influential group has argued that in the future economies such as the UK's will see a speeding up of the trends identified above. Influenced by figures such as Manuel Castells of Berkeley University in California, it has become common for policy makers to believe that a 'new economy' is rapidly developing which will increasingly be dominated by companies which are 'knowledge intensive' in nature. According to this 'upskilling thesis', lower-skilled jobs will be rarer and rarer in industrialised countries. Because they can be done far more cheaply in developing economies, they will increasingly be exported overseas. It follows that governments such as the UK's should prepare the workforce as best they can for the challenges of a 'high-skill, high-wage economy' in which those who do not have a relevant higher education are going to struggle to make a living.

Critics of Castells tend to look to the writings of a very different American academic guru figure – Harry Braverman. His theories derive from a marxian perspective as well as from observations of the activities of corporations in the 1960s and 1970s. This contrasting 'deskilling thesis' argues that businesses competing in capitalist economies will always look for ways of cutting their labour costs, and that they do this in part by continually reducing the level of skills required by the people they employ. It follows that, far from leading to a demand for higher-level skills and knowledge, the advent of an economy based on information and communication technologies will *over time* reduce such demand.

Both schools draw on widely documented trends to back up their positions. The up-skillers draw attention to the fact that the major growth areas in labour demand are in the higher-skilled occupational categories. Demand for graduates is increasing, demand for lower-skilled people is less strong, and is decreasing in some industries. They also draw attention to the emergence of skills shortages in many industries as employers find it steadily harder to recruit people with the abilities and experience they need.

By contrast, the down-skillers draw attention to the growth of call-centre-type operations which use technology to reduce the amount of knowledge and expertise required by customer services staff, and to the increasing use of bureaucratic systems which reduce the number of situations in which people have a discretion to make decisions. They also point to the strong growth in industries such as retailing and hotels which are characterised by employment of people who need only be low skilled and who are relatively low paid. They thus forecast a situation in which the workforce is heavily overqualified and in which graduates are increasingly employed in jobs for which no degree is necessary. They also argue that many of the 'skills' that employers say are in short supply are not in fact 'skills' at all, but merely 'attributes' or 'characteristics'. The target here is an evolving business language that refers to 'communication skills', 'interpersonal skills', 'team-working skills', 'problem-solving skills' and 'customer-handling skills'. These, it is argued, have nothing whatever to do with a knowledge-based economy and cannot be gained through formal education.

But who is right? The answer is profoundly important from a public policy point of view because decisions have to be taken today in order to ensure that the labour force is appropriately qualified to meet the needs of the economy in future decades. The answer is just as significant for organisations, not least because if the current labour force is seriously under skilled vis-à-vis future requirements, much of the onus for addressing the evolving 'gap' will fall on employers. Such a situation will also mean that current 'tight' labour market conditions remain and get tighter still, making effective recruitment and retention even harder to achieve than is currently the case.

As with all debates about future trends, it is impossible to state with certainty that one view is wrong and another right. So much depends on events and possible developments that are as yet unforeseeable. It is, for example, quite possible that the long period of economic growth the UK has enjoyed over fifteen years will come to an abrupt end and that a lengthy period of recession will follow. Were that to be the case, growth in the number of jobs of any kind, let alone at the higher-skill level, would be reduced or even cease altogether. Unemployment would increase and labour markets would loosen very considerably.

The most authoritative current predictions are probably those contained in the Leitch Review of Skills and in its associated documentation (*see* **www.hm-treasury.gov.uk**). Lord Sandy Leitch, a leading figure in the UK's financial services sector, was commissioned by the government to carry out a wide-ranging review of the country's skills base and of future skills gaps in 2004. His final report was published late in 2006 along with much of the research evidence on which he drew in reaching his conclusions. Of particular relevance to the debate we are considering here is the report written by Rachel Beaven and her colleagues from the Warwick Institute of Employment Research and Cambridge Econometrics looking at alternative skills scenarios for the UK economy through until 2020 (Beaven *et al.* 2005).

Leitch comes down strongly on the side of the up-skilling side of our debate. His view is that there will continue to be substantial growth in the number of jobs in the UK. He states that 'demand for skills will grow inexorably' as technology advances and globalisation of the world economy continues (Leitch 2006, p. 1). However, he also concludes that the existing skills base is far from 'world class' and that the UK is not nearly sufficiently well placed if it is to seize the opportunities presented, lift productivity levels and maintain its position as a leading international economy.

Beaven *et al.* (2005, p. 37) conclude that the number of jobs in the UK will grow to 30.1 million by 2020 (that is, a growth of over 2.3 million), but that there will at the same time be considerable further falls in the number of people employed in unskilled occupations (down by 845,000) and many skilled trades (down by 301,000) and in the number of administrative and secretarial jobs (down by 357,000). So much of the overall increase, and more besides, will be accounted for by the higher-skilled, higher-paid occupations. They estimate that demand for managers will grow by 889,000 and for professional and technical people by 1.65 million. The other major growth areas will be in occupations in the sales, customer services and personal services areas (up by 1.2 million by 2020). Importantly, this increased demand for labour will coincide with a period in which the size of the working population is projected to fall as the large cohort of people born between 1945 and 1964 – the 'baby-boom generation' – retire. Because there are many hundreds of thousands fewer UK-born individuals in succeeding cohorts, the actual number of new managers, professionals and service-sector workers that will need to be recruited in order to meet projected levels of demand will be up to eight times greater.

Meeting this demand, according to the Leitch Report, is going to require a very substantial lifting of the existing UK skills base. He concludes that the UK is not currently well placed to achieve this, and more importantly, that in significant respects major competitor nations are a good deal better placed. Over a third of adults in the UK do not 'hold the equivalent of a basic school-leaving qualification', 'almost half have difficulty with numbers' and 'one seventh are not functionally literate'.

We can thus conclude by asserting with some confidence that the long-term trend towards higher-skilled, professional occupations and away from unskilled and lower-skilled jobs will continue for the foreseeable future. For the time being at least, there will be a good deal more up-skilling than down-skilling in UK organisations. Moreover, it is clear from Lord Leitch's conclusions that meeting the demand for these jobs is going to be difficult without major investment in adult education and training on the part of both the government and employers. Encouraging the immigration of skilled workers from overseas will contribute to reducing skills gaps somewhat, but it will not help those whose existing levels of attainment and skill are at too low a level to enable them to find long-term employment in an economy based on higher-level skills and expertise.

From the point of view of employing organisations the future is most likely to involve a substantial further tightening of the labour market, lifting still further the advantages that will accrue to those who are best placed to recruit and then to retain the limited numbers of people who will have the most sought-after skills, knowledge and experience. The likelihood is therefore that the approaches described in this chapter, such as employer branding, overseas recruitment and effective retention strategies, will play an increasingly central role in organisations' HRM activities.

Activity 3.8

Assuming that Lord Leitch's predictions are broadly correct, what other HRM activities are likely to become increasingly important over the next twenty years in addition to those focused on improving the effectiveness of recruitment and retention practices in organisations?

SUMMARY PROPOSITIONS

3.1 Alternatives to filling a vacancy include reorganising the work; using overtime; mechanising the work; staggering the hours; making the job part time; subcontracting the work; using an employment agency.

3.2 Most people are recruited either internally or through informal channels. Alternative approaches involve advertising jobs in newspapers or on websites, using agencies and job centres, and through education liaison.

3.3 Employer branding involves actively selling the experience of working for an organisation by focusing on what makes the experience both positive and distinct.

3.4 Staff turnover tends to decrease in recessions and increase during economic booms. Contrary to much popular perception, average job tenure has not reduced substantially over the past thirty years.

3.5 While there are arguments that can be deployed in favour of modest staff turnover, it is generally agreed that too great a rate is damaging for an organisation.

3.6 Specific programmes which lead to improved retention include flexible benefits, better induction, the effective management of expectations, family-friendly initiatives, training opportunities and the improvement of line management in organisations.

3.7 The government anticipates that skills shortages will worsen in the future as the demand for people with specialised, higher-level skills outpaces growth in the supply of qualified people.

GENERAL DISCUSSION TOPICS

1 Why is it that the national newspapers which sell the fewest copies (broadsheets) dominate the market for recruitment advertising in the UK, while the more popular tabloids carry virtually none at all?

2 Staff turnover is generally low during recessions, but it increases substantially in firms which get into financial difficulty. What factors account for this phenomenon?

3 Think about your own experiences at work or those of close friends and family. What were the key factors that affected decisions to leave a particular job? What, if anything, could the employer have done to ensure that no resignation took place?

FURTHER READING

The Chartered Institute of Personnel and Development (CIPD) commissions a large survey each year on recruitment and retention issues which tracks all the major trends and provides authoritative evidence about employer practices. Each year the Confederation of British Industry (CBI) also carries out a major survey looking at staff turnover across the UK. These report the labour turnover rates among different groups as well as estimates of turnover costs.

Academic research on recruitment as opposed to selection processes is relatively undeveloped and there remain many central issues that have not been rigorously studied. In the USA the gap has been filled to some extent in recent years. The best summary and critique of this work is provided by Barber

(1998). Taylor and Collins (2000) provide a shorter treatment with an additional practical focus.

Martin Edwards (2005) has written one of the first serious analyses of academic thinking on the emerging concept of employer branding. His chapter appears in *Managing Human Resources: Personnel Management in Transition*, edited by Stephen Bach. It is entitled 'Employer and Employee Branding: HR or PR?'

Peter Hom and Rodger Griffeth (1995) provide by far the best source of information about academic research on turnover and staff retention issues in their *Employee Turnover*. It is now out of print, but is widely available in libraries. The same authors' more recent book (Griffeth and Hom, *Retaining Valued Employees*) remains in print.

REFERENCES

Auer, P., Berg, J. and Coulibaly, I. (2004) *Is a stable workforce good for the economy? Insights into the tenure-productivity-employment relationship*. Geneva: International Labour Organisation.

Barber, A.E. (1998) *Recruiting Employees: Individual and Organizational Perspectives.* Thousand Oaks, California: Sage.

Beaven, R., Bosworth, D., Lewney, R. and Wilson, R. (2005) *Alternative Skills Scenarios to 2020 for the UK Economy: A report for the Sector Skills Development Agency as a contribution to the Leitch Review of Skills*. Cambridge: Cambridge Econometrics.

Bevan, S., Barber, L. and Robinson, D. (1997) *Keeping the Best: a practical guide to retaining key employees*. Brighton: Institute for Employment Research.

Blanchflower, D.G., Saleheen, J. and Shadforth, C. (2007) *The Impact of Recent Migration from Eastern Europe on the UK Economy*. London: Bank of England.

Cappelli, P. (2000) 'A market-driven approach to retaining talent', *Harvard Business Review*, January/February, pp. 103–11.

Carroll, M., Marchington, M., Earnshaw, J. and Taylor, S. (1999) 'Recruitment in small firms: processes, methods and problems', *Employee Relations*, Vol. 21, No. 3, pp. 236–50.

CIPD (2003) *Recruitment and Retention 2003: survey report*. London: Chartered Institute of Personnel and Development.

CIPD (2005) *Recruitment, Retention and Turnover: Annual Survey Report 2005*. London: Chartered Institute of Personnel and Development.

CIPD (2006) *Recruitment, Retention and Turnover: Annual Survey Report 2006*. London: Chartered Institute of Personnel and Development.

CIPD (2007) *Recruitment, Retention and Turnover: Annual Survey Report 2007*. London: Chartered Institute of Personnel and Development.

Edwards, M. (2005) 'Employer and Employee Branding: HR or PR?', in S. Bach (ed.) *Managing Human Resources: Personnel Management in Transition*. Oxford: Blackwell.

Frankland, G. (2000) 'If you build it, they will come', *People Management*, 16 March, p. 45.

Gomez-Mejia, L. and Balkin, D. (1992) *Compensation, Organizational Strategy and Firm Performance*. Cincinnati, Ohio: South Western College Publishing.

Green, F., Felstead, A., Mayhew, K. and Pick, A. (2000) 'The impact of training on labour mobility: individual and firm-level evidence from Britain', *British Journal of Industrial Relations*, Vol. 38, No. 2.

Gregg, P. and Wadsworth, J. (1999) 'Job tenure, 1975–98', in P. Gregg and J. Wadsworth (eds) *The State of Working Britain*. Manchester: Manchester University Press.

Griffeth, R. and Hom, P. (2001) *Retaining Valued Employees*. Thousand Oaks, California: Sage.

Grugulis, I., Warhurst, C. and Keep, E. (2004) 'What's happening to 'Skill?', in C. Warhurst, I. Grugulis and E. Keep (eds) *The Skills That Matter*. Basingstoke: Palgrave.

Herzberg, F. (1966) *Work and the Nature of Man*. Cleveland, Ohio: World Publishing.

Hom, P. and Griffeth, R. (1995) *Employee Turnover*. Cincinnati, Ohio: South Western College Publishing.

IDS (2005) *Recruiting Foreign Workers*, IDS Study No. 807, October (pp. 7–16). London: Incomes Data Services.

IDS (2006) *Online Recruitment*, IDS Study No. 819, April. London: Incomes Data Services.

Iles, P. and Robertson, I. (1997) 'The impact of selection procedures on candidates', in P. Herriot (ed.) *Assessment and Selection in Organisations*. Chichester: Wiley.

IES (2002) *Free, fair and efficient? Open internal job advertising* (W. Hirsh, E. Pollard and P. Tamkin). Brighton: Institute of Employment Studies.

IRS (1999) 'Benchmarking labour turnover: annual guide 1999/2000', *Employee Development Bulletin*, No. 118, October.

IRS (2000) 'Improving retention and performance through induction', *Employee Development Bulletin*, No. 130, pp. 10–16, October.

IRS (2003) 'Better recruitment processes', *IRS Employment Review*, No. 780, 18 July.

IRS (2005) 'Online recruitment in the UK: 10 years older and wiser', *IRS Employment Review*, No. 822, 29 April, pp. 42–8.

IRS (2006) 'Building a McReputation to aid recruitment and retention', *IRS Employment Review*, No. 853, 18 August.

Leitch, S. (2006) *Prosperity for all in the global economy – world class skills. The Final Report of the Leitch Review of Skills*. London: HM Treasury.

Macaulay, C. (2003) 'Job mobility and job tenure in the UK', *Labour Market Trends*, November.

National Statistics (2006) *Labour Market Review*. Basingstoke. Palgrave Macmillan.

Newell, S. and Shackleton, V. (2000) 'Recruitment and selection', in S. Bach and K. Sisson (eds) *Personnel Management: A Comprehensive Guide to theory and practice*. Oxford: Blackwell.

Ritzer, G. (1996) *The Macdonaldisation of Society: an investigation into the changing character of contemporary social life*, revised edn. Thousand Oaks, California: Pine Forge.

Smith, P. (2008) 'Australian submarine fleet hit as crew choose to go underground', *Financial Times*, 11 March.

Sturges, J. and Guest, D. (1999) *Shall I Stay or Should I go?* Warwick: Association of Graduate Recruiters.

Taylor, S. and Collins, C. (2000) 'Organizational Recruitment: Enhancing the Intersection of Research and Practice', in C. Cooper and E. Locke (eds) *Industrial and Organizational Psychology*. Oxford: Blackwell.

Wanous, J.P. (1992) *Recruitment, Selection, Orientation and Socialization of Newcomers*. Reading, Mass.: Addison Wesley.

Winters, L.A. and Yusuf, S. (2007) *Dancing with Giants: China, India and the Global Economy*. Washington/Singapore: The World Bank and The Institute of Policy Studies.

Chapter 4

Selection

The objectives of this chapter are to:

1 Explain the importance of viewing selection as a two-way process

2 Examine the development and use of selection criteria

3 Evaluate the range of selection methods that are available (interviewing will be dealt with in detail in the Skills Package) and consider the criteria for choosing different methods

4 Review approaches to selection decision making

5 Explore the relationship between the validity of selection methods and their frequency of use

International professional football teams appear to be dependent on having a wealthy owner and an outstanding manager/coach, but there is a very high turnover among managers, mainly due to disappointing results on the field but also often due to a lack of rapport between owner and manager. Why should so many owners apparently fail to make sound appointments, requiring an expensive termination after such a short period? Perhaps they go about selection the wrong way. Make sure you do better – we consider in this chapter how you might!

The changing nature of HRM (Chapter 13) has led, amongst other things, to the devolution of many operational HR activities to line managers. Recruitment, the attraction of candidates to apply for a position, and selection, the decision over which candidate to appoint to a position, are now typically line-manager responsibilities and it thus becomes increasingly critical for line managers to understand selection processes and their role in them. Perhaps one of the most important aspects of this is to appreciate the flaws in various selection methods and the need to exercise subjective judgement within an apparently objective process. While the search for the perfect method of selection continues, in its absence HR and line managers continue to use a variety of imperfect methods to predict which applicant will meet the demands of the job most successfully, and/or be the best fit with the work group and culture of the organisation. Selection is increasingly important as more attention is paid to the costs of poor selection, in a very competitive market for talent. The costs of poor selection can be significant, including poor performance, additional training, demotivation of others, high levels of absence, and so on, in addition to the £4,333 the Chartered Institute of Personnel and Development (CIPD) (2007) found to be the average cost of filling a vacancy. This context has promoted greater attention to the applicant's perspective and increasing use of technology in selection. In addition equal opportunities legislation has underlined the importance of using well-validated selection procedures, so that the selection process discriminates fairly, and not unfairly, between applicants.

SELECTION AS A TWO-WAY PROCESS

The various stages of the selection process provide information for decisions by both the employer and the potential employee. While employment decisions have long been regarded as a management prerogative there is considerable evidence that the two-way nature of the process is now being widely acknowledged, and Lievens *et al.* (2002) suggest that labour market shortages have promoted a concern for the organisation's image and the treatment of applicants during the recruitment and selection process. We must also be concerned not only with the job to be done, but also with the work and the organisational context that is offered.

Throughout the selection process applicants choose between organisations by evaluating the developing relationship between themselves and the prospective employer. This takes place in the correspondence from potential employers; in their experience of the selection methods used by the employer; and in the information they gain at interview. Applicants will decide not to pursue some applications. Either they will have accepted another offer, or they will find something in their dealings with the organisation that discourages them and they withdraw. When large numbers of candidates withdraw it may be because the information provided by the organisation was sufficiently detailed, accurate and realistic that they were able to make a wise decision that they were not suited to the organisation and that time would be wasted by continuing. On the other hand, it might be that potentially admirable recruits were lost because of the way in which information was presented, lack of information, or the interpretation that was put on the 'flavour' of the correspondence. We have to remember that the applicant's frame of reference is very different from that of the manager in the organisation and selection processes should operate to meet the needs of both the organisation *and* the applicant. Papadopoulou *et al.* (1996), for example, demonstrated that candidates were influenced by the recruiter's ability to supply adequate and accurate information, which was what they expected from the interview. In addition they were influenced by the way the recruiter managed the interaction, so the recruiter's control of the interaction, their listening and in particular their ability to allow candidates to present themselves effectively are all important.

SELECTION CRITERIA

Unless the criteria against which applicants will be measured are made explicit, it is impossible to make credible selection decisions. It will be difficult to adopt the most appropriate selection procedure and approach, and difficult to validate the selection process. There are various ways to outline selection criteria.

Person specification

Selection criteria have typically been presented in the form of a person specification representing the ideal candidate. This covers such areas as skills, experience, qualifications, education, personal attributes, special attributes, interests and motivation (IRS 2002a). Individual job criteria contained in job descriptions and person specification are derived from the process of job analysis. Although it is reasonably easy to specify the factors that should influence the personnel specification, the process by which the specification is formed is more difficult to describe. Van Zwanenberg and Wilkinson (1993) offer a dual perspective. They describe 'job first – person later' and 'person first – job later' approaches. The first starts with analysing the task to be done, presenting this in the form of a job description and from this deriving the personal qualities and attributes or competencies that are necessary to do the task. The difficulty is in translating job demands into personal attributes as well as the constant change of job demands and tasks. The alternative approach suggested by van Zwanenberg and Wilkinson starts with identifying which individuals are successful in a certain job and then describing their characteristics. There is also a trend towards making the person specification appropriate for a broad band of jobs rather than one particular job.

Although the IRS found that person specifications were used by three-quarters of the organisations in their study, Lievens *et al.* (2002) challenge the use of traditional person specifications as jobs become less defined and constantly change, which has greatly influenced the increased use of competencies as selection criteria.

Competency-based criteria

In addition to, or sometimes instead of, a person specification, many organisations are developing a competency profile as a means of setting the criteria against which to select. Competencies have been defined as underlying characteristics of a person which result in effective or superior performance; they include personal skills, knowledge, motives, traits, self-image and social role. Organisations design competency frameworks which they draw on for a number of purposes, including selecting into the organisation applicants who have the desired competencies, for example, communication, team working and planning and organising. Woodruffe (2000) and Whiddett and Hollyforde (2003) are useful practical sources of information on how to use competencies in the selection process.

Until recently organisational criteria involving competencies were rarely made explicit and they were often used at an intuitive level. However, Townley (1991) argues that organisations are increasingly likely to focus on more general attitudes and values than narrow task-based criteria. Barclay (1999) explains how fit with the organisation is often expressed in terms of personality, attitudes, flexibility, commitment and goals, rather than the ability to do the specific job for which the person is being recruited. In many organisations, for example call centres, such selection approaches have led to a much greater emphasis on these competencies than on the education or experience typically demanded by the use of person specifications. Such organisational criteria are also important where jobs are ill defined and constantly changing. It should be noted, however, that using competencies as the only selection criterion is considered to be limiting and unhelpful (*see*, for example, Brittain and Ryder (1999) and Whiddett and Kandola (2000)). Critiques of selection based on competency have also included the danger of 'cloning', that is selecting very similar types into an organisation and thus limiting diversity, and that competencies are backward looking, focusing on what has previously made the organisation successful rather than the competencies that it may need for future success.

Next steps in selection criteria

As we discussed above, both person specifications and competency approaches have their critics. The search continues for criteria that will improve the process of selecting potential employees and we present information in the following Window on Practice on O2's approach to this, selecting on the basis of performance.

WINDOW ON PRACTICE

Performance-based selection at O2

Mobile firm O2 is planning to roll out performance-based selection following successful pilots in one of its call centres and its retail division. Selection is focused on a performance profile, rather than a traditional competency profile, and involves an evaluation interview that focuses on between four and six accomplishments in a candidate's career and what O2 describes as a 'talent assessment matrix' to rate skills and behaviours required to be successful in a specified role.

Having selected over 500 new employees using this method, O2 suggests that candidates are of a noticeably higher standard than those selected using competency-based methods and that it has been easier to identify less suitable candidates. It is also suggested that the process makes for a more effective interview, with 'more meaningful dialogue' and makes it easier to assess motivation and willingness to work.

While a significant investment has been required in helping managers to develop the new styles of questioning required, O2 suggests that this approach is the next generation of selection method, incorporating performance management and selection techniques. Potential candidates gain an insight into the objectives for the role and the organisation is better placed to assess their likelihood of achieving these objectives.

Source: Summarised from L. Philips (2007) 'O2 hires on Performance', *People Management*, 23 August.

Whatever approach is taken to determine selection criteria, the next step is to decide what methods to use when selecting employees and it is to this that we now turn.

Activity 4.1

1 Thinking about a role you have applied for, what approach has been taken to determining selection criteria?

2 How successful do you think this was?

3 Which of the other approaches could have been used and what would have been the effect of this on the selection process?

SELECTION METHODS

There are a wide range of selection methods, some used more widely than others. We consider the mechanics of each method, together with its effectiveness or 'predictive validity'. Predictive validity is the extent to which a selection method can predict a candidate's subsequent job performance and is clearly an important consideration in adopting a selection method. One might expect that methods with high predictive validity would be the most widely used but, as we shall see in the Key Debate later in the chapter, this is not always the case. We explore in that debate the reasons for, and implications of, the mismatch between validity and usage of selection methods. Figure 4.1 examines methods of selection used by respondents to the CIPD 2007 survey of recruitment, retention and turnover.

The most popular selection methods are clearly based around interviews and application forms, with assessment centres and other forms of testing also being used. We consider traditional methods of selection first and then more advanced methods.

FIGURE 4.1
Methods of
selection

	Used in some way	Not used	Rarely used	Occasionally used	Frequently used	2006 survey
Interviews following contents of CV/ application form (that is, biographical)	92	8	5	10	77	85*
Structured interviews (panel)	88	12	9	21	58	88
Competency-based interviews	86	15	6	17	63	85
Tests for specific skills	80	20	14	37	29	82
General ability tests	72	28	16	30	26	75
Literacy and/or numeracy tests	70	30	16	29	25	72
Telephone interviews	61	39	23	23	15	56
Personality/aptitude questionnaires	56	44	12	26	18	60
Assessment centres	47	53	12	19	16	48
Group exercises (for example, role playing)	46	54	18	18	10	48
Pre-interview references (academic or employment)	45	55	15	13	17	50(E) 48(A)
Online tests (selection)	30	71	10	11	9	25

Base: 843

*result in 2006 survey refers only to interviews following contents of CV/application form (that is biographical) as removed structured interviews (1:1) from this year's survey

'E' refers to employment reference and 'A' relates to academic reference results from the 2006 survey, as this year we have combined both categories.

Source: This figure is taken from Survey Report: Recruitment, Retention and Turnover (2007) with the permission of the publisher, the Chartered Institutue of Personnel and Development, London (www.cipd.co.uk).

Traditional methods of selection

Often referred to as 'the classic trio', traditional methods of selection comprise application forms, interviews and references.

Application forms

Application forms are a useful preliminary to employment interviews and decisions, either to present more information that is relevant to such deliberations, or to arrange information in a standard way. This makes sorting of applications and shortlisting easier and enables interviewers to use the form as the basis for the interview itself, with each piece of information on the form being taken and developed in the interview. While there is heavy use of CVs for managerial and professional posts, many organisations, especially in the public sector, require both – off-putting to the applicant but helpful to the organisation in eliciting comparable data from all applicants.

Some organisations have extended the application form to take a more significant part in the employment process. One way is to ask for very much more, and more detailed, information from the candidate.

Another extension of application form usage has been in weighting, or biodata, defined by Anderson and Shackleton (1990) as 'historical and verifiable pieces of information about an individual in a selection context usually reported on application forms'. Biodata is perhaps of most use for large organisations filling many posts for which they receive high numbers of applications. This method is an attempt to relate the characteristics of applicants to characteristics of a large sample of successful job holders. The obvious drawbacks of this procedure are first the time it takes and the size of sample needed, making it feasible only where there are many job holders in a particular type of position. Secondly, it smacks of witchcraft to the applicants who might find it difficult to believe that success in a position correlates with being, *inter alia*, the first born in one's family. Such methods are not currently well used and Taylor (2005) notes their controversial nature and perceived unfairness.

Application forms are increasingly available electronically; this not only speeds up the process but also enables 'key word' searches of the data on the forms (for alternative ways in which this may be carried out *see* Mohamed *et al.* (2001)), but there are questions about the legality of this method when used alone. Initial sifting of electronic applications often includes a variety of methods including material from an application form as shown in the Woolworths examples in the Window on Practice.

WINDOW ON PRACTICE

Multiple method interactive screening at Woolworths

Receiving a large number of CVs for a wide range of jobs Woolworths designed its interactive screening process to deal professionally and speedily with this volume. There are two stages in the interactive screening process: the first stage consists of biographical, competency and expectation matching, and the second comprises telephone screening.

First stage

Biographical screening This comprises a series of questions to check for required qualifications, experience and education. In addition there are 'killer questions' which are so crucial that if an inappropriate response is received the candidate is advised that their application is unlikely to be successful, although it

▶

is their choice if they wish to continue. Feedback is always given anyway at the end of this biographical exploration, where candidates may be advised perhaps to consider applying for a different job.

Competency screening Candidates are asked behavioural questions about their previous experiences to check whether their behaviours and attitudes match with the competency framework appropriate to the role for which they are applying.

Expectation matching Candidates are asked questions about what they expect or desire from a career with Woolworths. These are matched against the reality of the role and mismatches are followed up in the second stage of screening.

Second stage

From the first stage candidates are assessed as A (great candidate), B (possible) and C (not suitable). Telephone interviews with A candidates aim to hook them in and invite them to the next selection event, whereas with B candidates the interview will be more exploratory.

Woolworths maintains that screening has produced a greater quality of candidates for the next stage in the selection process, an assessment centre, and note that the conversion rate has increased to 40 per cent.

Source: Summarised from R. Suff (2005b) 'First-line filter: screening candidates for selection', *Employment Review*, No. 837, 16 December, pp. 44–48.

Case 4.1 at **www.pearsoned.co.uk/torrington** deals with the reliability of application forms and CVs.

Face-to-face interviews

We discuss the traditional interview and the skills involved in the Skills Package. We note here, however, that it is the most widely used method of selection (Figure 4.1), despite being widely criticised as lacking in validity, that is, failing adequately to predict how well a potential employee is likely to perform in a job (*see* Key Debate below).

Telephone interviewing

Telephone interviews can be used if speed is particularly important, and if geographical distance is an issue, as interviews with appropriate candidates can be arranged immediately. CIPD (2007) reports that 56 per cent of organisations use this method of selection, a figure which has doubled since 2003, and probably reflects its use as one of a combination of screening tools, as well as a test of telephone manner, where required. Murphy (2005) reports similar figures and growth from an IRS survey. Telephone interviews are best used as part of a structured selection procedure, rather than alone – generally as pre-selection for a face-to-face interview. However, they may also have an important role when selecting for jobs in which telephone manner is critical such as those of call centre and contact centre staff. There may be problems such as lack of non-verbal information, and difficulties getting hold of the applicant. However, a positive aspect is the concentration on content rather than the person. Applicants without experience of them can find telephone interviews daunting. Murphy (2005) refers to and replicates checklists for organisations and candidates in the most effective use of such interviews.

WINDOW ON PRACTICE

One large employer requests CVs from applicants, and, on the basis of these, invites a selected number to take part in a telephone interview. A date and time are given and an idea of the questions that will be asked so that the candidate can prepare. The interview takes about 15–20 minutes, and time is allowed for the candidate to ask questions of the interviewer as well. Candidates are also told in advance of the telephone interview that if they are successful at this stage they will be invited to a one-day assessment centre on a specified date. After the telephone interview candidates are notified in writing whether or not they will move on to the assessment centre stage of the selection procedure.

Activity 4.2

What are the advantages of using telephone interviews of the type described in the Window on Practice box? For what types of job would you use this approach to selection?

References

One way of informing the judgement of managers who have to make employment offers to selected individuals is the use of references. Candidates provide the names of previous employers or others with appropriate credentials and then prospective employers request them to provide information. Reference checking is increasing as organisations react to scandals in the media and aim to protect themselves from rogue applicants (IRS 2002b). There are two types: the factual check and the character reference.

The factual check

The factual check is fairly straightforward as it is no more than a confirmation of facts that the candidate has presented. It will normally follow the employment interview and decision to offer a post. It simply confirms that the facts are accurate. The knowledge that such a check will be made – or may be made – will help focus the mind of candidates so that they resist the temptation to embroider their story.

The character reference

The character reference is a very different matter. Here the prospective employer asks for an opinion about the candidate before the interview so that the information gained can be used in the decision-making phases. The logic of this strategy is impeccable: who knows the working performance of the candidate better than the previous employer? The wisdom of the strategy is less sound, as it depends on the writers of references being excellent judges of working performance, faultless communicators and – most difficult of all – disinterested. The potential inaccuracies of decisions influenced by character references begin when the candidate decides who to cite. They will have some freedom of choice and will clearly choose someone from whom they expect favourable comment, perhaps massaging the critical faculties with such comments as: 'I think references are going to be very important for this job' or 'You will do your best for me, won't you?'

Advanced methods of selection

The increasing costs of selection, coupled with the increasing recognition of the problems associated with 'the classic trio', have led organisations to consider more sophisticated methods of selection in order better to predict the likely job performance of a candidate. We discuss some of these below.

Testing

The use of tests in employment procedures is surrounded by strong feelings for and against. Those in favour of testing in general point to the unreliability of the interview as a predictor of performance and the greater potential accuracy and objectivity of test data. Tests can be seen as giving credibility to selection decisions. Those against them either dislike the objectivity that testing implies or have difficulty in incorporating test evidence into the rest of the evidence that is collected. Questions have been raised as to the relevance of the tests to the job applied for and the possibility of unfair discrimination and bias. Also, some candidates feel that they can improve their prospects by a good interview performance and that the degree to which they are in control of their own destiny is being reduced by a dispassionate routine.

Tests remain heavily used, and the key issue debated currently is the extent to which tests should be administered over the web. CIPD (2007) found 72 per cent of organisations using general ability tests, 70 per cent of organisations using literacy/numeracy tests and 56 per cent using personality tests and Murphy (2006) in an IRS survey found similar results.

Tests are chosen on the basis that test scores relate to, or correlate with, subsequent job performance, so that a high test score would predict high job performance and a low test score would predict low job performance.

WINDOW ON PRACTICE

Online testing at B&Q

B&Q has been using online psychological testing for managers, and this is being extended to all managerial and shop floor appointments. The system cost £12,000 to install and it is expected that costs will be recouped by the end of the first year of full use. B&Q has introduced this in a context of a growing company in a competitive recruitment market, and the tests are open to anyone who can access the website (**www.diy.com**). Tests are assessed as they are completed and feedback is immediately given to candidates to tell them if they can progress to the next stage of the selection procedure. B&Q argues that this approach avoids bias which may be present when initially assessing CVs. If candidates do not have online access a telephone test is available as an alternative.

Source: E. Davidson (2003) 'You can do it', *People Management*, Vol. 9, No. 4, 20 February, pp. 42–3.

Use and interpretation

Tests need to be used and interpreted by trained or qualified testers. Test results, especially personality tests, require very careful interpretation as some aspects of personality will be measured that are irrelevant to the job. The British Psychological Society (BPS) can provide a certificate of competence for occupational testing at levels A and B. Both the BPS and CIPD have produced codes of practice for occupational test use. It is recommended that tests are not used in a judgemental, final way, but to stimulate discussion with the candidate based on the test results and that feedback is given to candidates. The International Test Commission (**www.intest.com**) also provides guidelines on computer-based and Internet-delivered testing. In addition it is recommended in the CIPD code that test data alone should not be used to make a selection decision (which could contravene the 1998 Data Protection Act), but should always be used as part of a wider process where inferences from test results can be backed up by other sources. Norm tables and the edition date of a test are also important features to check. For example Ceci and Williams (2000) warn that intelligence is a relative concept and that the norm tables change over time – so using an old test with old norm tables may be misleading.

Problems with using tests

A number of problems can be incurred when using tests.

1 Tests are not outstanding predictors of future performance.
2 Validation procedures are very time consuming, but are essential to the effective use of tests. There are concerns that with the growth of web testing, new types of tests, such as emotional intelligence tests, are being developed without sufficient validation (Tulip 2002).

3 The criteria that are used to define good job performance in developing the test are often inadequate. They are subjective and may account to some extent for the mediocre correlations between test results and job performance.

4 Tests are often job specific. If the job for which the test is used changes, then the test can no longer be assumed to relate to job performance in the same way. Also, personality tests only measure how individuals see themselves at a certain time and cannot therefore be reliably reused at a later time.

5 Tests may not be fair as there may be a social, sexual or racial bias in the questions and scoring system. People from some cultures may, for example, be unused to 'working against the clock'.

6 Increasingly organisations are using competencies as a tool to identify and develop the characteristics of high performance. However, as Fletcher (1996) has pointed out, it is difficult to relate these readily to psychological tests. Rogers (1999) reports research which suggests the two approaches are compatible – but there is little evidence to support this so far.

WINDOW ON PRACTICE

Ensuring tests are 'fair and reasonable' and free from ethnic or sexual bias

Indirect discrimination would result when a test unfairly and unjustifiably disadvantages one race or sex compared with another, and test results need to be monitored to show that is not happening. Organisations need to be able to demonstrate that the test has been developed or tailored and assessed in relation to the job content and person specification. Alternative means of taking the test also need to be developed when the use of tests would disadvantage a disabled person.

Source: Summarised from M. Palmer (2002) 'Very testing testing', *People Management*, Vol. 8, No. 1, 10 January, pp. 18–19.

Activity 4.3

In what ways could you measure job performance for the following?

- A data input clerk
- A mobile plumber
- A call centre operator
- A supervisor

Case 4.2 at **www.pearsoned.co.uk/torrington** deals in more detail with methods of online selection.

Different types of tests

Aptitude tests

People differ in their performance of tasks, and tests of aptitude (or ability) measure an individual's potential to develop in either specific or general terms. This is in contrast to attainment tests, which measure the skills an individual has already acquired. When considering the results from aptitude tests it is important to remember that a simple relationship does not exist between a high level of aptitude and a high level of job performance, as other factors, such as motivation, also contribute to job performance.

Aptitude tests can be grouped into two categories: those measuring general mental ability or general intelligence, and those measuring specific abilities or aptitudes.

General intelligence tests

Intelligence tests, sometimes called mental ability tests, are designed to give an indication of overall mental capacity. A variety of questions are included in such tests, including vocabulary, analogies, similarities, opposites, arithmetic, number extension and general information. Ability to score highly on such tests correlates with the capacity to retain new knowledge, to pass examinations and to succeed at work. However, the intelligence test used would still need to be carefully validated in terms of the job for which the candidate was applying. And Ceci and Williams (2000) note that intelligence is to some extent determined by the context – so an individual's test score may not reflect capacity to act intelligently. Indeed practical intelligence, associated with success in organisations, may be different from the nature of intelligence as measured by tests (Williams and Sternberg 2001). Examples of general intelligence tests are found in IDS (2004).

Special aptitude tests

There are special tests that measure specific abilities or aptitudes, such as spatial abilities, perceptual abilities, verbal ability, numerical ability, motor ability (manual dexterity) and so on. An example of a special abilities test is the Critical Reasoning Test developed by Smith and Whetton (*see* IDS 2004).

Attainment tests

Whereas aptitude tests measure an individual's potential, attainment or achievement tests measure skills that have already been acquired. There is much less resistance to such tests of skills. Few candidates for a secretarial/administrative post would refuse to take a keyboard speed test, or a test on 'Word', 'PowerPoint' or 'Excel' software before interview. The candidates are sufficiently confident of their skills to welcome the opportunity to display them and be approved. Furthermore, they know what they are doing and will know whether they have done well or badly. They are in control, while they feel that the tester is in control of intelligence and personality tests as the candidates do not understand the evaluation rationale. Attainment tests are often devised by the employer.

Personality tests

The debate still rages as to the importance of personality for success in some jobs and organisations. The need for personality assessment may be high but there is even more resistance to tests of personality than to tests of aptitude, partly because of the reluctance to see personality as in any way measurable. There is much evidence to suggest that personality is also context dependent, and Iles and Salaman (1995) also argue that personality changes over time. Both of these factors further complicate the issue. Personality tests are mainly used for management, professional and graduate jobs, although there is evidence of their use when high-performance teams are developed.

Theories of human personality vary as much as theories of human intelligence. Jung, Eysenck and Cattell, among others, have all proposed different sets of factors/traits that can be assessed to describe personality. Based on research to date Robertson (2001) argues that it is now possible to state that there are five basic building blocks of personality: extroversion/introversion; emotional stability; agreeableness; conscientiousness and openness to new experiences. Myers–Briggs is a well-used personality test; for details *see* McHenry (2002).

It is dangerous to assume that there is a standard profile of 'the ideal employee' (although this may fit nicely with theories of culture change) or the ideal personality for a particular job, as the same objectives may be satisfactorily achieved in different ways by different people. Another problem with the use of personality tests is that they rely on an individual's willingness to be honest, as the socially acceptable answer or the one best in terms of the job are seemingly easy to pick out, although 'lie detector' questions are usually built in.

WINDOW ON PRACTICE

Online testing: the case for and against

CIPD (2007) reports that 25 per cent of respondents to its survey used online tests and there is much interest in developing this area. Tests can be used in one of three different ways:

- uncontrolled – anyone can register to use them on the open Internet;
- controlled – the candidate needs first to be registered by the organisation using the test, and their identity must be checked;
- supervised – as above, and a qualified tester from the organisation also logs on and ensures that time limits and other requirements are met.

Arguments for online testing:

- cheaper in the long run
- immediate analysis
- immediate feedback to candidate
- can be used for wider range of (lower-paid) jobs

- speeds processes and helps to retain potential candidates
- good for company image
- can use a wider range of different tests – e.g. video scenarios, followed by 'what would you do next?'
- can be convenient for applicants

Arguments against online testing:

- worries over confidentiality and security of personal data
- appears cold and impersonal
- open to misuse – who is actually completing the test?
- can encourage the rapid development of new tests which are not properly validated

Group selection methods and assessment centres

Group methods

The use of group tasks to select candidates is not new – the method dates back to the Second World War – but such measures have gained greater attention through their use in assessment centres. Plumbley (1985) describes the purpose of group selection methods as being to provide evidence about the candidate's ability to:

- get on with others
- influence others and the way they do this
- express themselves verbally
- think clearly and logically
- argue from past experience and apply themselves to a new problem
- identify the type of role they play in group situations

These features are difficult on the whole to identify using other selection methods and one of the particular advantages of group selection methods is that they provide the selector with examples of behaviour on which to select. When future job performance is being considered it is behaviour in the job that is critical, and so selection using group methods can provide direct information on which to select rather than indirect verbal information or test results. The increasing use of competencies and behavioural indicators, as a way to specifiy selection criteria, ties in well with the use of group methods.

There is a range of group exercises that can be used including informal discussion of a given topic, role plays and groups who must organise themselves to solve a problem within time limits which may take the form of a competitive business game, case study or physical activity.

Group selection methods are most suitable for management, graduate and sometimes supervisory posts. One of the difficulties with group selection methods is that it can be difficult to assess an individual's contribution, and some people may be unwilling to take part.

Activity 4.4

To what extent does a person's behaviour on these group selection tasks accurately reflect behaviour on the job? Why?

Assessment centres

Assessment centres incorporate multiple selection techniques, and group selection methods outlined above form a major element, together with other work simulation exercises such as in-basket tasks, psychological tests, a variety of interviews and presentations. Assessment centres are used to assess, in depth, a group of broadly similar applicants, using a set of competencies required for the post on offer and a series of behavioural statements which indicate how these competencies are played out in practice. Even assuming that the competencies for the job in question have already been identified, assessment centres require a lengthy design process to select the appropriate activities so that every competency will be measured via more than one task. Assessment centres have been proven to be one of the most effective ways of selecting candidates – this is probably due, as Suff (2005a) notes, to the use of multiple measures, multiple assessors and predetermined assessment criteria.

A matrix is usually developed to show how the required competencies and the activities link up together. In terms of running the centre, sufficient well-trained assessors will be needed, usually based on the ratio of one assessor for two candidates to ensure that the assessor can observe each candidate sufficiently carefully. Lists of competencies and associated behaviours will need to be drawn up as checklists and a careful plan will need to be made of how each candidate will move around the different activities – an example of which is found in Figure 4.2. Clearly candidates will need to be very well briefed both before and at the start of the centre.

At the end of the procedure the assessors have to come to agreement on a cumulative rating for each individual, related to job requirements, taking into account all the selection activities. The procedure as a whole, rather than each separate activity, can then be validated against job performance. The predictive validities from such procedures are not very consistent, but there is a high 'face validity' – a feeling that this is a fairer way of selecting people. Reliability can also be improved by the quality of assessor training, careful briefing of assessors and a predetermined structured approach to marking. The chief disadvantages of these selection methods are that they are a costly and time-consuming procedure, for both the organisation and the candidates. The time commitment is extended by the need to give some feedback to candidates who have been through such a long procedure which involves psychological assessment – although feedback is still not always available for candidates. Assessment centre use is increasing and CIPD (2007) found that 47 per cent of organisations in its survey used assessment centres for selection. Some organisations have been improving their centres (*see* IRS 2002c) by making the activities more connected or by using longer simulations or

FIGURE 4.2
An example of the scheduling of events – based on an assessment centre for a professional post (central government)

Day One Times	Activity	Who is involved
9.30–10.00	Introduction to centre	All
10.00–10.45	General discussion – given topics	All
10.45–11.15	Coffee	
11.15–12.00	General intelligence test	All
12.00–12.30	One-to-one interviews (30 mins each)	Candidates A, B, C
12.30–1.30	Lunch	
1.30–2.00	One-to-one interviews (30 mins each)	Candidates B, E, C
2.00–2.45	Spatial reasoning test	All
2.45–3.15	Coffee	
3.15–4.00	Personality test	All
4.00–4.30	One-to-one interviews (30 mins each)	Candidates C, F, D

Day Two Times	Activity	Who is involved
9.30–10.15	Verbal reasoning test	All
10.15–10.45	One-to-one interviews (30 mins each)	Candidates D, A, F
10.45–11.15	Coffee	
11.15–12.00	Critical thinking test	All
12.00–12.30	One-to-one interviews (30 mins each)	Candidates E, B, A
12.30–1.30	Lunch	
1.30–3.00	In-tray exercise	All
3.00–3.30	Coffee	
3.30–4.00	One-to-one interviews (30 mins each)	Candidates F, D, E

Note: Based on six candidates (A, B, C, D, E, F) and three assessors.

scenarios which are a reflection of real-life experience on the job, and are carrying out testing separately from the centre. Some are assessing candidates against the values of the company rather than a specific job, in view of the rapid change in the nature of jobs. Others, such as Britvic, are running a series of assessment centres which candidates must attend, rather than only one. A helpful text relating competency profiles and assessment centre activities is Woodruffe (2000) and IDS (2005) provides examples of different company experiences.

Work sampling/portfolios

Work sampling of potential candidates for permanent jobs can take place by assessing candidates' work in temporary posts or on government training schemes in the same organisation. For some jobs, such as photographers and artists, a sample of work in the form of a portfolio is expected to be presented at the time of interview. Managers and professionals who expect at some point to be changing jobs or careers should maintain regularly updated portfolios of their work experiences and achievements. This makes them constantly review how their careers and skill banks are developing and can enhance their employability by having a readily available and up-to-date bank of material from which to draw in approaching any new opportunity.

Other methods

A number of other less conventional methods such as physiognomy, phrenology, body language, palmistry, graphology and astrology have been suggested as possible selection methods. While these are fascinating to read about there is little evidence to suggest that they could be used effectively. Thatcher (1997) suggests that the use of graphology is around 10 per cent in Holland and Germany and that it is regularly used in France; in the UK he found 9 per cent of small firms (with fewer than 100 employees), 1 per cent of medium-sized firms (100–499 employees) and 5 per cent of larger firms used graphology as a selection method. In 1990 Fowler suggested that the extent of use of graphology is much higher in the UK than reported figures indicate, as there is some reluctance on the part of organisations to admit that they are using graphology for selection purposes. There are also concerns about the quality of graphologists – who can indeed set themselves up with no training whatsoever. The two main bodies in this field in the UK are the British Institute of Graphology and the International Graphology Association and both these organisations require members to gain qualifications before they can practise.

WINDOW ON PRACTICE

It is interesting to contrast different approaches to selection in different countries. Bulois and Shackleton (1996) note that interviews are the cornerstone of selection activity in both Britain and France, but that they are consciously used in different ways. In Britain, interviews are increasingly structured and criterion referenced, whereas in France the approach tends to be deliberately unstructured and informal. In France, the premise is that 'the more at ease the candidates are, the higher the quality of their answer', whereas in Britain they characterise the premise as 'the more information you get about an individual, the better you know him/her and the more valid and reliable your judgement is' (p. 129). Tixier (1996), in a survey covering the EU (but excluding France, Switzerland, Sweden and Austria), found that structured interviews were favoured in the UK, Scandinavia and Germany. This contrasted with Italy, Portugal and Luxembourg where unstructured styles were preferred.

Bulois and Shackleton identify selectors in Britain as more aware of the limitations of interviews and as attempting to reduce the subjectivity by also carrying out assessment centres and psychological tests; whereas in France these methods were identified as unnatural, tedious and frustrating. Interviews are much more likely to be supplemented by handwriting analysis in France – both methods being identified as valuable, flexible and cheap sources of information. Shackleton and Newell (1991) report that handwriting analysis was used in 77 per cent of the organisations that they surveyed in France compared with 2.6 per cent of the organisations they surveyed in the UK.

Both culture and employment legislation clearly have an influence on the selection methods adopted in any country and the way in which they are used.

FIGURE 4.3
A selection decision-making matrix

Selection criteria	Candidate 1	Candidate 2	Candidate 3	Candidate 4
Criterion a				
Criterion b				
Criterion c				
Criterion d				
Criterion e				
General comments				

FINAL SELECTION DECISION MAKING

The selection decision involves measuring each candidate against the selection criteria defined in the person specification, and not against each other. A useful tool to achieve this is the matrix in Figure 4.3. This is a good method of ensuring that every candidate is assessed against each selection criterion and in each box in the matrix the key details can be completed. The box can be used whether a single selection method was used or multiple methods. If multiple methods were used and contradictory information is found against any criterion, this can be noted in the decision-making process.

When more than one selector is involved there is some debate about how to gather and use the information and judgement of each selector. One way is for each selector to assess the information collected separately, and then for all selectors to meet to discuss assessments. When this approach is used, there may be some very different assessments, especially if the interview was the only selection method used. Much heated and time-consuming debate can be generated, but the most useful aspect of this process is sharing the information in everyone's matrix to understand how judgements have been formed. This approach is also helpful in training interviewers.

An alternative approach is to fill in only one matrix, with all selectors contributing. This may be quicker, but the drawback is that the quietest member may be the one who has all the critical pieces of information. There is a risk that all the information may not be contributed to the debate in progress. Iles (1992), referring to assessment centre decisions, suggests that the debate itself may not add to the quality of the decision, and that taking the results from each selector and combining them is just as effective.

KEY DEBATE: VALIDITY AND USE OF SELECTION METHODS

In this key debate, we consider the contradiction between the use of a selection method and its effectiveness. Research from CIPD (2007) demonstrates the usage of various methods of selection. Some of this data (Table 4.1) is combined with data from Beardwell *et al.* (2004) in order to consider the effectiveness of a method as compared to its usage. In considering effectiveness, we use a score of predictive validity which ranges from 0 to 1, where 0 indicates that a method never predicts effective job performance and 1 suggests that a method always predicts effective job performance. Effective job

TABLE 4.1 Selection method and predictive validity

Selection Method	Predictive validity	Usage (%)*
Assessment centres	0.68	47
Structured interviews	0.62	88
Work samples	0.55	80
Ability tests	0.54	72
Personality questionnaires	0.38	56
Unstructured interviews	0.31	92
References	0.13	45

Source: Beardwell *et al.* 2004 and * CIPD (2007).

performance is assessed using measures of performance, such as error rate, production rate, appraisal scores, absence rate or whatever criteria are important to the organisation. The higher the score for validity, the more effectively a selection method predicts effective job performance, and the data in Table 4.1 suggests that assessment centres are the most effective method of selection, predicting effectively how a candidate is likely to perform in a job approaching 70 per cent of the time.

Unstructured interviews and references, part of the 'classic trio' of selection methods, have predictive validity of 0.31 and 0.13, not very effective at all in predicting future job performance. You would expect these methods not to be widely used, yet the CIPD (2007) research suggests that unstructured interviews are used by 92 per cent of organisations. Given the evidence on the lack of effectiveness of such methods, why do they continue to be so widely used? We explore this in detail below, outlining, first, why unstructured interviews continue to be used and, secondly, why more advanced methods of selection are not adopted.

Perhaps the main reason why unstructured interviews continue to be so widely used is their 'face validity', that is, candidates expect to have an interview and would, perhaps, think it strange were this not part of the selection process. Building on this is the increasing focus on the two-way nature of selection which we discussed at the beginning of the chapter. If an organisation is to provide the candidate with the necessary information, negotiate on terms and conditions or role, sell itself to the candidate or start the communication process required for the formation of the psychological contract, described in Chapter 1, then an interview is a necessary event.

There are also more pragmatic considerations such as time and cost. Unstructured interviews are relatively cheap and quick to organise, and those involved in the selection process may lack the skill level needed to structure an interview effectively. Small and medium-sized firms (SMEs) in particular may lack the resources or expertise to engage in more advanced methods of selection. There is also a school of thought which suggests that managers may not be aware of the research that suggests that unstructured interviews are a poor predictor of effective job performance or, perhaps more tellingly, that even where they are aware, they believe that while others may struggle to identify sound potential candidates, they themselves can rise above all the problems inherent in the selection interview that is not structured to select a high-performing employee. Thus many managers rely on and are confident in their use of intuition – it is often said that decisions are made in the first few seconds of an interview, but this does not guarantee a good decision and both employers and employees may come to regret such decisions.

Turning then to consider why firms do not more widely adopt advanced methods of selection such as assessment centres, resource issues are an obvious explanation. Assessment centres involve a significant financial outlay and are expensive and onerous to administer. Time is also an issue as it typically takes a great deal of time to set up a centre and sufficient notice must be given to candidates to allow them to arrange their commitments so as to be available. This may also lead some candidates to resist attending an assessment centre if it requires a couple of days of their time. At senior levels, there may be a perception that such methods of selection are not appropriate to those already at a senior level.

In contrast our table shows that if the interview is *structured* its predictive validity doubles from 0.31 to 0.62, just slightly behind assessment centres. Using structured interviews costs only a moderate amount to set up in terms of interviewer training and is fairly cheap to administer.

For costlier methods of selection, great care needs to be taken in deciding whether the improvement in selection decision making justifies such costs. The abilities of the staff involved in the selection process is also an issue when using tests and assessment centres as only those staff who are appropriately qualified by academic qualification and/or attendance on a recognised course may administer psychological tests. This may again render such methods beyond the reach of many SMEs.

A further twist to this debate is the notion of objectivity in the selection process which is suggested by terms such as 'validity' which is a very precise, scientific term. Ultimately all selection decisions are subjective, involving as they do the judgement of one individual or a set of individuals on the likely job performance of another. It is perhaps this quest for objectivity that is behind the increasing focus on online tests as an objective method of screening and selecting candidates. Yet recognising and dealing with subjectivity is a necessary part of selection processes involving human beings. Thus in an ideal world we may adopt assessment centres and certainly it is wise to combine selection methods, given that accuracy in selection generally increases in relation to the number of appropriate selection methods used (IRS 2002d). Ultimately, we must balance the pros and cons, costs and validity of each method of selection in determining the method that will best serve our purpose and situation and proceed in the knowledge of the limitations we face.

SUMMARY PROPOSITIONS

4.1 Selection is a two-way process. The potential employer and the potential employee both make selection decisions.

4.2 The most well-used selection methods are application forms, interviews (including those conducted by video and telephone), tests, group selection procedures, assessment centres and references. There is increasing use of the Internet in applying many of these methods.

▶

> **4.3** A procedure for selection decision making needs to be agreed which can integrate all the selection information available.
>
> **4.4** Choice of selection methods must trade off a variety of factors; this means that the most valid methods are not always the most used ones.

GENERAL DISCUSSION TOPICS

1 It could be argued that the selection process identifies candidates who are competent in the selection process rather than candidates who are most competent to perform the job on offer. Discuss this in relation to all forms of selection.

2 'It is unethical and bad for business to make candidates undergo a selection assessment centre without providing detailed feedback and support.' Discuss.

FURTHER READING

International Journal of Selection and Assessment, Vol. 11, No. 2/3, June/September 2003.
This is a special edition of the journal and it is devoted to the role of technology in shaping the future of staffing and assessment. Contains some highly relevant articles, including, for example, using technology in the recruiting, screening and selection process; applicant and recruiter reactions to technology; Internet-based personality testing and privacy in Internet-based selection systems.

Lievens, F., van Dam, K. and Anderson, N. (2002) 'Recent trends and challenges in personnel selection', *Personnel Review*, Vol. 31, No. 5, pp. 580–601.

IRS (2002) 'Of good character: supplying references and providing access', *Employment Review*, No. 754, 24 June, pp. 34–6.
The latter is the second of a two-part series on references – this one concentrating on providing references and employee access to references about them. It is useful to read this in conjunction with *Employment Review*, No. 752, 27 May, entitled 'The check's in the post' (IRS 2002c) which focuses on the legal position and on the content and nature of references.

Murphy, N. (2006) 'Voyages of discovery: carrying out checks on job applicants', *Employment Review*, No. 850, 7 July, pp. 42–8.
This article reports the results of a survey into employer practices to check the background details of applicants, and is much broader than simply seeking references from previous employers. It covers the type of information that is checked on together with the mechanisms used.

Murphy, N. (2005) 'Selecting graduates: doing it on-line, on time', *Employment Review*, No. 836, 2 December, pp. 42–5.
This article provides a very good insight into the stages of the selection process for fast-track candidates in the Civil Service, and demonstrates how online tools have been designed to reflect the real nature of the job being applied for and how such tools integrate with an assessment centre. An example from Cadbury Schweppes is also included.

REFERENCES

Anderson, N. and Shackleton, V. (1990) 'Staff selection decision making into the 1990s', *Management Decision*, Vol. 28, No. 1.

Barclay, J. (1999) 'Employee Selection: a question of structure', *Personnel Review*, Vol. 28, No. 1/2, pp. 134–51.

Beardwell, I., Holden, L. and Claydon, T. (2004) *Human Resource Management: a contemporary approach*, Harlow: Financial Times Prentice Hall.

Boyatzis, R. (1982) *The Competent Manager*. Chichester: John Wiley.

Brittain, S. and Ryder, P. (1999) 'Get complex', *People Management*, 25 November, pp. 48–51.

Bulois, N. and Shackleton, V. (1996) 'A qualitative study of recruitment and selection in France and Britain: the attitudes of recruiters in multinationals', in I. Beardwell (chair), *Contemporary Developments in Human Resource Management*. Paris: Editions ESKA, pp. 125–35.

Ceci, S. and Williams, W. (2000) 'Smart Bomb', *People Management*, 24 August, pp. 32–6.

CIPD (2007) *Recruitment, Retention and Turnover: Annual Survey 2007*. London: Chartered Institute of Personnel and Development.

Davidson, E. (2003) 'You can do it', *People Management*, Vol. 9, No. 4, 20 February, pp. 42–3.

Fletcher, C. (1996) 'Mix and match fails to work on competencies', *People Management*, September.

Fowler, A. (1990) 'The writing on the wall', *Local Government Chronicle*, 26 January, pp. 20–8.

IDS (2004 update) *IDS Study Plus: Psychological Tests*, No. 770, Spring. London: Incomes Data Services.

IDS (2005) *Assessment Centres*, IDS Study No. 800. London: Incomes Data Services.

Iles, P. (1992) 'Centres of excellence? Assessment and development centres, managerial competence and human resource strategies', *British Journal of Management*, Vol. 3, pp. 79–90.

Iles, P. and Salaman, G. (1995) 'Recruitment, selection and assessment', in J. Storey (ed.) *Human Resource Management: A critical text*. London: Routledge.

IRS (2002a) 'Psychometrics: the next generation', *Employment Review*, No. 744, 28 January, pp. 36–40.

IRS (2002b) 'Focus of attention', *Employment Review*, No. 749, 15 April, pp. 36–41.

IRS (2002c) 'The check's in the post', *Employment Review*, No. 752, 27 May, pp. 34–42.

IRS (2002d) 'Setting the tone: job descriptions and person specifications', *Employment Review*, No. 776, 23 May, pp. 42–8.

Lievens, F., van Dam, K. and Anderson, N. (2002) 'Recent trends and challenges in personnel selection', *Personnel Review*, Vol. 31, No. 5, pp. 580–601.

McHenry, R. (2002) 'The Myers–Briggs Response', *People Management*, Vol. 8, No. 24, 5 December, p. 34.

Mohamed, A., Orife, J. and Wibowo, K. (2001) 'The legality of a key word search as a personnel selection tool', *Personnel Review*, Vol. 24, No. 5, pp. 516–22.

Murphy, N. (2005) 'Got your number: using telephone interviewing', *Employment Review*, No. 832, 30 September, pp. 43–5.

Murphy, N. (2006) 'Testing the waters: employers' use of selection assessments', *Employment Review*, No. 852, 4 August, pp. 42–8.

Palmer, M. (2002) 'Very testing testing', *People Management*, Vol. 8, No. 1, 10 January, pp. 18–19.

Papadopoulou, A., Ineson, E. and Williams, D. (1996) 'The graduate management trainee preselection interview', *Personnel Review*, Vol. 25, No. 4, pp. 21–37.

Plumbley, P.R. (1985) *Recruitment and Selection*, 4th edn. London: Institute of Personnel Management.

Robertson, I. (2001) 'Undue diligence', *People Management*, Vol. 7, No. 23, 22 November, pp. 42–3.

Rogers, G. (1999) 'All round vision', *People Management*, 2 July.

Shackleton, V. and Newell, S. (1991) 'Management selection: a comparative survey of methods used in top

British and French companies', *Journal of Occupational Psychology*, Vol. 64, pp. 23–36.

Suff, R. (2005a) 'Centres of attention', *IRS Employment Review*, No. 816, 28 January, pp. 42–8.

Suff, R. (2005b) 'First-line filter: screening candidates for selection', *Employment Review*, No. 837, 16 December, pp. 44–8.

Taylor, S. (2005) *Employee Resourcing*. London: IPD.

Thatcher, M. (1997) 'A test of character', *People Management*, 15 May.

Tixier, M. (1996) 'Employers' recruitment tools across Europe', *Employee Relations*, Vol. 18, No. 6, pp. 67–78.

Townley, B. (1991) 'Selection and appraisal: reconstituting social relations?', in J. Storey (ed.) *New Perspectives in Human Resource Management*. London: Routledge.

Tulip, S. (2002) 'Personality trait secrets', *People Management*, Vol. 8, No. 17, pp. 34–8.

van Zwanenberg, N. and Wilkinson, L.J. (1993) 'The person specification – a problem masquerading as a solution?', *Personnel Review*, Vol. 22, No. 7, pp. 54–65.

Whiddett, S. and Hollyforde, S. (2003) *The competencies handbook*. London: Institute of Personnel and Development.

Whiddett, S. and Kandola, B. (2000) 'Fit for the job?', *People Management*, 25 May.

Wilkinson, L.J. and van Zwanenberg, N. (1994) 'Development of a person specification system for managerial jobs', *Personnel Review*, Vol. 23, No. 1, pp. 25–36.

Williams, W. and Sternberg, R. (2001) *Success for Managers*. London: Lawrence Erlbaum Associates.

Woodruffe, C. (2000) *Development and Assessment Centres: Identifying and assessing competence*, 3rd edn. London: Institute of Personnel and Development.

Chapter 5

Performance management

The objectives of this chapter are to:

1 Outline the characteristics of a performance management system

2 Explain the stages of a typical performance management system

3 Review the implementation of performance management systems

4 Explore the processes and contribution of 360-degree/multi-rater feedback

His promises were, as he then was, mighty;
But his performance, as he is now, nothing.

Four hundred years ago William Shakespeare put this opinion about King Henry VIII into a speech by the first of his six wives, Katherine of Aragon. Today the same sentiment is frequently expressed by managers about members of staff for whom they are responsible. So often it seems that promise is not fulfilled in performance. Also people often seem to lack the confidence or the application to fulfil their potential. Central to the effectiveness of every manager is the need to conjure an effective performance from their people.

Managing individual performance in organisations has traditionally centred on assessing performance and allocating reward, with effective performance seen as the result of the interaction between individual ability and motivation. Increasingly, it is recognised that planning and enabling have a critical effect on individual performance, with goals and standards, appropriate resources, guidance and support from the individual's manager all being central.

The words 'performance management' are sometimes used to imply organisational targets, frameworks like the balanced scorecard, measurements and metrics, with individual measures derived from these. This meaning of performance management has been described by Houldsworth (2004) as a harder 'performance improvement' approach compared with the softer developmental and motivational approaches to aligning the individual and the organisation, which she suggests equates to good management practice. We adopt this as a very helpful distinction and in this chapter focus on the softer approach to employees and teams.

INTRODUCING PERFORMANCE MANAGEMENT

The idea of appraising performance has existed for many years and has revolved largely around an annual review of objectives between manager and subordinate. Traditional *performance appraisal* systems were usually centrally designed by the specialists, backwards focused on historic performance and often involved elaborate forms completed as a record of the process. These were not living documents and were generally stored in the archives of the HR department until the next round of appraisal meetings. In the last two decades, however, the concept of *performance management* has emerged which adopts a future-oriented, strategic focus, applied to all employees in an organisation and is line-manager owned. The focus of performance management is to maximise current performance and future potential, a preoccupation which arises from the pressures of globalisation and the associated requirement to create the competitive advantage needed to survive in an international marketplace. Human capital is an essential component in creating such competitive advantage (Mayo 2001) and performance management has a key role in developing human capital. We focus on performance management rather than appraisal in this chapter. Performance appraisal is relevant as it is an integral part of a performance management system, but we adopt the term *performance review* in order to avoid confusion with traditional appraisal systems. The Skills Package at the end of the book deals with the skills required for a performance review meeting in the context of a performance management system (PMS).

Defining performance management

Clark (2005) provides a useful definition of performance management, stating that the essence of it is:

> Establishing a framework in which performance by human resources can be directed, monitored, motivated and refined, and that the links in the cycle can be audited. (p. 318)

There is, however, often limited consideration given within discussions of performance management to what performance actually is. We adopt Brumback's (1998) definition of performance:

Performance means both behaviours and results . . . Not just the instruments for results, behaviours are also outcomes in their own right. (p. 265)

This definition has important implications for managing performance, as it requires focus not just on the outcomes, the 'whats', of performance, but also the behaviours adopted, the 'hows'. We explore later in this chapter the design of PMSs that attempt to manage both behaviours and outcomes.

There has clearly been a significant growth in recent years in the number of organisations attempting to manage performance. In the early 1990s, Bevan and Thompson (1992) found that just 20 per cent of the organisations they surveyed had introduced a PMS. Recent reports, however, indicate that 87 per cent of respondents operate a formal PMS, 37 per cent of these being new systems (CIPD 2005). As noted above, this increase reflects the growth in the number of organisations attempting to achieve sustainable competitive advantage through their human capital and suggests that performance management is now a key issue for organisations. We explore below the characteristics of PMSs and the processes commonly adopted when managing performance.

Characteristics of performance management systems

PMSs are closely tied into the objectives of the organisation, so that the resulting performance is more likely to meet organisational needs. Performance review is almost always a key part of the system, but is integrated with *performance planning*, which links an individual's objectives to business objectives to ensure that employee effort is directed towards organisational priorities. Support for *performance delivery*, through development plans, coaching and ongoing review, enables employee effort to be successful, performance is *assessed* and successful performance *rewarded and reinforced*.

The conceptual foundation of performance management relies on a view that performance is more than ability and motivation. It is argued that clarity of goals is key in enabling the employee to understand what is expected and the order of priorities. In addition goals themselves are seen to provide motivation, a view that is based on goal setting theory originally developed by Locke in 1968 and further developed with practical applicability (Locke and Latham 1990). Research to date suggests that for goals to be motivating they must be sufficiently specific, challenging but not impossible and set participatively. Also the person reviewed needs feedback on future progress.

The other theoretical base of performance management is expectancy theory, which states that individuals will be motivated to act provided they expect to be able to achieve the goals set, believe that achieving the goals will lead to other rewards and believe that the rewards on offer are valued (Vroom 1964). The characteristics of PMSs are summarised in Table 5.1.

TABLE 5.1 Characteristics of performance management systems

- Top-down link between business objectives and individual objectives (compared with performance appraisal where there may be no objectives, or objectives not explicitly linked to business objectives)
- Line manager driven and owned (rather than being owned by the HR function, as typically with performance appraisal)
- A living document where performance and development plans, support and ongoing review are documented as work progresses, and prior to annual review (rather than an archived document retrieved at appraisal time to compare achievement with intentions)
- Performance is rewarded and reinforced

FIGURE 5.1
Stages of
a typical
performance
management
system

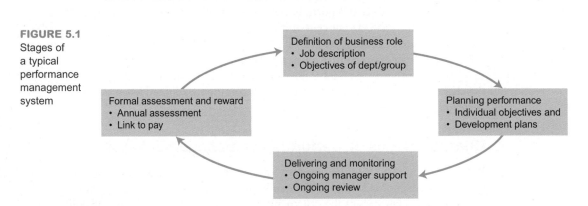

STAGES IN A PERFORMANCE MANAGEMENT SYSTEM

Figure 5.1 shows a typical system, the main stages of which are discussed below.

Business mission, values, objectives and competencies

There is an assumption that before it is able to plan and manage individual performance the organisation will have made significant steps in identifying the performance required of the organisation as a whole. In most cases this will involve a mission statement so that performance is seen within the context of an overriding theme. In addition many organisations will identify the strategic business objectives that are required within the current business context to be competitive and that align with the organisation's mission statement.

Many organisations will also identify core values of the business and the key competencies required. Each of these has a potential role in managing individual performance. Organisational objectives are particularly important, as it is common for such objectives to be cascaded down the organisation in order to ensure that individual objectives contribute to their achievement (for an example of an objective-setting cascade, *see* Figure 5.2). Similarly, key organisational competencies, that is, things the

FIGURE 5.2
An objective-
setting
cascade

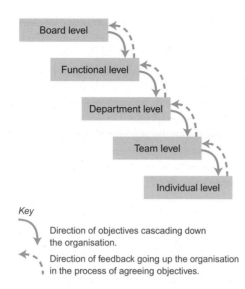

Key

Direction of objectives cascading down
the organisation.

Direction of feedback going up the organisation
in the process of agreeing objectives.

organisation must do well to succeed, can be translated into a competency framework (*see* Chapter 6 for further discussion of this) and employee behaviours are managed against this framework.

Planning performance: a shared view of expected performance

Individual objectives derived from department or team objectives and an agreed job description can be jointly devised by manager and employee and may focus on outcomes or behaviours. Objectives which are *outcome/results* oriented are tightly defined and include measures to be assessed. The objectives are designed to stretch the individual, and offer potential development as well as meeting business needs. It is helpful to both the organisation and the individual if objectives are prioritised. Many organisations use the 'SMART' acronym for describing individual objectives or targets:

- Specific
- Measurable
- Appropriate
- Relevant
- Timed

It is clearly easier for some parts of the organisation than others to set targets. There is often a tendency for those in technical jobs, such as computer systems development, to identify purely technical targets, reflecting the heavy task emphasis they see in their jobs. Moving staff to a different view of how their personal objectives contribute to team and organisational objectives is an important part of the performance management process. An objective for a team leader in systems development could be:

To complete development interviews with all team members by end July 2007. (Written March 2007)

Clearly, the timescale for each objective will need to reflect the content of the objective and not timescales set into the PMS. As objectives are met, managers and their staff need to have a brief review meeting to look at progress in all objectives and decide what other objectives should be added, changed or deleted. Five or six ongoing objectives are generally sufficient for one individual to work on at any time. A mix of objectives about new developments and changes as well as routine aspects of the job is generally considered to be appropriate.

The critical point about a *shared* view of performance suggests that handing out a job description or list of objectives to the employee is not adequate. Performance expectations need to be understood and, where possible, to involve a contribution from the employee. For example, although key accountabilities may be fixed by the manager, they will need to be discussed. Specific objectives allow for and benefit from a greater degree of employee input as employees will have a valid view of barriers to overcome, the effort involved and feasibility. However, difficulties have been experienced with purely 'what' objectives as there may be appropriate and inappropriate ways of achieving an objective. For example, a manager with an objective to ensure that another department agrees to a plan of action could achieve this in different ways. The manager may pressure susceptible members of the other department and force agreement through without listening to the other department's perspective. This may alienate the other department and damage future good relations. Alternatively the manager could adopt a collaborative approach so that the needs of both departments are met, providing a sound basis for future cooperation between the departments. As suggested in Brumback's definition of performance, the 'how' is also very important and more sophisticated systems now incorporate *behavioural targets* through the use of competencies and identifying competency profiles for particular jobs. The IDS (2005), for example, reports that 89 per cent of its respondents that used performance review measured employees against objectives or goals, with 56 per cent measuring against competencies. Williams (2002) further argues that as individuals cannot always control their results it is important to have behavioural targets as well as output targets.

Planning the support, development and resources necessary for employees to achieve their objectives is imperative. Without this support it is unlikely that even the most determined employees will achieve the performance required. It is also recommended that there is a personal development plan; this also would underpin the achievement of objectives.

Delivering and monitoring performance

While the employee is working to achieve the performance agreed, the manager retains a key enabling role. Organising the resources and off-job training is clearly essential. So too is being accessible. There may well be unforeseen barriers to the agreed performance which the manager needs to deal with, and sometimes the situation will demand that the expected performance needs to be revised. The employee may want to sound out possible courses of action with the manager before proceeding, or may require further information. Sharing 'inside' information that will affect the employee's performance is often a key need, although it is also something that managers find difficult, especially with sensitive information. Managers can identify information sources and other people who may be helpful.

Ongoing *coaching* during the task is especially important as managers guide employees through discussion and by constructive feedback. They can refer to practical job experiences to develop the critical skills and competencies that the employee needs, and can provide job-related opportunities for practice. Managers can identify potential role models to employees, help to explain how high achievers perform so well, and oil the organisational wheels. *See* Chapter 6 and the Skills package for further information on coaching skills.

Employees carry out ongoing review to plan their work and priorities and also to advise the manager well in advance if the agreed performance will not be delivered by the agreed dates. Joint employee/manager review ensures that information is shared. For example, a manager needs to be kept up to date on employee progress, while the employee needs to be kept up to date on organisational changes that have an impact on the agreed objectives. Both need to share perceptions of how the other is doing in their role, and what they could do that would be more helpful.

These reviews are normally informal, although a few notes may be taken of progress made and actions agreed. They need not be part of any formal system and therefore can take place when the job or the individuals involved demand, and not according to a pre-set schedule. The review is to facilitate future employee performance, providing an opportunity for the manager to confirm that the employee is 'on the right track', redirecting him or her if necessary. They thus provide a forum for employee reward in terms of recognition of progress. A 'well done' or an objective signed off as completed can enhance the motivation to perform well in the future. During this period evidence collection is also important. In the Scottish Prison Service (IDS 2003) line managers maintain a performance monitoring log of their team members' positive and negative behaviours in order to provide regular feedback and to embed the practice of ongoing assessment. Employees are expected to build up a portfolio of evidence of their performance over the period to increase the objectivity of reviews and to provide an audit trail to back up any assessment ratings. It is also during this part of the cycle that employees in many organisations can collect 360-degree feedback, that is feedback from a range of people, to be used developmentally and as part of an evidence base.

WINDOW ON PRACTICE

Performance management at Orange

To meet a very competitive environment and the convergence of a number of businesses Orange recognised that it needed to make its performance management process more robust. There were a number of concerns with the existing system including the system of rating on a five point scale; executives feeling that HR owned the process; employees feeling that objective setting often did not support the business and some feelings of lack of support and direction.

The new system has five core principles:

- one clear cascade process for objectives
- reward should stay linked to performance
- a balance between 'what' and 'how' objectives
- process needs to be owned by the business
- performance should be clearly and consistently differentiated across the ratings

The design of the system was led by senior representatives of the core businesses and a decision was made to keep the best bits of the current system and incorporate 'snippets of good stuff' from elsewhere, rather than looking for a 'best practice' model used elsewhere to implement.

The five point ratings scale was kept but the labels attached to each point were changed to demonstrate that the mid-point was a good place to be (which was used previously when employees had met their objectives and were doing a good job, and which had caused disagreements). The new scale ranged from 'unacceptable' (one); 'getting there' (two); 'great stuff' (three, the mid-point); 'excellent' (four) and 'exceptional' (five). The distribution curve used to ensure consistent ratings was abandoned in favour of 'calibration' which takes place at various levels and involves a manager sharing the ratings they have given to their direct reports with other managers at their level and providing justification for their ratings being prepared to explore and discuss their views. Objective setting is now linked into the organisation's 'Balanced Scorecard' approach they have adopted with Vice Presidents' objectives being set at the same time (and published on the intranet) and cascaded down the organisation. Objectives are weighted to ensure prioritisation and staff must have two or three behavioural ('how' or input) objectives. Orange has a profit sharing scheme for non-managers called 'success share', and now performance ratings are used to determine the proportion received by each individual. For managers the bonus scheme has altered giving senior managers more flexibility to allocate rewards for each point on the five point scale, without having to manipulate ratings.

Source: R. Johnson (2006) 'Orange Blossoms', *People Management*, Vol. 12, No. 21, pp. 56–60, 26 October.

Formal performance review/assessment

Regular formal reviews are needed to concentrate on developmental issues and to motivate the employee. Also, an annual review and assessment is needed, of the extent to which objectives have been met, and this may well affect pay received. In many organisations, employees are now invited to prepare an initial draft of achievement against objectives, for example Microsoft and AstraZeneca (IDS 2003). Some organisations continue to have overall assessment ratings which have to conform to a forced distribution, requiring each team/department to have, say, 10 per cent of employees on the top point, 20 per cent on the next point, and so on, so that each individual is assessed relative to others rather than being given an absolute rating. These systems are not popular and Roberts (2004) reports how staff walked out in a part of the Civil Service over relative assessment. AstraZeneca does not encourage its managers to give an overall rating to staff at all as its research suggested that this was demotivating (IDS 2003). Behaviourally anchored rating scales (BARS) and behavioural observation scales (BOS) are other specific methods of linking ratings with behaviour at work, although evidence suggests that these are not widely used (Williams 2002).

A more recent development is the electronic collection of information on which to base performance review, for example, various forms of electronic surveillance system. There are increasing examples of how activity rates of computer operators can be recorded and analysed, and how the calls made by telephone sales staff can be overheard and analysed. Sewell and Wilkinson (1992) describe a Japanese electronics plant where the final electronic test on a piece of equipment can indicate not only faults but the individual operator responsible for them. On another level some companies test the performance of their sales staff by sending in assessors acting in the role of customer (Newton and Findlay 1996), often termed 'mystery shoppers'. Research by the Institute for Employment Studies (IRS 2001), however, has found that review is only seen as fair if the targets set were seen as reasonable, managers were seen to be objective and judgements were consistent across the organisation.

Reward

Performance management may have a number of aims, the most common, however, are developmental and judgemental. Developmental aims may include training and employee growth, whereas judgemental aims relate to issues such as pay and promotion. While it is argued that there is a tension between developmental and judgemental aims, Houldsworth (2003) notes that many organisations try to use their PMS to achieve both. Armstrong and Baron (2005) argue that PMS should be developmentally focused, even suggesting that the term 'performance management and development' may be more appropriate. Many systems, however, still include a link with pay, but Fletcher and Williams (1992) point to some difficulties experienced. Some public and private organisations found that the merit element of pay was too small to motivate staff, and sometimes seen as insulting. Although performance management organisations were more likely than others to have merit- or performance-related pay (Bevan and Thompson 1992), some organisations have regretted its inclusion. Armstrong and Baron (1998a) report that staff almost universally disliked the link with pay, and a manager in one of their case study companies reported that 'the whole process is an absolute nightmare' (p. 172). Clark (2005) provides a good discussion of the problems with the pay link and we include a detailed discussion of performance-related pay in Chapter 7.

There are forms of reward other than monetary and the Institute of Employment Studies (IRS 2001) found that there was more satisfaction with the system where promotion and development, rather than money, was used as a reward for good performance. The increased emphasis on development may have led to a decline in the use of performance-related pay. Whereas in the 1992 IPD survey 85 per cent of organisations claimed to link performance management to pay (Bevan and Thompson 1992), Armstrong and Baron (1998a) found that only 43 per cent of survey respondents reported such a link. However, 82 per cent of the organisations visited had some form of performance-related pay (PRP) or competency-based pay, so the picture is a little confusing. They suggest that a view is emerging of performance management which centres on 'dialogue', 'shared understanding', 'agreement' and 'mutual commitment', rather than rating for pay purposes. To this end organisations are increasingly suggesting that employees take more ownership of performance management (*see* Scott 2006 for a good example) and become involved in collecting self-assessment evidence throughout the year (IDS 2005). While these characteristics may feature in more sophisticated systems, Houldsworth (2003) reports that 77 per cent of organisations link performance assessments with pay, and it appears that many organisations are trying to achieve both development and reward outcomes. She also contrasts systems driven by either performance development or performance measurement, finding that the real experience of developmental performance management is that it is motivational, encourages time spent with the line manager, encourages two-way communication and is an opportunity to align roles and training with business needs. Alternatively, where there is a measurement focus, performance management is seen as judgemental, a chance to assess and get rid of employees, emphasises control and getting more out of staff, raises false expectations and is a way to manage the salaries bill.

Activity 5.2

Think of the performance appraisal or performance management system at your place of work.

- To what extent does it focus on development and to what extent does it focus on reward?

- How, and how well, are each of these purposes achieved? Explain why this is.

- What would you do to improve the system, and what impacts would these actions have?

IMPLEMENTATION AND CRITIQUE OF PERFORMANCE MANAGEMENT

Performance management needs to be line driven rather than HR driven, and therefore mechanisms need to be found to make this happen. The incorporation of line managers alongside HR managers in a working party to develop the system is clearly important as doing so not only takes account of the needs of the line in the system design, but also demonstrates that the system is line led (Williams 2002). Training in the introduction and use of the system is also ideally line led, and Fletcher and Williams (1992) give us an excellent example of an organisation where line managers were trained as 'performance management coaches' who were involved in departmental training and support for the new system. However, some researchers have found that line managers are the weak link in the system (see, for example, Hendry et al. 1997). The then Department of Trade and Industry (DTI) now the Department for Business, Enterprise and Regulatory Reform (see IRS 2001) notes that any system is only as good as the people who put it into operation. See Case 5.1 at **www.pearsoned.co.uk/torrington** which deals with the introduction of a PMS.

WINDOW ON PRACTICE

Fletcher and Williams (1992) report on a scheme that was introduced by training a series of nominated line manager coaches from each department of an organisation. They had then to take the message back to their colleagues and train them, tailoring the material to their department (Personnel/Training providing

▶

▶ the back-up documentation). These were serving line managers who had to give up their time to do the job. Many of them were high-flyers, and they have been important opinion leaders and influencers – though they themselves had to be convinced first. Their bosses could refuse to nominate high-quality staff for this role if they wished, but they would subsequently be answerable to the Chief Executive. This approach was taken because it fits with the philosophy of performance management (i.e. high line-management participation), and because it was probably the only way to train all the departmental managers in the timescale envisaged.

Source: Summarised from C. Fletcher and R. Williams (1992) *Performance Management in the UK: Organisational Experience*. London: IPM, p. 133.

Bevan and Thompson (1992) found incomplete take-up of performance management, with some aspects being adopted and not others. They noted that there was a general lack of integration of activities. This is rather unfortunate as one of the key advantages of performance management is the capacity for integration of activities concerned with the management of individual performance. This problem is still apparent. Hendry *et al.* (1997) reported the comments of Phil Wills from GrandMet, that there is still little understanding of what an integrated approach to performance management means. Williams (2002) suggests that there is still confusion over the nature of performance management and that it is expected to deliver in too many areas, for example, training and development, pay, careers and bonuses (IRS 2001). The conflict between these aims means that the results are typically unsatisfactory.

Performance management seems to suffer from the same problems as traditional appraisal systems. Armstrong and Baron (1998a) report, for example, that over half the respondents to their survey feel that managers give their best ratings to people that they like, and over half the managers surveyed felt that they had not received sufficient training in performance management processes. They also report (1998b) that the use of ratings was consistently derided by staff and seen as subjective and inconsistent.

In terms of individual objective setting linked to organisational performance objectives, there are problems when strategy is unclear and when it evolves. Rose (2000) also reports a range of problems, particularly the fact that SMART targets can be problematic if they are not constantly reviewed and updated, although this is a time-consuming process. Pre-set objectives can be a constraining factor in such a rapidly changing business context, and they remind us of the trap of setting measurable targets, precisely because they are measurable and satisfy the system, rather than because they are most important to the organisation. He argues that a broader approach which assesses the employee's accomplishments as a whole and their contribution to the organisation is more helpful than concentrating on pre-set objectives. Williams (2002) also notes that there is more to performance than task performance, such as volunteering and helping others. He refers to this as contextual performance; it is sometimes referred to as collegiate behaviour.

Often a PMS is seen as imposed by the HR function and there may be little ownership of the system by line managers. Similarly, if paperwork has to be returned to the HR function it may well be seen as a form-filling exercise for someone else's benefit and with no practical value to performance within the job. There is an increasing literature indicating that appraisal can have serious negative consequences for the employee (IRS 2005) such as demotivation and reduced performance.

A further concern with SMART targets is that they inevitably have a short-term focus, yet what is most important to the organisation is developments which are complex and longer term, which are very difficult to pin down to short-term targets (see, for example, Hendry et al. 1997). In this context systems which also focus on the development of competencies will add greater value in the longer term. Armstrong and Baron (1998b) do note that a more rounded view of performance is gradually being adopted, which involves the 'how' as well as the 'what', and inputs such as the development of competencies. There is, however, a long way to go adequately to describe performance and define what is really required for organisational success. It is also noted with concern that most performance management research in conducted in a western setting (Vance et al. 1992) and that there is limited understanding of PMS in different cultures.

More fundamentally Egan (1995) argues that the problem with appraisal not only relates to poor design or implementation, but is rooted deeply in the basic reaction of organisational members to such a concept. There is an increasing body of critical literature addressing the role and theory of appraisal. These debates centre on the underlying reasons for appraisal (see, for example, Barlow 1989; Townley 1993; Newton and Findlay 1996) and the social construction of appraisal (see, for example, Grint 1993). This literature throws some light on the use and effectiveness of performance appraisal in organisations arguing that, rather than being for the benefit and development of employees, it is a mechanism for management control and monitoring of employees which leads to work intensification and stress.

WINDOW ON PRACTICE

Applicability of appraisal in different cultural settings

The way that an appraisal process is used can be affected by the cultural context in which it takes place. For example, Varma et al. (2005) compared the use of performance appraisal in manufacturing organisations in the USA and India using statistical analysis. They found that interpersonal effect (the like/dislike relationship between supervisor and subordinate) appeared to have no impact in performance appraisal ratings given in the USA but that in India supervisors inflated the rating of low performers. They suggested that this might be due to local cultural norms and a collectivist Indian culture, as opposed to an

▶

▶ individualistic US culture, and a greater concern in India for positive relationships. Another example is an event experienced by one of the authors of this book when running a course on performance appraisal in the Czech Republic some time after the Velvet Revolution. Managers on the course said that the use of performance appraisal would be entirely unacceptable at that time as workers would associate it with what had gone before under the Communist regime. Apparently every year a list was published in order of the highest to the lowest performer. Whilst this list was claimed to represent work performance the managers said that in reality it represented degrees of allegiance to the Communist Party and was nothing to do with work performance.

EVALUATION OF PERFORMANCE MANAGEMENT SYSTEMS

We discussed earlier the key role of PMSs in developing human capital to achieve sustainable competitive advantage. Given this, it is somewhat disappointing that there is little evidence to demonstrate a correlation between the existence of a PMS and organisational performance in the private sector (Armstrong and Baron 1998a). These authors do report, however, that 77 per cent of organisations surveyed regarded their systems as effective to some degree and Houldsworth (2003), using the Henley and Hay Group survey of top FTSE companies and public sector respondents, reports that 68 per cent of organisations rated their performance management effectiveness as excellent. It would be interesting, however, to know how these perceptions were arrived at, given that few organisations have formal mechanisms for evaluating their PMS (Williams 2002). While Houldsworth *et al.* (2005) propose that performance management practice is now more sophisticated and better received by employees, we suggest that it still remains an act of faith.

KEY DEBATE: 360-DEGREE FEEDBACK

360-degree feedback, a very specific term used to refer to feedback from a variety of sources, is increasingly being used both within PMSs and as a separate development activity. Despite this, it is a relatively new practice, a recent CIPD survey (CIPD 2005) indicating that only 14 per cent of respondents had 360-degree feedback systems, suggesting that this emerging aspect of performance management is worthy of fuller consideration. Interest in 360-degree feedback may arise either as an HR specialist considering the implementation and operation of such a system, or as a line manager subject to and participating in this type of feedback system.

The nature of 360-degree feedback

This approach to feedback refers to the use of the whole range of sources from which feedback can be collected about any individual.

> The systematic collection and feedback of performance data on an individual or group derived from a number of stakeholders. (Ward 1997, p. 15)

Thus feedback is collected from every angle on the way that the individual carries out their job: from immediate line manager; peers; subordinates; more senior managers; internal customers; external customers; and from individuals themselves. It is argued that this breadth provides better feedback than relying on the line manager only, who will only be able to observe the individual in a limited range of situations, and thus 360-degree feedback provides a better way to capture the complexities of performance. Hodgetts *et al.* (1999) report that more than 70 per cent of United Parcels Service employees found that feedback from multiple sources was more useful in developing self-insight than feedback from a single source. Individuals, it is argued, will find feedback from peers and subordinates compelling and more valid (*see*, for example, Borman 1998 and Atwater *et al.* 2002), and Edwards and Ewen (1996, p. 4) maintain that:

> No organizational action has more power for motivating employee behaviour change than feedback from credible work associates.

Such all-round feedback enables the individual to understand how they may be seen differently (or similarly) by different organisational groups, and how this may contrast with their own views of their strengths and weaknesses. This provides powerful information for the development of self-awareness. While 360-degree feedback may be collected using informal methods, as shown in the Window on Practice box on Humberside TEC, the term itself is a registered trade mark, and refers to a very specific method of feedback collection and analysis which was devised in the United States (*see* Edwards and Ewen 1996, p. 19), and they suggest that 'simplistic, informal approaches to multi-source assessment are likely to multiply rather than reduce error'. However, informal approaches are sometimes used quite successfully as an alternative to a survey questionnaire and statistical analysis.

WINDOW ON PRACTICE

Using an informal approach to 360-degree feedback at Humberside TEC

Storr (2000) reports on a 360-degree feedback process which is quite different from the survey approach. It is a process which has gradually been built up from upward appraisal for team leaders, has been piloted and has gradually become standard. The process is owned by the appraisees, and is different because it is

▶

▶ carried out face to face rather than using a paper system, and by all raters at the same time in a group-based approach for 90 per cent of individuals. It is a dialogue rather than a survey, and the only rule is that every individual must carry out at least one per year. The purpose of the system is to 'improve performance and enable people to learn and grow' (p. 38). Each group has a trained facilitator who supports both appraisers and appraisees. Different individuals have reacted differently to the approach, as might be expected: one individual said that they see it as empowerment, and many found that there was a great advantage in seeing the world from other people's point of view. Storr reports on one individual who received similar feedback from the group to that which she had received previously, from her manager, but hearing it from the six members of the group had a much stronger effect on her. Individuals often used their first experience of the process in a general way to ask the group what they should start doing, stop doing, continue doing or do differently. Over time, however, individuals began to ask more specific questions.

Source: Summarised from F. Storr (2000) 'This is not a circular', *People Management*, 11 May, pp. 38–40.

Formal approaches may be more widely adopted but may not be appropriate in all circumstances and organisations are advised to consider a number of issues when deciding whether or not to adopt 360-degree feedback. First, are the organisation's culture and structure appropriate? 360-degree feedback typically thrives in flatter organisational structures with lower levels of management control where employees are empowered and risks, and subsequent mistakes, are tolerated. Secondly, there are design issues: for example, will the system's aims be focused on development or pay? The debate on this in PMSs is mirrored broadly, but more intensely, in respect of 360-degree feedback. While there is evidence that some organisations do use such feedback to drive pay (Mabey 2001), there is strong opinion that 360-degree feedback should be developmentally focused (Armstrong and Baron 2005). Indeed, Mabey (2001) suggests that feedback is seriously compromised when the purpose of ratings is decision making rather than development. Table 5.2 outlines the difference in approach required in systems that focus on decision making on issues like pay and those that are development driven. The two purposes adopt very different approaches, reinforcing the difficulty in attempting to both develop and judge individuals using the same system.

Further considerations are skill levels in the organisation and the extent to which the participants have the skills to make the feedback work in a positive and constructive way and communication, that is, whether staff fully understand and support the system and whether they trust the process. It can be seen that many organisations will have to undertake a significant amount of work before introducing a system and that 360-degree feedback is not necessarily appropriate in all circumstances.

TABLE 5.2 360-degree feedback design features by purpose

Design feature	Purpose	
	Decision making	**Development only**
'Owner' of the feedback	Organisation	Participant
Questionnaire content	Core competencies	Job-specific competencies
Length of questionnaire	Shorter (30–50 items)	Longer (80+ items)
Response scales	Encourage between-person comparisons	Encourage within-person ranking of skills
Ratee participation	Required	Voluntary
Administration schedule	As required (e.g. annual)	Ad hoc (on request)
Report format	Between-person comparisons	Within-person comparisons
Copy of results	Participant and supervisor	Participant only
Share results with raters?	Expected or required	Optional or discouraged
Action plan	Required	Recommended
Typical uses	• Performance management • Succession planning • Staffing • Pay (e.g. bonuses)	• Employee development • Career planning • Training

Source: D. Bracken, C., Timmreck, J. Fleenor and L. Summers (2001) '360-degree feedback from another angle', *Human Resource Management*, Vol. 40, No. 1, p. 13.

Activity 5.3

1 Think of your current or previous role, in paid employment or any other capacity, and:

- Identify one or two critical incidents (such as making a presentation or attending an important meeting for the first time).

- Identify a longer-term activity you have been involved in (such as a project group or working party).

2 For both of these identify who could have provided you with constructive feedback, and why, and what specific questions you would have asked of them.

3 Now think ahead. What plans can you make to incorporate feedback into an up-coming one-off or longer-term activity?

360-degree feedback processes

The formal process is a survey using a carefully constructed questionnaire for all the contributors of feedback. This questionnaire may be bought off the peg, providing a well-tested tool, or may be developed internally, providing a tool more precisely matched to the needs of the organisation. Whichever form is used, the essence is that it is based on behavioural competencies (for a more detailed explanation of these *see* Chapter 6). The design of the questionnaire is crucial to the system's success and the following points, drawn from a recent CIPD factsheet on the topic (**www.cipd.co.uk**), outline key considerations in questionnaire design.

- Questions should be relevant to the recipient's job. If they are not, the recipient will not be motivated to change or understand what changes are required.
- Each question should be concise, use plain English, and omit qualifiers, such as 'when appropriate' and 'as necessary'. Vague, complex questions rarely produce clear feedback.
- Each question should be similar to the other questions used to measure a particular competency, and be different from all other questions relating to other competencies. Muddled competencies make muddled feedback.
- Questions should set standards. For example, an item in a questionnaire worded 'Makes decisions' is not in itself a question, and any rating of a person against this statement is not helpful, as the decisions made could be unclear, late, autocratic or wrong.

Additionally it may be appropriate for some free-text questions to be included that allow those completing the questionnaire to provide an explanation of the ratings they have given. While such explanations are harder to analyse, the recipient can look for themes and common patterns that emerge in the comments.

WINDOW ON PRACTICE

Johnson (2001) reports on the merger between two pharmaceuticals companies – UniChem from the UK and Alliance Sante from France to form Alliance UniChem. In an attempt to focus managers from diverse cultures on a single vision the HR department concentrated on all aspects of performance management, in particular 360-degree feedback which was felt to be a pragmatic and practical tool. Four key values were identified, excellence, service, innovation and partnership, and competencies were drawn up to reflect these. The process had to be introduced very sensitively as 360-degree feedback was virtually unheard of in three countries covered by the company – Italy, Spain and Portugal, and in France it was seen very much as an American tool and regarded with considerable suspicion.

The most senior managers went through the process first, and it was then piloted in different countries. The tool was developed to be used in five different languages, and the customised package adopted came with development activities for each competency, and coaching sessions to ensure that feedback was not interpreted without analysis and support. The whole process formed part of a self-development programme.

Source: Summarised from R. Johnson (2001) 'Doubled entente', *People Management*, Vol. 7, No. 9, 3 May, pp. 38–9.

Those providing feedback will be asked to score, on a given scale, the extent to which the individual displays the competencies specified. Using a well-designed questionnaire, distributed to a sufficient number of contributors and employing appropriate analysis tools, should provide reliable and valid data for the individual. Many organisations feel it necessary to use software systems in 360-degree feedback, in view of the vast amount of data that is generated. This clearly has cost implications for the process but provides information to individuals that is seen as highly credible.

The feedback is usually presented to the individual in the form of graphs or bar charts showing comparative scores from different feedback groups, such as peers, subordinates, customers, where the average will be provided for each group, and single scores from line manager and self. The feedback should be concise and easy to understand; often the use of graphics can help this (*see* Figure 5.3). In most cases the individual will have been able to choose the composition of the contributors in each group, for example which seven subordinates, out of a team of 10, will be asked to complete the feedback questionnaire. But beyond this the feedback will be anonymous as only averages for each group of contributors will be reported back, except for the line manager's score. While this is a generally accepted principle of 360-degree feedback, one of the few studies of managers subject to such feedback suggests that many managers would prefer the system to be open rather than confidential (Mabey 2001).

The feedback will need to be interpreted by an internal or external facilitator in a face-to-face meeting. It is generally recommended that the person receiving the feedback

FIGURE 5.3
A 360-degree feedback profile

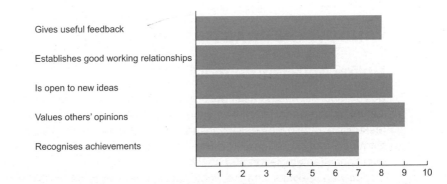

Source: This figure is taken from Managing Performance: Performance Management in Action (2005) written by M. Armstrong and A. Baron with the permission of the publisher, the Chartered Institutue of Personnel and Development, London (www.cipd.co.uk).

will need some training in the nature of the system and how to receive feedback, and the contributors will need some training on how to provide feedback. The principle behind the idea of feedback is that the person receiving it can then use this information to change their behaviours and to improve performance, by setting and meeting development goals and an action plan.

Reported benefits include a stronger ownership of development goals, a climate of constructive feedback, improved communication over time and an organisation which is more capable of change as continuous feedback and improvement have become part of the way people work (Cook and Macauley 1997). It is also suggested that 360-degree feedback helps to create new insights that promote a greater awareness of how the person being reviewed impacts on others and presents a more rounded view of performance. One study suggests that participants in a 360-degree feedback process are also more likely to have a positive view of their employing organisation (Mabey 2001). Useful texts on designing and implementing a system include Edwards and Ewen (1996) from the US perspective and Ward (1998) from the UK perspective. A brief 'how to do it guide' is Goodge and Watts (2000).

For an in-depth example of 360-degree feedback *see* Case 5.2 at **www.pearsoned.co.uk/torrington**.

360-degree feedback online

One feature of 360-degree feedback that appears to be in increasing usage is that of online feedback, which removes the need for paper copies of the questionnaires, making distribution and collation of the questionnaires much quicker and easier. Online feedback is suggested to make the feedback both more confidential and more complete, and indeed the person being reviewed can specify the competencies on which they particularly require feedback. The feedback can be quickly provided, online, to the person being reviewed who can then be responsible for the management of the feedback. While seemingly attractive, there can be significant costs attached to implementing online 360-degree feedback systems and so choice of software provider is important.

WINDOW ON PRACTICE

Online 360-degree feedback

Bexley Council, a large local government organisation, aimed to change their culture to one where there was improved communication, more teamwork and a responsive, employee-centred attitude. Their chosen mechanism for this was the introduction of an online 360-Degree feedback system. The administration, questionnaire completion and analysis were all computerised and managed by the software provider and the whole process proved to be flexible and efficient and to provide timely results.

There were two phases to the project. In Phase I, managers and their teams used the systems to appraise one another on the required competency behaviours. After Phase I there was a strong view that communication within and between the participating teams had improved. Managers felt that the appraisal discussions had a structure that was previously missing, allowing many performance related issues to be raised and resolved for the first time.

The online system meant that in Phase II, comparisons could be made over time. The 360-degree feedback system allowed the managers and team members to see how these results compared with those of Phase I. They were therefore able to assess the outcome of interventions and training programmes that had been implemented as part of this programme. The systems are now in use throughout the organisation on a regular basis. The process continues to produce better individual and team performance, greater communication, and increased employee participation and motivation. Bexley Council has now been rated as a highly performing council.

Source: Human Factors International, business psychology and strategy consultants, www.hfi.com. Adapted by the authors.

Difficulties and dilemmas in 360-degree feedback

As with all processes and systems there needs to be clarity about the purpose of 360-degree feedback. Most authors distinguish between developmental uses, which they identify as fairly safe and a good way of introducing such a system, and other uses such as to determine pay awards. There seems to be an almost universal view that using such data for pay purposes is not advisable. Ward (1998) provides a useful framework for considering the different applications of this type of feedback, and reviews in some detail other applications such as using 360-degree feedback as part of a training course to focus attention for each individual on what they need to get out of the course. Other applications he suggests include using 360-degree feedback as an approach to team building, as a method of performance appraisal/management, for organisation development purposes and to evaluate training and development. Edwards and Ewen (1996) suggest that it can be used for nearly all HR systems, using selection, training and development, recognition and the allocation of job assignments as examples.

Most approaches to 360-degree feedback require anonymity for those providing feedback as well as clarity of purpose. Anonymity can be difficult to maintain with a small team, so those providing feedback may feel uncomfortable about being open and honest. In their research, Pillutla and Ronson (2006) demonstrate how feedback from colleagues may be biased and warn against recruitment, reward and promotion decisions being made on the basis of such feedback. The dangers of collusion and bias need to be eliminated, and it is suggested that the appropriate software systems can achieve this, but they are of course expensive, as are well-validated off-the-peg systems.

Follow-up is critical and if the experience of 360-degree feedback is not built on via the construction of development goals and the support and resources to fulfil these, the process may be viewed negatively and may be demotivating. There is an assumption that the provision of such feedback will motivate the individuals receiving it to develop and improve their performance, but Morgan and Cannan (2005) found very mixed results in their Civil Service research. One-third of their respondents were not motivated to act on the feedback and in this case felt that the 360-degree process was an isolated act with lack of follow-up, depending heavily on the proactivity of the individuals involved, and with little support given.

London *et al.* (1997) report concerns about the way systems are implemented, and that nearly one-third of respondents they surveyed experienced negative effects. Atwater and his colleagues (2002) found some negative reactions such as reduced effort, dissatisfaction with peers who provided the feedback and a lower commitment to colleagues. Fletcher and Baldry (2001) note that there are contradictions in the results from 360-degree feedback so far, and they suggest that further research is needed on how feedback affects self-esteem, motivation, satisfaction and commitment. The DTI (2001) suggests that sufficient resources need to be devoted to planning a system and that it should be piloted before general use. Clearly, 360-degree feedback needs to be handled carefully and sensitively and in the context of an appropriate organisational climate so that it is not experienced as a threat. Atwater *et al.* (2002) suggest that to counteract any negative effects it is important to prepare people for making their own ratings and on how they can provide honest and constructive feedback to others, ensure confidentiality and anonymity of raters, make sure the feedback is used developmentally and owned by the person being rated (for example they may be the only person to receive the report), provide post-feedback coaching and encouragement and encourage people to follow up the feedback they have received. Other problems identified include an over-reliance on technology and systems that are too bureaucratic.

There are a number of processes recommended to address some of the problems identified above and we present these in Table 5.3.

We have discussed in this 'Key debate' the increasing prominence of 360-degree feedback within PMSs and explained the reasons for and the benefits of this. We also, however, consider the problems of operationalisation and organisational structure for 360-degree feedback and suggest that, as with PMSs more generally, while such systems are sound in theory, many organisations have a long way to go in practice to implement them successfully.

TABLE 5.3 360-degree feedback: criteria for success

Active support of top management

Commitment to the process based on briefing, training and understanding the benefits

Use of feedback data as basis for development

Questionnaire reflects typical and significant aspects of behaviour

Well-delivered and comprehensive training programmes

No one feels threatened by the process

Questionnaires are reasonably easy to complete

Bureaucracy is minimised

Source: This table is taken from Managing Performance: Performance Management in Action (2005) written by M. Armstrong and A. Baron with the permission of the publisher, the Chartered Institutue of Personnel and Development, London (www.cipd.co.uk).

SUMMARY PROPOSITIONS

5.1 Employee performance management systems (PMSs) have risen in prominence due to their role in developing human capital in order to achieve sustainable competitive advantage.

5.2 Performance is comprised of both the 'what' and the 'how' and both these aspects of performance should be managed.

5.3 PMSs should link business objectives and individual objectives, be line manager owned, be an ongoing process and reward and reinforce performance.

5.4 Current trends in sophisticated PMSs include greater employee ownership, emphasis on the 'how' as well as the 'what', emphasis on evidence collection from both manager and employee, upward feedback to the line manager as well as downward feedback to the employee.

5.5 There is a tension between using PMSs developmentally or judgementally. Many organisations try to do both but are unlikely to be successful in this.

5.6 There are many critiques of PMSs and little evaluative evidence to demonstrate their benefits.

5.7 360-degree feedback is increasingly being used to provide individuals with a basis for changing behaviour and improving performance.

5.8 There is again a tension between using the process developmentally and linking it directly to pay awards.

5.9 Online 360-degree feedback is growing in importance and use.

GENERAL DISCUSSION TOPICS

1 Performance management is suggested to be fundamental to an organisation's attempts to achieve sustainable competitive advantage. Explain why this is and to what extent the use of performance management is likely to be successful in contributing to this.

2 360-degree feedback may have many advantages, but there is the argument that it can never really work because of the built-in biases, such as marking a boss well because you're due for a pay rise; marking yourself low so that you can be happily surprised by others' evaluations; marking peers down to make oneself look better. Discuss as many built-in biases as you can think of, and suggest how they might be tackled and whether substantive improvements could be made.

FURTHER READING

Cunneen, P. (2006) 'How to improve performance management', *People Management*, Vol. 12, No. 1, pp. 42–3.

Kuvaas, B. (2006) 'Performance Appraisal satisfaction and employee outcomes: mediating and moderating roles of work motivation', *International Journal of Human Resource Management*, Vol. 17, No. 3 pp. 504–22.

Poon, J. (2004) 'Effects of performance appraisal politics on job satisfaction and turnover intention', *Personnel Review*, Vol. 33, No. 3, pp. 322–34.

These articles reflect a stream of research looking at the outcomes of appraisal from the employee perspective, in particular focusing on job satisfaction, intention to quit and commitment. Comparing articles provides an interesting across-countries comparison, with savings banks being investigated in Norway by Kuvaas and a cross-sector study of part-time MBA students in Malaysia being carried out by Poon.

Swinburne, P. (2001) 'How to use feedback to improve performance', *People Management*, Vol. 7, No. 11, 31 May, pp. 46–7.
Short but extremely helpful and full of practical detail. Excellent guidelines on the 'do's and don'ts' of giving feedback and some very useful tips for receiving feedback.

Mabey, C. (2001) 'Closing the circle: participant views of a 360-degree feedback programme', *Human Resource Management Journal*, Vol. 11, No. 1, pp. 41–53.
A useful article in that it presents a summary of the views of managers involved in the 360-degree process, rather than the more usual HR specialist perspective.

Ward, P. (1997) *360-degree feedback*. London: Institute of Personnel and Development.
A detailed and insightful text which presents material both on 360-degree processes and on the issues surrounding such systems. Also uses some informative case study material.

REFERENCES

Armstrong, M. and Baron, A. (1998a) *Performance Management – The New Realities*. London: Institute of Personnel and Development.

Armstrong, M. and Baron, A. (1998b) 'Out of the Tick Box', *People Management*, 23 July, pp. 38–41.

Armstrong, M. and Baron, A. (2005) *Managing Performance: Performance Management in Action*. London: Chartered Institute of Personnel and Development.

Atwater, L., Waldman, D. and Brett, J. (2002) 'Understanding and optimising multi-source feedback', *Human Resource Management*, Vol. 41, No. 2, Summer, pp. 193–208.

Barlow, G. (1989) 'Deficiencies and the perpetuation of power: latent functions in management appraisal', *Journal of Management Studies*, Vol. 26, No. 5, pp. 499–518.

Bevan, S. and Thompson, M. (1992) 'An overview of policy and practice', in *Personnel Management in the UK: an anaylsis of the issues*. London: IPM.

Borman, W. (1998) '360 ratings: an analysis of assumptions and a research agenda for evaluating their validity', *Human Resource Management Review*, Vol. 7, pp. 299–315.

Bracken, D., Timmreck, C., Fleenor, J. and Summers, L. (2001) '360 degree feedback from another angle', *Human Resource Management*, Vol. 40, No. 1, p. 13.

Brumback, G.B. (1998) 'The Complete Guide to Performance Appraisal', *Personnel Psychology*, Vol. 51, No. 1, pp. 265–9.

CIPD (2005) *Performance Management: Survey Report*. London: Chartered Institute of Personnel and Development.

Clark, G. (2005) 'Performance Management Strategies' in G. Salaman, J. Storey and J. Billsberry (eds) *Strategic Human Resource Management: Theory and Practice*. London: The Open University in association with Sage.

Cook, S. and Macauley, S. (1997) 'How colleagues and customers can help improve team performance', *Team Performance Management*, Vol. 3, No. 1.

DTI (2001) *360 degree feedback: Best practice guidelines* (Prof C. Farrell).

Edwards, M.R. and Ewen, A.J. (1996) *360 Degree Feedback*. New York: Amacom, American Management Association.

Egan, G. (1995) 'A clear path of peak performance', *People Management*, 18 May, pp. 34–7.

Fletcher, C. and Baldry, C. (2001) 'Multi-source feedback systems: a research perspective', in I. Robertson and C. Cooper (eds) *Personnel Psychology and HRM*. Chichester: John Wiley and Sons Ltd.

Fletcher, C. and Williams, R. (1992) *Performance Management in the UK: Organisational experience*. London: Institute of Personnel Management.

Goodge, P. and Watts, P. (2000) 'How to manage 360° feedback', *People Management*, 17 February, pp. 50–2.

Grint, K. (1993) 'What's wrong with performance appraisals? – a critique and a suggestion', *Human Resource Management Journal*, Vol. 3, No. 3, pp. 61–77.

Hendry, C., Bradley, P. and Perkins, S. (1997) 'Missed a motivator?', *People Management*, 15 May, pp. 20–5.

Hodgetts, R., Luthans, F. and Slocum, J. (1999) 'Strategy and HRM initiatives for the '00s: environment redefining roles and boundaries, linking competencies and resources', *Organizational Dynamics*, Autumn, p. 7.

Houldsworth, E. (2003) 'Managing Individual performance', paper presented to the CIPD National Conference, Harrogate, 22–24 November.

Houldsworth, E. (2004) 'Managing Performance', in D. Rees and R. McBain (eds) *People Management: Challenges and Opportunities*. Basingstoke: Macmillan.

Houldsworth, E., Jirasinghe, D. and Everall, K. (2005) 'How can HR get the measure of performance management?', *People Management*, Vol. 11, No. 16, 11 August, p. 48.

IDS (2003) 'Performance Management', IDS Studies, No. 748, April. London: IDS.

IDS (2005) 'Performance Management', IDS Studies, No. 796, April. London: IDS.

IRS (2001) 'Performance appraisal must try harder', *IRS Employment Trends*, No. 724, March, pp. 2–3.

IRS (2005) 'Appraisals (2): learning from practice and experience', *IRS Employment Review*, No. 829, 12 August, pp. 13–17.

Johnson, R. (2001) 'Doubled entente', *People Management*, Vol. 7, No. 9, 3 May, pp. 38–9.

Locke, E. (1968) 'Towards a theory of task performance and incentives', *Organisational Behaviour and Human Performance*, Vol. 3, No. 2, pp. 157–89.

Locke, E. and Latham, G. (1990) *A Theory of Goal Setting and Task Performance*. Englewood Cliffs, NJ: Prentice-Hall.

London, M., Smither, J. and Adsit, D. (1997) 'Accountability: the achilles heel of multi-source feedback', *Group and Organizational Dynamics*, Vol. 22, No. 2, pp. 162–84.

Mabey, C. (2001) 'Closing the circle: participant views of a 360-degree feedback programme', *Human Resource Management Journal*, Vol. 11, No. 1, pp. 41–53.

Mayo, A. (2001) *The Human Value of the Enterprise: Valuing People as Assets – Monitoring, Measuring, Managing*. London: Nicolas Brealey.

Morgan, A. and Cannan, K. (2005) '360° feedback: a critical enquiry', *Personnel Review*, Vol. 34, No. 6, pp. 663–80.

Newton, T. and Findlay, P. (1996) 'Playing God? – the performance of appraisal', *Human Resource Management Journal*, Vol. 6, No. 3, pp. 42–58.

Pillutla, M. and Ronson, S. (2006) 'Survival of the similar', *People Management*, Vol. 12, No. 6, 23 March, pp. 36–7.

Roberts, Z. (2004) 'Q&A: "We must move on"', *People Management*, Vol. 10, No. 10, 20 May, pp. 16–17.

Rose, M. (2000) 'Target Practice', *People Management*, 23 November, pp. 44–5.

Scott, A. (2006) 'Intensive care', *People Management*, Vol. 12, No. 9, 4 May, pp. 38–40.

Sewell, G. and Wilkinson, B. (1992) 'Someone to watch over me: surveillance, discipline and the just-in-time process', *Sociology*, Vol. 26, pp. 271–89.

Storr, F. (2000) 'This is not a circular', *People Management*, 11 May, pp. 38–40.

Townley, B. (1993) 'Performance appraisal and the emergence of management', *Journal of Management Studies*, Vol. 30, No. 2, pp. 27–44.

Vance, C.M., McClaine, S.R., Boje, D.M. and Stage, D.H. (1992) 'An examination of the transferability of traditional performance appraisal across cultural boundaries', *Management International Review*, Vol. 32, No. 4, pp. 313–26.

Varma, A., Pichler, S. and Srinivas, E. (2005) 'The role of interpersonal affect in performance appraisal: evidence from two samples – the US and India', *International Journal of Human Resource Management*, Vol. 16, No. 11, pp. 2029–44.

Vroom, V. (1964) *Work and Motivation*. Chichester: John Wiley.

Ward, P. (1997) *360-degree feedback*. London: Institute of Personnel and Development.

Ward, P. (1998) 'A 360 degree turn for the better', *People Management*, 9 February.

Williams, R. (2002) *Managing Employee Performance*. London: Thompson Learning.

CHAPTER 6

People development

The objectives of this chapter are to:

1 Review the context and importance of learning and development in the UK

2 Identify the value of learning and development to the organisation and the individual

3 Discuss the role of the line manager in learning and development, with special emphasis on coaching

4 Explain the use and value of competencies in learning and development

5 Explore a range of development methods

6 Debate the value of e-learning

Skills shortages?

Which do you believe poses the greater danger to the future of the UK or you personally: global warming or terrorism? Taking the one you have chosen, would you say that it's a bigger threat to the country or you than avian flu? And how do all these three rate against the skills shortage as menaces to our national prosperity?

Yes, that's right – the skills shortage.

What's that? You say you weren't aware there was a skills shortage?

. . . this is Peter Kingston the *Guardian's* Further Education Editor, writing in 2007, and he goes on to say:

▶

> ▶ Why is there no national frisson over forecasts about Britain
> meandering into a state of low-skills equilibrium in which most
> businesses bumble along with poorly trained workers directed by
> inadequate managers to produce low-grade goods and services?

He goes on to propose potential reasons for the lack of interest in and
attention to these skills shortages: perhaps it's a dull topic, perhaps people
and businesses don't believe there is a problem since the economy has
been doing comparatively well, perhaps it's recognised as a problem, but
someone else's problem.

Kingston notes that historically the UK has paid less attention to skills
development than, say, France or Germany and that our skills gap has
always been a concern, but that demographic changes now mean that it is
imperative that something is done about it.

Source: P. Kingston (2007) 'Short Changed', *People Management*, Vol. 13, No. 16,
pp. 28–31.

Remedying skills deficiencies requires that both organisations and individuals commit
themselves to people development, yet this has often been a neglected area. In this
chapter we first look at the UK learning and development context before exploring the
value that employee development has for employers and individuals. In more practical
terms we examine the role of the line managers and competencies in people development
before looking at specific development methods, the key debate focusing on the
contribution of e-learning.

THE UK LEARNING AND DEVELOPMENT CONTEXT

In the UK, people development has traditionally been seen as a cost rather than
an investment and this is underlined by our voluntarist approach, meaning that
organisations choose to invest as much or as little as they think fit in the development
of their employees, with the government's role limited to *encouraging* learning and
development rather than intervening. In countries where the government intervenes,
such as France, companies are forced to pay an annual levy to the government and can
only claim it back if they can show evidence that they have spent this amount of money
on developing employees. High levels of skills are critical in promoting high performance
and wealth as a country, and there is a view that the UK's lack of attention to
development means that it will remain a low-wage, low-skills economy (Keep and
Mayhew 1999), with the emphasis on competing on price rather than quality.

In recent years in the UK there has been a governmental focus on measures to
increase our skills levels and reduce skills gaps, and there is some evidence from the WER
(Workplace Employee Relations) survey that training for core employees has increased

between 1998 and 2004 (Kersley *et al.* 2006). However, despite these efforts evidence of skills gaps remains (*see*, for example, Phillips 2006a). In 2007 the Leitch Report identified the need for significantly more investment in skills if the UK is to compete effectively in the world and has set national targets for increases in skills qualifications attained by 2020. The report suggested, and the government has put in place, a variety of mechanisms to achieve this, including a voluntary pledge from employers to increase their learning and development. There is a further suggestion in the report that if this voluntary approach does not work then more forceful measures may be taken.

Alternatively it has been suggested that it is not a lack of investment in learning and development that is the problem but the way such investment is distributed, that is, who it is spent on and the content of the development initiative. It is generally agreed that learning and development spend is unevenly distributed. It is often the people at the lower end of the hierarchy that miss out, and Westwood (2001) reports that:

> **Access to workforce development is unequal with managers and professionals or those with a degree up to five times more likely to receive work based training than people with no qualification and/or unskilled jobs. (p. 19)**

Broader development is concentrated on those at the beginning of their careers and those in more senior and specialist posts. Part-timers and those with fewer qualifications to begin with seem to miss out in terms of development and the WER survey found that professionals, associated professionals, managers and those with most qualifications receive most training rather than low-skilled workers. The highest levels of learning and development are generally found in larger organisations, especially the public sector.

The Leitch Report may be very useful in encouraging a broader distribution of learning and development, the focus being on improving lower-level skills via increasing those attaining qualifications at this level.

Activity 6.1

Consider the learning and development you have achieved to date in your career, or interview a family member or a friend if you have yet to begin your work career.

1 What type of development have you (or your interviewee) received?

2 Who requested the development?

3 How easy or difficult was it to gain the development that you (or your interviewee) desired?

4 How useful was that training and development in doing your job and in gaining a job move or enhanced job duties?

5 What role did your (or your interviewee's) line manager play in this development?

A further problem is that in the UK a great deal of money is spent on development that does not last very long. In terms of learning content there is evidence to suggest that much development is related to induction and particularly health and safety and this does nothing to drive the development of a knowledge-based economy. Most learning and development is reactive, that is addressing short-term problems rather than proactively focusing on the long-term strategic needs of the organisation. In addition to the Leitch Report and its associated initiatives there is currently a range of other initiatives (for example Investors in People), bodies (for example Learning and Skills Councils), and reports in the UK which are aimed at increasing and improving skills via learning and development. If you wish to read more about this you can consult a specialist learning and development text, such as Harrison (2005).

THE VALUE OF LEARNING AND DEVELOPMENT TO ORGANISATIONS AND INDIVIDUALS

The problem with people development is that it is very difficult to provide compelling evidence that it really does improve performance and provide a clear business benefit. Supporters claim that it improves recruitment, motivation and retention; enhances individuals' skills, knowledge and attitudes appropriate for the job they are doing to enable them to do it better; and prepares employees to take on different and sometimes higher-level roles in the organisation. In this way learning and development can be seen as an investment in improving business performance. In a more general sense the pace of change in business today means that there is a constant need for new skills to be developed in order for the organisation to remain competitive. Continuous development is a key part of enhancing the value of the employee capital in any organisation and this is generally seen as the way in which organisations gain competitive advantage.

For some the end of the last paragraph will be seen as rhetoric which is all well and good, but in the everyday business context there are problems associated with development activities: people may require time off the job and the costs of internal or external learning and development specialists, courses and materials have to be met. Development activities may also provide employees with the skills and qualifications they need to get a better job elsewhere and hence they may leave the organisation which provided the development. For the line manager people development may therefore cause considerable problems, but many of these potential problems result from the way that learning and development is carried out (for example, it does not need to take place off the job) and the lack of supporting mechanisms (such as job moves within the company) and other rewards for employees who have achieved high levels of skill.

Activity 6.2

1 What particular problems might a line manager anticipate if all the employees in their team were entitled to seven days' off-the-job training per year backed up by line manager coaching support?

2 How might these problems be reduced?

3 What general barriers might individuals experience when asked to attend an employee development event? (You may wish to focus on a specific area of development such as interviewing skills, sales skills, or learning a new software package).

4 How might these barriers be reduced?

The focus of learning and development has moved from instructor-led training, with an emphasis on trainers identifying the content of what is delivered to learners, to self-directed development with an emphasis on integrating learning with job tasks so that it becomes highly relevant to the job and job performance. This involves learners and their managers taking the lead and identifying what they need to learn and both developing a greater awareness of the processes of learning, with specialist trainers being called upon for support and facilitation when needed. This shift underlines the importance of the line manager in learning and development.

THE LINE MANAGER AND LEARNING AND DEVELOPMENT

When learning and development is seen as the responsibility of the learning and development specialist or the HR function it often has the unfortunate impact of separating learning and development activities from the line manager and the individual doing the job. As the focus has shifted from the trainer to the learner, the importance of learning on the job has risen. This means that the role of the line manager is critical as they work with an individual to determine the latter's learning needs, to agree on the best ways these needs should be met, to support and enable the application of skills learned on an off-the-job development event, and to provide ongoing feedback, guidance, coaching and review. In the 2007 Learning and Development Survey (CIPD 2007) increasing line manager involvement in development was reported.

Line managers are also increasingly responsible for their group's learning and development budget and a development specialist ideally acts in a facilitative role providing information, guidance, appropriate processes and support to the line manager. It is to be hoped that the intimate involvement of the line manager means that all development activities are central to the job role that the individual is currently doing

129

or about to do, and that such learning and development activity strengthens the working relationship between manager and employee.

The involvement of the line manager can also go beyond working with individuals that they manage to contributing to the development of a competency framework in the organisation (which we explore in the following section), acting as assessors on development centres, contributing to the design of a developmentally based performance management system (*see* Chapter 5), acting as trainers themselves in running courses on aspects of strategic initiatives in the organisation and adapting these to meet departmental needs. Development centres can be defined as centres where the behaviour of a group of employees with potential for further job moves is assessed as they carry out a range of relevant activities over the course of, say, a couple of days, with the assessment then used to draw up a development plan for each individual who attended the centre.

WINDOW ON PRACTICE

The line manager's role in learning and development: experiences of six organisations

Sue Hutchinson and John Purcell carried out case studies of the line manager's role in six organisations: Wiltshire County Council, Defence Logistics Organisation/Defence Procurement Agency (DLO/DPA) (part of the Ministry of Defence), Standard and Poor (publishing and part of McGraw-Hill), Halcrow (engineering design and consultancy), John Lewis Partnership (retail store) and Wincanton (logistics and distribution). Through research into these companies they identified the line manager's role as being fundamental in the following areas:

- **Induction activities**: for example making arrangements for new starters to shadow others or work alongside them and identifying a 'buddy' to guide the new starter.
- **Giving access to challenging work or being a member of a project team**: providing the best route for learning by doing new things.
- **Encouraging job rotation and multiskilling**: so that individuals are better able to contribute to the work of a whole section.
- **Coaching and guidance**: where the manager works on a one-to-one basis with an individual in solving a particular business problem.
- **The provision of informal training activities**: where the whole team gets together, for example over lunch, to discuss a new development or issue. This can be led by the manager or a team member and tends to be around technical rather than soft skills.
- **Arranging for a secondment**: for an individual to work in another area to build networks and broaden experience.

- **Identification of an external training programme**: where there is nothing appropriate internally, for example attending conferences for professional employees.
- **Providing formal training**: actually delivering this, for example health and safety training.
- **Responsibility for career development and promotion**: sometimes a shared responsibility between the HR function and the line manager.
- **Emphasising knowledge sharing**: for example encouraging problem solving groups and developing a localised culture of learning.

Source: This text is adapted from Change Agenda: Learning and the Line: The role of line managers in training, learning and development (2007) written by S. Hutchinson and J. Purcell with the permission of the publisher, the Chartered Institutue of Personnel and Development, London (www.cipd.co.uk).

The role of the line manager in learning and development can therefore potentially be very wide ranging, but this may bring with it a range of problems, the most prevalent being the demand for time as line managers increasingly work under the pressure to produce more and more. Adding on further tasks in the form of people development may simply mean that line managers have the responsibility but not the time to fulfil that responsibility as well as they may wish. In addition line managers are often not well prepared for their role as a people developer, may never have anticipated this as part of their role, and may not consider development activities as one of their natural strengths or preferences. Where managers *are* able to acquire the relevant skills, time issues may still pose problems.

The line manager's coaching role

Coaching is an informal approach to individual development based on a close relationship between the individual and one other person, either internal or external to the organisation. The coach is often the immediate manager, who is experienced in the task, and as coach helps the learner to develop by giving them the opportunity to perform an increasing range of tasks, and by helping them to learn from their experiences. They work to improve the learner's performance by asking searching questions, actively listening, discussion, encouragement, understanding, counselling and providing information and honest feedback. The manager coach is usually in a position to create development opportunities for the learner when this is appropriate. For example, a line manager can delegate attendance at a meeting, or allow an employee to deputise, where this is appropriate to the individual's development needs. Alternatively they can create the opportunity for a learner to join a working party or can arrange a brief secondment to another department. Coaches can share 'inside' information with the individual they are coaching to help them understand the political context in which they are working. For example, they are able to explain who will have most influence on a decision that will be made, or future plans for restructuring within a department.

Activity 6.3

'If line managers devote a significant amount of time to people development the job will never get done.'

Put the case for and against this comment.

Skilled managers can adapt their coaching style to suit the individual they are coaching, from highly directive at one end of the scale to non-directive at the other. The directive approach is highly structured by the manager with plenty of advice and guidance. The non-directive approach allows the learner to structure the meeting while the line manager concentrates on asking questions to allow the learner to work things out for themselves. The style needed may change over time, as the learner gains more confidence and experience, and the ability to switch styles is important. A useful text on the practical skills of coaching is Pemberton (2006). In an exploratory study Carroll and Gillen (2001) found a variety of barriers to line manager acceptance of a teaching/coaching role, in particular lack of interpersonal competence, lack of time, performance pressures, and a feeling that the teaching role was not valued and was the role of the HR department. This same article also provides some excellent material on what makes an effective coach. The CIPD (2006) found that competing business pressures and lack of coaching skills and experience within the organisation were the greatest barriers to coaching, and IDS (2006a) suggests that given the emphasis in coaching on honest self-reflection, there will be barriers in organisations where the culture is not one of openness and honesty. IDS also points out that coaching has been seen as a remedial tool but that it probably has more to offer as a development opportunity for turning good performers into excellent ones. In a similar vein Purcell and his colleagues (2003) revealed a strong relationship between effective coaching and guidance from the line manager and employee satisfaction, commitment and motivation leading to employees being prepared to put in that bit of extra effort. You may find it helpful at this point to refer to the coaching section in the Skills Package at the end of the book.

Line manager coaching brings challenges in respect of boundaries and Hall draws these out well (Hall 2007). One boundary is the extent to which the manager takes a counselling role; the manager needs to be aware of when counselling activity becomes more personal and where referral to a qualified therapist is the most appropriate course of action. Another ethical issue is that coaching activity usually enhances the relationship between the line manager coach and individual and whilst this is positive up to a point there is a boundary beyond which the relationship can become potentially abusive. For example, a closer relationship might mean that the manager takes advantage of the learner by asking them to do unreasonable levels of extra work or using them to pass on messages to their peers, which they should be communicating themselves. Thirdly, managers may need to adopt a different style at times, for example when the context demands urgent action with directive managerial behaviour. Whilst time is an ever-present concern for line managers, coaching is often possible in brief conversations and does not necessarily need to be planned in advance.

THE USE OF BEHAVIOURAL COMPETENCIES IN LEARNING AND DEVELOPMENT

Before a manager coaches an employee or arranges other forms of development for them it is important for the development need to be clearly identified. Organisations have increasingly used competencies to define the behaviour associated with high performance in a role, and as such they can be used directly as a way of identifying employee development needs. Organisations usually produce their own framework of competencies, and attached to the definition of the competency there will be a list of behaviours that indicate that this competency is being used. Frameworks often group competencies together in the form of clusters (*see* the example in Figure 6.1).

In some organisations the behavioural indicators are defined at different levels of sophistication, as can be seen in the Window on Practice which examines practice at Connexions (a state-provided careers service for people of all ages), and some organsiations provide both positive and negative behavioural indicators, as in the example from the Police Force in the following Window on Practice.

FIGURE 6.1
Typical content of a competency framework

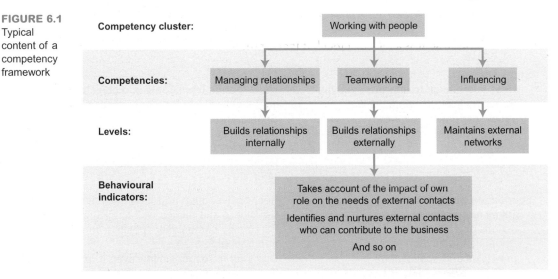

Source: This figure is taken from The Competencies Handbook (1999) written by S. Whiddett and S. Hollyforde with the permission of the publisher, the Chartered Institutue of Personnel and Development, London (www.cipd.co.uk).

WINDOW ON PRACTICE

An example of behavioural skills with level definitions from Connexions

Working with others

The ability to work constructively within a group/team environment

Level definitions	Examples of actions demonstrated at each level
Stage Three – Contributes to organisational success by defining, planning and implementing strategies for the future and building strategic relationships and alliances – Manages and allocates available resources, including financial, capital and people to best meet current and future requirements (2 of 4)	– Is able to recognise opportunities for organisation-wide networking – Develops and maintains strategic partnerships and alliances – Understands the strategic implications of working within different cultures (3 of 4)
Stage Two – Able to transfer knowledge – Challenges procedures – Develops best practice – Provides leadership to others (4 of 6)	– Builds confidence in others to take further responsibility – Provides constructive feedback to others on performance and impact on others – Maximises networking opportunities (3 of 7)
Stage One – Uses information to improve systems – Regularly acts on own initiative – Takes responsibility for own actions and decisions	– Understands team goals and objectives and works proactively for team success – Shares knowledge, skills and experience openly and honestly – Volunteers to work in projects or subcommittees – Helps others to achieve goals (4 of 10)
Foundation stage – Takes responsibility for own actions and decisions – Understands fundamental principles and applications – Refers to others for guidance – Follows procedures and processes	– Responsive, open and friendly in manner – Considers and relates well to all kinds of people – Personally enthusiastic, positive and approachable – Owns up to responsibility, even if mistakes happen – resilient (4 of 9)

Source: Connexions Cheshire and Warrington, but there is a national framework.

WINDOW ON PRACTICE

A sample competency from the Police Force

Respect for Race and Diversity – A

Behaviour category

● Considers and shows respect for the opinions, circumstances and feelings of colleagues and members of the public, no matter what their race, religion, position, background, circumstances, status or appearance.
● Understands other people's views and takes them into account. Is tactful and diplomatic when dealing with people, treating them with dignity and respect at all times. Understands and is sensitive to social, cultural and racial differences.

Positive Indicators

● Sees issues from other people's viewpoints
● Is polite and patient when dealing with people, treating them with respect and dignity
● Shows understanding and sensitivity to people's problems, vulnerabilities and needs
● Makes people feel valued by listening and supporting their needs and interests
● Understands what offends and adapts own actions accordingly
● Respects confidentiality wherever appropriate

(this is a selection from a full list of 13)

Negative Indicators

● Does not consider other people's feelings
● Does not encourage people to talk about personal issues
● Makes situations worse with inappropriate remarks, language or behaviour
● Is thoughtless and tactless when dealing with people
● Is dismissive and impatient with people
● Does not respect confidentiality
● Uses humour inappropriately

(this is a selection from a full list of 11)

Source: Police (Cheshire Constabulary, however these are national competencies).

Activity 6.4

How could a line manager assess an individual's competence in respect for race and diversity. Think of as wide a range of approaches as possible and use the positive and negative behaviours listed in the police force Window on Practice to help you.

Competencies comprise a complex mix of factors such as skill, personality, motives, self-image and so on. If these are the elements of competency, some of them can be developed, some can be modified and some can be measured, but not all, and this leads us to the way that competencies can be used most constructively in an organisation. Competencies can be used as an integrating mechanism in terms of people management so that once a competency framework has been devised it can be used not only for learning and development, but for recruitment and selection, appraisal and the allocation of rewards. This means that the competencies appropriate to business success are consistently applied and also that a consistent message is experienced by employees. In addition those competencies that are especially difficult to develop can be highlighted in the recruitment and selection process so that such competencies are brought into the organisation.

Our focus in this chapter is learning development where line managers can use competencies to:

- identify an individual's strengths and weaknesses (via observation in the job, employee reflection or on a development centre) and hence development needs
- draw up a development plan in conjunction with the employee to address weaknesses
- provide the external and other support, resources and work opportunities needed in the plan
- provide coaching and feedback to the individual on their development and monitor progress

Whilst this may sound remedial, this is not necessarily the case as competencies for future roles may be identified and worked on in advance, as can competencies for changes and new ways of working that are being introduced wholesale into the organisation.

Whilst competency frameworks are now heavily used by organisations this approach has been criticised due to the complex process required to research the appropriate competencies for the organisation, and perhaps more importantly, the fact that such competencies, due to the research process itself, will be inevitably backward looking rather than future oriented. In addition competency frameworks may not include every aspect that is critical to superior performance. Furthermore, while one set of competencies may result in high performance this does not necessarily mean that such performance may not be achieved via a different set of competencies. It is also important to remember that changes in behaviour may be due to factors other than competencies, for example increased or different resources.

We have been focusing on personal behavioural competencies in this section and such competencies can be described as something which an individual inputs into the job that they do. You will, however, come across a different type of competence contained within National Vocational Qualifications (NVQs). These are expressed in terms of job standards, in other words they express the job tasks that an individual can do (or is learning to do) and as such are termed 'outputs', in other words job achievements. NVQs are national qualifications which have brought together a wide and unstructured range of previous vocational qualifications and are heavily promoted by the government and used as relevant measures in the Leitch Review.

METHODS OF LEARNING AND DEVELOPMENT

Although there are concerns that the use of competencies may not be perfect managers still frequently use them to identify individual development needs. Once these are identified, the manager and the individual need to decide the best way for the appropriate competencies to be developed. It may be by improving underlying knowledge, practical skills or attitude development, or a combination of these.

Off-job methods: education and training courses

These may include educational courses leading to a qualification (such as an MBA) or consultancy courses. The latter vary in length from a half-day to several weeks, and are run by consultants or professional bodies for all comers. They have the advantage that they bring together people from varying occupational backgrounds and are not, therefore, as introspective as in-house courses and are popular for topical issues, such as changes in legislation or new procedures required by government bodies. They are, however, often relatively expensive and superficial, despite their value as sources of industrial folklore, by which we mean the swapping of experiences among course members.

The most valuable courses of this type are those that concentrate on specific skills such as developing time management, interviewing or disciplinary skills; or on imparting new knowledge as when a new national initiative or a change in legislation is introduced. Such a course can provide an interpretation of the development, but also the opportunity to share views and reactions with fellow employees to ensure that one's own feelings are not idiosyncratic or perverse.

In-house courses are often similar in nature to consultancy courses, and are sometimes run with the benefit of some external expertise. In-house courses can be particularly useful if the learning needs to relate to specific organisational procedures and structures, or if it is geared to encouraging employees to work more effectively together in the organisational environment. The drawbacks of in-house courses are that they suffer from a lack of breadth of content, and there is no possibility of learning from people in other organisations.

Alternatively, there are outdoor-type courses which are sometimes known as Outward Bound, after the organisation that pioneered them. Outdoor courses attempt to develop skills involved in working with and through others, and aim to increase self-awareness and self-confidence through a variety of experiences, including outdoor physical challenges. More recently there has been increasing use of learning experiences based on drama, which engage participants in improvisation through role play and exercises. Other forms of simulation such as games and computer simulations may be used in addition to role play.

One of the major concerns with these different types of off-job courses and activities is the difficulty of ensuring transfer of learning back to the workplace. As part of their research on the contribution of off-job courses to managers Longenecker and Ariss (2002) asked managers what helped them retain what they had learned and transfer it to the workplace. Developing goals/plans for implementing new skills was most frequently identified. In addition managers said that it helped to review materials immediately after the programme; be actively involved in the learning itself; make a report to peers/superiors on what they had learned; review material and development plans with their mentor/manager; and include development goals in performance reviews. It is generally agreed that a supportive climate helps transfer (for example line manager interest and involvement and development having a high priority in the organisation). Santos and Stewart (2003), for example, found that transfer was more likely if reward such as promotion or pay was attached to developmental behaviour change, and also where there was a helpful management climate in terms of pre- and post-course briefings and activities. Currently there are number of more creative approaches where experiential job-related activities are included on courses as shown in the Window on Practice.

WINDOW ON PRACTICE

Experiential activities

Brockett (2006) explains how EDF Energy aims to improve customer service via experiential course activities for engineers, dispatch and call-centre workers. During the course participants play the role of guests at a sixtieth birthday party. Cake, music and decorations accompany this. Half-way though the party there is a surprise power cut represented by a blackout and audio recording of family members becoming distressed and stumbling about in the dark. The aim was to let course members experience what their customers experience when they have a power cut so that they can better understand the effect that it has on people's lives. Performance improvements followed in terms of repair times, accuracy of estimated repair times and increase in commendation letters from the public. This suggests that an experience, especially in the shoes of the customer, can have a powerful impact on employee perceptions and behaviours.

Phillips (2006b) provides an example of BUPA care staff in a retirement home. As part of a 'Personal Best' programme aimed at improving customer service staff took the role of residents so as to see life through their customer's eyes. So for example they were fed puréed food and were hoisted in a mechanical sling from a chair into a bed. As a result staff behaviour towards residents has changed, for example explaining the hoisting procedure to residents and doing it more slowly.

Sources: J. Brockett (2006) 'Energy firm gets party vibe', *People Management*, Vol. 12, No. 10, 18 May, p. 12 and L. Phillips (2006b) 'BUPA Stars', *People Management*, Vol. 12, No. 22, 9 November, pp. 30–2.

Learning on the job

Manager coaching and other internal and external coaching

We have discussed line manager coaching above, but there is increasing use of external coaches, especially for more senior managers, or specially trained internal coaches; 'coaching' has become very much a professional occupation with its own code of ethical practice.

Many organisations are now providing or arranging intensive training for designated internal coaches who operate broadly in the organisation, just in a coaching role, and qualifications to reflect this are increasingly becoming available. This is quite different from the basic training in coaching that line managers are likely to receive. External executive coaching is often provided by consultancies and specialist coaching organisations. Various forms of coaching may include career coaching, performance coaching, skills coaching, business coaching and life coaching. Given the increasing professionalisation of coaching it is not surprising that the quality of the coaching experience is receiving attention. There is increasing supervision of practice, in a way that is similar to supervision for counsellors, which involves regular meetings with a more experienced practitioner to explore their client relationships and reflect on practice. A CIPD study carried out by the Bath Consultancy Group (Arney 2006) found that close to half the coaches received regular supervision, and that supervision was a fast-growing practice. Such individual supervision is carried out with a mind to client confidentiality; however, there is also a growing trend for group supervision of coaches and also for organisations to want to collect common themes discussed in coaching sessions as these can be used to inform organisational thinking (Arney 2006). Both these approaches put client confidentiality at greater risk, as personal information may be shared intentionally or unintentionally with a wider group.

WINDOW ON PRACTICE

Coaching at the Medical Research Council (MRC) and Unilever

Hall (2006) reports on the arrangement that external coaching company 'Laughing Phoenix' has made with the MRC which involves coaching the 30 most senior HR professionals. One of the conditions of the agreement was that the company would feed back recurring themes to the MRC so that it could align coaching with the wider business picture.

Unilever has contacted internal coaches regularly to 'harvest some of the intelligence they had gathered from their clients', again keen to pick up recurring themes, helping the organisation know which areas to tackle and help the coaches understand the context of their work.

Source: L. Hall (2006) 'Inside Job', *People Management*, Vol. 12, No. 16, 10 August, pp. 34–6.

The number of organisations aiming to develop a coaching culture was 80 per cent in the 2006 CIPD survey, with 79 per cent already using some coaching activities.

Mentoring

Mentoring offers a wide range of advantages for the development of the mentee or protégé, and the mentor may occasionally be the individual's immediate manager, but usually it is a more senior manager in the same or a different function. Mentoring generally focuses on activities which enhance career advancement, giving an individual exposure and visibility and sponsorship. In addition there is often an emphasis on developing a sense of competence, clarity of identity and effectiveness in the managerial role. A mentoring relationship may include some coaching and guidance as well as emotional support, and the mentor also acts as a role model of how to get on in the organisation.

The drawbacks to mentoring include the risk of over-reliance on one source of guidance, potentially being alienated from other sources of expertise, the difficulty of dealing with conflicting views in an unequal relationship, and the sense of loss experienced when a mentor leaves. Perceived benefits, however, considerably outweigh any drawbacks; however, mentoring needs to be well done and the dangers that mentees may pick up a mentor's bad habits minimized.

Mentors are also seen as responsible for developing talent, and while a mentor/protégé relationship might not naturally occur, mentoring may be encouraged or formalised. For example, in some organisations all new graduates are attached to a mentor as soon as they join. The difficulties of establishing a formal programme include the potential mismatch of individuals, unreal expectations on both sides and the time and effort involved.

WINDOW ON PRACTICE

Mentoring at Fifteen

Liam Black, Director of Fifteen (Jamie Oliver's project to turn disadvantaged youngsters into cooks) initiated a structured programme to turn six members of staff into qualified mentors able to support the more vulnerable youngsters to aid retention. The staff are from different companies run by Olliver and are not directly working with the youngsters. The six are working towards a Certificate in Workplace Mentoring from the Oxford School of Coaching and Mentoring (accredited by John Brookes University), which is suitably tailored to their work-based needs. The programme is a six-month blended learning package and the mentors will work with the youngsters setting goals, developing coping strategies and building their often non-existent self-esteem.

Source: P. Cottee (2006) 'Oliver's Army', *People Management*, Vol. 12, No. 19, 28 September, pp. 44–5.

Peer relationships

Although mentor relationships have been shown to be related to high levels of career success, not all developing individuals have access to such a relationship, and even formal schemes are often reserved for specific groups such as new graduate entrants. Supportive peer relationships at work are potentially more widely available to the individual and offer a number of benefits for the development of both parties. The benefits that are available depend on the nature of the peer relationship and these range from information sharing, career strategising, giving job-related feedback, to emotional support, personal feedback and friendship. Most of us benefit from one or a number of peer relationships at work but often we do not readily appreciate their contribution towards our development. Peer relationships most often develop on an informal basis and provide mutual support. Some organisations, however, formally appoint an existing employee to provide such support to a new member of staff through their first 12–18 months in the organisation. These relationships may, of course, continue beyond the initial period. The name for the appointed employee will vary from organisation to organisation, and sometimes the word 'buddy', 'coach' or 'mentor' is used – which can be confusing!

Activity 6.5

Consider each significant peer relationship that you have at work. Where does each fit on the continuum of relationships described above, and what contributions does it make towards your development?

If you are in full-time education consider the contribution that each of your relationships (whether at university, home or work) has to your development.

Self-development

Natural learning is learning that takes place on the job and results from an individual's everyday experience of the tasks that they undertake. Natural learning is even more difficult to investigate than coaching, mentoring or peer relationships, and yet the way that we learn from everyday experiences, and our level of awareness of this, is very important for our development. To some extent self-development may be seen as a conscious effort to gain the most from natural learning in a job, and to use the learning cycle as a framework. The learning cycle is a way of explaining how we learn from our experiences and has four stages:

- Having an experience (for example, carrying out an appraisal interview)
- Reflecting on that experience (thinking about what happened and trying to understand it – for example, every time I made criticisms Joe became very defensive)
- Developing a theory about what happened (for example, maybe he was defensive because the criticisms came from me, and if I had given him some space to talk first, he might have raised the criticisms himself and had more ownership of them)
- Pragmatic planning (for example, how am I going to test out this theory in the next appraisal interview? What will I say? How will I do it?)

And so the cycle continues with the next experience.

Self-development can be focused in specific skills development, but often extends to attitude development and personal growth.

Activity 6.6

The video *Groundhog Day* can be viewed as a journey of self-development. Watch the video and answer the following questions:

1 How did Phil's attitudes change and how was this reflected in his behaviour?

2 What do you think Phil learned?

3 How did he learn it?

4 Why is personal development so difficult?

The emphasis in self-development is that each individual is responsible for, and can plan, their own development, although they may need to seek help when working on some issues. Self-development involves individuals in understanding how learning happens and analysing the strengths and weaknesses of the way that they personally learn, and the competencies they display at work – primarily by means of questionnaires and feedback from others. This analysis may involve 360-degree feedback which we discussed in Chapter 5, and may initially begin on a self-development course, or with the help of a facilitator, but would then be continued by the individual back on the job. From this analysis individuals, perhaps with some help at first, plan their development goals and the way that they will achieve them, primarily through development opportunities within the job.

Many of the activities included in self-development are based on observation, collecting further feedback about the way they operate, experimenting with different approaches and in particular reviewing what has happened, why and what they have learned. Self-development, however, is not a quick fix as it requires a long-term approach and careful planning and dedication, in addition to a certain amount of soul searching.

Self-development groups

Typically, a group of individuals is involved in a series of meetings where they would jointly discuss their personal development, organisational issues and/or individual work problems. The idea is that they have a supportive environment in which to discuss their personal development. Group members may help each other by asking searching questions, offering suggestions and providing constructive feedback. Groups may begin operating with a leader who is a process expert, not a content expert, and who therefore acts as a facilitator rather than, but not to the complete exclusion of, a source of information. A process expert is a person who is skilled in understanding and managing group processes, but may have no understanding of what the group is discussing. A content expert is someone who understands exactly what the group is discussing and has more knowledge than they do, but may not know anything about how groups work. The group itself is the primary source of information and may operate without outside help as its members' process skills develop. The content and timings of the meetings can be very flexible, although they will require a significant level of energy and commitment if they are to operate well.

Learning logs

Learning logs are a mechanism for learning retrospectively as they encourage a disciplined approach to learning from opportunistic events. The log may be focused around one particular activity and is usually designed to encourage the writer to explain what happened, how they have reflected on this, what conclusions they have made and what future learning actions they wish to make. Alternatively logs can be used in the form of a daily or weekly diary.

Activity 6.7

Identify a management skills area that you need to develop. (You may find it particularly helpful to choose an interpersonal area, for example, assertiveness, influencing others, presentation, being more sociable, contributing to meetings, helping others.) Even if you are currently a full-time student you will find that you need to employ a wide range of management skills.

Keep a learning diary over the next few weeks, logging anything that is relevant to your development area.

At the end of the period review what you have learned in your development area and also what you have learned about the learning cycle.

Learning contracts

There is increasing use of learning contracts, sometimes used within more formalised self-development groups; on other management courses; as part of a mentoring or coaching relationship; or in working towards a competency-based qualification. These contracts are a formal commitment by the learner to work towards a specified learning goal, with an identification of how the goal might be achieved. They thus promote a proactive approach to learning.

The value of learning contracts for individuals depends on them choosing to participate, their identification of the relevant goal and the importance and value they ascribe to achieving it. A learning contract will only be effective with commitment, because ultimately the individual learner has to make it happen. The Window on Practice uses a helpful format which could be adopted in devising your own learning contract.

WINDOW ON PRACTICE

David wanted to improve his influencing skills and has sent the following draft learning contract to his manager for discussion:

Goal

To improve my influencing skills with both peers and more senior managers.

Specific objectives

- To prepare for influencing situations.
- To try to understand better the perspective of the other.
- To identify the interpersonal skills required – probably active listening, reflecting, summarising, stating my needs, collaboration (but maybe more).
- To be able to identify that I have had more influence in decisions made.

Activities

- Watch a recommended video on influencing skills.
- Re-read my notes from the interpersonal skills course I attended.
- Watch how others in my department go about influencing.
- Ask other people (supportive ones) how they go about it.
- Identify possible influencing situations in advance, and plan for what I want and what might happen.
- Reflect back on what happened, and work out how to do better next time.
- Ask for feedback.

Resources

- Video.
- Notes.
- The support of others.

Assessment

- I could ask for feedback from colleagues and my manager.
- My own assessment may be helpful.
- Make a log over time of decisions made and my originally preferred outcome.

KEY DEBATE: IS E-LEARNING THE FUTURE OF LEARNING AND DEVELOPMENT?

As technology enables interesting and interactive presentation of distance learning materials, there is evidence of considerable enthusiasm on the part of organisations to pursue this approach to development, and take advantage of the opportunities it presents. CIPD (2003) reports that one of the most significant changes in learning and development over the last five years is the increased use of e-learning, although it is still most heavily used by IT staff, but by 2006 only a quarter of respondents to the CIPD Learning and Development survey say that it has significantly altered learning and development offerings. E-learning can be defined as 'learning that is delivered, enabled or mediated by electronic technology' (Sloman and Rolph 2003, p. 1).

E-learning covers a wide variety of approaches from using CD-ROMs to the company intranet and the Internet. More sophisticated approaches do not confine e-learning to interactive learning at a distance. Increasingly, synchronous learning is used where all participants log on at the same time, with a tutor or facilitator being available online. Individuals can progress through material alone or network with others to complete a task and use chat rooms and have a dialogue with the tutor. Videoconferencing can also be used to bring participants together at the same time. For example, some MBAs have been delivered via videoconferencing rather than classroom-based teaching.

The advantages of e-learning are that:

- Learning can often take place at a convenient time, for example when the job is less busy, meaning that it is less disruptive.
- Learning does not usually have to be planned to fit in with the demands of a job and can be used opportunistically as time becomes available.
- Learning does not have to take place during working hours.
- E-learning can be cost effective when delivering a unit to a large number of employees.
- Modules or units can be completed when topics are relevant to job demands, rather than according to a schedule determined by others.
- When a learning need is identified development via e-learning can take place immediately; there is no need to wait for a slot on a course.
- Large numbers of employees can all be trained at the same time, for example where there is a new product launch, rather than waiting for a slot on a course.
- E-learning means that the training delivered is always consistent and not dependent on tutor or manager skills.
- Learners can take as long as they need to progress rather than being constrained by a timetable that applies to all.
- The material produced for e-learning is sustainable and easy to update.
- E-learning can encompass virtual reality in training, for example preparing employees to deal with dangerous situations where it would be inappropriate to rely solely on learning on the job.

Hammond (2001), for example, describes the case of Cisio which is constantly launching new IT-based products. The company has moved from 90 per cent classroom-based training for its sales representative to 80 per cent online training so that the large numbers of representatives can experience training immediately the product is launched. Channel Four (Cooper 2001) has a strategy to replace much of its classroom teaching activity with interactive learning, and the London Emergency Services are using virtual reality training to prepare employees for emergency events. For example Prickett (1997) reports how Hendon Police Training College uses virtual reality to prepare officers to deal with siege and hostage situations.

However, in spite of the advantages of e-learning the paragraph at the beginning of this section demonstrates that progress has been very modest despite high expectations. One of the reasons for this is that whereas organisations are often enthusiastic there has been much evidence of employees being unwilling to use e-learning. E-learning can be a solitary activity and is often very dependent on individual self-discipline, and there are some learners who will simply find that an interactive computer-based learning unit does not compare with the conviviality and action associated with attending a course. Thus motivation dwindles unless there is other support to encourage learners to complete the units they need. Lack of computer literacy is another barrier for many employees. At one level, all that may be required is the acquisition of basic computer skills, but at a higher level, even employees who have good everyday computer skills may have some difficulty with more sophisticated packages involving synchronous learning and joint learner tasks, bulletin boards and group/tutor dialogues, and they will need time to learn how particular packages work and how to use the facilities. If the right preparation and support is not made available employees can easily be put off by one difficult experience in which they found they could not keep up with the rest of the synchronous learning group. In some organisations access to the appropriate equipment was a problem for employees who did not have a personal computer on their desks.

There was much initial euphoria about what e-learning could contribute but increasingly it has been recognised that motivating learners is critical and most organisations now have much more realistic expectations of what e-learning can achieve, and often have to improve and re-launch e-learning solutions before they bed in. The support provided may well be critical, as may the way in which such methods are introduced and used. Sloman and Rolph (2003) found that e-learning has been implemented in a variety of ways, from being introduced as a sweeping ambitious change to small incremental changes to the organisation's approach to development, and from a mandatory change to an offer to volunteers.

WINDOW ON PRACTICE

A different slant on e-learning!

Virtual Reality has been around for many years in the gaming world but it is only recently that learning and development professionals have begun to grasp the potential that this technology has to offer.

For example, 'Second Life'™ produced by Linden, is a site that can be used just for fun, but also for learning and development. In this 'second life' world an individual creates a virtual persona, called an avatar and engages with other avatars, involving themselves in making and selling things, education, discussion groups and so on as in the real world.

Organisations that use it as a vehicle for people development may have a custom version of the world built for them, sometimes re-creating their office, store or campus so that the learners experience a virtual world which mirrors their real one.

Virtual worlds can be used to give individuals experience of trying out new skills, learning new ideas and making mistakes. There is the potential for individuals to 'meet' and engage with others that would be difficult in the real world. One way that virtual worlds can be used for people development is for there to be a 'scripted' approach. This means that some of the avatars are controlled to create situations which can then be discussed afterwards. 'Open access' (that is not scripted) learning may also be used, for example for team exercises where teams address a challenge and are given feedback, just an on an 'outdoor' team training event.

Sources: www.secondlife.com; CIPD (2008) 'Virtual Worlds and learning: using Second Life as Duke Corporate Education' CIPD case study from www.cipd.co.uk; Syedain H (2008) 'Out of this world' *People Management*, Vol 14 No 8, pp 20-23, 17 April

The difficulties experienced with e-learning have focused some organisations on understanding where e-learning fits with other approaches to learning and using it in ways that provide the most value. For example e-learning can be very effectively used before a face-to-face course to do pre-work so that for example all attendees are starting from a roughly similar knowledge base. In this case those employees who have the knowledge base already can be exempt and e-learning enables the others to get up to speed before the course begins. Similarly e-learning can be used effectively for course briefings and general preparation, such as the completion and analysis of pre-course questionnaires and other pre-work which saves time at the beginning of the event itself.

At the end of a course e-learning can be used for refreshers, for self-checking of understanding and planning how to apply the learning gained on the course. Similarly e-learning can be used in combination with manager coaching. This has led to the term 'blended learning' which is often used to indicate the blending of e-learning with face-to-face learning experiences, while others use it more broadly to indicate 'a range of ways that e-learning can be delivered when combined with multiple additional routes that support and facilitate learning' (Sloman and Rolph 2003, p. 6).

WINDOW ON PRACTICE

Hills and Francis (1999), for example, suggest that computer-based learning is a solitary activity, and that social contact and interaction were a necessary ingredient in learning. They assessed the use of their local computer-based training centres in Lloyds TSB, and found that some were used much more than others. The extent of use was not related to geographical accessibility, but instead to the support provided by the centre administrator, before, during and after learning sessions, and also the support of local managers.

Blended learning is increasingly used to indicate a blend of any approaches to learning, and there is evidence that learning and training now involve a much wider range of activities (CIPD 2006). For example Pickard (2006) reports on the blended learning approach at the Department for Work and Pensions which integrates self-managed learning, coaching and e-learning.

Our conclusion is that e-learning has a critical role to play but that it would be dangerous to see it as the answer to all learning needs and the future of learning and development at work. Its value is best exploited where it is the most appropriate approach to meeting key development needs, such as preparing for dangerous tasks by using virtual reality, and where it can be combined with other learning activities to ensure a more complete learning experience and where it particularly suits the learning style of the individual learner.

WINDOW ON PRACTICE

Julie Scumming at AXA

Clarke (2006) recounts a very inventive learning experience at AXA, highly job based and involving a variety of activities. The exercise started with a Christmas card from a fictitious employee, Julie Scumming. Posters followed announcing her arrival and then her fictitious husband entered the offices, shouting. After this there were diary entries on the intranet from both Julie and her boss which staff began to follow, and picked up the story that Julie was a devout Christian who felt she was being discriminated against and bullied by her boss and peers. Dummy tabloid articles were circulated, a stand-up row in the canteen was performed by actors. Sticky notes were put on computers saying not to get 'stuck like Julie', and an Advent calendar counted down the days to the main event which was a tribunal hearing for managers. When the tribunal panel retired to consider their verdict actors acted out scenes which had led up to the tribunal. Meanwhile employees could log on to discussion forums to express their views about the case, and there was a poll about the anticipated results. Involvement in all of this was voluntary but many staff participated. The objective was to raise awareness about discrimination issues. Responses to questionnaires after the event demonstrated that managers were more aware of religious discrimination issues.

Source: E. Clarke (2006) 'Julie Diligent', *People Management*, Vol. 12, No. 14, 13 July, pp. 32–43.

SUMMARY PROPOSITIONS

6.1 In the UK we have a voluntarist approach to employee development, with the government *encouraging* employers to engage in learning and development rather than intervening.

6.2 People development has the potential to improve business performance and an increasing number of employers see training and development as an important business investment.

6.3 Learning and development has moved from being instructor led to an emphasis on training on the job, self-development and line-manager coaching.

6.4 Behavioural competencies are increasingly used as a means of identifying and expressing employee development needs.

6.5 There is a wide range of people development methods including formal off-job education; internal and external consultancy courses; and informal coaching, mentoring, peer support, and self-development, encompassing learning contracts and learning logs.

6.6 E-learning has transformed approaches to learning but is most effectively used when blended with other methods.

GENERAL DISCUSSION TOPICS

1   A heavy emphasis on people development is absolutely critical in underpinning the new psychological contract. Revisit the Key debate in Chapter 1 before you begin your discussion.

2   What are the advantages of providing learning and development experiences to employees who are over 60, and what barriers might there be to this? You may wish to come back to this question once you have read Chapters 9 and 10.

FURTHER READING

Wilson, C. (2007) *Best Practice in Performance Coaching*. London: Kogan Page.
This useful book is a good starting point for any manager beginning to coach employees; it also provides detailed information for line managers with more experience. Practical case histories are included as well as useful tools and models.

REFERENCES

Arney, E. (2006) 'Insider's Guide', *People Management*, Vol. 12, No. 23, 23 November, pp. 40–2.

Brockett, J. (2006) 'Energy firm gets party vibe', *People Management*, Vol. 12, No. 10, 18 May, p. 12.

Carroll, S. and Gillen, D. (2001) 'Exploring the teaching function of the managerial role', *Journal of Management Development*, Vol. 21, No. 5, pp. 330–42.

CIPD (2003) *Training and Development 2003: Survey Report*. London: Chartered Institute of Personnel and Development.

CIPD (2006) *Training and Development 2006: Survey Report*. London: Chartered Institute of Personnel and Development.

CIPD (2007) *Learning and Development: Annual Survey*. London: Chartered Institute of Personnel and Development.

Clarke, E. (2006) 'Julie Diligent', *People Management*, Vol. 12, No. 14, 13 July, pp. 32–43.

Clutterbuck, D. and Megginson, D. (2005) *Making coaching work: Creating a Coaching Culture*. London: Chartered Institute of Personnel and Development.

Cooper, C. (2001) 'Connect Four', *People Management*, February.

Hall, L. (2006) 'Inside Job', *People Management*, Vol. 12, No. 16, 10 August, pp. 34–6.

Hall, L. (2007) 'Costume Change', *People Management*, Vol. 13, No. 7, 5 April, pp. 42–3.

Hammond, D. (2001) 'Reality Bytes', *People Management*, January.

Harrison, R. (2005) *Learning and Development*. London: IPD.

Hills, H. and Francis, P. (1999) 'Interaction Learning', *People Management*, July.

Hutchinson, S. and Purcell, J. (2007) *Change Agenda: Learning and the Line: The role of line managers in training, learning and development*. London: Chartered Institute of Personnel and Development.

IDS (2006a) 'Coaching in the Workplace', HR Studies No. 831, October. London: IDS.

IDS (2006b) 'E-Learning', HR Studies No. 818. London: IDS.

Keep, E. and Mayhew, K. (1999) 'The assessment: knowledge, skills and competitiveness', *Oxford Review of Economic Policy*, Vol. 15, No. 1, pp. 1–15.

Kersley, B., Alpin, C., Forth, J., Bryson, A., Bewley, H., Dix, G. and Oxenbridge, S. (2006) *Inside the Workplace: Findings from the 2004 Workplace Employment Relations Survey*. London: Routledge.

Kingston, P. (2007) 'Short Changed', *People Management*, Vol. 13, No. 16, pp. 28–31.

Leitch, S. (2006) *Leitch Review of Skills: Prosperity for all in the Global economy: Final Report*. London: HMSO, December.

Longenecker, C. and Ariss, S. (2002) 'Creating competitive advantage through effective management education', *Personnel Review*, Vol. 21, No. 9, pp. 640–54.

Pemberton, C. (2006) *Coaching to Solutions: A Manager's toolkit for Performance delivery*. Oxford: Butterworth-Heinemann.

Phillips, L. (2006a) 'UK's IT skills gap remains wide', *People Management*, Vol. 12, No. 23, 23 November, p. 12.

Phillips, L. (2006b) 'BUPA Stars', *People Management*, Vol. 12, No. 22, 9 November, pp. 30–2.

Pickard, J. (2006) 'Suits Ewe', *People Management*, Vol. 12, No. 12, 15 June, pp. 36–7.

Prickett, R. (1997) 'Screen Savers', *People Management*, 26 June, pp. 36–8.

Purcell, J., Kinnie, N., Hutchinson, S., Rayton, B. and Swart, J. (2003) *Understanding the People Performance Link: Unlocking the black box*, Research report. London: Chartered Institute of Personnel and Development.

Santos, A. and Stewart, M. (2003) 'Employee perceptions and their influence on training effectiveness', *Human Resource Management Journal*, Vol. 13, No. 1, pp. 27–45.

Sloman, M. and Rolph, J. (2003) *E-learning: The learning curve – The change agenda*. London: Chartered Institute of Personnel and Development.

Westwood, A. (2001) 'Drawing a line – who is going to train our workforce?', in CIPD (ed.) *The Future of Learning for Work*. London: Chartered Institute of Personnel and Development.

CHAPTER 7

Reward management

The objectives of this chapter are to:

1 Set out the different elements that can make up a reward package

2 Evaluate the major alternative methods of setting base pay rates

3 Introduce incentive payments and discuss their major advantages and disadvantages

4 Explain the causes and significance of current trends in the provision of occupational pensions

5 Explore the potential of flexible benefits systems in the UK context

6 Explain the concept of 'total reward' and explore the reasons for its increasing prominence

7 Debate the merits of individual performance-related pay (PRP)

The past two decades have seen substantial increases in the level of affluence enjoyed by most who live and work in the UK. Wages have increased at a faster rate than price inflation, a much higher proportion of income being spent on luxury goods and services than was the case in the 1970s and 1980s. In 1984, the British Social Attitudes Survey reported that 24 per cent of UK residents classed themselves as 'living comfortably', while 26 per cent were 'finding it hard' or 'very hard' to live on their incomes. Eighteen years later the figures had changed to 39 per cent and 16 per cent respectively (Bromley 2003).

However, this increased affluence has been accompanied by a very considerable rise in inequality. The standard measure of equality in a society is the gini coefficient. On this index a score of 0 would indicate a completely equal distribution of wealth among all in a country, while a score of 1 would indicate that all the wealth was held by a single individual. The World Bank calculates gini coefficients for most countries each year, enabling changes over time to be tracked alongside differences between countries. In 2007 the UK's gini coefficient was .36. This is the highest it has been for many decades. In 1977 the UK's score was just .24, since when it has steadily increased. This means that wealth in the UK is now spread less equally than in all other major European countries, some of which have the lowest gini coefficients in the world. In 2007, Denmark was the most equal society according to the World Bank with a gini coefficient of just .24 (UNDP 2008).

The increased inequality in the UK is in large part explained by increased dispersion of earnings. People at the lower end of the income scale have benefited from increased affluence to a far lesser degree than those at the top end, and continue to do so.

In 2008 around 2.9 million people in the UK (10 per cent of the working population) were earning over £35,000 a year, 290,000 (1 per cent) were earning over £100,000 a year, while 47,000 people were reported to be earning over £350,000 a year (Giles 2008). The Chief Executives of the 100 biggest companies in the UK enjoyed base pay rises averaging 7 per cent in 2007 taking their average salaries from £663,000 to £711,000. This is broadly equivalent to the salary paid to Premiership footballers and means that their average weekly salary is greater than the average annual income of the bottom fifth of households – £12,000 a year. In practice, however, Chief Executives of top companies earn much more. Their annual bonuses increased by 20 per cent in 2007, giving an average figure for cash-based remuneration to 1.35 million (Wilman 2008).

Reward is central to the employment relationship. While there are many people who enjoy working and who would continue working even if they won a large sum in a lottery, most of us work mainly because it is our only means of earning the money we need to sustain us and our families in the style to which we are accustomed. How much we are paid and in what form therefore matters hugely to us. It helps determine which jobs we choose to do, which employers we seek work with and, to a significant extent, how much effort we put into our work. For these reasons effective reward management is also very important for employers. Getting it wrong makes it much harder to recruit and retain good people and much easier to demotivate those already in the organisation. Pay also matters because money spent on salaries, benefits and other forms of reward typically amounts to well over half an organisation's total costs. It is thus a major determinant both of profitability and of competitive advantage for commercial businesses. In the public sector the cost of rewarding staff is determined by and, in turn helps determine, the level of taxes that we pay.

There are two central questions that employers should ask when determining the approach they intend to take in managing reward:

1 What principles should we use to determine how much each person in the organisation should be paid?
2 What form should the reward package we offer take?

This is not an area of HR activity in which 'best practice' is readily identified. There are no simple answers to these two questions which can be said to apply equally well across different organisational scenarios. Instead it is necessary for managers to devise distinct reward strategies which are tailored to meet the needs of their circumstances and the expectations of the people they either employ or hope to employ in the future.

In this chapter we address each of these two questions in turn. We start by reviewing the major alternative mechanisms that organisations use to determine pay levels, going on to look at each of the major elements that make up the typical pay package. We give particular attention to the recent emergence of 'total reward' perspectives, explaining why they are likely to become increasingly central to future management thinking about reward. Our 'Key debate' in this chapter concerns the case for and against performance-related pay – one which is fascinating because of the very polarised positions the major protagonists have taken as it has raged over several decades. In Chapter 9 you can read about the ways in which payment systems are regulated in law.

MANAGEMENT OBJECTIVES

When making decisions about what kind of payment system is most appropriate, managers should start by thinking about what objectives they are seeking to achieve. These are likely to include the following:

1 To minimise expenditure on wages and salaries over the long term.
2 To attract and retain staff of the desired calibre, experience and qualifications.
3 To motivate the workforce so as to maximise organisational performance.
4 To direct effort and enthusiasm in specific directions and to encourage particular types of employee behaviour.
5 To underpin and facilitate the management of organisational change.

It is the diversity of these objectives, relating to competition in both product and labour markets, that makes reward management a complex and fascinating area of practice. There is no one payment system or form of incentive that can achieve all the above for all groups of staff in an organisation, so managers are necessarily required to weigh up the advantages and disadvantages before making judgements based on a balanced assessment of likely outcomes. Moreover, it is not an area in which doing nothing is an option, simply because all employers have to have some form of mechanism, however ad hoc in nature, in order to pay their employees.

SETTING BASE PAY

One of the most important decisions in the development of reward strategies concerns the mechanism or mechanisms that will be used to determine the basic rate of pay for different jobs in the organisation. It is possible to identify four principal mechanisms for the determination of base pay. They are not entirely incompatible, although one tends to be used as the main approach in most organisations: external market comparisons, internal labour market mechanisms, job evaluation and collective bargaining.

External market comparisons

Here focus is on recruiting and retaining staff, rates being set which are broadly equivalent to 'the going rate' for the job in question. Specialists refer to these comparisons as *external relativities*. Some employers consciously pay over the market rate in order to secure the services of the most talented employees. Others 'follow the market', by paying below the going rate while using other mechanisms such as flexibility, job security or longer-term incentives to ensure effective recruitment and retention. In either case the decision is based on an assessment of what rate needs to be paid to compete for staff in different types of labour market.

There are several possible sources of intelligence about market rates for different job types at any one time. A great deal of salary information is published in trade journals, particularly in respect of hard-to-recruit groups such as computer staff. More detailed information can be gained by joining one of the major salary survey projects operated by firms of consultants or by paying for access to their datasets. Information on specific types of job, including international packages for expatriate workers, is collected by specialised consultants and can be obtained on payment of the appropriate fee. White (2000, pp. 44–5) identifies a range of other sources of UK pay data including the Confederation of British Industry's Pay Databank and the Office of Manpower Economics. In addition there are more informal approaches such as looking at pay rates included in recruitment advertisements in papers, at job centres and on web-based job-board sites. New staff often bring with them a knowledge of pay rates for types of job in competitor organisations and can be a useful source of information. Finally, it is possible to join or set up salary clubs. These consist of groups of employers, often based in the same locality, who agree to share salary information for mutual benefit.

Internal labour market mechanisms

In most larger organisations with clear hierarchies much recruitment is from within, existing staff being promoted in preference to hiring outsiders. Where this occurs employees have to compete with one another for promotion, leading to the development of internal labour markets. Comparisons with what other organisations are paying then become less significant than comparisons with the pay of fellow employees. The result is a need for managers to focus on *internal differentials* when setting pay rates. Fair distribution of rewards between different levels in the hierarchy is important, but it is also desirable to use pay levels as a means of encouraging would-be promotees to maximise their effort. An interesting metaphor used is that of the sports tournament in which an organisation's pay structure is likened to the prize distribution in a knock-out competition such as is found, for example, at the Wimbledon Tennis Championships. Here the prize money is highest for the winner, somewhat lower for the runner-up, lower again for the semi-final losers and so on down the rounds. The aim, from the point of view of the tournament organisers, is to attract the best players to compete in the first round, then subsequently to give players in later rounds an incentive to play at their peak. According to Lazear (1995, pp. 26–33), the level of base pay for each level in an organisation's hierarchy should be set according to similar principles. The level of pay for any particular job is thus set at a level which maximises performance lower down the hierarchy among employees competing for promotion. The actual performance of the individual receiving the pay is less important.

Job evaluation

Job evaluation involves the establishment of a system which is used to measure the size and significance of jobs. It results in each job being scored with a number of points, establishing in effect a hierarchy of all the jobs in the organisation ranging from those which require the most knowledge and experience and which carry a great deal of responsibility (i.e. senior management and specialist professional jobs) to those which require least knowledge and experience and require the job holder to carry relatively low levels of responsibility. Each job is then assimilated to an appropriate grade and payment distributed accordingly. The focus is thus on the relative worth of jobs within an organisation and on comparisons between these rather than on external relativities and comparisons with rates being paid by other employers. Fairness and objectivity are the core principles, an organisation's wage budget being divided among employees on the basis of an assessment of the nature and size of the job each is employed to carry out.

Usage of job evaluation has increased markedly in recent years. It is currently used by just over half of public sector organisations in the UK and by 15 per cent of companies operating in the private sector (CIPD 2007, p. 10). One of the main reasons is its use as a tool in organisation restructuring and in harmonising the terms and conditions enjoyed by different groups of employees, for example following a merger or acquisition, or the signing of a single-status agreement with a trade union. Another important reason for the increased use of job evaluation is the need to comply with the Equal Pay Act 1970, as modified in 1984, which places as central in assessing equal pay claims the question of whether or not a job evaluation scheme is in use.

The most widely used job evaluation schemes are analytical in nature, being based on points-rating systems, under which each job is examined in terms of factors such as skill, effort and responsibility. Each factor is given a weighting indicating its value relative to the others and for each factor there are varying degrees. A score is then given depending on how demanding the job is in terms of each factor, with the overall points value determining the relative worth of each job – and hence its grade in the organisation's pay structure. The points values eventually derived for each job can then be plotted on a graph or simply listed from the highest to the lowest to indicate the ranking. Then – and only then – are points ratings matched with cash amounts, as decisions are made on which points ranges equate with various pay grades. This process

FIGURE 7.1
Job evaluation
analysis

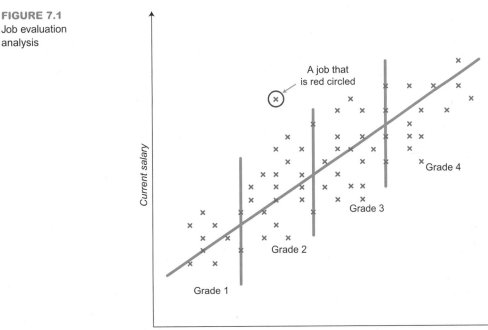

is illustrated in Figure 7.1, each cross representing a job. The most common approach involves using a graph on which one axis represents the *current* salary for each job evaluated and the other the number of *job evaluation points* awarded. A line of best fit is then drawn and each job assigned to a grade. Salary-modeling software is widely available to help with this process.

WINDOW ON PRACTICE

A widely used proprietary scheme is the Hay Guide Chart-Profile Method, which is particularly appropriate for the evaluation of management jobs. The method is based on an assessment of four factors; know-how, problem solving, accountability and working conditions. Jobs are assessed by using each of three guide charts, one for each factor. A profile is then developed for the job showing the relationship between the factors, a ranking is eventually produced and the rates of pay of the jobs considered in order to produce a new pay structure. At this stage comes one of the greatest advantages of this system. The proprietors have available a vast amount of comparative pay data on different undertakings using their system, so their clients not only can compare rates of pay within their organisation (differentials and internal relativities) but also can examine their external relativities.

Collective bargaining

The fourth approach involves determining pay rates through collective negotiations with trade unions or other employee representatives. Thirty years ago this was the dominant method used for determining pay in the UK, negotiations commonly occurring at industry level. The going rates for each job group were thus set nationally and were adhered to by all companies operating in the sector concerned. Recent decades have seen a steady erosion of these arrangements, collective bargaining being decentralised to company or plant level in the manufacturing sector, where it survives at all. Meanwhile the rise of service sector organisations with lower union membership levels has ensured that collective bargaining arrangements now cover only a minority of UK workers. According to Kersley *et al.* (2006, p. 180) only 40 per cent now have any of their terms and conditions determined in this way, collective bargaining over any kind of issue continuing in only 27 per cent of workplaces. The experience of many other countries is similar, but there remain regions such as Eastern Europe and Scandinavia where collective bargaining remains the major determinant of pay rates. Where separate clusters of employees within the same organisation are placed in different bargaining groups and represented by different unions, *internal relativities* become an issue for resolution during bargaining.

In carrying out negotiations the staff and management sides make reference to external labour market rates, established internal pay determination mechanisms and the size of jobs. However, a host of other factors come into the equation too as each side deploys its best arguments. Union representatives, for example, make reference to employee need when house prices are rising and affordable accommodation is hard to find. Both sides refer to the balance sheet, employers arguing that profit margins are too tight to afford substantial rises, while union counterparts seek to gain a share of any increased profits for employees. However good the case made, what ultimately makes collective bargaining different from the other approaches is the presence of industrial muscle. Strong unions which have the support of the majority of employees, as is the case in many public sector organisations, are able to ensure that their case is heard and taken into account. They can thus 'secure' a better pay deal for their members than market rates would allow.

Activity 7.1

Which of the four mechanisms outlined above do you think is usually most efficient for setting the following?

- Base pay

- Annual cost of living increases

- Executive remuneration packages

- Bonus schemes

THE ELEMENTS OF PAYMENT

Once the mechanisms for determining rates of pay for jobs in an organisation have been settled, the second key strategic decision relates to the make-up of the pay package. Here there is a great deal of potential choice available. What is included and to what extent are matters which should be decided with a view to supporting the organisation's objectives and encouraging the necessary attitudes and actions on the part of employees. The payment of an individual will be made up of one or more elements from those shown in Figure 7.2. Fixed elements are those that make up the regular weekly or monthly payment to the individual, and which do not vary other than in exceptional circumstances. Variable elements can be varied by either the employee or the employer.

Basic rate

The irreducible minimum rate of pay is the basic. In most cases this is the standard rate also, not having any additions made to it. In other cases it is a basis on which earnings are built by the addition of one or more of the other elements in payment. In the UK as many as 60 per cent of employees receive no additional payments at all beyond their basic pay (Grabham 2003, p. 398).

FIGURE 7.2 potential elements of payment

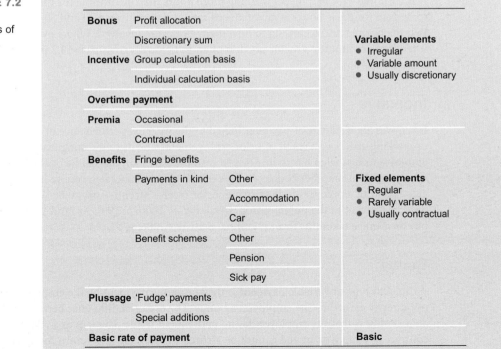

Bonus	Profit allocation		
	Discretionary sum		**Variable elements**
Incentive	Group calculation basis		• Irregular
	Individual calculation basis		• Variable amount
			• Usually discretionary
Overtime payment			
Premia	Occasional		
	Contractual		
Benefits	Fringe benefits		
	Payments in kind	Other	**Fixed elements**
		Accommodation	• Regular
		Car	• Rarely variable
	Benefit schemes	Other	• Usually contractual
		Pension	
		Sick pay	
Plussage	'Fudge' payments		
	Special additions		
Basic rate of payment			**Basic**

Plussage

Sometimes the basic has an addition to recognise an aspect of working conditions or employee capability. Payments for educational qualifications and for supervisory responsibilities are quite common, as are 'fudge' payments to compensate individuals for undertaking activities that others are unwilling to take on.

Benefits

Extras to the working conditions that have a cash value are categorised as benefits and can be of great variety. They include pensions, company cars, sick pay, health insurance, luncheon vouchers, subsidised meals and discount purchase schemes.

Premia

Where employees work at inconvenient times – or on shifts or permanently at night – they receive a premium payment as compensation for the inconvenience. This is for inconvenience rather than additional hours of work. Shift premia are received by 11 per cent of UK workers (Grabham 2003, p. 399), accounting on average for around 6 per cent of their total pay (National Statistics 2006, p. 9).

Overtime

It is customary for employees working more hours than are normal for the working week to be paid for those hours at an enhanced rate, usually between 10 and 50 per cent more that the normal rate according to how many hours are involved. Where overtime is paid it tends to account for a major portion of an individual's gross pay (18.2 per cent on average in 2006).

Incentive

Incentives are elements of payment linked to the working performance of an individual or working group, as a result of prior arrangement. The distinguishing feature is that the employee knows what has to be done to earn the payment, though he or she may feel very dependent on other people, or on external circumstances, to receive it. In the UK, 44 per cent of employees in the private sector receive incentive payments, compared with only 19 per cent in the public sector (Kersley *et al.* 2006, p. 190). Around 10 per cent of pay on average takes this form (National Statistics 2006, p. 9).

Bonus

A different type of variable payment is the gratuitous payment by the employer that is not directly earned by the employee: a bonus. The essential difference between this and an incentive is that the employee has no entitlement to the payment as a result of a contract of employment and cannot be assured of receiving it in return for a specific performance. The most common example of this is the Christmas bonus.

If your employer offered you a 'remuneration package', which could be made up from any of the items in Figure 7.2 provided that the total cost was no more than £X, what proportion of each item would you choose and why? Does your answer suggest ideas for further development of salary policies?

INCENTIVES

While incentive payment systems are common in the UK, there are millions of employees who do not receive this kind of reward and many employers who use them only in a limited way (often in the remuneration of senior managers). It is thus perfectly possible, and some would argue desirable, to recruit, retain and motivate a workforce by paying a simple, fixed rate of pay for each job in the organisation. There is other equipment in the HR manager's toolkit which can be used to reward effort and maintain good levels of job satisfaction. The most fundamental question is therefore whether or not to use an incentive payment system at all. In the opinion of Sisson and Storey (2000, pp. 123–4) many organisations in the UK have introduced schemes in recent years for 'ideological reasons' as a means of impressing stock market analysts, reinforcing management control or undermining established collective bargaining machinery. These, they suggest, are poor reasons which have generally met with little long-term success. Incentive schemes should only be used where they are appropriate to the needs of the business and where they can clearly contribute to the achievement of organisational objectives.

There is a long tradition in the academic literature of hostility to incentive schemes in general and those which focus on the individual in particular. In 1966, Frederick Herzberg argued that pay was a 'hygiene factor' rather than a 'motivator'. He claimed that its capacity to motivate positively was limited, while it can very easily demotivate when managed poorly. It follows that there is little to be gained and a great deal to lose from the introduction of incentive schemes. Others (for example, Thompson 2000) have focused on the way that incentives are perceived by employees as tools of management control which reduce their autonomy and discretion. This, it is argued, causes resentment and leads to dissatisfaction and industrial conflict. A third source of criticism is the considerable additional costs which invariably mount up when organisations introduce incentive schemes. Cox (2006, p. 1493) labels these 'costly side-effects' and shows that they are both considerable and largely unanticipated at the time a new scheme is introduced.

A different school of thought argues in favour of incentives on the grounds that they reward effort and behaviours which the organisation wishes to encourage. As a result they not only are a fair basis for rewarding people, but also can enhance organisational effectiveness and productivity. Advocates of *expectancy theory* hold this position with their belief that individual employees will alter their behaviour (e.g. by working harder or prioritising their actions differently) if they believe that in so doing they will be rewarded with something they value. Hence, where additional pay is a valued reward, employees will seek it and will work to secure it. A positive outcome for both employer and employee is achievable provided the incentive is paid in return for a form of employee behaviour which genuinely contributes to the achievement of organisational objectives.

In addition, many reward specialists point to a significant *sorting effect* which leads employees who are willing and able to perform to a higher standard to be attracted to jobs in which their superior relative contribution will be properly rewarded. At the same time, it is argued, existing employees who perform relatively poorly are more likely to seek alternative employment than colleagues who perform well and are rewarded for doing so. Hence, over time, the quality of employees rises as a result of the presence of incentive schemes. Conversely, of course, it can be plausibly argued that employers who fail to recognise superior individual contribution in their payment systems are more likely to lose higher-performing people because they perceive themselves to be being inadequately rewarded for their skills and efforts. The major types of incentive payment system are the following: payment by results (PBR), performance-related pay (PRP), skills-based pay and profit sharing.

Payment by results

Historically, the most widely used incentive schemes have been those which reward employees according to the number of items or units of work they produce or the time they take to produce them. In the UK piecework schemes such as these are less common than used to be the case because they are mainly associated with jobs in sectors such as manufacturing and agriculture which have long been in decline. However, PBR is still widely used in some shape or form by employers of manual workers, and it is apparent that new schemes are commonly introduced in manufacturing organisations (Cox 2006). Much more common nowadays is another form of PBR – the payment of sales commission.

PBR schemes are often problematic and regularly need to be modified if they are to retain their impact on productivity. The chief criticisms levelled at them are their tendency to reward quantity of output rather than quality and the way that the workers who are subject to them are often unable to predict what their take-home pay will be in a particular week or month. They also tend, in effect, to 'punish' workers when an organisation's systems fail or the actions of fellow employees prevent people from maximising their individual output. Moreover, as time passes, employees who are subject to PBR schemes tend to find ways of making the system work in their interest, reducing the extent to which there is a meaningful link between effort expended and reward gained. So there is a continual need for managers to evaluate the effectiveness of particular approaches and to introduce new systems on a regular basis.

Performance-related pay

While there are many different types of PRP scheme available, all involve the award of a pay rise or bonus payment to individual employees following a formal assessment of their performance over a defined period (normally the previous year). Two distinct varieties of scheme can be identified:

1 **Merit-based systems** involve the immediate supervisor undertaking an appraisal of each subordinate's work performance during the previous year. This will typically be done following a formal appraisal interview and often requires the completion of standard documentation drawn up by an HR department. A proportion of future remuneration is then linked to a score derived from the supervisor's assessment.

2 **Goal-based systems** are more objective, but are not appropriate for all kinds of job. They are, however, particularly well suited for the assessment of managerial work. Here the supervisor and subordinate meet at the start of the appraisal period and agree between them a list of objectives which the appraisee will seek to meet during the coming months. At the end of the year the employee is assessed on the basis of which objectives have or have not been met. A score is then derived and a bonus payment or pay rise awarded.

In recent years PRP schemes have become a great deal more common across all industrial sectors. They have always been hugely controversial leading to a vigorous and ongoing debate between those who favour their use and those who believe them to be seriously counterproductive. We will examine these arguments in more detail in the 'Key debate' section below.

Activity 7.3

Make a list of five jobs that you consider would be best rewarded by a merit-based system and five more that are best rewarded via the goal-based approach.

Skills-based pay

These systems reward employees for the skills or competencies which they acquire. They are particularly prevalent as a means of rewarding technical staff, but there is no reason why the principle should not be extended to any group of employees for whom the acquisition of additional skills might benefit the organisation. The most obvious effect is to encourage multiskilling and flexibility enabling the organisation to respond more effectively and speedily to the needs of customers. A multiskilled workforce may also be slimmer and less expensive. In addition it is argued that, in rewarding skills acquisition, a company will attract and retain staff more effectively than its competitors in the labour market. The operation of a skills-based reward system is also proof that the sponsoring employer is genuinely committed to employee development.

However, a skills-based pay system will only be cost effective if it results in productivity increases which are sufficient to cover the considerable costs associated with its introduction and maintenance. A business can invest a great deal of resources both in training its workforce to attain new skills, and in rewarding them once those skills have been acquired, only to find that the cost of the scheme outweighs the benefit gained in terms of increased flexibility and efficiency. Furthermore, in assisting employees to become more highly qualified and in many cases to gain NVQs, an employer may actually find it harder to retain its staff in relatively competitive labour markets. The other major potential disadvantage is associated with skills obsolescence. Where a business operates in a fast-moving environment and needs to adapt its technology regularly, a skills-based payment system can leave the organisation paying enhanced salaries for skills which are no longer significant or are not required at all.

Profit sharing

There are a number of different ways in which companies are able to link remuneration to profit levels. In recent years the government has sought to encourage such schemes and has actively promoted their establishment with advantageous tax arrangements. Underlying government support is the belief that linking pay to profits increases the employee's commitment to his or her company by deepening the level of mutual interest. As a result, it is argued that such schemes act as an incentive encouraging employees to work harder and with greater flexibility in pursuit of higher levels of take-home pay. Other potential advantages for employers described by Pendleton (2000, pp. 346–51) are better cost flexibility, changed attitudes on the part of employees and the discouragement of union membership. There are two major types of scheme.

1 **Cash-based schemes** pay out a bonus, calculated as a proportion of annual profits, which are then subject to tax and national insurance in the same way as base pay. Gainsharing is a variation on cash-based profit sharing which links bonuses to costs saved rather than profit generated in a defined period. So if a workforce successfully achieves the same level of output at lower overall cost, the gain is shared between employer and employees.
2 **Share-based schemes** involve employees being awarded shares rather than cash. In the UK there are government-sponsored schemes in operation which involve favourable tax treatment, the purpose being to increase commitment by giving employees a significant financial stake in the future of the business they work for, while at the same time helping to align employees' interests with those of shareholders. Traditionally senior managers have been paid, in part, through share-based reward systems, but companies are increasingly seeing an advantage in extending these arrangements to a greater proportion of their staff.

The obvious disadvantage of the schemes described above from the employee's point of view is the risk that pay levels may decline if the company fails to meet its expected profit levels. If no profit is made it cannot be shared and profit-based incentives therefore vary in magnitude from year to year. For these reasons it is questionable to assert that profit-sharing schemes do in fact act as incentives. Unlike PRP awards they do not relate specifically to the actions of the individual employee. Annual profit levels are clearly influenced by a whole range of factors which are both internal and external to the company. An employee may well develop a community of interest with the company management, shareholders and other employees but it is unlikely seriously to affect the nature of his or her work. Furthermore of course, both poor and good performers are rewarded equally in profit-related schemes.

The authors analysing the 2004 Workplace Employment Relations (WER) Survey (Kersley *et al.* 2006, pp. 190–91) concluded that around 40 per cent of the workplaces in their sample operated either a payment by results or a merit-pay incentive scheme, while 21 per cent operated some form of share-ownership scheme. Around 30 per cent paid profit-related bonuses to at least some employees. Even allowing for a strong degree of overlap between schemes as a result of employers operating different payment systems simultaneously, these figures suggest that incentive payments form at least some part of some peoples' reward packages in a majority of UK workplaces. The 2004 WER Survey also found evidence of substantial growth in the incidence of individual PRP systems since the previous survey conducted in 1998. The CIPD's annual survey of reward practice covers a much smaller sample of employers, but it too suggests both high usage of incentives in the UK and considerably increased usage of incentives over recent years. In 2007 70 per cent of its respondents reported using 'cash-based/incentive plans', 64 per cent used individual-based schemes, 27 per cent used team-based schemes, while 53 per cent used schemes that 'are driven by business results'. While such approaches are used by a sizeable minority of employers in the public and voluntary sectors, it is in the private sector that activity is focused (CIPD 2007).

BENEFITS

Employee benefits commonly used to be known as 'fringe benefits', suggesting a peripheral role in the typical pay packet. The substantial growth in the value of most benefits packages over the past ten or twenty years means that the title 'fringe' is no longer appropriate. An increasing proportion of individual remuneration is made up of additional perks, allowances and entitlements which are mostly paid in kind rather than cash. The total value of benefits 'paid' by employers to employees commonly represents between 20 per cent and 50 per cent of an organisation's salary budget, depending on what is included. Pensions alone can easily account for 20 per cent, to which must be added the costs of providing some or all of the following: company cars, sick pay, meals, live-in accommodation, parking facilities, private health insurance, crèche facilities, mobile phones, Christmas parties, staff discounts, relocation expenses and any holiday or maternity allowances paid in excess of the required statutory minima. Smith (2000, p. 153) shows that these extra elements of pay are distributed unevenly between members of staff. Those earning at the top of the scale (especially directors and senior managers) tend to gain rather more than average employees, 30 per cent or 40 per cent of their take-home pay being accounted for by benefits of various kinds.

Occupational pensions

The role of employers in providing pensions has moved up the public policy agenda for several reasons in recent years, but underlying all of them are the long-term demographic trends which have called into question the ability of the established UK pension system to provide an adequate income to older people after they retire. For many years now life expectancy has been increasing markedly while, at the same time, fewer children are being born. These trends are leading to a steady rise in the *dependency ratio*, by which is meant the proportion of retired people vis-à-vis working people in the economy. At present in the UK 27 per cent of the adult population is aged over 65. By 2050 according to the Government Actuary, the proportion will be 48 per cent (Turner 2004, p. 4). Demographic trends are thus leading us steadily towards a situation in which the funding of adequate pensions using established approaches is going to become harder and harder to achieve.

Until the 1990s the UK could boast that it had one of the most extensive and well-funded systems of occupational pension provision in the world. Well over half of the workforce were members of reasonably generous, well-funded occupational pension schemes provided for them by their employers, while millions of retired employees drew a substantial income from the schemes which supplemented their state pensions. Unfortunately this long-established system is in terminal decline. Employers are less likely to offer membership of occupational schemes than they were, and where they still do so, it is on a less satisfactory financial basis when seen from the perspective of most employees. A combination of factors is responsible, but the core problem is the hugely increased costs that are now associated with the provision of good pensions for staff. This is due to taxation changes, to increased life expectancy and to the need to keep topping up pension funds whenever the stockmarket suffers falls of the kinds it has in recent years.

In 2002 Lord Turner, a former Director General of the Confederation of British Industry (CBI) was appointed by the Department for Work and Pensions to lead an extensive review of future pension provision in the UK. The government accepted the vast majority of its recommendations and included them in the Pensions Act 2007 which aims to encourage later retirement and significantly greater levels of saving into pension funds. From 2012 employers who do not provide a superior occupational pension or a Group personal pension (GPP) will be required to pay a contribution of 3 per cent of all employees' earnings between £5,000 and £33,000 a year into a personal account. Employees will pay a contribution of 4 per cent, a further 1 per cent being paid in as a result of tax relief. Employees will be permitted to opt out, but they will be automatically enrolled by their employer either into an occupational scheme or into the new personal accounts scheme. The latter will be commercially provided but will operate within strict government regulations.

Activity 7.4

The UK has always been unusual in having such a substantial occupational pensions sector. There is a similar system in the Netherlands and in the Republic of Ireland, but in most EU countries most employers see no reason why they should be involved in the provision of pensions. Why do you think these differences persist?

Occupational schemes do not generally pay their pensioners in the pay-as-you-go manner operated by the state, but create a pension fund, which is managed separately from the business. The advantage of this is that should the organisation become bankrupt, the pension fund cannot be seized to pay debtors because it is not part of the company. The money in the pension fund is invested and held in trust for the employees of the company at the time of their retirement. However, where a company becomes insolvent at a time when its pension fund is in deficit, employees can lose all or part of their pensions. Occupational funds take two main forms:

1 **Defined benefit schemes** remain the common form in the public sector, but two-thirds of the private sector schemes have now been closed to new members (National Association of Pension Funds 2007). Here contributions are made into a single organisation-wide fund which is invested on behalf of members by a fund manager. Retired employees then draw a pension from the fund calculated according to a defined formula. Most defined benefit schemes take the final salary form, in which the value of the pension is determined by the level of salary being received by each individual at the time of retirement. In the private sector it is common for this to be calculated on a 'sixtieths' basis, whereby the retiree is paid an annual pension equivalent to one-sixtieth (1.67 per cent) of their final salary multiplied by the number of years' pensionable service they have completed. In the public sector it is usual for the figure to be based on 'eightieths', with a tax-free lump sum being paid in addition at the time of retirement. Examples of final salary calculations are given in Table 7.1.

2 **Defined contribution schemes** (also known as money purchase schemes) are organised in a totally different way from defined benefit arrangements. Employees and employers both contribute a fixed percentage of current salary to these schemes, usually 5 per cent or 6 per cent on a monthly basis. The pension benefits received are then entirely dependent on the money that has been contributed and the way that

TABLE 7.1 Final salary schemes: examples of various contribution periods with a 1/60th and a 1/80th scheme

Sixtieths scheme	
Final salary	= £24,000
Contributions for 5 years	= $1/60 \times 24{,}000 \times 5$
Pension	= £2,000 per year
Final salary	= £24,000
Contributions for 25 years	= $1/60 \times 24{,}000 \times 25$
Pension	= £10,000 per year
Final salary	= £24,000
Contributions for 40 years	= $1/60 \times 24{,}000 \times 40$
Pension	= £16,000 per year
Eightieths scheme	
Final salary	= £24,000
Contributions for 25 years	= $1/80 \times 24{,}000 \times 25$
Pension	= £7,500 per year
Lump sum	= $3/80 \times 24{,}000 \times 25 = £22{,}500$

it has been invested. Where investments perform well, a good level of pension can be gained. Where investments are disappointing, the result is a low level of pension. Further uncertainty derives from the way that money purchase schemes result in the payment of a lump sum which must be used to buy an annuity from an insurance company from which a weekly or monthly income is paid for life. Annuity rates vary considerably from year to year, and there is also considerable variation between the deals offered by different providers. In essence this means that the risk associated with pension investments is carried by the employee in a defined contribution arrangement, rather than by the employer as in a final salary scheme.

In recent years there has been a strong trend away from defined benefit schemes and towards defined contribution provision. At the time of writing 66 per cent of all UK schemes are of the money purchase variety, compared with only 5 per cent in 1990 (National Association of Pension Funds 1992 and 2007). The majority of newly established schemes take the defined contribution form, while many organisations now offer only a money purchase scheme to new employees.

GPPs are alternative arrangements set up by an employer instead of an occupational pension scheme. From a legal and taxation perspective a GPP is no different from any individual personal pension arrangement, but charges are lower because the employer is able to arrange a bulk discount. The scheme is administered by an insurance company, the employer making contributions as well as the employee. Pensions are calculated on the same basis as in an occupational money purchase scheme, but tend to be smaller because employees are responsible for paying some of the administrative charges. A key difference is that a GPP is contract based rather than trust based. This means that unlike an occupational pension there is no board of trustees appointed to oversee the running of the scheme; instead a contract is signed with an external provider.

Stakeholder pensions are a form of government-sponsored pension arrangement. These are aimed primarily at middle income earners who do not have access to an occupational scheme. A stakeholder pension scheme can be operated by an employer, a financial services company or a trade union. Such schemes operate along money purchase lines and are regulated by established authorities. Charges are kept low because providers are obliged to follow minimum standards set by the government. Employers are not obliged to make contributions to a stakeholder pension, but must provide access to one through their payroll. If employees join a scheme, for example one provided by their trade union, the employer is therefore obliged to make deductions via the payroll out of pre-tax income.

Activity 7.5

Which of these types of occupational pension scheme would you find most attractive at the current stage in your career? Under what circumstances might you change your preference?

Aside from giving advice and taking overall responsibility for pensions issues, HR managers are concerned with determining their organisations' pension policy. Is an occupational pension to be offered? If so, what form should it take? What level of contribution is the employer going to make? It is quite possible to make a judgement in favour of generous occupational provision simply on paternalistic grounds. Many organisations have thus decided that they will offer pensions because it is in the interests of their staff that they should. Occupational schemes represent a convenient and tax-advantageous method of providing an income in old age; it therefore makes sense to include a pension in the total pay and benefits package. The problems with such a commitment, particularly in the case of defined benefit schemes, are the cost and the fact that the long-term financial consequences are unpredictable. This, combined with the fact that many employees do not seem to appreciate the value of an occupational pension, is one of the reasons that many employers have been questioning their commitment to final salary schemes and to pension provision in general.

Flexible benefits

Flexible benefits or 'cafeteria plans' have proliferated in the United States over recent years where they are specifically recognised in the tax regime. By contrast, take-up of the idea in the UK has tended to be slow. However, there is unquestionably a great deal more interest in the approach developing among UK employers.

The approach involves giving individual employees a choice as to how exactly their pay packet is made up. The overall value of the package is set by the employer, but it is for employees to choose for themselves what balance they wish to strike between cash and the different kinds of benefit. This helps ensure that employees are only provided with benefits of which they are aware and which they appreciate. Resources that would otherwise be wasted by providing unwanted benefits are thus saved. The employer gets maximum value per pound spent, while at the same time allowing employees to tailor their own 'perfect' benefits mix. The result should be improved staff retention and a better motivated workforce.

WINDOW ON PRACTICE

In 1998 a large-scale merger took place between two of the world's largest professional services firms – Price Waterhouse and Coopers & Lybrand. The merged firm, called PricewaterhouseCoopers, employs 150,000 people in 150 different countries. While the two organisations were culturally similar, they had rather different traditions in the provision of benefits. Rather than continue with different people employed on different sets of terms and conditions, partners decided to harmonise everyone as soon as was possible. This process was made a great deal easier and less contentious by the decision to develop a new flexible benefits scheme called 'Choices'. It allows employees to trade cash for additional holiday, a choice of car, childcare vouchers, retail vouchers, insurance of various kinds and a pension. No one was required to alter their existing benefits package as a result of the merger unless they wished to.

Source: O. Franks and D. Thompson (2000) 'Rights and rites of passage', *People Management*, 17 February.

Flexible benefits plans take many different forms, the main distinction being between those that are 'fully flexible' and those that allow a degree of flexibility within prescribed limits. A degree of restriction is more common, a compulsory core of benefits being compulsory, with flexibility beyond that. Under such a scheme everyone might be required to take four weeks' holiday and invest in a minimal pension, but be allowed freedom to determine whether or not they wished to benefit from private health insurance, gym membership, discounts on company products or whether or not they want a company car. A third approach is administratively simpler but is more restrictive in terms of employee choice. This involves 'prepackaging' a number of separate benefits menus designed to suit different groups of employees (rather like a pre-set banquet menu in a Chinese restaurant). Employees must then opt for one package from a choice of five or six, each having the same overall cash value. One is typically tailored to meet the needs of older staff, another is for those with young families, a third for new graduates and so on.

TOTAL REWARD

So far in this chapter we have focused on transactional or tangible rewards, by which we mean those which are financial in nature. But it is important to remember that employees also value the intangible (or relational) rewards which they gain from coming to work. These include opportunities to develop both in terms of their career and more generally as a human being, the social life which is associated with working in communal settings, recognition from managers and colleagues for a job well done and for the effort expended, and more generally from a sense of personal achievement. Increasingly the opportunity to work flexibly so as to achieve a better 'work-life balance' is discussed in this context too.

A trend towards viewing reward policies and practices as extending well beyond the realms of payment has led to widespread interest in the concept of 'total reward' which involves managers viewing the way that they reward employees in the round, taking equal account of both the tangible and intangible ingredients that together help to make work and jobs 'rewarding' in the widest sense of the word. The idea is effectively illustrated in graphical form by Armstrong and Brown (2006, p. 25) in their model adapted from work by the Towers Perrin reward consultancy (*see* Figure 7.3). Here four distinct categories of rewards are identified, the implication being that each has equal potential significance as a source of reward from the employee perspective.

The change in perspective away from a narrow focus on payment towards a broader focus on 'total reward' has come about largely because of developments in the commercial environment. Year on year, organisations operating in the private sector are facing greater competitive pressure in their product markets leading them to search for ways of reducing their costs while retaining or improving the levels of quality they achieve. In the public sector competitive forces increasingly play a role too, but here pressure to keep costs down come primarily from tax payers seeking good value for their money. The trouble is that these pressures are being faced simultaneously with tighter labour market conditions, making it difficult for employers to recruit, retain and motivate the staff they need without substantially increasing pay levels.

FIGURE 7.3

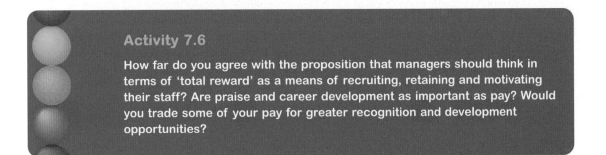

Source: Adapted from M. Armstrong and D. Brown (2006) *Strategic Reward: Making it Happen*. London: Kogan Page.

Activity 7.6

How far do you agree with the proposition that managers should think in terms of 'total reward' as a means of recruiting, retaining and motivating their staff? Are praise and career development as important as pay? Would you trade some of your pay for greater recognition and development opportunities?

WINDOW ON PRACTICE

Total reward at the Crown Prosecution Service

In 2006 the Crown Prosecution Service (CPS) launched a new reward system which was heavily influenced by the 'total reward' concept. Until 1996 when responsibility for reward management was devolved, the CPS's 8,500 staff were paid on standard terms and conditions which were negotiated nationally

▶

▶ for civil servants working across all government departments. After devolution incremental changes were introduced that aimed to meet the particular needs of the CPS, culminating in this major overhaul. Labelled 'Invest', the new approach aims to underpin the Service's evolving agenda.

The first priority for the CPS is to successfully manage a major programme of expansion. New responsibilities taken over from the police require that the CPS employs 300 new lawyers and 500 new administrators. 'Invest' is designed to increase the attractiveness of a career within the CPS and to help retain staff more effectively. An explicit objective of the service is to make itself 'an employer of choice' for lawyers and people seeking a career in public administration. A second aim is substantially to improve performance. The CPS has as its central corporate objective a mission to become recognised as 'a world-class prosecution authority'. This requires cultural change and the acquisition by staff of a range of new skills and attributes.

The new strategy aims to meet these objectives in a number of ways. First, a job evaluation system has been introduced to ensure that each job is fairly graded according to the skills its holders require and the responsibilities they shoulder. Secondly, a new performance appraisal system has come into effect to strengthen links between pay and individual effort and contribution. The existing civil service benefits package has been enhanced with new elements such as childcare services and a counselling service, the whole package being promoted with greater coherence at the recruitment stage. A major element is enhanced training and development opportunities for staff, allowing easier career progression within the service. Employees are sponsored to attain professional qualifications, while e-learning packages have also been developed to support career development. Finally flexible working initiatives have been developed, including a great deal more homeworking, which aim to meet the needs both of the service and its employees. In the future it is intended to introduce long-service awards and to recognise individual achievements with formal letters of recognition from senior managers.

Source: Adapted from R. Suff (2006) 'Inverting in Excellence at the Crown Prosecution Service' *IRS Employment Review* No. 841, 17 February, pp. 24–7.

KEY DEBATE: DOES PRP WORK?

The relative merits of performance-related pay (PRP) are the subject of a fierce and fascinating debate between managers, consultants, government ministers, academics, trade unionists and other authorities. Opinion is hugely divided. On the one hand there are those who support the approach both in principle and in practice, on the other are critics who fiercely oppose its use, arguing that PRP systems are fundamentally flawed and thus cannot meet their objectives however carefully they are designed. A third group is prepared to accept that PRP can work in limited circumstances, but argue that most schemes that are introduced disappoint in practice and have a demotivating effect as far as employees are concerned.

On the whole, in the UK, managers, consultants and government ministers tend to argue in favour of PRP, while academic researchers take a negative view. The former persist in their belief that PRP works well and should be extended to cover a greater portion of the workforce. The latter see such a policy as an excellent example of the worrying 'knowing-doing gap' that has, in their view, bedevilled reward management practice in the UK for many years (Armstrong *et al.* 2005, p. 4). This explains why coverage of PRP schemes in the UK has grown substantially in recent years (particularly in the public sector) in spite of the presence of a growing body of evidence that raises serious doubts about their effectiveness.

The case for PRP

There is no question that PRP, particularly systems of the goal-based variety (*see* above), has many theoretical attractions when seen from a management perspective:

- It serves to attract and retain good performers, creating incentives for the most talented and hard-working people to earn more than they would be able to earn under a system which pays a flat rate irrespective of personal performance.
- It is the fairest available system because it distributes rewards according to the efforts and skills that people contribute.
- It motivates people by rewarding them for putting in additional effort or achieving specific objectives.
- It provides a means whereby managers can exercise control over people's priorities without the need for close supervision.
- It provides a means of rewarding people for their efforts without the need to promote them upwards into jobs for which they might be less well suited.
- It reinforces the individual employment relationship at the expense of the collective, undermining the influence of trade unions.
- It forces managers and staff to commuicate directly, regularly and specifically about roles, duties, expectations and development needs.

In short PRP aims to provide a flexible and cost-effective means of distributing rewards fairly between the good and poorer performers while also contributing towards improved organisation performance. Moreover, it is based on principles to which most people, employees as well as managers, seem to adhere (Brown and Armstrong 2000, pp. 11–13). Most of us are very happy to see individuals rewarded for superior performance and/or effort and would like payment decisions to be based on such criteria. The problems arise when attempts are made to put the principles into practice. A system which is fair and objective in theory can easily fail to achieve these objectives when implemented.

The case against PRP

Occupational psychologists tend to question the ability of PRP to motivate positively (e.g. Kohn 1993), while sociologists see it as a means of reinforcing management control at the expense of worker autonomy (e.g. Hendry *et al.* 2000). A further source of criticism has come from those who suspect that PRP is used as a means of perpetuating gender inequality in payment matters (e.g. Rubery 1995). However, the most colourful and damning criticisms have come from management thinkers such as W. Edwards Deming who advocate Total Quality Management approaches and for whom PRP represents exactly the wrong kind of initiative to introduce:

> It leaves people bitter, crushed, bruised, battered, desolate, despondent, dejected, feeling inferior, some even depressed, unfit for work for weeks after receipt of rating, unable to comprehend why they are inferior. It is unfair, as it ascribes to the people in a group differences that may be caused totally by the system they work in. (Deming 1986, p. 75).

The whole basis of Deming's philosophy is the substitution of 'leadership' for 'supervision', removing organisational hierarchies and managing people with as little direction and control as possible. Management thinkers such as Deming see PRP as having the opposite effect. It reinforces the hierarchy, enhances the power of supervisors and strengthens management control.

For many critics, including those cited above, PRP has fundamental flaws which cannot be overcome. Kohn (1993), for example, argues that incentives can only succeed in securing temporary compliance. Their use cannot change underlying attitudes, while the attempt to make such changes ultimately damages the long-term health of an organisation by undermining relationships and encouraging employees to focus on short-term aims.

PRP stifles innovative thinking, constructive criticism and creativity. Instead people focus simply on achieving specific tasks in the most unchallenging way they can find. Moreover, it tends to undermine teamworking as people concentrate their efforts on achieving their own individual objectives rather than directing their efforts towards a common good.

The research evidence

The research evidence is patchy on the question of how far incentives actually lead to performance improvements at the organisational level. Some studies suggest a correlation between superior performance and some types of PRP scheme (e.g. Huselid 1995, Piekkola 2005 and Gielen *et al.* 2006), while others (e.g. Thompson 1992 and Pearce *et al.* 1985) have found no significant evidence of any link. In any case, as Corby *et al.* (2005, pp. 5–6) point out, there are very few published studies which focus on performance or productivity levels before and after the introduction of a new scheme. What we have is correlation studies which link superior organisational performance to the presence of incentive schemes, but no proof of any causal relationship.

Interview-based studies tend to show that when implemted, PRP often fails to meet expectations and can have negative effects. Systems fail as often as they succeed. The arguments are summarised well by Gomez-Mejia and Balkin (1992, pp. 249–55), Cannell and Wood (1992, pp. 66–101), Pfeffer (1998, pp. 203–4) and Purcell (2000). The major points made by these authors are as follows:

- Employees paid by PRP, especially where the incentive is substantial, tend to develop a narrow focus to their work. They concentrate on those aspects which they believe will initiate payments, while neglecting other parts of their jobs.
- PRP, because of its individual nature, tends to undermine teamworking. People focus on their own objectives at the expense of cooperation with colleagues.
- PRP, because it involves managers rating employees, can lead to a situation in which a majority of staff are demotivated when they receive their rating. This occurs where people perceive their own performance to be rather better than it is considered to be by their supervisors – a common situation. The result is a negative effect on the motivation of the staff who are unexceptional, but loyal and valued. These are often the very people on whom organisations depend most.
- Employees are rarely in a position wholly to determine the outcomes of their own performance. Factors outside their control play an important role, leading to a situation in which the achievement or non-achievement of objectives is partially a matter of chance.
- Even the most experienced managers find it difficult to undertake fair and objective appraisals of their employees' performance. Subjective judgements are often taken into account leading to perceptions of bias. Some managers deliberately manipulate ratings for political reasons, allowing their judgement to be coloured by the effect they perceive the outcome will have on particular employees. Low ratings are thus avoided, as are very high ratings, where it is perceived this will lead to disharmony or deterioration of personal relationships.
- In organisations subject to swift and profound change, objectives set for the coming year may become obsolete after a few months. Employees then find themselves with an incentive to meet goals which are no longer priorities for the organisation.
- PRP systems tend to discourage creative thinking, the challenging of established ways of doing things and a questioning attitude among employees.
- Budgetary constraints often lead managers to reduce ratings, creating a situation in which excellent individual performance is not properly rewarded.
- It is difficult to ensure that each line manager takes a uniform approach to the rating of their subordinates. Some tend to be more generously disposed in general than others, leading to inconsistency and perceptions of unfairness.
- When the results of performance appraisal meetings have an impact on pay levels, employees tend to downplay their weaknesses. As a result development needs are not discussed or addressed.
- PRP systems invariably increase the pay bill. This occurs because managers fear demotivating their staff by awarding low or zero rises in the first years of a system's operation. Poorer performers are thus rewarded as well as better performers.

It is nonetheless reasonable to question the research methods used by some of the critics of PRP. Many of those who have looked at the issue from a psychological standpoint (e.g. Herzberg 1966 and Kohn 1993) have based their conclusions, to an extent, on laboratory studies (Taylor 2000, p. 21). They have not observed or questioned individual managers or employees about their experiences, but have instead conducted controlled experiments in universities using volunteers and observing their reactions to different types of situation. This rather artificial setting makes it reasonable to question how generalisable their findings are to real workplaces.

Secondly, it is fair to point out that many writers looking at PRP from a sociological background make little attempt to disguise their political objections to PRP – particularly as regards its use in the public sector. Hendry *et al.* (2000) and Thompson (2000) fall into this category. For them PRP is associated with the individualisation of the employment relationship, the undermining of trade unions and the reinforcement of management control. These are developments of which they make it clear they strongly disapprove. It follows that they are likely to be predisposed to criticise PRP, to emphasise its flaws and to downplay its advantages.

Using PRP effectively

Despite the problems described above it is possible to implement PRP successfully, as is shown by the experience of case study companies quoted by Brown and Armstrong (2000), IRS (2005a, 2005b) and IDS (2005). It will only work, however, if it is used in appropriate circumstances and if it is implemented properly. Part of the problem with PRP has been a tendency in the HR press to portray it as universally applicable and as a panacea capable of improving performance dramatically. In fact it is neither, but is one of a range of tools that have a useful if limited role to play in some situations. Gomez-Mejia and Balkin (1992) specify the following favourable conditions:

- Where individual performance can be objectively and meaningfully measured.
- Where individuals are in a position to control the outcomes of their work.
- Where close teamworking or cooperation with others is not central to successful job performance.
- Where there is an individualistic organisational culture.

In addition, Brown and Armstrong (2000) rightly point to the importance of careful implementation and lengthy preparation prior to the installation of a scheme. Moreover, they argue that PRP should not be looked at or judged in isolation from other forms of reward, both extrinsic and intrinsic. Success or failure can hinge on what else is being done to maximise motivation, to develop people and to improve their job security.

Ultimately PRP has one great advantage which no amount of criticism can remove: it helps ensure that organisational priorities become individual priorities. Managers can signal the importance of a particular objective by including it in a subordinate's goals for the coming year. If the possibility of additional payment is then tied to its achievement, the chances that the objective concerned will be met increases significantly.

WINDOW ON PRACTICE

Many job descriptions for supervisory positions include reference to responsibility for ensuring that the appropriate health and safety at work regulations are adhered to. Few supervisors, however, if left to themselves would see this aspect of their work as a priority. In one organisation known to the authors it was decided to try to raise the profile of health and safety issues by including objectives in this field into managers' annual performance targets. It therefore became clear that the level of PRP in the following year would, in part, be determined by the extent to which the health and safety objectives had been met. The result was the swift establishment of departmental health and safety committees and schemes whereby staff could bring safety hazards to the attention of supervisors.

Activity 7.7

Having read about the arguments and the evidence in favour of and against PRP systems, what is your view of their effectiveness? To what extent do you think PRP could be used in paying the following groups and how?

- school teachers
- police officers
- supermarket check-out operators
- journalists

SUMMARY PROPOSITIONS

7.1 There are four main alternative methods of setting base pay rates: external labour market comparisons, internal labour market mechanisms, job evaluation and collective bargaining.

7.2 The main elements of payment are basic rate, plussage, benefits, premia, overtime, incentives and bonus.

▶ 7.3 Incentive payment schemes either involve the payment of a bonus or form the basis of incremental progression systems. In either case, the reward should represent at least 7 per cent of salary if there is to be a meaningful incentive effect.

7.4 Performance-related pay systems are either merit based or goal based. They have been the subject of notable debate in recent years, many researchers finding a mismatch between their theoretical attractions and practical outcomes.

7.5 Skills-based pay involves linking incentives to the achievement of defined competencies or qualifications. It rewards what people bring to the job rather than the results of their efforts. Profit-sharing schemes have been promoted by governments for many years. They can be either cash based or share based.

7.6 Between 20 per cent and 50 per cent of the typical employer's pay bill is spent on the provision of supplementary benefits, a large proportion accounted for by occupational pensions. Evidence suggests that most employees do not appreciate the true financial value of such benefits.

7.7 In theory flexible benefits plans have a great deal to offer employees. It is likely that their use will grow more widespread in the next few years.

7.8 Competition in product and labour markets has led employers increasingly to think in terms of 'total reward' when developing reward strategies. This involves incorporating all management initiatives, which may have the effect of adding value to the experience of working in an organisation.

GENERAL DISCUSSION TOPICS

1 Do you think it is possible to identify 'best practice' in payment policy? What elements would you consider should make up any such package?

2 In what circumstances might it be appropriate to base individual payment on team performance?

3 Draw up three flexible benefits packages; one aimed at new graduates, one at employees in their thirties, and one for those aged over 50.

FURTHER READING

The Chartered Institute of Personnel and Development (CIPD) carries out a big annual survey of reward management policy and practice which is published in February each year. It can be downloaded from the Institute's website. In addition CIPD publishes the results of other research projects that focus on reward. Two recent examples are the report of a symposium held in 2005 at which academics and practitioners who specialise in reward matters met to discuss developments in the field (Armstrong *et al.* 2005) and a series of papers by John Purcell and Sue Hutchison published in 2006 and 2007 summarising their research on the role played by line managers in the implementation of reward initiatives.

An excellent chapter by Ian Kessler entitled 'Remuneration Systems', in S. Bach (ed.) (2005) assesses the recent research into all major aspects of reward strategy and policy that has been undertaken in the UK. All aspects are discussed, including regulatory developments and the ever-present search for links between reward practice and improved organisational performance.

REFERENCES

Armstrong, M. and Brown, D. (2006) *Strategic Reward: Making it Happen*. London: Kogan Page.

Armstrong, M., Thompson, P., Brown, D. and Cotton, C. (2005) *Reward Management: Report on a one-day conference held on 13th July 2005, organised jointly by e-reward and the Chartered Institute of Personnel and Development*. London: Chartered Institute of Personnel and Development.

Bromley, C. (2003) 'Has Britain become immune to inequality?', in A. Park, J. Curtice, K. Thomson, L. Jarvis and C. Bromley (eds) *British Social Attitudes. The Twentieth Report*. London: National Centre for Social Research.

Brown, D. and Armstrong, M. (2000) *Paying for Contribution: real performance-related pay strategies*. London: Kogan Page.

Cannell, M. and Wood, S. (1992) *Incentive Pay: Impact and Evolution*. London: IPM.

CIPD (2007) *Reward Management: Annual Survey Report 2007*. London: Chartered Institute of Personnal and Development.

Corby, S., White, G. and Stanworth, C. (2005) 'No news is good news? Evaluating new pay systems', *Human Resource Management Journal*, Vol. 15, No. 1, pp. 4–24.

Cox, A. (2006) 'The outcomes of variable pay systems: tales of multiple costs and unforeseen consequences', *International Journal of Human Resource Management*, Vol. 16, No. 8, pp. 1475–97.

Deming, W.E. (1986) *Out of the Crisis: Quality, Productivity and Competitive Position*. Cambridge: Cambridge University Press.

Franks, O. and Thompson, D. (2000) 'Rights and rites of passage', *People Management*, 17 February.

Gielen, A.C., Kerkhofs, M.J.M. and Van Ours, J.C. (2006) *Performance-related pay and labor productivity*. IZA Discussion Paper 2211. Berlin: Institute for the Study of Labor (IZA).

Giles, C. (2008) 'Very rich get richer under Labour', *Financial Times*, 17 January.

Gomez-Mejia, L. and Balkin, D. (1992) *Compensation, Organizational Strategy and Firm Performance*. Cincinnati, Ohio: South Western Publishing.

Grabham, A. (2003) 'Composition of Pay', *Labour Market Trends*, August.

Hendry, C., Woodward, S., Bradley, P. and Perkins, S. (2000) 'Performance and rewards: cleaning out the stables', *Human Resource Management Journal*, Vol. 10, No. 3, pp. 46–62.

Herzberg, F. (1966) *Work and the Nature of Man*. Cleveland, Ohio: World Publishing.

Huselid, M. (1995) 'The impact of HRM practices on turnover, productivity and corporate performance', *Academy of Management Journal*, June.

IDS (2005) 'Bonus Schemes', IDS Studies No. 794. London: Incomes Data Services.

IRS (2005a) 'Pay 4 Performance at Yorkshire Water', *IRS Employment Review* No. 833, pp. 31–5.

IRS (2005b) 'Performing flexible reward at Severn Trent Water', *IRS Employment Review* No. 834, pp. 30–3.

Kersley, B., Alpin, C., Forth, J., Bryson, A., Bewley, H., Dix, G. and Oxenbridge, S. (2006) *Inside the Workplace: Findings from the 2004 Workplace Employment Relations Survey*. Abingdon: Routledge.

Kessler, I. (2005) 'Remuneration Systems' in S. Bach (ed.) *Managing Human Resources: Personnel Management in Transition*, 4th edn. Oxford: Blackwell.

Kohn, A. (1993) 'Why Incentive Plans Cannot Work', *Harvard Business Review*, September–October, pp. 54–63.

Lazear, E.P. (1995) *Personnel Economics*. Boston: Massachusetts Institute of Technology.

NAPF (1992) *Seventeenth Annual Survey of Occupational Pension Funds*. London: National Association of Pension Funds.

NAPF (2007) *Annual Survey of Occupational Pension Funds 2006*. London: National Association of Pension Funds.

National Statistics (2006) *2006 Annual Survey of Hours and Earnings*. London: National Statistics.

Pearce, J.L., Stevenson, W.B. and Perry, J.L. (1985) 'Managerial compensation based on organizational performance: A time series analysis of the effects of merit pay', *Academy of Management Journal*, Vol. 28, pp. 261–78.

Pendleton, A. (2000) 'Profit-sharing and employee share ownership', in R. Thorpe and G. Homan (eds) *Strategic Reward Systems*. London: FT/Prentice Hall.

Pfeffer, J. (1998) *The Human Equation: Building profits by putting people first*. Boston: Harvard Business School Press.

Piekkola, H. (2005) 'Performance-related pay and firm performance in Finland', *International Journal of Manpower*, Vol. 7, No. 8, pp. 619–35.

Purcell, J. (2000) 'Pay per view', *People Management*, 3 February, pp. 41–3.

Purcell, J. and Hutchinson, S. (2006) *Rewarding Work: The Vital Role of Line Managers*. London: Chartered Institute of Personnal and Development.

Rubery, J. (1995) 'Performance-related pay and the prospects for gender pay equity', *Journal of Management Studies*, Vol. 32, No. 5, pp. 637–54.

Sisson, K. and Storey, J. (2000) *The Realities of Human Resource Management*. Buckingham: Open University Press.

Smith, I. (2000) 'Benefits', in G. White and J. Druker (eds) *Reward Management: A Critical Text*. London: Routledge.

Suff, R. (2006) 'Investing in Excellence at the Crown Prosecution Service', *IRS Employment Review* No. 841, 17 February, pp. 24–7.

Taylor, S. (2000) 'An Introduction to Strategic Reward', in R. Thorpe and G. Homan (eds) *Strategic Reward Systems*. London. Financial Times/Prentice Hall.

Thompson, M. (1992) *Pay and Performance: The Employer Experience*. Institute of Manpower Studies Report No. 218. London: IMS.

Thompson, M. (2000) 'Salary progression systems', in G. White and J. Druker (eds) *Reward Management: A Critical Text*. London: Routledge.

Turner, A. (2004) *Pensions: Challenges and Choices. The First Report of the Pensions Commission*. London, HMSO.

UNDP (2008) *Human Development Reports*. United Nations Development Programme. Available online at: **http://hdrstats.undp.org**.

White, G. (2000) 'Determining pay', in G. White and J. Druker (eds) *Reward Management: A Critical Text*. London: Routledge.

Wilman, J. (2008) 'Executive pay rises above inflation', *Financial Times*, 10 March.

CHAPTER 8

Employee relations

The objectives of this chapter are to:

1 Identify the major strategic choices that employers face in the employee relations field

2 Introduce the main methods used by employers to involve employees in decision making

3 Assess the extent of information sharing and its purpose

4 Set out the case for formal and informal consultation with employees and their representatives

5 Explore the role and future of trade unions

Employees want to hear it 'straight' from the boss's mouth!

In a much-visited video clip on Google, Steve Ballmer, Microsoft's Chief Executive, can be seen bouncing around the stage to dance music, screaming, whooping and exhorting his hyped-up audience to: 'COME AARN, GED UP'. He then pauses, panting, before shouting at the top of his voice: 'I HAVE FOUR WORDS FOR YOU: I – LOVE – THIS – COMPANY . . . YEAHHHS!'

Mr Ballmer evidently took to heart – and to the extreme – that cliché of leadership that you can never communicate enough with your employees. Chief Executives routinely pay homage to communication and boast about the ways they 'reach out' to their people – through 'town hall' meetings, site visits, newsletters, open doors and, now, blogs.

▶

▶ Those on the receiving end, however, are often left feeling bemused or, worse, cheated. What employees really want, according to a new survey, is straight-talkers who keep them up to date with bad, as well as good, news. They also want leaders who stay true to themselves instead of putting on a performance or preaching through PowerPoint.

A survey of 1,000 employees suggests that they regard communicating with staff as a more important leadership quality than having a clear vision for the company. Only 40 per cent say their boss communicates effectively. The 'considerate' ones talk directly to staff rather than through managers or the media, invite feedback and value people's views. About a third of employees have bosses like this – considerate, sincere and motivating.

On the other hand, a third say their bosses fail to provide enough information about plans, communicate too late or not at all and talk at them rather than having a conversation. These 'controlling' communicators also tend to underestimate the intelligence of their workers and how far they can trust them. They are keener to talk to industry peers than to their staff.

Many respondents complain of the lack of face-to-face contact with their leaders. 'Nobody at floor level ever gets asked their opinion, even though they are the ones dealing directly with the customers and the ones with the real experience of what people need,' says one employee.

Another says that, if she was in charge, she would 'try to remember who works for me, and why, and their names; show some interest in what they have to say and actually try to act on it; be less aloof and proud and feel free to admit when I am wrong or need help'.

'Leaders can learn to tell the truth, to admit what they don't know and to admit mistakes,' says Jeffrey Pfeffer, professor of organisational learning at Stanford's Graduate School of Business. 'They can also learn to be less controlling. People want to make decisions at work and have some control and responsibility, just as they do in other spheres of their lives.'

Source: Alison Maitland (2006), *Financial Times*, 1 December (abridged by the authors).

The term 'employee relations' describes the study of the employment relationship between employer and employee. Historically, it has been concerned to look at collective relationships managed between trade unions (on behalf of employees) and employers. For reasons that we will explore in the Key debate later in this chapter, this collective emphasis in the employment relationship has diminished and there is an increasing focus on the individual level at which the employment relationship is managed between line manager and employee. As the extract above shows, a key element of managing this relationship is communication with employees and involving them in decision-making processes. We open this chapter with a brief discussion of employee relations strategy, before discussing in detail mechanisms of employee involvement and communication. We close with a consideration of the reasons for trade union decline and its implications.

STRATEGIC CHOICES

Most organisations in the UK do not have a clearly identifiable employee relations strategy which their managers can readily articulate. At no point have managers at senior levels determined what the general approach or philosophy of the organisation should be towards the relationship it has with its employees either individually or collectively. While it may be possible to identify the operation of a clear management style or the presence of definable employee relations culture, these have not in most cases been shaped in a deliberate or coherent manner by managers (Blyton and Turnbull 2004, p. 121). Instead, pragmatism reigns and employee relations issues only get given serious attention at senior levels when problems arise (Keenoy 1992, p. 97).

The reason for this is that there is often only limited scope for individual managers or teams of managers, however senior, to determine the nature of the employment relationships in an organisation. Whereas a reward strategy or an employee development strategy can be thought through, devised and then introduced by managers with relative ease, altering, let alone shaping, the direction of employee relations is far harder to achieve. This is because the nature of the employment relationship in an organisation is controlled to a considerable extent by the attitudes, outlook and responses of employees. While managers can often readily get employees to *do* what they want them to, they cannot do more than influence their hearts and minds. As a result, even if a strategic approach to employee relations is developed, there is no guarantee that it will be successfully implemented and the extent of its success will always be difficult to measure objectively and accurately.

Moreover, the defining characteristics of the employment relationship in most organisations are heavily determined by the nature of the work that is being carried out and the way that it is organised. For example, a new manufacturing plant which mass-produces goods via assembly lines is inevitably going to develop different kinds of employment relationships with its staff than would be the case in a new shop, hotel, hospital or government department. All of these workplaces will develop clearly differentiated cultures derived from the complexity of work that they carry out, the nature of customer interaction, the extent of competition and the nature of the skills and qualifications their staff possess. Once established, workplace cultures are difficult to change, and this means that the nature of established employment relationships is difficult to change too.

Despite these difficulties, it can be strongly argued that organisations are more effective when their senior managers do think strategically about the employment relationship and develop policies and practices which help them to achieve clearly articulated objectives. There are strategic choices to be made in the field of employee relations and it is better that these should be considered and rational, rather than determined in an ad hoc, inconsistent and reactive fashion.

Management control

Employees and their employers share some interests in common, but what they aim to get from their relationship also varies considerably. There is thus an ever-present need, from a management perspective, to supervise what employees are doing and, more generally, to exercise a degree of control over a workplace. However, the nature of the control that is exercised varies from organisation to organisation, and this is largely a matter determined by management.

The central choice is between the two fundamentally different control strategies identified by Friedman (1977): 'direct control' and 'responsible autonomy'. The former involves close supervision by managers who determine what work is done, when and by whom. This is a model of control that is often seen as being similar to that used in the armed forces, although its origins lie as much in the ideas of F.W. Taylor and the school of scientific management which sought to organise work in the way that an engineer might design a machine. Responsible autonomy, by contrast, is both subtler and a great deal more pleasant from the employees' point of view. It is also believed by many managers to be more desirable because it leads to less conflict with staff, and more cost effective because less management time needs to be spent supervising the activities of others. Here the organisation sets the objectives, communicating clearly to its staff what it wants them to achieve, but it allows employees as much autonomy as is practicable to decide how and when they meet these objectives. The scope for responsible autonomy obviously varies greatly between jobs, as most sales representatives, for instance, have scope for varying their hours, the sequence of their calls and the way in which they approach and deal with customers, while those working on an assembly line or as a supermarket check-out operator have much less scope. The important thing for managers to remember is that almost all have *some* scope.

Labour-market orientation

In recent years most labour markets have tightened, making it harder for employers to recruit and retain good performers. Staff who are unhappy now have more alternative employment opportunities open to them and can thus either switch employers, or credibly threaten to do so if they find that their objectives from an employment relationship are not being met. Effective employee relations practices can aid staff retention because of their influence on job satisfaction.

One strategic choice for employers in response to tightening labour market conditions is to seek to acquire the status of an 'employer of choice' or even that of *the* employer of choice in their industry. This involves being more attractive to prospective employees than competitor organisations, in order to hold on to the services of high performers. Positioning an organisation as an employer of choice can be expensive in the short term, but reaps dividends over time because fewer people are required, and those that are employed help ensure that the organisation meets its objectives more effectively and efficiently than its rivals, sustaining competitive advantage. Employee relations strategies therefore have to be developed that will increase employee satisfaction and decrease dissatisfaction.

Taylor (2001, p. 15), drawing on the work of Michael White and Stephen Hill, states that contemporary research into what employees want to achieve from the employment relationship consistently reports a desire, above other possibilities, for the following:

- an interesting job
- employment security
- a feeling of positive accomplishment
- influence over how their job gets done

This strongly suggests that there are substantial long-term dividends to be gained by employers who develop sophisticated employee relations strategies. Effective employee involvement practices are central, as are approaches to supervision which combine responsible autonomy with strong positive feedback mechanisms. Involving employees in the management of change is particularly important so as to minimise perceptions of insecurity. Above all, an employer of choice requires an employee relations strategy which is built around a view of employees as individuals with different personalities, attributes and ambitions. A traditional approach which views employees as a mass group of people with identical aspirations is unlikely to deliver jobs which individuals find interesting or fulfilling. We develop this idea in detail in this chapter, outlining mechanisms for employee involvement and communication.

Not all labour markets are tight, and while they have tightened considerably over the long term in most parts of the UK, it is important to recognise that there are areas of high unemployment both in this country and overseas. Moreover, in all countries, there are groups of people who lack sufficient basic skills or whose skills have become obsolete. In such conditions employers are not required to become employers of choice in order to recruit and retain effective staff. People may prefer jobs which are interesting, secure and satisfying, and may desire a degree of influence over how they do their jobs, but management do not have to provide such employment for reasons of commercial necessity. Where competitive pressures require organisations to minimise costs in order to survive and prosper, a rather different employee relations strategy is appropriate. Policies are likely to be highly standardised, employee involvement is limited and few formal opportunities for positive feedback are provided. Jobs are designed first and foremost around the need of the organisation to maximise its efficiency rather than around the needs or aspirations of employees.

Activity 8.1

Think of an organisation that seeks to position itself as an 'employer of choice' – recruitment advertising is often a good indicator of this. How does it do this and what effect do you think this will have on employee relations within the organisation?

EMPLOYEE INVOLVEMENT

It is quite possible to run a successful business without involving employees in management activities to any meaningful extent, but the chances of sustained success are higher when employees are involved. The same is true of organisations in the public and voluntary sectors. Objectives are more effectively and efficiently achieved if employees have some say in decision making, especially as it affects their own areas of work. This is for two principal reasons.

1 Managers may be paid more than their staff, have bigger offices and drive more expensive cars, but that does not mean that they always know best. There is no fount of wisdom exclusive only to managers. Ultimately it is for managers to make decisions and to be held accountable, and these can be tough to make. But the chances that they will make the right decision are enhanced if they listen to the views of others and allow their own ideas to be subjected to a degree of scrutiny and constructive criticism. Moreover, involvement allows managers to tap into the ideas and suggestions of staff. The best new ideas often originate from people lower down organisational hierarchies because they are closest to the operational coalface and often to customers.

2 Employees like being involved. They appreciate having their opinions listened to and acted upon, particularly in matters that directly concern their day-to-day activities. The chances of them being positively satisfied with their work are thus greatly improved if they are genuinely able to be involved. The knock-on effects include lower staff turnover, lower levels of absence, the ability to attract more recruits and higher levels of performance. The effective management of change is especially enhanced by employee involvement because people are always happier to support what they helped to create.

Employee involvement activity comes in many different forms. It can be formal or informal, direct or indirect, one-off or sustained over time, central to an organisation's core business or relatively peripheral. In recent years the number and extent of such programmes has increased. This is partly due to the requirements of the law (*see* Chapter 9) and partly because they have a part to play in many of the more common, contemporary HRM initiatives we have discussed elsewhere in this book – becoming an 'employer of choice', 360-degree appraisal and employee engagement, for example.

Our aim here is to discuss the major forms employee involvement takes, explore the difficulties that can be experienced in the implementation of initiatives and to evaluate their contribution to the achievement of an organisation's objectives.

TERMINOLOGY

A variety of labels are used to describe employee involvement initiatives singly and collectively. While some writers have sought to make distinctions between them, there is no generally accepted usage. Hence you will read not just about 'involvement', but also about 'employee participation', 'industrial democracy', 'empowerment' and, in the most recent literature, about 'employee voice'. Each of these terms differs subtly and suggests a

FIGURE 8.1
The escalator
of participation

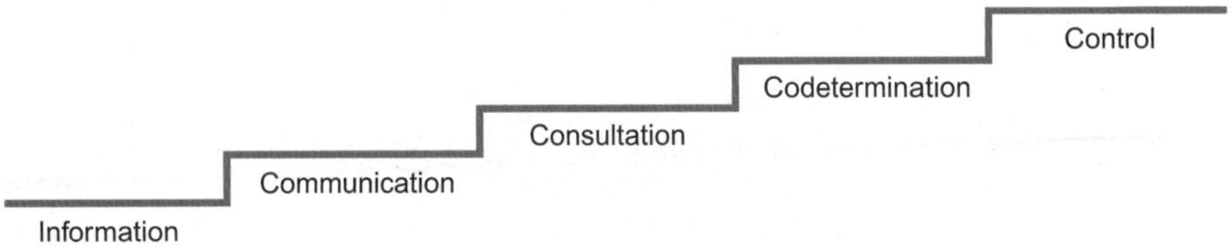

Escalator steps (bottom to top): Information, Communication, Consultation, Codetermination, Control

Source: Reprinted with permission from M. Marchington and A. Wilkinson (2005) 'Direct participation and involvement', in S. Bach (ed.) Managing *Human Resources: Personnel Management in Transition*, 4th edn. Oxford: Blackwell, Fig. 15.1, p. 401.

different perspective, but all to a greater or lesser extent are used to describe a situation in which employees are given, gain or develop a degree of *influence* over what happens in an organisation. The extent and nature of that influence, however, varies considerably.

Marchington and Wilkinson (2005, p. 401) helpfully distinguish between the major categories of involvement with their 'escalator' model. The focus here is on the extent of participation and influence (*see* Figure 8.1).

At the bottom of the escalator are organisations where there is no involvement at all, employees are provided with only the information necessary to do their jobs with no opportunity to respond, managers taking all decisions without taking any meaningful account of what employees might think. By contrast, at the top of the escalator are organisations or parts of organisations which are controlled by employees rather than by a distinct group of managers. Employee control is very rare in the UK at the level of the organisation, although there are one or two examples of companies, for example the John Lewis Partnership, which are communally owned and run by staff in a partnership arrangement. However, a substantial degree of control is much more often exercised by employees at the level of an individual department or team within a larger organisation.

WINDOW ON PRACTICE

Loch Fyne Oysters is an example of a very successful company which is owned by its employees.

Based at the head of Loch Fyne in Argyll, the company runs the largest oyster farm in the UK, a mussel farm, a smokehouse for the processing of salmon, a world-famous restaurant and a shop. Products are sold to retailers, hotels and restaurants in 22 countries. The company employs 120 people and has a turnover of £11 million. It was founded in 1977 by a local landowner and a biologist, Johnnie Noble and Andy Lane, who built it up steadily over 25 years. When Mr Noble died suddenly in 2003 at a time when the company needed an injection of funds, it was put on the market. The company would have been taken over by a large corporation had Andy Lane not found a way of securing the necessary funds while also transferring ownership to the employees.

▶

▶   This was achieved by entering into an agreement with the Baxi Trust which
invested £2 million to buy 50 per cent of the shares, with the promise of a
7 per cent return for 15 years. The shares are held in an employee trust. Each
year a number are purchased using the company's profits and distributed among
staff with more than three years' service. Further shares are also purchased
by the trust each year, so that over time the company will become owned in
its entirety by its staff. No one is permitted to own more than 5 per cent of the
company, while two board members are elected by the staff. Loch Fyne Oysters
is run like any other company, except that there is necessarily more emphasis
placed on communicating, consulting and involving employees in decision
making. Openness with staff, together with increased development opportunities,
has led to improved customer service, increased staff morale and a substantial
improvement in productivity.

In between 'information' and 'employee control', there are three further stages, each in turn representing a deepening of the extent of involvement. The first is 'communication', signalling a very limited degree of involvement. At this stage employer and employees simply exchange information. Managers disclose defined classes of information, ensuring that employees are aware of the decisions they are taking, the economic situation and their objectives. Employees are also given an opportunity to respond, to voice concerns or put their own ideas forward. But decision making remains exclusively in the management realm. The next step up the escalator is 'consultation'. Here information is exchanged, often through formalised channels. Decision making is still the responsibility of managers, but full and proper consideration is given to the views expressed by staff (or their elected representatives) before key decisions are taken. Finally, a further step up the escalator takes us to co-determination or joint decision making. This is relatively rare in a formal sense in the UK, although it happens informally all the time. But it is very common indeed in northern European countries where the law requires the agreement of a Works Council before significant decisions affecting employment can be taken.

At each of these stages involvement initiatives can be either direct or indirect in nature. The term 'direct involvement' relates to situations in which managers enter into a dialogue with, consult with or co-determine decisions with employees as individuals. People thus have a direct input in some shape or form. By contrast, the term 'indirect employee involvement' refers to a situation in which employers take account of employee views through the filter of a representative institution. This may be a trade union, or it may be another kind of body such as a works council, a working party or a consultative committee. Either way, direct involvement is restricted to representatives of the workforce as a collective group.

Academic research into employee involvement often encompasses payment arrangements such as profit sharing and employee share ownership schemes which are referred to as types of 'financial participation'. These help to develop a community of interest between employers and their staff and can lead to situations in which individual employees cast votes at annual general meetings.

INFORMATION SHARING

According to the 2004 Workplace Employment Relations Survey formal systems of communication between managers and employees are present in the vast majority of UK organisations (Kersley *et al*. 2006, p. 135). In many cases, however, the communication is carried out at the local level (e.g. line managers meeting with employees individually), there being no formal mechanisms provided for more senior managers to communicate directly with their staff or vice versa. Moreover, where a degree of formality is reported it can be limited simply to the posting of important data on noticeboards or ad hoc circulation of information by e-mail. As a result, a substantial minority of UK employees are reported to believe that they are not kept informed about what their companies are doing (45 per cent) or are not even given sufficient information to do their jobs effectively (35 per cent) (ORC International 2004, cited by IRS 2005a).

The extent to which the disclosure of information by managers can be regarded as a form of employee involvement is debatable. After all, merely being told about an organisation's plans or its financial results does not in any way give employees influence. Nonetheless it can help to make employees feel a sense of involvement or at least of inclusion in the circle of those 'in the know'. It also enables employees, either individually or collectively, to exercise informal influence locally, simply because they are in a position to develop and articulate credible alternative approaches to those their immediate line managers would otherwise impose. Alternatively they are in a position to help improve or refine their strategies. It is often rightly stated that 'knowledge is power' and it therefore follows that spreading relevant knowledge beyond the ranks of management to employees is an empowering activity. This is why managers will frequently hold back information from their staff while also letting it be known that they are doing so. Except in a crisis situation in which there is a need to promote calm and keep everyone focused on their jobs, often no conceivable damage would be done to the organisation by disclosing the information; labelling it 'confidential' and refusing to disclose it serves to enhance managers' own sense of personal authority and power.

However reluctant line managers may be to share information to which they are privy, there is substantial evidence to back up the view that regular, extensive information sharing has positive outcomes for organisations. This occurs because it improves levels of commitment among staff (*see* Peccei *et al*. 2005) and because in a practical sense it helps everyone to clarify what their role is in the wider organisation. It thus enhances communication and coordination across divisions. It also helps to prevent false understanding developing among staff thanks to the inevitable 'rumour mills' that operate in all organisations.

Two-way communication, by contrast, especially when it takes the form of a formal exercise, clearly falls into the category of employee involvement. Staff are being asked to respond to a suggested new approach, asked their opinion, being invited to make suggestions for improvements or given an opportunity to point out flaws in current systems or management thinking. Provided the exercise is not merely cosmetic, and that the views of staff are given serious consideration, influence is gained. We discuss below some of the most common methods of information sharing.

Team briefing

Team briefing is an initiative that attempts to do a number of different things simultaneously. It provides authoritative information at regular intervals, so that people know what is going on, the information is geared to achievement of production targets and other features of organisational objectives, it is delivered face to face to provide scope for questions and clarification, and it emphasises the role of supervisors and line managers as the source of information:

Team briefings are often used to cascade information or managerial messages throughout the organisation. The teams are usually based round a common production or service area, rather than an occupation, and usually comprise between four and fifteen people. The leader of the team is usually the manager or supervisor of the section and should be trained in the principles and skills of how to brief. The meetings last for no more than 30 minutes, and time should be left for questions from employees. Meetings should be held at least monthly or on a regular prearranged basis (Holden 1997, p. 624).

With goodwill and managerial discipline, team briefing can be a valuable contributor to employee involvement, as it deals in that precious commodity, information. Traditionally, there has perhaps been a managerial view that people doing the work are not interested in anything other than the immediate and short term and that the manager's status partly rests on knowing what others do not know. For this reason all the managers and supervisors in the communications chain have to be committed to making it a success, as well as having the training that Holden refers to above.

Team briefing gets easier once it is established as a regular event. The first briefing will probably go very well and the second will be even better. It is important that management enthusiasm and commitment do not flag just as the employees are getting used to the process.

During economic recessions there is a boost to the team briefing process because so many managements have so much bad news to convey. When you are losing money and profitability, there is a great incentive to explain to the workforce exactly how grim the situation is, so that they do not look for big pay rises. Whatever the economic climate, team briefing continues to be used widely and was found to operate in a majority of organisations featured in the 2004 WER Survey (Kersley *et al.* 2006, p. 135).

Sometimes, instead of cascading information down a management hierarchy, senior managers in larger organisations like to brief larger groups of employees about significant developments directly. Roadshows or 'interactive executive sessions' of this kind are common and are seen by managers as being almost as effective a means of passing information to employees as more conventional forms of team briefing (IRS 2005b).

Quality circles

Originating in Japanese firms, quality circles comprise small groups of employees (10–15 maximum) who meet regularly to generate ideas aimed at improving the quality of products and services and of organisational productivity. They can also be used as problem-solving groups and as a means by which employee opinion is transmitted to senior management. Some quality circles consist of staff who work together within a team or organisational function, others are cross-functional and focus on interdepartmental issues.

These sorts of practice have several objectives, such as to increase the stock of ideas within an organisation, to encourage cooperative relations at work and to legitimise change. These practices are predicated on the assumption that employees are recognised as a (if not the) major source of competitive advantage for organisations, a source whose ideas have been ignored in the past or who have been told that 'they are not paid to think' (Marchington 2001, p. 235).

Not only, therefore, are quality circles a potential source of useful ideas for improving systems and saving costs, they also give people a welcome opportunity to contribute their thoughts and experience. A general positive impact on employee attitudes should thus result.

News sheets

Another common form of employee involvement occurs through the regular publication of in-house journals or news sheets in either paper or electronic form. On one level they simply provide a means by which information concerning finances, policy and proposed change can be transmitted by managers to employees. This is a limited form of employee involvement which does little more than improve the extent to which employees are informed about what is going on elsewhere in their organisations. This will engender a perception of greater involvement and belonging, but does not directly involve employees in any type of decision making. For that to occur, the news sheet must be interactive in some way. It may, for example, be used as a means by which employees are consulted about new initiatives, or may provide a forum through which complaints and ideas are voiced.

WINDOW ON PRACTICE

One marketing company called BI increased its profitability and halved its staff turnover, in part, by introducing a range of employee involvement initiatives (IRS 2006). The early years had seen company revenues decline markedly, leading to a pay freeze and staff turnover of 60 per cent.

▶

▶   In 2004, following the appointment of a new chief executive and HR director, a wide range of measures were introduced to tackle these problems. Improving employee involvement was a priority to signal very clearly the adoption of a new mangement style, to promote a positive culture and to encourage staff to identify problems and possible solutions. The initiatives included the following:

- weekly e-mail bulletins to staff from senior managers explaining major developments
- annual letters to staff from the MD thanking them and setting out key achievements
- quarterly company meetings at which all staff are briefed about financial matters and strategy
- an intranet site updated daily with fresh information about the company's activities
- monthly meetings at which the HR director talks in confidence to 10 randomly selected employees about their concerns
- regular meetings of a 'people forum' at which representatives from each team are consulted about developments

As a result of these involvement activities many changes were made to operational processes and also to HR practices. Hours of work were made more flexible, and staff discouraged from working more hours than was necessary. A scheme was also introduced to allow people to trade some of their salary for additional holiday.

Attitude surveys

Regular surveys of employee opinion are very useful from a management point of view, particularly where there are no unions present to convey to management an honest picture of morale and commitment in the organisation. In order to be effective (that is, honest), responses must be anonymous, individuals stating only which department they work in so that interdepartmental comparisons can be made. It also makes sense to ask the same questions in the same format each time a survey is carried out, so that changes in attitude and/or responses to initiatives can be tracked over time.

The major problems with attitude surveys are associated with situations in which they reveal serious problems which are then not properly addressed. This can easily lead to cynicism and even anger on the part of the workforce. The result is a poorer employee relations climate than would have been the case had no survey taken place. It is counterproductive to involve employees if their contribution is subsequently ignored, yet this appears to happen in many of the organisations where regular surveys are conducted. IRS (2005a) found that the main reasons employers in their sample gave for carrying out employee surveys were to 'take the pulse of the organisation' and to 'demonstrate commitment to employee views'. Only a minority subsequently used the information gathered to shape decision making, even in the HR arena.

Suggestion schemes

A common system of formal bottom-up communication employed by organisations involves encouraging staff to make suggestions about how practices and processes could be improved to make them more effective, efficient or safe. Employees are often best placed to observe in detail what happens operationally on the front line because they have the greatest level of interaction on a day-to-day basis with customers, equipment and organisational procedures. Managers often only become aware of problems when their employees report them, so without such information they can have no opportunities for improving things. So it makes sense to encourage staff to put forward suggestions; and having a formal scheme enhances the chances that they will do so. IRS (2005b) describes several types of scheme and draws together from these examples some good practice points. IRS argues that employees should be recognised financially or otherwise when they make a suggestion which is taken up, that systems for submitting ideas should be as uncomplicated as possible, that feedback should be given to all who submit ideas, that past suggestions should be revisited periodically and that schemes must be regularly publicised to remind staff of their existence. IRS also found that organisations are increasingly benefitting from schemes which operate electronically. Suggestions are submitted via e-mail or a form placed on an intranet and filed systematically by an evaluator. Feedback is then given electronically and the successes of the whole scheme publicised regularly through e-mail bulletins sent to all staff.

 You will find further information on employee involvement activities in Case 8.1 on this book's companion website, **www.pearsoned.co.uk/torrington**.

Activity 8.3

Despite plenty of evidence that demonstrates how beneficial two-way information sharing can be for organisations, only a minority of non-union employers operate formal systems. Why do you think this is? What are the likely consequences? What arguments would you use to persuade a team of managers of the need to listen to the views of staff and to take them seriously?

CONSULTATION

After information sharing, the next step up the 'employee involvement escalator' is consultation. Here employees are asked either directly, or through representatives, to express views which management take into account when making decisions. Such processes fall short of negotiation or co-determination because there is no ultimate expectation of agreement if the views of staff and management diverge. In some organisations regular meetings are held to enable consultation to take place about a wide range of issues. In others consultation exercises take place irregularly and focus on specific areas such as organisational restructuring or policy changes. Consultation is generally regarded as a hallmark of good management. An employer who fails to consult properly, particularly at times of significant change, is likely to be perceived as being unduly autocratic. The result will be dissatisfaction, low levels of motivation, higher staff turnover and poorer levels of customer service. Moreover, consultation has important advantages as a means by which good ideas are brought forward and weak ones challenged.

In workplaces where unions are recognised it is usual for consultation to take place over a range of issues through permanent consultative institutions. The joint consultative committee (JCC) is the most common form, being a forum in which managers and staff representatives meet on a regular basis. In more traditional unionised organisations JCCs are kept distinct from negotiating forums – despite the fact that the membership is often the same. A clear divide is thus established between areas which are to be the subject of negotiation (typically terms and conditions of employment) and matters which are the subject of consultation such as health and safety or training. In recent years 'partnership agreements' have become more common, there has been a shift from negotiation towards consultation, the aim of these being to downplay the adversarial nature of the union-employer relationship and to widen the range of topics about which both sides can engage constructively.

JCCs are only found in 14 per cent of UK workplaces employing over ten people, but they are present in a majority of those employing over two hundred (Kersey *et al.* 2006, pp. 126–7). It is unusual for the very largest workplaces not to have some form of consultative forum which meets periodically, although in some multisite corporations formal consultation with employee representatives is restricted to the corporate level and does not take place in individual workplaces. JCCs are four times as common in union workplaces than in those where unions are not recognised (Kersley *et al.* 2006, p. 127) suggesting that they are mostly still used in parallel with collective bargaining machinery. However, some researchers (e.g. Kelly 1998) have argued that they are used in some workplaces as a substitute for collective bargaining or as a means of discouraging the development of a union presence. Managers in such workplaces believe that unions are less likely to gain support and request recognition if the employer keeps its staff informed of issues that affect them and consults with them before taking decisions. Consultative forums in non-union firms also provide a means whereby managers can put their case effectively without the presence of organised opposition.

From a management perspective, the great danger is that people come to believe that management is not genuinely interested in hearing their views or in taking them on board. Rose (2001, p. 391) refers to this approach as a 'pseudo-consultation' in which managers are really doing little more than informing employees about decisions that have already been taken. Cynicism results because there is perceived to be an attempt on the part of managers to use consultative forums merely as a means of legitimising their decisions. They can say that consultation has taken place, when in truth it has not. Pseudo-consultation typically involves assembling employees in large groups with senior managers present. The management message is then put across strongly and a short time is given for others to respond. In such situations employees have no time to give proper consideration to the proposals and are likely to feel too intimidated to articulate criticisms. The result is often worse in terms of employee morale and engagement with the changes than would have been the case had no consultation been attempted.

Even where managers genuinely intend to undertake meaningful consultation, they can very easily create an impression that it is no more than a 'pseudo' exercise. It is therefore important to avoid the approaches outlined in the above paragraph. Employees should be informed of a range of possible ways forward (not just the one favoured by management) and invited to consider them in small groups. The results of their deliberations can then be fed back to senior managers and given proper consideration. In this way the appearance of pseudo-consultation, as well as the reality, can be avoided.

KEY DEBATE: THE ROLE AND FUTURE OF TRADE UNIONS

The most significant and fundamental recent trend in UK employee relations has been the substantial decline in the number of people joining trade unions and taking part in trade union activity. In the UK membership levels reached a historic peak in 1979, when it was recorded that over 13 million people (58 per cent of all employees) were members of listed trade union organisations. In almost every year since then the number has declined as people have let their membership lapse, older members have retired and younger people have not replaced them. By 2005 membership among employees stood at 7.4 million and represented just 25.8 per cent of the working population (DTI 2007, p. 1). The rate of decline has reduced somewhat in recent years, some unions reporting modest increases in their membership levels, but trade union density (i.e. the percentage of employees in membership) has fallen every year for all but two of the past thirty years. By 2004 49 per cent of UK workplaces employing over 25 people stated that they employed no union members at all (Kersley *et al.* 2006, p. 110), while in hundreds of thousands more unions have no influence of any significance. For most employees, therefore, the norm is now to work in a non-union workplace.

The reasons for the decline in unionisation have long been debated by academic researchers and by the trade unions themselves. The issue remains the subject of considerable controversy and has by no means been settled. Despite the publication of a huge amount of evidence on the possible antecedents, no genuine consensus has been established. As a result, there is also little agreement about what the trade unions can now do, if indeed there is anything they can do, to arrest the decline in their membership levels and embark on a successful process of renewal.

Trade union leaders have tended in the past to place the blame for their decline on the actions of governments, particularly those of the conservative administrations of 1979–97 when union density fell fastest (Bryson 2007, p. 183).

During the 1980s a series of hostile employment acts passed on to the statute books which did not help the union cause and were intended to reduce their power. The only serious full-frontal legal attack on the ability of unions to recruit members came in the form of regulations which made it impossible to sustain closed shop agreements whereby membership of a specific trade union was a necessary precondition of employment in certain workplaces. This represented a major reform, affecting over five million employees who worked in closed shops (Dunn and Gennard 1984). Other legislative changes are often cited as having had a powerful, if less direct, impact. For example, a series of measures (still on the statute book) made it harder than it had been for unions to organise strikes and other forms of industrial action. Secondary action (sometimes known as sympathy action) was effectively outlawed, while secret ballots of union members and week-long cooling-off periods started to be required ahead of any action. These measures had the effect of reducing the influence of trade unions, and hence can be claimed to have made people less likely to see a point in becoming members. The same kind of effect is said to have followed the privatisation of state-run corporations and the decentralising of collective bargaining in the public sector.

As an explanation for much of the union decline, however, this argument lacks credibility when subjected to scrutiny. First and foremost, it ignores the fact that substantial declines in union membership were a feature of the employee relations scene in the vast majority of industrialised countries in the 1980s and 1990s, including those which had governments that were favourable to their cause (Vissa 2002). Indeed the decline was a good deal steeper and faster in several other major OECD countries including Australia, Austria, France, New Zealand and the USA where unions lost more than half their members in the last quarter of the twentieth century (Blanchflower 2007, p. 3). Secondly, it is notable that the decline in union membership in the UK continued after 1997 with the election of the Labour government which swiftly introduced measures designed to enhance the position of trade unions in the workplace (e.g. compulsory recognition laws and the right for all to be represented by a union official at serious grievance and disciplinary hearings).

A second commonly advanced explanation is the impact of industrial restructuring. According to this point of view unions declined simply because the types of workplace in which they have historically been recognised and have been able to attract large numbers of members have also declined in number. In their place types of workplace which have not traditionally been unionised have become much more numerous. Established industries in which union membership is the norm have declined (e.g. mining, shipbuilding, heavy manufacturing industry). The jobs that have been lost have been replaced by those in the service sector in which union membership is a great deal rarer (e.g. call centres, hospitality, tourism, retailing). The size of the average workplace has declined too, and this has had an adverse impact on the propensity of employees to join a union. There are far fewer large factories employing thousands on assembly lines than there used to be, and many more small-scale office and hi-tech manufacturing operations. Management styles in small workplaces, even when part of a much larger group, inevitably tend to be more ad hoc and personal. Grievances, disputes and requests for a pay rise are thus discussed and settled in face-to-face meetings or informally between people who know each other well, without the need to involve a trade union.

This explanation carries more weight, but there are problems with it. Metcalf (2005), for example, argues that only a small proportion of the total loss of members in the last thirty years can be ascribed to industrial restructuring. He points out that union density in manufacturing is actually relatively low (27 per cent or so), so the loss of jobs in that sector can only have had a relatively marginal effect. Moreover, we have seen considerable growth since 1997 in the number of public sector jobs – a sector in which union density is particularly high (64 per cent). He is also keen to slay the myth that a major reason for union decline is the increase in the proportion of jobs held by women. Contrary to popular perception women are just as likely to join unions as men are where a union exists and since 2003 more union members have been female than male.

In recent years a third explanation has achieved greater recognition and acceptance (*see* Metcalf 2005 and Bryson 2007). It is simply argued that people have become less interested in joining unions, see no real point in doing so and do not believe that they will gain by joining. Metcalf focuses in particular on the reduction in what is known as the 'union wage premium', by which is meant the additional amount of money earned by union members when compared with non-union members. In the 1980s this stood at 10 per cent, giving people a clear incentive to join unions and take part in their activities. The premium fell to 5 per cent by 2004 and, according to Bryson (2007, p. 197) has now dropped to 'a statistically non-significant three per cent'. More generally, Bryson (2007, p. 190) presents evidence that people do not have great faith in unions to make a real difference to their working lives. In non-union workplaces 66 per cent believe that having a union would 'make no difference', while a further 14 per cent assert that unions would make matters worse. The view is more favourable in unionised workplaces, but even here over 40 per cent of employees do not think that the presence of a union has any positive impact. These surveys do not demonstrate that people are actively hostile to unions or to the prospect of joining; rather, the picture that emerges is one of widespread indifference and disinterest. There is a sense that unions are no longer seen as being of relevance to working life as they were in the past.

Part of the explanation may lie in the development in recent years of tight labour market conditions making it relatively easy for people who are dissatisfied with their jobs to secure alternative employment. In particular, the proliferation of small workplaces in the private services sector means that alternative employment is readily available for suitably qualified people. When receptionists, shop workers, sales executives, call-centre staff or IT people are dissatisfied with their work, their workplace or their managers, they can simply look for another job and resign. They do not need to move house to find work and were unlikely, in the recent economic climate, to suffer any decline in income. Their jobs thus matter less to them than was the case in the days of the steel town, the mining village or the city suburb in which one big employer provided the lion's share of all employment. In short, there is now less need to join a union because there are other ways of resolving problems at work and relieving discontent.

Another interesting possible explanation for the disinterest in union membership could be the rise more generally in society of a greater sense of individualism. This trend is difficult to quantify or measure in any clear, objective way, but it is widely recognised by leading sociologists as being the most significant single contemporary social trend (*see* Giddens 2006 and Puttnam 2001). Could it simply be that as time passes people are generally becoming less community focused in their orientation, less concerned with notions of solidarity or collective action and more concerned with forging their own individual identities and their own economic destinies? Evidence in support of this idea is provided by the statistics on union density among different age groups (DTI 2007, p. 7). Membership is far higher among older people than among their younger colleagues, suggesting that a significant shift in attitudes has occurred across the generations. Union density among over-fifties is 35 per cent, while among 35–49-year-olds it is 34 per cent. Among the 25- to 34-year-old age group it falls to 24 per cent, while only 10 per cent of those aged 16 to 24 are members.

It is difficult to reach any firm, definitive conclusions about the causes of trade union decline. In practice it is likely that all the above explanations are to some extent 'factors' which help explain what has happened. Whatever the precise cause there is no question that the future outlook for trade unions in the present economic and political climate looks bleak. The question of whether continued trade union decline is inevitable has been considered by many and, as with most debates about the future, this one is characterised by diverse views. From a trade union perspective there are grounds for pessimism, despite years of new initiatives aimed at recruiting new members in the private sector. Not only has the proportion of younger people who choose to join unions declined dramatically, but we continue to see the fastest growth rates in industries which have not traditionally been unionised. With the exception of some jobs in the public sector, the fastest-growing professions are all ones that have very low rates of union density (e.g. technicians, consultants, software engineers, nursery nurses, hairdressers and beauticians). These factors lead Metcalf (2005) to calculate that 'long run union density will be around 20 per cent, implying a rate of 12 per cent in the private sector'.

The alternative view rests first of all on the observation that trade unions have been through periods of decay before and have later recovered. Kelly (1998) shows how union membership declined steeply during the 1920s and early 1930s, density falling as low as 22 per cent in 1933, only to recover again afterwards. His theory of 'long waves' in industrial relations leads him to conclude that workers will only ever put up with so much 'exploitation and domination' by employers, before beginning to unite to fight back. Others take heart from research which shows that many employees in the non-union sectors (including young people) are neither strongly opposed to unions, nor unwilling to countenance joining a union in the future. Fifty per cent of those asked in a poll in 2001 said that they would be either 'very likely' or 'fairly likely' to join if one were available at their workplace (Charlwood 2003, p. 52), while positive attitudes to unions appear to be just as common among non-members as they are among members (Prowse and Prowse 2006). These figures suggest that unions could create a renaissance for themselves if they could find more effective ways of organising and marketing themselves in the private services sector, and in garnering greater positive enthusiasm for their activities among an indifferent public.

SUMMARY PROPOSITIONS

8.1 Few organisations have a coherent employee relations strategy despite such strategies supporting the achievement of organisational objectives.

8.2 Strategic choices for employee relations include the extent of management control exercised and the desire to become an 'employer of choice'.

8.3 Genuine employee involvement serves to increase commitment and to improve decision making in organisations.

8.4 Information sharing is common in the UK. Team briefing, news sheets and suggestion schemes are the most common mechanisms adopted.

8.5 The use of formal consultation processes is common in larger UK organisations. Joint Consultative Committees are found in most unionised workplaces.

8.6 Trade union membership has seen substantial decline over recent decades and there is debate as to the future role of Trade unions in the UK employment relationship.

GENERAL DISCUSSION TOPICS

1   What are the main considerations when deciding whether to adopt a 'responsible autonomy' approach to management control?

2   How far do you agree with the view that information sharing barely constitutes employee involvement at all?

3   In what ways would you like to see increased or decreased employee involvement in UK organisations, and why?

FURTHER READING

Dundon, T. *et al.* (2005) 'The management of voice in non-union organisations: managers' perspectives', *Employee Relations*, Vol. 27, No. 3 pp. 307–19.
In this article Tony Dundon and his colleagues explore the views of managers about the role played by consultative fora in seven non-union organisations. They conclude that commentators have often been too hasty to dismiss these practices as inconsequential or ineffective.

Storey, J. (ed.) (2005) *Adding Value through Information and Consultation*. Basingstoke: Palgrave Macmillan/Open University.

Harley, B., Hyman, J. and Thompson, P. (2005) *Participation and Democracy at Work: Essays in Honour of Harvie Ramsay*. Basingstoke: Palgrave Macmillan.
Two books of articles by leading academic researchers which between them cover every aspect of informing, consulting and involving employees.

REFERENCES

Blanchflower, D.G. (2007) 'International patterns of union membership', *British Journal of Industrial Relations*, Vol. 45, No. 1, pp. 1–28.

Blyton, P. and Turnbull, P. (2004) *The Dynamics of Employee Relations*. Basingstoke: Palgrave Macmillan.

Bryson, A. (2007) 'New Labour, New Unions?', *British Social Attitudes Survey: The Twenty-third report*. London: National Centre for Social Research.

Charlwood, A. (2003) 'Willingness to unionize amongst non-union workers', in H. Gospel and S. Wood (eds) *Representing Workers: union recognition and membership in Britain*. London: Routledge.

DTI (2007) *Trade Union Membership 2006* (H. Grainger and M. Crowther). London: Department of Trade and Industry/National Statistics.

Dundon, T., Wilkinson, A., Marchington, M. and Ackers, P. (2005) 'The management of voice in non-union organisations: managers' perspectives', *Employee Relations*, Vol. 27, No. 3, pp. 307–19.

Dunn, S. and Gennard, J. (1984) *The Closed Shop in British Industry*. London: Macmillan.

Friedman, A. (1977) *Industry and Labour: Class struggle at work and monopoly capitalism*. London: Macmillan.

Giddens, A. (2006) *Sociology*, 5th edn. London: Polity Press.

Holden, L. (1997) 'Employee Involvement', in I. Beardwell and L. Holden (eds) *Human Resource Management*, 2nd edn. London: Pitman.

IDS (2005a) 'Suggestion Schemes', IDS Study No. 812. London: Incomes Data Services.

IDS (2005b) 'Information and Consultation Arrangements', IDS Study No. 790. London: Incomes Data Services.

IRS (2005a) 'Dialogue or monologue: is the message getting through?', *IRS Employment Review*, No. 834, October.

IRS (2005b) 'More questions than answers? Employee surveys revealed', *IRS Employment Review*, No. 820, March.

IRS (2006) 'BI bounces back with culture of employee engagement', *IRS Employment Review*, No. 839. January.

Keenoy, T. (1992) 'Constructing control', in J.F. Hartley and G.M. Stephenson (eds) *Employment Relations: The Psychology of Influence and Control at Work*. Oxford: Blackwell.

Kelly, J. (1998) *Rethinking Industrial Relations: mobilization, collectivism and long waves*. London: Routledge.

Kersley, B., Alpin, C., Forth, J., Bryson, A., Bewley, H., Dix, G. and Oxenbridge, S. (2006) *Inside the Workplace: Findings from the 2004 Workplace Employment Relations Survey*. Abingdon: Routledge.

Marchington, M. (2001) 'Employee Involvement at Work', in J. Storey (ed.) *Human Resource Management: A Critical Text*, 2nd edn. London: Thomson Learning.

Marchington, M. and Wilkinson, A. (2005) 'Direct participation and involvement', in S. Bach (ed.) *Managing Human Resources: Personnel Management in Transition*, 4th edn. Oxford: Blackwell.

Metcalf, D. (2005) 'Trade unions: resurgence or perdition? An economic analysis', in S. Fernie and D. Metcalf (eds) *Trade Unions: Resurgence or Demise?* London: Routledge.

Peccei, R., Bewley, H., Gospel, G. and Willman, P. (2005) 'Is it good to talk? Information disclosure and organisational performance in the UK', *British Journal of Industrial Relations*, Vol. 43, No. 1, pp. 11–39.

Prowse, P.J. and Prowse, J.M. (2006) 'Are non-union workers different to their union colleagues? Evidence from the public sevices', *Industrial Relations Journal*, Vol. 37, No. 3, pp. 222–41.

Puttnam, R. (2001) *Bowling Alone*. New York, Simon & Schuster.

Rose, E. (2001) *Employee Relations*. London: Financial Times/Prentice Hall.

Taylor, R. (2001) *The Future of Employment Relations*. London: ESCR Future of Work Seminar Series.

Vissa, J. (2002) 'Why fewer workers join unions in Europe: a social custom explanation of membership trends', *British Journal of Industrial Relations*, Vol. 40, No. 3, pp. 403–30.

CHAPTER 9

Employment regulation

The objectives of this chapter are to:

1 Demonstrate the great increase in the regulation of workplaces and labour markets in recent decades

2 Explain and illustrate the major principles of discrimination law and the defences that employers can deploy when accused of unlawful actions in this area

3 Introduce unfair dismissal law, setting out the grounds on which it is lawful to dismiss an employee and how an employment tribunal determines whether such dismissals are reasonable

4 Summarise the major principles underpinning the criminal and civil law aspects of health and safety law

5 Set out the major family-friendly employment rights that have been introduced in recent years

6 Debate the extent to which employment law is best characterised as a benefit or a burden from the point of view of employing organisations

In August 2006 Helen Green, an assistant company secretary employed in London won her case in the High Court. She had suffered two nervous breakdowns which were due, it was found, to Ms Green having been bullied at work by five colleagues. Over a period of four years she claimed to have been verbally abused, ignored and denigrated by them to such an extent that she became seriously ill, at one point being placed on 'suicide watch' in hospital. On her return to work following the first breakdown, she found that little had changed and she suffered a relapse a few months later. Her

▶

▶ employment was subsequently terminated when it became clear that she was unlikely to be able to return to work in the foreseeable future. Having found in favour of Ms Green, her former employers, Deutsche Bank, were ordered to pay her compensation of £35,000 for pain and suffering, £25,000 for disadvantage in the labour market, £128,000 for lost earnings and a massive £640,000 for loss of future earnings and pension. In addition to this total of £828,000 damages, the bank was ordered to pay Ms Green's legal costs, taking its total payout to around £1.5 million – and that is before taking its own costs into account.

The day after the ruling and on subsequent days the newspapers covered the story in some depth. This was partly because of the size of the award (sizeable indeed for a woman who was earning £45,000 a year prior to her breakdown), partly because Ms Green is a good-looking young woman whose photograph editors were keen to publish, and partly because the nature of the 'bullying and harassment' that she had suffered appeared to many to have amounted to no more than the kind of banter and political game-playing that goes on regularly in the majority of larger UK organisations.

Many opinion articles and letters appeared in the papers. Some supported Ms Green, arguing that it was about time employers were required to take bullying of the kind she had suffered more seriously. Many, however, were critical, in one case accusing her of acting like a 'gold-digging cry-baby' who had seriously put back the cause of women seeking careers in the financial services industry. The net result was a great deal of negative publicity for Deutsche Bank, particularly when it later emerged in newspaper interviews that the bank had sought both to undermine Ms Green's case by suggesting that her breakdowns were due to unfortunate circumstances in her earlier life (she had been sexually abused by her adoptive father) and had tried unsuccessfully to find evidence to demonstrate that her mother had suffered from a serious mental illness.

Yet in many respects it can be plausibly argued that Deutsche Bank was unlucky in this case. It had after all kept Helen Green's job open for her and had paid her a full salary for over two years before dismissing her. The bank had promoted her twice before her breakdown, had provided a counselling service and had sent her on a stress-management training programme. Moreover, some of the specific incidents that had led to Ms Green's breakdowns do appear on the face of it to be childish in nature and unlikely to offend most people to anything like the same extent. They included removing her name from a circulation list, hiding her post, blowing raspberries at her and, on one occasion, a colleague 'crossing her arms in a very dramatic way and staring at Ms Green'.

Whatever the rights and wrongs of the ruling in this case, it demonstrates very clearly how employers can easily find themselves on the wrong side of the law in their dealings with employees and how the results can be costly in terms of compensation, staff time and lost reputation.

Sources: BBC 2006, Tait 2006, Guest 2006 and *The Times* 2006.

A REGULATORY REVOLUTION

As was pointed out in Chapter 1, one of the most important contemporary developments which has shaped HR practice in organisations has been the seemingly relentless increase, year on year, of new employment regulation. Forty years ago it was commonly and correctly stated that UK workplaces and labour markets were among the most lightly regulated in the industrial world. It was a long-standing tradition for the state to make a virtue of not intervening in the relationship between employers and employees except when it was absolutely necessary to do so. As a result, with the exception of basic health and safety entitlements, laws preventing the exploitation of child workers and the basic principle that the terms of all contracts of employment were legally enforceable, there was hardly any such thing as 'employment law' in the UK. Since then the position has wholly reversed. Though still less tightly regulated than some European countries, the UK now has one of the most highly regulated labour markets in the world. The effect has been seriously to limit the extent to which managers have freedom to run their organisations as they please.

The revolution began properly in the early 1970s with the introduction of unfair dismissal law and of specialised labour law courts called Industrial Tribunals (now renamed Employment Tribunals) to hear cases brought by aggrieved individuals. These developments were followed by the establishment of the right for women to take a period of paid maternity leave following the birth of a child and to return to their jobs afterwards, a right not to be discriminated against on grounds of sex, marital status, race, ethnicity or national origin, and a right for men and women to be paid equal pay for equal work. Health and safety law was consolidated and extended so that the same principles and the same type of inspection regime now apply in all workplaces. The 1980s saw the introduction of further measures, for the most part with a European origin. Extensive rights for workers whose organisations passed from one owner or 'controlling body' to another were introduced, while the extent of health and safety law and equal pay law was substantially extended. The Thatcher and Major governments (1979–97) expressed their dislike of the Continental approach to employment regulation which they saw as placing an unnecessary and counterproductive burden on business and as a disincentive to job creation, but they did not repeal the new individual employment rights established by their predecessors in any fundamental way. Indeed, 1995 saw a substantial augmentation of employment rights with the passing of the Disability Discrimination Act. Earlier a variety of measures were introduced which remain on the statute book aimed at reducing the number of strikes and restricting the rights of employers to take account of someone's trade union membership or non-membership when making recruitment decisions.

After 1997 however, following the election of the Blair government, the pace at which new law was introduced sped up very considerably. This was partly because the government believed it was the right thing to do and it had been elected on that platform, but also importantly as a result of the introduction of a wide range of significant new employment rights at the European level. For example, we have seen major extensions of discrimination law into new areas. As a result it is now unlawful to discriminate on grounds of sexual orientation, religion or belief, age or because someone is employed on either a fixed-term or a part-time contract. We have also seen a very substantial extension of family-friendly employment rights, so that most women are now entitled to a year's maternity leave, fathers can take periods of paid paternity leave, while parents of young children and adult carers have gained the right to request flexible working. Other major new employment rights have included the National Minimum Wage, the Working Time Regulations, compulsory trade union recognition where a majority of a workforce vote for it, a degree of protection for 'whistleblowers', a raft of new data protection rights, a ban on smoking in public places (including workplaces), collective consultation rights, regulations concerning the employer's right to intercept e-mails and phone calls and a right for all to be accompanied by a union official or work colleague at serious disciplinary and grievance meetings. Moreover, further extensions are planned for the future, most notably in the area of maternity and paternity rights.

It is important to appreciate that in most instances the passing of a new Act of Parliament or of sets of regulations issued under these Acts is very often the start of a process of law making rather than the end. This is because statutes typically lack detail on how principles should be applied in different circumstances. It often takes a further five to ten years for sufficient numbers of test cases to be brought before the courts in order that definitive judgments can be made about precise points of interpretation. Hence, at the time of writing (Spring 2008), it is impossible with real certainty to give definitive advice about many important aspects of age discrimination law, despite its having been introduced in 2006. What exactly is and is not lawful, for example in the wording of recruitment advertisements, has yet to be established. In a year or two the courts will get the opportunity to make rulings about whether it is generally lawful to advertise for a 'youthful' or an 'experienced' person, but as yet they have not done so.

DISCRIMINATION LAW

Most anti-discrimination law is now covered by European treaties or directives and thus applies in all member states of the EU. Central to the achievement of this harmonisation was the issuing in 2000 of the Equal Treatment Framework Directive which required the governments of all the member states to introduce new law and, where necessary, to amend their existing laws in order to ensure that it complied with the core principles set out in the directive. As a result, across the EU there is now regulation to deter the discrimination at work on the following grounds:

- sex
- race, ethnicity and national origin
- sexual orientation
- religion or belief
- age
- disability

In each case the details differ somewhat, but the same broad principles apply. Below we illustrate these by describing sex discrimination law at some length, going on briefly to explain how and why some of the other fields of discrimination law employ slightly different approaches.

Sex discrimination law

In the UK, extensive law in the area of sex discrimination has been on the statute books since the passing in 1975 of the Sex Discrimination Act. This has been amended on several occasions since then and has been interpreted in different ways as a result of new case law, but the core tenets have always remained the same.

As matters stand there are four separate headings under which a case can be brought: direct sex discrimination, indirect sex discrimination, sexual harassment and victimisation.

Direct sex discrimination

Direct discrimination is straightforward. It occurs simply when an employer treats someone unfavourably and when sex or marital status is an important factor in this decision. In judging claims the courts use the 'but for' test, asking whether the woman would have received the same treatment as a man (or vice versa) but for her sex. Examples of direct sex discrimination include advertising for a man to do a job which could equally well be done by a woman, failing to promote a woman because she is pregnant or dismissing a married woman rather than her single colleague because she is known to have a working husband.

If an employer is found to have discriminated *directly* on grounds of sex or marital status, except in one type of situation, there is no defence. The courts cannot, therefore, take into account any mitigating circumstances or make a judgment based on the view that the employer acted reasonably. Once it has been established that direct discrimination has occurred, proceedings end with a victory for the applicant.

The one exception operates in the area of recruitment, where it is possible to argue that certain jobs have to be reserved for either women or men. For this to be acceptable the employer must convince a court that it is a job for which there is a 'genuine occupational qualification'. The main headings under which such claims are made are as follows:

- authenticity (e.g. acting or modelling jobs)
- decency (e.g. lavatory or changing room attendants)
- personal services (e.g. a counsellor engaged to work in a rape crisis centre)

Direct discrimination on grounds of pregnancy or maternity is assumed automatically to constitute unlawful sex discrimination. This means that there is no defence of reasonableness whatever the individual circumstances. It is thus unlawful to turn down a job application from a well-qualified woman who is eight months pregnant, irrespective of her intentions as regards the taking of maternity leave.

Indirect sex discrimination

Indirect discrimination is harder to grasp, not least because it can quite easily occur unintentionally. It occurs when a 'provision, criterion or practice' is set or operated which

There are, however, some significant differences in the case of age discrimination and disability discrimination law:

- In age discrimination law it is permissible to discriminate directly if the act is objectively justified. In such cases the same defence that applies in cases of indirect discrimination must be complied with if the employer is to be able to show that it has acted lawfully, namely that the act of discrimination amounted to 'a proportionate means of achieving a legitimate aim'.
- In age discrimination law (at least as of 2008) it is lawful for employers to retire staff mandatorily at the age of 65 or at a later age provided they comply with a statutory procedure. This involves writing to employees as they approach the set retirement age and offering them the chance to request an opportunity to work beyond that date.
- In disability discrimination law it is not possible to bring a claim of 'indirect discrimination' as defined above. The Disability Discrimination Act 1995 is solely concerned with direct discrimination, harassment and victimisation. This means that an individual has no basis for claiming that an organisation's policies or practices favour able-bodied people in general terms more than disabled people.
- Positive discrimination in favour of disabled people is entirely lawful. This is simply because there is no protection provided in discrimination law for able-bodied people.
- Disability discrimination law permits employers to discriminate against a disabled person, a job applicant or an existing employee who becomes seriously ill, provided they have first genuinely considered whether any 'reasonable adjustments' could be made to enable that person to work or continue working. This typically involves adjusting working practices to accommodate someone's particular needs or making alterations to premises.

Activity 9.1

The only situation in UK law when positive discrimination can occur is in the selection of parliamentary candidates. Here it is lawful for political parties to draw up 'all women shortlists' to help ensure that a reasonable number of female candidates are elected to represent safe seats. Many commentators, however, argue that unless employers are permitted generally to discriminate positively in favour of minority or under-represented groups a truly equal society will never be created (see Fredman 2002). The problem, it is argued, is that discrimination law aims to promote 'equality of opportunity' rather than 'equality of outcome', and this is not sufficient to bring about radical social change. Some go as far as to argue that employers should be required to discriminate positively in certain circumstances.

What is your view about positive discrimination? Should the law be changed or should it remain as it is? Justify your answer.

Remedies

Victorious claimants in discrimination cases are awarded damages of two kinds. First they can claim from the employer compensation for any financial losses they have sustained as a result of the unlawful discrimination they have suffered. This may be very limited, but where someone has resigned or been dismissed there can be extensive sums awarded to compensate for lost earnings and potential future losses. The second category is 'injury to feelings'. The sums awarded here range from £500 for one-off incidents that cause very limited distress (e.g. being turned down for a job at the shortlisting stage when the individual had little expectation of being successful at interview) up to £25,000 where someone has, for example, been subjected to a lengthy campaign of racial harassment.

Equal pay law

The Equal Pay Act 1970 was the first legislation promoting equality at work between men and women. It came into force in December 1975 and was subsequently amended by the Equal Pay (Amendment) Regulations 1983. The Act is solely concerned with eliminating unjustifiable differences in the treatment of men and of women in terms of their rates of pay and other conditions of employment. It is thus the vehicle that is used to bring a case to tribunal when there is inequality between a man's contract of employment and that of a woman. In practice the majority of cases are brought by women and concern discriminatory rates of payment, although there have been some important cases focusing on aspects of pension provision brought by men. The Act, as amended in 1983, specifies three types of claim that can be brought. These effectively define the circumstances in which pay and other conditions between men and women should be equal:

1 **Like work**: where a woman and a man are doing work which is the same or broadly similar – for example where a woman assembly worker sits next to a male assembly worker, carrying out the same range of duties.
2 **Work rated as equivalent**: where a man and a woman are carrying out work which, while of a different nature, has been rated as equivalent under a job evaluation scheme.
3 **Work of equal value**: where a man and a woman are performing different tasks but where it can be shown that the two jobs are equal in terms of their demands, for example in terms of skill, effort and type of decision making.

Unlike sex discrimination law where the 'but for' test permits the use of hypothetical comparators, in order to bring a case under the Equal Pay Act the claimant must be able to point to a comparator of the opposite gender with whom he or she wishes to be compared. The comparator must be employed by the same employer and at an establishment covered by the same terms and conditions. When an equal value claim is brought which an employment tribunal considers to be well founded, an 'independent expert' may be appointed to carry out a job evaluation exercise in order to establish whether or not the two jobs being compared are equal in terms of the demands they make.

Employers can employ two defences when faced with a claim under the Equal Pay Act. First, they can seek to show that a job evaluation exercise has been carried out which indicates that the two jobs are not like, rated as equivalent or of equal value. To succeed the job evaluation scheme in use must be both analytical and free of sex bias. Secondly, the employer can claim that the difference in pay is justified by 'a genuine material factor not of sex'. For this to succeed, the employer has to convince the court that there is a good business reason for the unequal treatment and that there has thus been no sex discrimination. Examples of genuine material factors that have proved acceptable to the courts are as follows:

- different qualifications (e.g. where a man has a degree and a woman does not)
- performance (e.g. where a man is paid a higher rate than a woman because he works faster or has received a higher appraisal rating)
- seniority (where the man is paid more because he has been employed for several years longer than the woman)
- regional allowances (where a man is paid a London weighting, taking his pay to a higher rate than that of a woman performing the same job in the Manchester branch)

The courts have ruled that differences in pay explained by the fact that the man and woman concerned are in separate bargaining groups, by the fact that they asked for different salaries on appointment or because of an administrative error are not acceptable genuine material factor defences. It is possible to argue that a difference in pay is explained by market forces, but evidence has to be produced to satisfy the court that going rates for the types of work concerned are genuinely different and that it is therefore genuinely necessary to pay the comparator at a higher rate.

When a claimant wins an equal pay claim he or she is entitled to have their pay equalised with that of their chosen comparator and is also paid compensatory back-pay for a period of up to six years.

UNFAIR DISMISSAL LAW

Unlike discrimination law, unfair dismissal law is covered by UK legislation and is not an area of regulation that the EU has to date sought to harmonise across member states. This means that as in most UK-based employment law the key rights only apply to 'employees' and not to all 'workers'. This distinction is important because the employee category only includes people who are accepted by an employment tribunal to be working under 'a contract of service'. In practice it means that significant and growing groups such as agency workers, casual workers and homeworkers are often excluded from bringing cases on the grounds that their employment status is that of an independent contractor working under a 'contract for services' rather than that of an employee. Unfair dismissal law is further restricted in most situations to people who have completed a year's continuous service as an employee in the same employment at the time that their dismissal takes effect. This means that employers are usually acting within the law if they dismiss someone who has yet to complete a year's service, even if they carry out the dismissal without following a fair or customary procedure or for an unfair reason.

Indeed, when someone is dismissed with less than a year's service they are not entitled in law to be given an explanation. The one-year restriction on qualification applies except where the reason for the dismissal is one of those listed below which are classed as 'automatically unfair' or 'inadmissible'. A further requirement is that the claim form is lodged at the tribunal office before three months have elapsed from the date of dismissal. Unless there are circumstances justifying the failure to submit a claim before the deadline, claims received after three months are ruled out of time.

When faced with a claim of unfair dismissal, and where it is not disputed that a dismissal took place, an employment tribunal asks two separate questions:

- Was the reason for the dismissal one which is classed by the law as legitimate?
- Did the employer act reasonably in carrying out the dismissal?

Where the answer to the first question is 'No', there is no need to ask the second because the dismissed employee will already have won his or her case. Interestingly the burden of proof shifts as the tribunal moves from considering the first to the second question. It is for the employer to satisfy the tribunal that it dismissed the employee for a legitimate reason. The burden of proof then becomes neutral when the question of reasonableness is addressed.

Automatically unfair reasons

Certain reasons for dismissal are declared in law to be inadmissible or automatically unfair. Where a tribunal finds that one of these was the principal reason for the dismissal, it finds in favour of the claimant (i.e. the ex-employee) whatever the circumstances of the case. In practice, therefore, there is no defence that an employer can make to explain its actions that will be acceptable to the tribunal. The list of automatically unfair reasons for dismissal has grown steadily in recent years as new employment rights have come on to the statute book:

- dismissal for a reason relating to pregnancy or maternity
- dismissal for a health and safety reason (e.g. refusing to work in unsafe conditions)
- dismissal because of a spent conviction
- dismissal for refusing to work on a Sunday (retail and betting workers only)
- dismissal for a trade union reason
- dismissal for taking official industrial action (during the first twelve weeks of the action)
- dismissal in contravention of the part-time workers or fixed-term employees regulations
- dismissal for undertaking duties as an occupational pension fund trustee, employee representative, member of a European Works Council or in connection with jury service
- dismissal for asserting a statutory right
- dismissal for a reason connected with the transfer of an undertaking (i.e. when a business or part of a business changes hands or merges with another organisation) in the absence of a valid economic, technical or organisational reason

Potentially fair reasons

From an employer's perspective it is important to be able to satisfy the tribunal that the true reason for the dismissal was one of those reasons classed as potentially fair in unfair dismissal law. Only once this has been achieved can the second question (the issue of reasonableness) be addressed. The potentially fair grounds for dismissal are as follows:

- lack of capability or qualifications: if an employee lacks the skill, aptitude or physical health to carry out the job, then there is a potentially fair ground for dismissal
- misconduct: this category covers the range of behaviours that we examine in considering the grievance and discipline processes: disobedience, absence, insubordination and criminal acts. It can also include taking industrial action
- redundancy: where an employee's job ceases to exist, it is potentially fair to dismiss the employee for redundancy
- statutory bar: when employees cannot continue to discharge their duties without breaking the law, they can be fairly dismissed. Most cases of this kind follow disqualification of drivers following convictions for speeding, drunk or dangerous driving. Other common cases involve foreign nationals whose work permits have been terminated
- some other substantial reason: this most intangible category is introduced in order to cater for genuinely fair dismissals for reasons so diverse that they could not realistically be listed. Examples have been security of commercial information (where an employee's husband set up a rival company) or employee refusal to accept altered working conditions
- dismissals arising from official industrial action after twelve weeks have passed
- dismissals that occur on the transfer of an undertaking where a valid ETO (economic, technological or organisational) reason applies
- mandatory retirements which follow the completion of the procedures set out in the Employment Equality (Age) Regulations 2006 (*see* above)

Determining reasonableness

Having decided that potentially fair grounds for the dismissal exist, the tribunal then proceeds to consider whether the dismissal is fair in the circumstances. The test used by the tribunal in reaching decisions about the fairness of a dismissal is that of the reasonable employer. Tribunal members are not required to judge cases on the basis of what they would have done in the circumstances or what the best employers would have done. Instead they have to ask themselves whether what the employer did in the circumstances of the time fell within a possible band of reasonable responses. In practice this means that the employer wins the case if it can show that the decision to dismiss was one that a reasonable employer *might* conceivably have taken.

In assessing reasonableness tribunals always take a particular interest in the procedure that was used. They are also keen to satisfy themselves that the employer has acted broadly consistently in its treatment of different employees and that it has taken into account any mitigating circumstances that might have explained a deterioration in an employee's conduct or performance. In addition, they are required to have regard to the size and resources of the employer concerned. Higher standards are thus expected of a large PLC with a well-staffed HR department than of a small owner-managed business employing a handful of people. The former, for example, might be expected to give two or three warnings and additional training before dismissing someone on grounds of incapability. One simple warning might suffice in a small business which relied heavily on an acceptable level of performance from the individual concerned. Another factor that is taken into consideration is consistency. If one person is dismissed and another retained when they are both guilty of the same act of misconduct or are both equally poor performers, the dismissal will usually be unfair in law.

The most common reason for dismissal is misconduct. Here the law makes an important distinction between 'gross misconduct' and 'ordinary misconduct', there being different expectations about how the 'reasonable' employer handles each category.

- **Gross misconduct** occurs when an employee commits an offence which is sufficiently serious to justify summary dismissal. To qualify, the employee must have acted in such a way as to have breached their contract and must have known (or ought to have known) at the time they committed the act that it might be classed as 'gross misconduct'. In practice this means that their actions must be 'intolerable' for any reasonable employer and, in most cases, in breach of well-established and clearly communicated workplace rules.
- **Ordinary misconduct**, by contrast, involves lesser transgressions, such as minor breaches of rules and relatively insignificant acts of disobedience, insubordination, lateness, forgetfulness or rudeness. In such cases the employer is deemed by the courts to be acting unreasonably if it dismisses as a result of a first offence. The dismissal would only be fair if, having been formally warned at least once, the employee failed to improve his/her conduct.

Employers have a wide degree of discretion when it comes to deciding what exactly does and does not constitute gross misconduct, and this will vary from workplace to workplace. For example, a distinction can be made between uttering an obscene swear word in front of colleagues (ordinary misconduct) and swearing obscenely to a customer (gross misconduct).

Another key principle in misconduct cases concerns procedure. Whether the individual is dismissed summarily for gross misconduct or after a number of warnings for ordinary misconduct, the tribunals look to see if a reasonable procedure has been used. The main questions that an employment tribunal asks when faced with such cases are as follows:

- Was the accusation thoroughly, promptly and properly investigated by managers before the decision was made to dismiss or to issue a formal warning?
- Was a formal hearing held at which the accused employee was given the opportunity to state their case and challenge evidence brought forward by managers?
- Was the employee concerned permitted to be represented at the hearing by a colleague or trade union representative?
- Was the employee treated consistently when compared with other employees who had committed similar acts of misconduct in the past?

Only if the answers to all these questions is 'Yes' will a tribunal find a dismissal fair. They do not, however, expect employers to adhere to very high standards of evidence gathering such as those employed by the police in criminal investigations. Here, as throughout employment law, the requirement is for the employer to act reasonably in all the circumstances, conforming to the principles of natural justice and doing what it thought to be right at the time, given the available facts.

WINDOW ON PRACTICE

In the past fifteen years employment tribunals have had to come to grips with a new type of dismissal case, situations in which people are dismissed for downloading and storing pornographic images from the Internet. Tribunals have had to consider whether or not such actions constitute gross misconduct (leading to summary dismissal without notice), or whether they should be considered as ordinary misconduct, in which case summary dismissal for a first offence would be regarded as being unfair.

Cases have been decided in different ways depending on the clarity of established rules and procedural matters. In *Parr* v. *Derwentside District Council* (1998), Mr Parr was summarily dismissed having been caught by his employers accessing pornography from his computer while at work. He claimed that he had visited the site concerned by accident, had got himself stuck in it and had subsequently 'revisited it only because he was disturbed by the prospect that entry could easily be made by children'. His claim for unfair dismissal failed because the employers had used a fair procedure and because they were able to show that Mr Parr had broken established codes of conduct.

By contrast, in *Dunn* v. *IBM UK Ltd* (1998), a summary dismissal occurring in similar circumstances was found to fall outside the 'band of reasonable responses'. In this case the employers were found not to have investigated the matter properly and not to have convened a fair disciplinary hearing, the whole matter having been handled far too hastily. Moreover, there was no company policy on Internet usage for Mr Dunn to have broken and he was unaware that he had done anything that would be construed as gross misconduct. He won his case, but had his compensation reduced by 50 per cent on the grounds that he was partly responsible for his own dismissal.

In a third case, *Humphries* v. *VH Barnett & Co* (1998), a tribunal stated that in normal circumstances the act of accessing pornography from the Internet while at work should not be construed as gross misconduct unless such a policy was made clear to employees and established as a workplace rule. However, in this case, the tribunal decided that the pictures downloaded were so obscene that Mr Humphries could be legitimately treated as having committed an act of gross misconduct.

Source: IDS (1999) 'Downloading pornography', *IDS Brief*, No. 637, May.

Poor performance is the second most common reason for dismissing staff. The law allows employers to determine for themselves what constitutes an acceptable level of performance in a job, provided of course that a consistent approach to all employees is followed. However, such dismissals are only considered to be reasonable (and hence fair in law) if the employee concerned has both been formally warned about their poor performance at least once and given a reasonable opportunity to improve. Formality in this context means that a formal hearing has been held at which the employee has been entitled to be represented and after which there has been a right of appeal to a more senior manager.

The requirement on employers to warn an employee formally that their performance is unsatisfactory, and the subsequent requirement to give the employee concerned support during a reasonable period in which they have an opportunity to improve, means that dismissals on grounds of poor performance can take several weeks or months to carry through. Moreover, during this time relationships can become very strained because formal action has been taken and a formal warning given. For these reasons managers often seek to avoid dismissing in line with the expectations of the law, instead seeking to dress up poor performance dismissals as redundancies or cases of gross misconduct. However, employment tribunals are very aware of this tendency and always find dismissals that occur in such circumstances to be unfair.

Remedies

When a claimant wins an unfair dismissal case they can only claim compensation for financial losses that have been sustained directly as a result of the dismissal. There is a requirement that claimants demonstrate that they have sought to mitigate their losses by applying for other jobs and by claiming any state benefits for which they qualify. The basic award is calculated according to age, salary and length of service, but the wage aspect is capped so awards are rarely more than a few thousand pounds. The further compensatory award takes account of lost earnings, potential lost future earnings and pension entitlements. It too is capped at a level set by the government (£63,000 in 2008). Successful claimants can also ask to be reinstated in their jobs or re-engaged by the employer who dismissed them, but such remedies are rarely sought and even more rarely granted in practice.

Activity 9.2

In what circumstances do you think a dismissed employee might welcome reinstatement or re-engagement, and in what circumstances might the employer welcome it?

HEALTH AND SAFETY LAW

Health and safety law can be neatly divided into two halves, representing its criminal and civil spheres. The first is based in statute and is policed both by the Health and Safety Executive and by local authority inspectorates. The second relies on the common law and allows individuals who have suffered injury as a result of their work to seek damages against their employers. The former is intended to be preventative, while the latter aims to compensate individuals who become ill as a result of their work.

Criminal law

Health and safety inspectors potentially wield a great deal of power, but their approach is to give advice and to issue warnings except where they judge that there is a high risk of personal injury. They visit premises without giving notice beforehand in order to inspect equipment and make sure that the appropriate monitoring procedures are in place. They have a general right to enter premises, to collect whatever information they require and to remove samples or pieces of equipment for analysis. Where they are unhappy with what they find, inspectors issue *improvement notices* setting out recommended improvements and requiring these to be put in place by a set date. In the case of more serious lapses, where substantial risk to health is identified, the inspectors issue *prohibition notices* which prevent employers from using particular pieces of equipment until better safety arrangements are established. Breach of one of these statutory notices is a criminal offence, as is giving false information to an inspector. Over a thousand prosecutions are brought each year for non-compliance with a Health and Safety Executive Order, leading to fines of up to £20,000.

Prosecutions are also brought after injuries have been sustained where it can be shown that management knew of risks and had not acted to deal with them. Where fatalities result and an employer is found guilty of committing corporate manslaughter, fines of several hundred thousand pounds are levied. Moreover, in some cases custodial sentences have been given to controlling directors held to have been individually liable.

The Health and Safety at Work etc. Act 1974 is the source of most health and safety law in the UK, under which more detailed sets of regulations are periodically issued. Its main purposes are as follows:

- to secure the health, safety and welfare of people at work
- to protect the public from risks arising from workplace activities
- to control the use and storage of dangerous substances
- to control potentially dangerous environmental emissions

The Act places all employers under a general duty 'to ensure, as far as is reasonably practicable, the health, safety and welfare at work' of all workers. In addition there are specific requirements to maintain plant and equipment, to provide safe systems of working, to provide a safe and healthy working environment, to consult with trade union safety representatives, to maintain an accident reporting book and to post on a noticeboard a copy of the main provisions contained in the 1974 Act.

Since 1974 numerous sets of regulations have been issued, many of a very specialised nature, to add to the more general principles established in the Health and Safety at Work

Act. The most significant have been the following, most of which originate at the European level:

- The First Aid Regulations 1981 place employers under a general duty to provide adequate first aid equipment and facilities.
- The Control of Substances Hazardous to Health (COSHH) Regulations 1988 concern the safe storage and usage of potentially dangerous substances.
- The Management of Health and Safety at Work Regulations 1992 place a variety of duties on employers. Examples include regulations on the safe lifting of heavy loads, the prolonged use of video display units (VDUs) and the particular health and safety needs of pregnant workers.
- The Health and Safety (Consultation with Employees) Regulations 1996 require employers to consult collectively with their employees about health and safety matters irrespective of whether a trade union is recognised.
- The Working Time Regulations 1998 limit the working week to 48 hours in most lines of work, but permit employers to request that employees sign opt-out agreements so that they can be asked to work for longer. A right to twenty-eight days' paid holiday each year also forms part of the regulations.
- The Health Act 2006 bans smoking in public spaces, including most workplaces and company vehicles in England. Equivalent legislation has been passed by the Scottish parliament and the Welsh and Northern Irish assemblies.

Activity 9.3

1 Devise a health and safety policy for your organisation or one with which you are familiar. Include information about:

- general policy on health and safety
- specific hazards and how they are to be dealt with
- management responsibility for safety
- how the policy is to be implemented

Or:

2 Obtain the Health and Safety Policy from any organisation and assess the policy in the light of these four points.

Civil law

While distinct in origin and nature from the criminal sanctions, civil cases relating to health and safety are often brought alongside criminal proceedings in connection with the same incident. When someone is seriously injured or suffers ill health as a direct result of their work the health and safety authorities will bring a criminal prosecution,

(Taylor and Emir 2006, p. 5). Finally, to this additional cost burden we can plausibly add lost opportunity costs. Although these are impossible to quantify at all accurately, it is reasonable to ask to what extent benefits could accrue if managers were free to devote the time they spend dealing with employment law matters on value-adding activities instead.

A further argument contends that the effect of employment law, even if it is not the intention of legislators, is to harm the career interests of those groups who are afforded the most legal protection (e.g. ethnic minorities, disabled people and mothers with dependent children). This occurs because it makes organisations less likely to employ them. There is less evidence to back this argument up, but some surveys carried out among owners and managers running small businesses suggest that there is a real practical impact. The Institute of Directors, for example, reported that 45 per cent of their members believe recent extensions to maternity rights have created 'a disincentive to hiring women of prime child-bearing age' (Lea 2001, p. 56), while US-based economists such as Richard Epstein (2002, p. 8) have long argued that in practice 'equal opportunity', when imposed by government, 'leads to less opportunity'.

The main arguments in favour of employment law relate to social justice and the need to reduce the extent to which people suffer unreasonably at the hands of prejudiced, negligent or bullying managers abusing the power their position gives them. It is necessary to protect employees via the law, just as it is necessary to protect other vulnerable groups from injustice. Such arguments are strong, straightforward and accepted by most, although disagreements will always persist about where the balance should lie between protecting the interests of employees and those of employers. However, there are also influential economic arguments in favour of extensive employment protection legislation. The implication here is that regulation of the employment relationship does not just benefit employees, but that organisations and the economy generally have also stood to gain from its extension in recent decades.

There are a number of distinct strands that make up the economic argument in favour of employment law. The first has been used on many occasions by ministers introducing new legislation in the face of business opposition. It was very effectively articulated in the government white paper entitled 'Fairness at Work' (DTI 1998) where it is simply argued that the most productive workplaces, particularly in the service sector which now accounts for the vast majority of UK jobs, are those in which people are managed effectively and fairly. In requiring managers to treat their staff with dignity, fairness and in an equitable manner, employment regulation helps to raise employment standards. In turn this has positive benefits for businesses in terms of higher levels of motivation and productivity, lower levels of staff turnover and a healthy, high-trust employee relations climate. Employment law, it is argued, should hold no fears whatever for good employers. All it aims to do is to bring all employment practice up to that same broad standard.

The second strand of the argument relates directly to the issue of growing skills shortages which we discussed in Chapter 3. The starting point here is the view that the inability of many employers to recruit and retain people with the skills and experience that they need constitutes a significant national economic problem, which holds back economic growth (*see* Frogner 2002). It follows that the amelioration of skills shortages should properly be a significant public policy objective. Improving employment standards by forcing employers to treat their employees well helps to achieve this because it makes work more attractive than it otherwise would be. It follows that more people with a choice about whether to work or not choose to do so in a world of regulated employment than would if the employment relationships were unregulated. The result is a higher economic participation rate as women with young children, people with long-term ill health issues and those who could afford to retire if they wanted to put their skills, at least for part of the time, at the disposal of the economy. High standards also help to attract into the country highly skilled migrant workers from overseas who might otherwise choose to work elsewhere.

The final, third strand of the argument concerns the UK economy's competitive position internationally. It is argued that highly developed economies such as the UK's cannot sustain themselves in the face of competition from developing and newly industrialised countries by competing on the basis of cost. There is no future for such a business strategy because wage levels in China, India and elsewhere are invariably much lower than those in the UK and, as a result, the goods and services that they produce will always be far cheaper. It follows that the UK needs clearly to position itself as a high-wage, knowledge-based economy which produces innovative hi-tech goods and provides upmarket services. In order to achieve this organisations need to be encouraged to work in partnership with their employees and, particularly, to invest in their training. There is little economic incentive for employers to devote resources to extensive employee development programmes in environments characterised by high staff turnover and low-trust employment relationships. Government thus needs to intervene to push employers in this direction and employment law is one of several public policy tools that are used to achieve this. The long-term aim is thus to help sustain economic growth in a rapidly changing and highly competitive business environment.

The most persuasive conclusion to reach is that employment regulation is both a burden and a benefit to UK employers, although it is of less benefit to and a much greater burden for smaller businesses without the expertise and resources to ensure that they are managing within its requirements. It is a burden because it adds substantial costs and because it limits the freedom managers have to run their businesses as they might wish. However, it is also a benefit because it helps to raise employment standards throughout the country making work more attractive to skilled migrants and to people who have skills and experience that they might otherwise choose not to use in the employment context. In the process it contributes to reduced staff turnover, helps to encourage later retirement and helps to create the conditions in which superior individual performance is more likely and, crucially, in which low-trust, adversarial industrial relations are less likely to emerge.

Activity 9.4

Where do you stand in this debate about employment legislation? Does it serve to underpin economic prosperity or reduce international competitiveness? What further measures would you welcome and which would you oppose?

SUMMARY PROPOSITIONS

9.1 In the space of a single generation UK workplaces have gone from being among the least regulated in the world to being among the most highly regulated.

9.2 Discrimination law has grown rapidly in recent years, extending to new grounds such as age, sexual orientation and religion or belief. Equal pay law requires men and women to be paid the same wage for doing work which is the same or which can be shown to be of equal value unless the employer can justify a difference on grounds other than sex.

9.3 The main grounds on which an employee can be dismissed without the likelihood of an unfair dismissal claim are lack of capability, misconduct, redundancy, statutory bar, some other substantial reason and fair mandatory retirement. If an employee is dismissed on one of the above grounds, the dismissal must be procedurally acceptable and fair in the circumstances.

9.4 The legal framework for health and safety includes both the criminal and civil law. The former is policed by health and safety inspectors; the latter provides a vehicle for those who suffer illness or injury as a result of their work to claim damages.

9.5 Family-friendly employment law has been very much extended in recent years and will be further extended in the future. It aims to help people better combine their work and domestic responsibilities.

9.6 Employment regulation increases the cost burden for employers and reduces their freedom of action, but in helping to ensure that reasonably high minimum standards are maintained in employee relations it also brings economic advantages to organisations.

GENERAL DISCUSSION TOPICS

1 How far do you think that UK discrimination law is effective in achieving its aims? What could be done to make it more effective?

2 In some countries a dismissal cannot be made until *after* a tribunal hearing, so that its 'fairness' is decided before it takes effect. What do you see as the benefits and drawbacks of that system?

FURTHER READING

An excellent book which analyses UK employment regulation in the round, explaining its purpose and debating its strengths and weaknesses from a variety of perspectives is *Perspectives on Labour Law* by A.C.L. Davies.

Sandra Fredman has written extensively on discrimination law. The key debates are discussed concisely and effectively in her book entitled *Discrimination Law*.

There are several good textbooks on employment law. Those aimed primarily at management students rather than lawyers include those written by Janice Nairns (2007), David Lewis and Malcolm Sargeant (2007) and Stephen Taylor and Astra Emir (2009).

REFERENCES

BBC (2006) 'Bullied City worker wins £800,000', BBC News website, 1 August.

CBI (2000) *Cutting through red tape: the impact of employment legislation*. London: Confederation of British Industry.

CIPD (2002) *Employment Law: Survey Report*. London: Chartered Institute of Personnel and Development.

Davies, A.C.L. (2004) *Perspectives on Labour Law*. Cambridge: Cambridge University Press.

DTI (1998) *Fairness at Work*, White Paper, May 1998, CM. 3968. London: Department of Trade and Industry.

Epstein, R. (2002) *Equal Opportunity or More Opportunity? The Good Thing About Discrimination*. London: Civitas.

ETS (2007) *Annual Report 2006–7*. London: Employment Tribunal Service.

Fredman, S. (2002) *Discrimination Law*. Oxford: Oxford University Press.

Frogner, M.L. (2002) 'Skills Shortages', *Labour Market Trends*, January.

Guest, K. (2006) 'Why I deserve every penny of the £800,000, by the bullied City exec', *The Independent*, 6 August.

IDS (1999) 'Downloading pornography', *IDS Brief*, No. 637, May. London: Incomes Data Services.

Lea, R. (2001) *The Work-Life Balance and all that: The re-regulation of the labour market*. London: Institute of Directors.

Lewis, D. and Sargeant, M. (2007) *Essentials of Employment Law*, 9th edn. London: Chartered Institute of Personnel and Development.

Nairns, J. (2007) *Employment Law for Business Students*, 3rd edn. London: Longman.

Tait, N. (2006) 'Courts take bullying by the horns', *Financial Times*, 6 August.

Taylor, S. and Emir, A. (2009) *Employment Law: An Introduction*. Oxford: Oxford University Press.

The Times (2006) Letters page, 8 August.

CHAPTER 10

Diversity in employment

The objectives of this chapter are to:

1   Define what we mean by diversity in employment

2   Explain the importance of diversity in employment

3   Explore the implications of diversity in employment for line managers

4   Explain how organisations can become more diverse

5   Debate the value of the management of diversity approach and the equal opportunities approach in achieving successful diversity in employment

The need to achieve equality, and latterly diversity, in employment has been on the business agenda since the initial legislation in 1975 which was designed to enable everyone in society to have the same chance of success as the initially dominant group in employment (white males).
So why:

- are only 10 per cent of FTSE directors, 20 per cent of MPs and 26 per cent of top civil servants women? (EOC 2007)
- is the employment rate for ethnic minorities only 59 per cent compared with 75 per cent for white people? (Smethurst 2007)
- are people with a disability 29 per cent less likely to be employed than able-bodied people? (Phillips 2007a)
- have women not yet achieved equal pay? (*see*, for example, Dobbs 2007)
- are people with a disability under-represented in professional and managerial jobs? (Skills and Enterprise Network 2000)

The Chair of the Equalities Review Panel, Trevor Phillips, said, 'It will take many years to remove the remaining barriers to equality. In some cases, unless we accelerate progress, it is unlikely that disadvantage will ever be overcome' (Phillips 2007b).

At the same time white working class males now report feeling ignored, neglected and disparaged by society according to a Radio 4 programme in March 2008. Some listeners who called openly put down the efforts that organisations make to become more diverse, for example one claimed that employers are only interested in an applicant's attitudes to diversity and not in the skills needed to do the job. Commentators spoke of the natural loyalty that white working class males have to their country which is part of their identity. This attitude was praised as a strength in the earlier twentieth century, yet callers said displaying such attitudes now labelled them as racist and discriminatory.

To achieve a successfully diverse workforce the challenge remains to further improve the opportunities for minority groups (however defined) whilst at the same time continuing to support and value the dominant group so they do not feel discounted. A tall order!

In today's world of globalisation and demographic change the workforce is becoming increasingly diverse and it is more important than ever for organisations to develop and manage equal opportunity and diversity strategies that attract and retain talent to improve workforce performance and so promote their competitive position.

WHAT DO WE MEAN BY DIVERSITY IN EMPLOYMENT?

For many years the achievement of diversity has been bandied about in boardrooms, offices, shops and factory floors, but what does it really entail? Managing diversity is the more recent term often adopted by organisations that seek to achieve what might previously have been termed equality of opportunity in employment. Whilst equality of opportunity focuses on disadvantaged groups in employment (such as women, ethnic minorities, older people, people with a disability and so on) with the aim of ensuring they are not unfairly discriminated against, diversity aims to improve the position of these groups via a broader approach which is inclusive of all employees. The CIPD (2005, p. 2) suggests the central theme of diversity as:

> valuing everyone as individuals – as employees, customers, clients and extending diversity beyond what is legislated about to looking at what's positively valued.

The focus is on valuing, not just managing to cope with difference and aiming to be fair to all employees, and it suggests a more proactive approach than equal opportunities. In focusing on each individual and what he or she has to offer, the emphasis on 'needy' groups, such as black and ethnic minority groups and people with a disability, is diminished, and all forms of support which the organisation provides such as extra training, flexible hours and so on are available to everyone and not just those groups which have been labelled as 'disadvantaged'. It also suggests the business benefits of a rich and varied people resource.

In the key debate at the end of this chapter we critically assess the comparative advantages and disadvantages of and difference between these two approaches. For now we focus on encouraging and managing *diversity* in employment, treating this, as do most organisations, as a generic approach which includes both the more proactive approach of enabling all individuals within the organisation to make the most of the potential they have to offer, as well as aspects of the original equal opportunities approach.

In order to do this effectively, organisations not only need to comply with legislation and produce policies which support equality and diversity, but also need constantly to examine their practices as discrimination can be very subtle and is often part of the culture of an organisation (sometimes called institutional discrimination) so that managers and other employees are unaware that they are discriminating. For example holding social/networking events in a pub excludes Muslims which may not only lead to their discomfort but have disadvantages for career progression. Culture is notoriously difficult to change and yet this is essential successfully to achieve diversity.

WINDOW ON PRACTICE

Gender segregation at Deloitte Touche

McCracken (2000) reports how Deloitte Touche were good at recruiting women and felt they had achieved equal opportunities, but they were finding that women were leaving at a much higher rate than men and few women were made partners. On investigating the situation they found that women were leaving, not for domestic reasons as they had anticipated, but due to the male-dominated culture. Men were assigned high-visibility assignments in manufacturing, financial services, acquisitions and mergers, whereas women were offered non-profit organisations, healthcare and retail. They also found that women were genuinely assessed on their performance levels, but that men were also assessed on their potential, which women missed out on.

Deloitte Touche made efforts to change these practical features of working life and also tried to promote work-life balance. Having identified the real problems in achieving equality they found that more women partners were coming through and that money was being saved as they were losing fewer talented women.

Source: Summarised from: D. McCracken (2000) 'Winning the talent war for women: sometimes it takes a revolution', *Harvard Business Review*, November–December, pp. 159–65.

WHY IS DIVERSITY IN EMPLOYMENT IMPORTANT?

The successful management of diversity is claimed to have clear business benefits and to make an organisation more competitive. On a simple level if the employer invests in ensuring that all employees are valued and given the opportunities to develop their potential, they are enabled to make their maximum contribution. The CIPD (2006a) suggests that business benefits can be summed up in three broad statements; that diversity: enhances customer relations and market share; enhances employee relations and reduces labour costs; and improves workforce quality and performance in terms of diverse skills, creativity, problem solving and flexibility.

For example, a company that discriminates, directly or indirectly, against older or disabled people, women, ethnic minorities, people with different sexual orientations or other minority groups will be curtailing the potential of available talent, and employers are not well known for their complaints about the surplus of talent. The financial benefits of retaining staff who might otherwise leave due to lack of career development or due to the desire to combine a career with family are stressed, as is the image of the organisation as a 'good' employer and hence its attractiveness to all members of society as its customers. A relationship between a positive diversity climate and job satisfaction and commitment to the organisation has also been found (Hicks-Clarke and Iles 2000). Although the impact on performance is more difficult to assess, it is reasonable to assume that more satisfied and committed employees will lead to reduced absence and turnover levels. In addition, the value of different employee perspectives and different types of contribution is seen as providing added value to the organisation, particularly when organisational members increasingly reflect the diverse customer base of the organisation. This provides a way in which organisations can better understand, and therefore meet, their customer needs.

IMPLICATIONS FOR LINE MANAGERS

Equal opportunities was initially seen as the remit of the HR department, but managing diversity increasingly centres on the role of the line manager and achieving diversity in employment brings a variety of challenges for line managers. One major challenge concerns personal self-awareness, a second is about developing this in members of their team and a third is about the interplay between diversity and team performance. Before you read on try Activity 10.1.

Activity 10.1

A leading supermarket advertised and interviewed for the job of shelf-stacker on the night shift. The job involved minor warehousing duties and the shift system included either a Friday or Saturday night, or sometimes both, every week.

What potentially false assumptions might be made about the following candidates and how could you argue against those assumptions?

- An Asian female of 29 years who is currently working in a variety of roles in the family business which comprises three large corner shops. She still lives at home but wants to widen her groceries/retail experience.

- A single white 26-year-old male who has a well-established job record including warehousing and forklift truck driving on a night shift for three years. This candidate is unemployed as he left his previous job to move back to the area and his long-term friends.

- A white female aged 55 years who has retired early from teaching on the grounds of ill health. In the whole of her last year at work she was off sick with stress. Since then she has had a year involving strenuous travelling. She says she is now fully recovered and wants a mindless job.

At the most basic level a manager needs internally to challenge any assumptions they make about each individual employee who works for them, for example assuming that a woman with two small children, or man of 68 are less interested than others in career progression, attending training or working overtime or overseas. Some assumptions are so deep and subtle that a manager is unaware that they are applying them to a situation where, for example, they need to decide to whom they should offer a special project, the opportunity to deputise or to travel to complete an assignment. It can be easy to accept the rhetoric and the dialogue of diversity, but this means nothing if it is not acted upon, and this requires a level of internal commitment to diversity. By focusing on self-awareness and being prepared to learn different ways of thinking, line managers not only change their own behaviour, but in so doing act as role models for those working for them.

There are other ways in which line managers shape the behaviour of those working for them, for example by discussing the challenge of diversity and why it is important, and using coaching to encourage their work group to begin to challenge their own assumptions. This is no easy task as such assumptions have been built up over years and are therefore very difficult to change. Encouraging diversity training for their team, including themselves, and being prepared to experiment in the allocation of assignments may all be useful.

The key task of the line manager is to promote cooperation and high performance within their team and it is here that diversity brings other challenges. If diversity initiatives are perceived as offering extras to minority groups, or a way of promoting people because they are female, black or gay rather than because they are the most skilled candidate, then diversity will cause resentments which will undoubtedly hinder team performance. Managers have a key role in making all group members feel valued.

WINDOW ON PRACTICE

The line manager's dilemma

One of the means that organisations use to check whether they are achieving diversity is to produce statistics grouping staff in a series of levels in terms of their seniority or pay. Within each of these levels the staff mix can be broken down by race, gender, age, sexuality, religion, disability and so on. Such statistics often demonstrate that senior positions remain dominated by white males whilst junior positions are dominated by minority groups.

In an effort to redress the balance organisations that are seriously trying to achieve diversity will encourage managers to, for example, promote members of minority groups where this is possible and appropriate.

If a line manager promoted from within their work group a member of a minority group who was not the best candidate for the job in terms of ability, competencies, experience and qualifications (or however the person specification for the job is defined) then other group members will understandably feel resentful. Performance in the group may suffer due to the limited skills of the appointee and cooperation may be compromised. The line manager may also be compromised legally as positive discrimination is not permitted in the UK. (Positive discrimination is deliberately discriminating in favour of a member of a minority group).

Alternatively the line manager may appoint the best qualified candidate (however expressed) and minority group members may feel that the obvious candidate got the job as usual, and that they will never get the chance to progress. Thus feelings of disillusionment and frustration are created. This may result in reduced engagement and effort and perhaps the decision to leave the organisation; in addition the statistical make-up of the workforce does not change.

The third approach that a line manager may adopt is to make efforts to ensure that the competencies, skills and experiences of minority groups are enhanced so that they are in a better position to compete fairly for promotions. This may involve extra coaching and arranging additional mentoring for individuals, as well as making sure they get opportunities to deputise, network, carry out special projects and so on to increase both their skills and their profile in the organisation. Whilst this may be a more subtle approach to encouraging diversity it may still result in claims of unfairness from majority groups who may want to know why they did not receive the extra coaching and experiences. The answer is not simple but does involve supporting and developing **all** team members and working to engage all members in the pursuit of diversity. A real challenge.

Activity 10.2

1 Identify as many ways as you can that a line manager could use to make an individual employee feel valued.

2 For each approach explain why the action would make the employee feel valued.

3 What things might a manager do which make an employee feel not valued or undervalued?

4 For each explain why this would have an effect on the employee.

5 Explain how the manager can avoid each of these approaches.

ACHIEVING SUCCESSFUL DIVERSITY IN ORGANISATIONS

Every organisation is different

Organisations will be starting from different positions in achieving successful diversity, and may be aiming for slightly different outcomes, and approaching issues in different ways. All of this will depend on the context, history, culture and size of the organisation, so there is no simple formula. Large organisations, for example, tend to have made more progress than smaller ones. We have used the word 'successful' to indicate that diversity is more than getting the numbers right, but includes positive attitudes and values which can promote improved performance.

WINDOW ON PRACTICE

The Policy Research Institute on Ageing and Ethnicity (PRIAE), which is an independent charity, carried out a survey of 300 businesses, funded by the EU to assess the contribution of ethnic minorities to small and medium-sized enterprises (SMEs). More than three-quarters of the respondents reported that they had less than 10 per cent of employees who were either black or from an ethnic minority. Ninety per cent of respondents had less than 10 per cent of black or ethnic minority managers, and 35 per cent of respondents had no black or ethnic minority managers.

Few could put a figure on the ethnic composition of their customers, and only a third of respondents felt that greater diversity would lead to better business performance.

Source: *People Management* (2007) 'SMEs are lagging behind on diversity', *People Management*, Vol. 13, No. 7, 5 April, p. 12.

Organisations may broadly be categorised into four groups depending on their approach to diversity.

1 **Avoidance**. This is typical of organisations in the UK before the initial diversity legislation in the UK, and for some organisations even after this date. In the UK such avoidance risks legal penalties, as we have seen in Chapter 9 on Employment regulation. Furthermore, different countries will have a different stance on diversity and different discrimination issues to resolve. Such difference in itself is a real challenge in our world of global business.

WINDOW ON PRACTICE

How multinationals might manage diversity in a global context

Cooke (2007) reports on the inaugural Global Workforce Roundtable summit organised by Boston College where academics and senior executives from multinationals presented and discussed their latest research findings. In summarising the conference Cooke identified confusions over the definition of diversity, and different expectations in different countries. In particular the author identifies that, in comparison with western countries where many differences are protected by law and enshrined in company policies, in many developing countries such as India and China inequalities are accepted and unchallenged. Also the demographics in these countries are different, and a key issue in China is discrimination in respect of the rural migrant workforce, and in India in respect of the caste system. All this questions whether the American definition of managing diversity is inadequate. The author suggests that the development of definitions and initiatives relevant to local needs could be considered.

These issues are key and yet complex for multinationals.

Source: F. L. Cooke (2007) 'How multinationals might manage diversity in a global context', *People Management*, Vol. 13, No. 1, 11 January, p. 51.

2 **Compliance**. This covers organisations which are concerned with avoiding legal consequences and which therefore aim to ensure that discrimination law is followed. Such organisations may focus on explicit forms of discrimination, such as advertisements and recruitment procedures but may neglect implicit and informal discrimination such as that at Deloitte Touche which is discussed in the first Window on practice in this chapter. The organisations' focus will be on reducing individual bias and stereotyping and on producing appropriate policies and procedures. Some statistics are likely to be produced, for example to check that the employee mix within an organisation represents the local population mix, or the employee mix at different hierarchical levels, but often these findings are not acted upon.

3 **Valuing diversity**. This covers organisations where there is a much higher level of diversity awareness and a clear belief in the business value of diversity. Such organisations are more likely to tackle the organisational culture and combine efforts to change the culture to one of valuing difference as well as developing the attitudes of individuals within the organisation. Statistics are likely to be more sophisticated and to be based on investigating whether high-level jobs, training, promotions, secondments and so on are equally available to all according to their ability and potential. Statistical results are also more likely to be thoroughly studied and used to create policy and procedural changes and practices where there appears to be a negative impact on some minority groups.

WINDOW ON PRACTICE

Age equality at Derby City Council

Platman reports that in Derby City Council potential applicants would phone to find out if there was any point in applying for a particular job, expecting that their older age would rule them out. The council felt that age discrimination restricted the pool of applicants and that they had to get rid of signals that age was not valued. The council now has a code of practice which centres on dignity at work, and this applies to both councillors and employees. The aim of the code is to ensure that ageist behaviour, attitudes and language are avoided. The intention is to put across the message that the council values the experience of older employees, and older employees are now specifically encouraged to apply for further training and promotions.

Source: Summarised from K. Platman (2002) 'Matured Assets', *People Management*, Vol. 8, No. 24, 5 December, pp. 40–2.

Thus they will tackle the organisational barriers to discrimination which can be informal, subtle and pervasive, as the gender-based equal pay example in Table 10.1, indicates. Many of these barriers fall within the prerogative of the manager to influence if only he or she will question their approach and the traditional way of doing things. Senior managers inspire an examination of the organisation's culture

TABLE 10.1 Barriers to the achievement of gender-based equal pay

Starting pay is frequently individually negotiated	As men usually have higher previous earnings this means they can negotiate a higher starting rate
Length of service	Men generally have longer service and fewer career breaks, and while this may result in greater experience early in a career it is less of a performance-influencing factor as general length of service increases
Broadbanding	There is a lack of transparency in such systems and there is a lack of structured progression, managers are likely to have high levels of discretion and may be unaware of biases
Lack of equal access to bonus payments	There is evidence that appraisal ratings and assessments discriminate unfairly against minority groups
Market allowances not evenly distributed	Such allowances are more likely to be given to men
Different pay structures and negotiating bodies	As some jobs are done primarily by women and some primarily by men, direct comparisons are harder to make
Job evaluation	Such schemes often perpetuate old values and may be subject to managerial manipulation

Source: Based primarily on material in IDS (2004) 'Employers move on equal pay', IDS Report No. 897, January, pp. 10–18.

to uncover ways in which various minority groups may be disadvantaged (which is sometimes termed 'institutional' discrimination).

4 **Sharing the value of diversity.** The last group of organisations comprises those that have made significant progress in valuing diversity and are so convinced that the valuing of difference is an asset that they take time to demonstrate this to other organisations and try and involve the local community in a gradual process of change.

We have identified four slightly idealised but very different approaches to the management of diversity. Fundamental to all but the first is the development of appropriate policies, strategies and plans, and fundamental to the most progressive two levels is the importance of culture change, so we consider these two aspects in some more detail below.

Equal opportunities and diversity policies, strategies and plans

Kersley *et al.* (2006) found that 73 per cent of organisations in the Workplace Employee Relations (WER) survey had equal opportunities or diversity policies or a statement, and this compares with 64 per cent in 1998. The public sector were more likely to have such policies (97 per cent, a level unchanged from the last survey) and larger organisations were more likely to have policies than smaller ones, which means that 88 per cent of the labour force is in organisations where such a policy exists. Clearly the existence of policy or statement depends on the nature of organisations surveyed. It would also be a mistake to assume that all policies cover all potentially disadvantaged groups (*see*, for example, EOR 1999b), and there is evidence that as legislation begins to cover new groups these are more likely to be covered. Whilst the CIPD (2006b) found 93 per cent of organisations which responded to their survey did have a diversity policy, the disadvantaged groups covered by these were very variable, and many did not cover all the groups for whom there is legislative protection.

In the WER survey the existence of a policy was positively associated with the existence of processes aimed at preventing discrimination such as job evaluation and monitoring of recruitment, selection, promotion and pay. However, these activities were still only carried out by a minority of such organizations. Despite the prevalence of policies there is always the concern that having a policy is more about projecting the right image than about reflecting how the organisation operates. For example, Hoque and Noon (1999) found that having an equal opportunities statement made no difference to the treatment of speculative applications from individuals who were either white or from an ethnic minority group and that 'companies with ethnic minority statements were more likely to discriminate *against* the ethnic minority applicant'. The Runnymede Trust (2000) in a survey on racial equality found that the way managers explained their equal opportunities policy was different from employee views about what happened in practice. Creegan *et al.* (2003) investigated the implementation of a race equality action plan and found a stark difference between paper and practice. Line managers who were responsible for implementing the plan were operating in a devolved HR environment and so had to pay for advice, training and support from HR. The consequence of this was that in order to protect their budgets they were reluctant to seek help. Employees felt that there was no ownership of the strategy or the plan within the organisation by senior or middle managers. Woodhams and Lupton (2006) found a disconnection between policy and practice in small organisations, and that whilst the presence of an HR specialist meant policies were more likely, this seemed to have no effect on implementation.

Activity 10.3

What can managers do to encourage diversity policy to be consistently put into practice, rather than just remaining organisation rhetoric?

Changing the culture

Changing culture is clearly a key part of any process for managing diversity. In 1995 Her Majesty's Inspectorate of Constabulory (HMIC) stressed the business case for diversity in the police force. The police force, over a number of years, has made considerable efforts to increase the recruitment and promotion of members of ethnic minorities (*see*, for example, EOR 1997). It began to tackle the issues of why individuals from different ethnic backgrounds would not even apply to the police for a career (for example, they may be seen, within some ethnic groups, as traitors for doing so). Some progress was made but the McPherson Report (1999) highlighted the issue of institutional racism, and further efforts were made to reduce discrimination. However, in 2004 there was still clear evidence of discriminatory cultures and attitudes, as evidenced by the television programme about the racist attitudes of new recruits into Manchester police. On Radio 4 on 20 January 2004 the Ali Desai case was discussed and it was argued that the metropolitan police service was racist in the way that it applied discipline to officers, picking up on smaller issues for racial minority groups than for white officers. The changes required to manage diversity effectively should not be underestimated.

WINDOW ON PRACTICE

Arriva: dramatic results on diversity

Arriva embarked on a diversity programme in 2003 and claims that it has stimulated a change in workforce profile and reduced employee turnover. This is a key outcome as one of the drivers behind the programme was to become an employer of choice in response to predicted demographic and legislative changes, recruitment challenges and a need to reflect the broader community in order to stay ahead in business. The company was aware, for example, that the company was a traditional white male environment, with bus driving, for example, being seen as a man's job. Arriva began by setting up a diversity committee made up of senior leaders from across the businesses to review progress and measures of success. In addition a Diversity Best Practice Forum was set up with responsibility for delivering the diversity agenda. Diversity behaviours were included in management and leadership competencies and individuals at all levels all have objectives linked to diversity.

Training was a key part of the company's approach to diversity and accomplished in two phases. The first was very innovative and a drama-based training organisation started off the programme called Managing and Valuing Difference. They prepared by researching what actually happened in the business and identified current key issues relating to diversity. Scenarios were then acted out and participants encouraged to be involved by interactive exercises and discussions. The aim was to create an understanding in the workforce of diversity and the business case for it, to help people appreciate the differences in others and where people felt able to challenge unacceptable behaviour. The second part of the training involved Arriva staff who volunteered to be trained as facilitators and the use of video scenarios. This second part of the training addressed 'Valuing and welcoming difference'.

In addition it was decided to extend flexible working and strengthen the role of minority groups. For example, there was a women's networking event attended by the chief executive with a view to encouraging, developing and retaining women in senior management. A recruitment monitoring process was also introduced to

▶

▶ help decide how to allocate resources on diversity. For example, in one part of the business it might be to target under-represented groups and produce a tailored approach to recruitment advertising, whilst in another it may be to have greater involvement in the local community. Open days have been held to encourage the recruitment of women bus drivers where existing women drivers also attend to share their views. Two-part application forms are used so that any personal data is separate from the application form and cannot bias shortlisting, and the use of male and female mentors has proved successful.

Source: Adapted from Wolff C. (2007) 'Arriva: dramatic results on diversity', *Equal Opportunities Review*, No. 160, January, pp. 5–11.

KEY DEBATE: MANAGING DIVERSITY OR EMPHASISING EQUALITY?

So far we have only briefly indicated the main difference between an equal opportunities approach and a management of diversity approach and have generally treated managing diversity as encompassing aspects of both approaches. However there is a continuing debate concerning the type of action that should be taken to alleviate the disadvantages that minority groups encounter. One school of thought supports legislative action, which we considered in detail in the chapter on employment regulation, and this approach is generally referred to as the equal opportunities approach. The other argues that this will not be effective and that the only way to change fundamentally is to alter the attitudes and preconceptions that are held about these groups. This second perspective is embodied in the managing diversity approach. The initial emphasis on legislative action was adopted in the hope that this would eventually affect attitudes. The labels 'equal opportunities' and 'management of diversity' are used inconsistently, and to complicate this there are different perspectives on the meaning of managing diversity, so we shall draw out the key differences which typify each of these approaches, and offer some criticism of their conceptual foundations and effectiveness.

The equal opportunities approach

The equal opportunities approach seeks to influence behaviour through legislation so that discrimination is prevented. It has been characterised by a moral and ethical stance promoting the rights of *all* members of society. The approach concentrates on the equality of opportunity rather than the equality of outcome found in more radical approaches. The approach is based on the understanding that some individuals are discriminated against, for example in the selection process, due to irrelevant criteria. These irrelevant criteria arise from assumptions based on the stereotypical characteristics attributed to them as members of a socially defined group, for example that women will not be prepared to work away from home due to family commitments; that a person with a disability will have more time off sick. As these assumptions are not supported by any evidence, in respect of any individual, they are regarded as irrelevant. The equal opportunities approach therefore seeks to formalise procedures so that relevant, job-based criteria are used (using job descriptions and person specifications), rather than irrelevant assumptions. The equal opportunities legislation provides a foundation for this formalisation of procedures, and hence procedural justice. As Liff (1999) points out, the use of systematic rules in employment matters which can be monitored for compliance is 'felt fair'. In line with the moral argument, and emphasis on systematic procedures, equal opportunities is often characterised as a responsibility of the HR department.

The rationale, therefore, is to provide a 'level playing field' on which all can compete on equal terms. Positive action (providing extra support to minority groups to put them in a better position to compete), not positive discrimination, is allowable in order that some may reach the level at which they can compete equally. For example, British Rail has given members of minority groups extra coaching and practice in a selection test for train drivers, as test taking was not part of their culture so that, when required to take a test, they were at a disadvantage.

Equal opportunities approaches stress disadvantaged groups, and the need, for example, to set targets for those groups to ensure that their representation in the workplace reflects their representation in wider society in occupations where they are under-represented. There are at present small numbers of ethnic minorities employed as firefighters, as police officers and in the armed forces (*see* IDS 2006 for an air force example) and small numbers of women in senior management roles. These targets are not enforceable by legislation, as in the United States, but organisations have been encouraged to commit themselves voluntarily to improvement goals, and to support this by putting in place measures to support disadvantaged groups such as special training courses and flexible employment policies.

Differences between socially defined groups are glossed over, and the approach is generally regarded as one of 'sameness'. That is, members of disadvantaged groups should be treated in the same way as the traditional employee (white, male, young, able-bodied and heterosexual), and not treated differently due to their group membership, unless for the purpose of providing the 'level playing field'.

Problems with the equal opportunities approach

There is an assumption in the equal opportunities approach that equality of outcome will be achieved if fair procedures are used and monitored. In other words this will enable any minority groups to achieve a fair share of what employment has to offer. Once such minority groups become full participating members in employment, the old stereotypical attitudes on which discrimination against particular social groups is based will gradually change, as the stereotypes will be shown to be unhelpful.

The assumption that fair procedures or procedural justice will lead to fair outcomes has not been borne out in practice, as we have indicated. In addition there has been criticism of the assumption that once members of minority groups have demonstrated their ability to perform in the organisation, this will change attitudes and beliefs in the organisation. This is a naïve assumption, and the approach has been regarded as simplistic. Attitudes and beliefs appear to have changed little. Other criticisms point out that the legislation does not protect all minority groups (although it is gradually being extended); and there is a general lack of support within the organisation, partly because equality objectives are often not linked to business objectives. Shapiro and Austin (1996), among others, argue that equal opportunities has usually been the concern of the HR function. The focus of equal opportunities is on formal processes and yet it is not possible to formalise everything in the organisation. Recent research suggests that this approach alienated large sections of the workforce (those not identified as disadvantaged groups) who felt that there was no benefit for themselves, and indeed that their opportunities were damaged. Others felt that equal opportunities initiatives had resulted in the lowering of entry standards, as in the London Fire and Civil Defence Authority (EOR 1996). This has the potential to create divisions in the workforce. Lastly, it is the individual who is expected to adjust to the organisation, and 'traditional equal opportunities strategies encourage a view that women (and other groups) have a problem and need help' (Liff 1999, p. 70).

In summary the equal opportunities approach is considered simplistic and to be attempting to treat the symptoms rather than the causes of unfair discrimination.

The management of diversity approach

The management of diversity approach concentrates on individuals rather than groups, and includes the improvement of opportunities for *all* individuals and not just those in minority groups. Hence managing diversity involves everyone and benefits everyone, which is an attractive message to employers and employees alike. Thus separate groups are not singled out for specific treatment. Kandola and Fullerton (1998, p. 4), who are generally regarded as the main UK supporters of a managing diversity approach, express it this way:

> The basic concept of managing diversity accepts that the workforce consists of a diverse population of people consisting of visible and non-visible differences . . . and is founded on the premiss that harnessing these differences will create a productive environment in which everyone feels valued, where all talents are fully utilized and in which organizational goals are met.

And (1998, p. 11) they contest, in addition, that:

> if managing diversity is about an individual and their contribution . . . rather than about groups it is contradictory to provide training and other opportunities based solely on people's perceived group membership.

So the focus is on valuing difference rather than finding a way of coping fairly with it. Whereas the equal opportunities approach minimised difference, the managing diversity approach treats difference as a positive asset. Liff (1996), for example, notes that from this perspective organisations should recognise rather than dilute differences, as differences are positive rather than negative.

This brings us to a further difference between the equal opportunities approach and the managing diversity approach which is that the managing diversity approach is based on the economic and business case for recognising and valuing difference, rather than the moral case for treating people equally. Rather than being purely a cost which may threaten the bottom line, equal treatment offers benefits for competitiveness.

Managing diversity highlights the importance of culture. The roots of discrimination go very deep, and the Macpherson Report (1999), for example, identifies institutional racism as a root cause of discrimination in the police force. Culture is important in two ways in managing diversity: first, organisational culture is one determinant of the way that organisations manage diversity and treat individuals from different groups. Equal opportunity approaches tend to concentrate on behaviour and, to a small extent, attitudes, whereas management of diversity approaches recognise a need to go beneath this, as the CIPD (2005) points out, diversity requires 'a mutual respect, obligation to and appreciation of others, irrespective of difference' (p. 17). So changing the culture to one which treats individuals as individuals and supports them in developing their potential is critical, although the difficulties of culture change make this a very difficult task.

Secondly, depending on the approach to the management of diversity, the culture of different groups within the organisation comes into play. For example, recognising that men and women present different cultures at work and that this diversity needs to be managed, is key to promoting a positive environment of equal opportunity, which goes beyond merely fulfilling the demands of the statutory codes. For example, Masreliez-Steen (1989) explains how men and women have different perceptions, interpretations of reality, languages and ways of solving problems, which, if properly used, can be a benefit to the whole organisation, as they are complementary. She describes women as having a collectivist culture where they form groups, avoid the spotlight, see rank as unimportant and have few but close contacts. Alternatively, men are described as having an individualistic culture, where they form teams, 'develop a profile', enjoy competition and have many superficial contacts. The result is that men and women behave in different ways, often fail to understand each other and experience 'culture clash'. However, the difference is about how things are done and not about what is achieved. However, we must be aware that here we have another stereotypical view which simplifies reality.

The fact that women, for example, have a different culture, with different strengths and weaknesses, means that women need managing and developing in a different way, needing different forms of support and coaching. Women more often need help to understand the value of making wider contacts and how to make them. Attending to the organisation's culture suggests a move away from seeing the individual as the problem, and requiring that the individual needs to change because they do not fit the culture. Rather, it is the organisation that needs to change so that traditional assumptions of how jobs are constructed and how they should be carried out are questioned, and looked at afresh, since structures, cultures and practices of organisations advantage the dominant group by being developed from their skills and lifestyles. This is the very heart of institutional discrimination, and so difficult to address as these are matters which are taken for granted and largely unconscious. The trick, as Thomas (1992) spells out, is to identify 'requirements as opposed to preferences, conveniences or traditions'.

Table 10.2 summarises the key differences between equal opportunities and managing diversity.

Finally, managing diversity is considered to be a more integrated approach to implementing equality. Whereas equal opportunities approaches were driven by the HR

TABLE 10.2 Major differences between 'equal opportunities' approaches and 'management of diversity' approaches

Aspect	Equal opportunities	Managing diversity
Purpose	Reduce discrimination	Utilise employee potential to maximum advantage
Approach	Operational	Strategic
Case argued	Moral and ethical	Business case – improve profitability
Whose responsibility	HR/personnel department	All managers
Focuses on	Groups	Individuals
Perspective	Dealing with different needs of different groups	Integrated
Benefits for employees	Opportunities improved for disadvantaged groups, primarily through setting targets	Opportunities improved for all employees
Focus on management activity	Recruitment	Managing
Remedies	Changing systems and practices	Changing the culture
Monitoring success	Changed processes	Business outcomes

function, managing diversity is seen to be the responsibility of all managers. And, as there are business reasons for managing diversity it is argued that equality should not be dealt with as a separate issue, as with equal opportunities approaches, but integrated strategically into every aspect of what the organisation does; this is often called mainstreaming.

Activity 10.4

Interview five people who are in employment and ask them a set of questions to help you explore whether the emphasis in their organisation is on managing diversity or equal opportunities. Then explore their feelings about the organisation's approach and how well they think it is working.

If you are or have been employed you could of course use your own organisation in place of one of the interviews.

Problems with the managing diversity approach

While the management of diversity approach was seen by many as revitalising the equal opportunities agenda, and as a strategy for making more progress on the equality front, this progress has been slow to materialise. In reality, there remains the question of the extent to which approaches have really changed in organisations. Redefining equal opportunities in the language of business benefits may just be a way of making it more palatable in today's climate, and Liff (1996) suggests that retitling may be used to revitalise the equal opportunities agenda.

It has been pointed out by Kirton and Greene (2003) that only a small number of organisations are ever quoted as management of diversity exemplars, although the numbers are now increasing, and EOR (1999b) notes that even organisations which claim to be managing diversity do not appear to have a more diverse workforce than others, and neither have they employed more minority groups over the past five years.

Apart from this there are some fundamental problems with the management of diversity approach. The first of these is its complexity, as there are differing interpretations. Miller (1996) highlights two different approaches to the management of diversity. The first is where individual differences are identified and celebrated, and where prejudices against groups are exposed and challenged via training. The second, more orthodox, approach is where the organisation seeks to develop the capacity of all, thus focusing on individuals. This debate between group and individual identity is a fundamental issue:

> Can people's achievements be explained by their individual talents or are they better explained as an outcome of their gender, ethnicity, class and age? Can anything meaningful be said about the collective experience of all women or are any generalisations undermined by other cross-cutting ideas? (Liff 1997, p. 11)

The most common approach to the management of diversity is based on individual contribution, Miller's second approach, rather than group identity, and in this approach differences are seen as random and nothing to do with the membership of a social group. So groups are not highlighted and all should be treated fairly and encouraged to develop their potential. The advantage of this approach is that it is inclusive and involves all members of the organisation. The alternative emphasis in the management of diversity, which Miller pointed out first, is that of *valuing differences* based on the membership of different social groups. Following this approach would mean recognising and highlighting differences, and being prepared to give special training to groups who may be disadvantaged and lack self-confidence, so that all in the organisation feel comfortable. Liff's (1997) conclusion is that group differences cannot be ignored, because it is these very differences which hold people back, and ignoring them may reduce diversity awareness and reduce the special support these groups may need.

The attractive idea of business advantage and benefits for all may divert attention from disadvantaged groups and result in no change to the status quo. If differences are not recognised, then it is difficult to question the norms and standards of the dominant group.

On the other hand, a management of diversity approach may reinforce group-based stereotypes, when group-based characteristics are identified and used as a source of advantage to the organisation. For example, it has been argued, in respect of women, that as these differences were treated previously as a form of disadvantage, women may be uncomfortable using them to argue the basis for equality. Others argue that a greater recognition of perceived differences will continue to provide a rationale for disadvantageous treatment.

In addition to this dilemma within managing diversity approaches, the literature provides a strong criticism of the business case argument, which has been identified as contingent and variable (Dickens 1999). Thus the business case is unreliable because it will only work in certain contexts. For example, where skills are easily available there is less pressure on the organisation to promote and encourage the employment of minority groups. Not every employee interacts with customers so if image and customer contact are part of the business case this pressure will only apply to some jobs and not others. Also some groups may be excluded. For example, there is no systematic evidence to suggest that disabled customers are attracted by an organisation which employs disabled people. UK managers are also driven by short-term budgets and the economic benefits of equality may only be reaped in the longer term. Indeed as Kirton and Greene (2003) conclude, the business case is potentially detrimental to equality, when, for example, a cost–benefit analysis indicates that pursuing equality is not an economic benefit.

The CIPD (2006a) argues that the evidence of performance improvements resulting from diversity is scanty and identifies the need to go beyond the rhetoric of the business case for diversity and conduct more systematic research and monitoring to demonstrate the outcomes of diversity policies. It also points to the importance of a conducive environment in gaining benefits. Furthermore it recites problems which can result from a more diverse workforce which include increased conflict, often resulting in difficulties in devising solutions, and poorer internal communication, with increased management costs due to these issues.

In terms of implementation of a diversity approach there are also difficulties. We have identified above the complexity of some of the varying ideas which come under the banner of diversity and this in itself is a barrier to implementation. Foster and Harris (2005) in their research in the retail sector found that it was a concept that lacked clarity for line managers in terms of both what it is and how to implement it within anti-discrimination laws, and some were concerned that it may lead to feelings of unfairness and claims of unequal treatment.

There are also concerns about whether diversity management, which originated in the USA, will travel effectively to the UK where the context is different, especially in terms of the demographics and the history of equality initiatives.

Lastly, managing diversity can be seen as introspective as it deals with people already in the organisation, rather than with getting people into the organisation.

Equal opportunities or managing diversity?

Are equal opportunities and managing diversity completely different things? If so, is one approach preferable to the other? For the sake of clarity, managing diversity is often characterised as different from equal opportunities. However, as we have seen, managing diversity covers a range of approaches and emphases, some closer to equal opportunities, some very different.

However, much of the management of diversity suggests that it is superior to and not compatible with the equal opportunities approach (*see* Kandola *et al.* 1996). There is, however, increasing support for equal opportunities and managing diversity to be viewed as mutually supportive and for this combination to be seen as important. Dickens (2006) suggests that social justice and economic efficiency are increasingly being presented as complementary, although there is so far a lack of guidance about how such complementarity can be achieved in practice.

While legislation on its own (equal opportunities approach) cannot change attitudes, it is important as a symbol and does change some behaviour which might otherwise have been discriminatory, by setting minimum standards.

SUMMARY PROPOSITIONS

10.1 There has been an emphasis on equality and diversity for over thirty years and yet progress has been very slow. At the same time the emphasis on diversity appears to have had a negative impact on some white males in UK society, particularly in relation to employment.

10.2 Terminology differs but most organisations combine efforts at complying with legislation and providing special support for minority groups to achieve equal opportunities, as well as a management of diversity approach where difference is valued and all employees should be able to access similar support.

10.3 The current focus on managing diversity is supported by the business case argument that diversity increases organisational competitiveness.

10.4 Organisations and their cultures, processes and structures are founded on the needs of the majority group and individuals from other groups are expected to adapt to this norm. This explains why progress towards equality has been very slow, and why there is currently much more focus on these issues.

10.5 Equal opportunities approaches and the management of diversity are best viewed, not as alternatives, but as complementary approaches which need to be interrelated.

GENERAL DISCUSSION TOPICS

1   Discuss Liff's (1997) question:
'Can people's achievements be explained by their individual talents or are they better explained as an outcome of their gender, ethnicity, class and age? Can anything meaningful be said about the collective experience of all women or are any generalisations undermined by other cross-cutting ideas?' (p. 11).

▶

> **2** In North America 'positive discrimination' is permitted so that it is legal to discriminate positively in favour of minority groups. Discuss whether this would be an appropriate approach in the country in which you are located. Identify points in favour and against and the way in which such an approach would best be implemented if it were decided upon.

FURTHER READING

Ryan, M.K., Haslam, S.A., Wilson-Kovacs, M.D., Hersby, M.D., Kulich, C. (2007) *Managing Diversity and the Glass Cliff*. London: Chartered Institute of Personnel and Development.
A good introduction to the glass cliff phenomenon whereby women and marginalised groups are often placed in senior positions in circumstances where organisations are in crisis and there is a high risk of failure.

Mattis, M. (2001) 'Advancing women in business organisations', *Journal of Management Development*, Vol. 20, No. 4, pp. 371–88.
This article examines the role of key players such as middle and first-line managers in supporting gender diversity initiatives. A wide range of case examples are used and the article provides a range of practical activities to support gender diversity.

WEB LINKS

www.equalityhumanrights.com
http://www.cadbury.com/ourresponsibilities/employ
mentpractices/Pages/diversityandopportunity.aspx

REFERENCES

CIPD (2005) *Managing Diversity: Linking Theory and Practice to business performance*. London: Chartered Institute of Personnel and Development.

CIPD (2006a) *Managing Diversity: Measuring Success*. London: Chartered Institute of Personnel and Development.

CIPD (2006b) *Diversity in Business: How much progress have employers made? First findings*. London: Chartered Institute of Personnel and Development.

Cooke F.L. (2007) 'How multinationals might manage diversity in a global context', *People Management*, Vol. 13, No. 1, 11 January, p. 51.

Creegan, C., Colgan, F., Charlesworth, R. and Robinson, G. (2003) 'Race equality policies at work: employee perceptions of the "implementation gap" in a UK local authority', *Work, Employment and Society*, Vol. 17, No. 4, pp. 617–40.

Dickens, L. (1999) 'Beyond the business case: a three pronged approach to equality action', *Human Resource Management Journal*, Vol. 9, No. 1, pp. 9–19.

Dickens, L. (2006) 'Re-regulation for gender equality: from 'either/or' to 'both'', *Industrial Relations Journal*, Vol. 37, No. 4, pp. 299–309.

Dobbs, C. (2007) 'Patterns of Pay: results of the Annual Survey of Hours and Earnings, 1997–2006', *Economic* and Labour Market Review, Vol. 1, No. 2, February, pp. 44–51.

Ellis, C. and Sonnenfield, J.A. (1994) 'Diverse approaches to managing diversity', Human Resource Management, Vol. 33, No. 1, Spring, pp. 79–109.

EOC (2007) Sex and power: who runs Britain? Manchester: Equal Opportunities Commission.

Equal Opportunities Review (1996) 'Ethnic minorities in the fire service', No. 68, July–August.

Equal Opportunities Review (1997) 'Ethnic minorities in the police service', No. 73.

Equal Opportunities Review (1998) 'Tackling Age bias: code or law?', No. 80, July–August.

Equal Opportunities Review (1999a) 'BT: Championing women in a man's world', No. 84, March–April, pp. 14–20.

Equal Opportunities Review (1999b) 'Equal Opportunities Policies: An EOR survey of employers', No. 87, September–October.

Foster, C. and Harris, L. (2005) 'Easy to say, difficult to do: diversity in retail management', Human Resource Management Journal, Vol. 15, No. 3, pp. 4–17.

Hicks-Clarke, D. and Iles, P. (2000) 'Climate for diversity and its effects on career and organizational attitudes and perceptions', Personnel Review, Vol. 29, No. 3.

Hoque, K. and Noon, M. (1999) 'Racial discrimination in speculative applications: new optimism six years on?', Human Resource Management Journal, Vol. 9, No. 3, pp. 71–82.

Humphries, J. and Rubery, J. (1995) Research Summary of the Economics of Equal Opportunity. Manchester: Equal Opportunities Commission.

IDS (2004) 'Employers move on equal pay', IDS Report No. 897, January, pp. 10–18.

IDS (2006) 'Promoting Race Equality', IDS HR Studies No. 825. London: IDS.

Jackson, B.W., LaFasto, F., Schultz, H.G. and Kelly, D. (1993) 'Diversity', Human Resource Management, Vol. 31, Nos 1 and 2, Spring/Summer, pp. 21–34.

Kandola, P. and Fullerton, J. (1994, 2nd edn 1998) Managing the Mosaic. London: Institute of Personnel and Development.

Kandola, R., Fullerton, J. and Mulroney, C. (1996) 1996 Pearn Kandola Survey of Diversity Practice Summary Report. Oxford: Pearn Kandola.

Kersley, B., Alpin, C., Forth, J., Bryson, A., Bewley, H., Dix, G. and Oxenbridge, S. (2006) Inside the Workplace: Findings from the 2004 Workplace Employment Relations Survey. London: Routledge.

Kirton, G. and Greene, A. (2003) The dynamics of managing diversity: a critical approach. Oxford: Butterworth Heinemann.

LaFasto, F. (1992) 'Baxter Healthcare Organisation', in B.W. Jackson, F. LaFasto, H.G. Schultz and D. Kelly, Human Resource Management, Vol. 31, Nos 1–2, Spring/Summer.

Liff, S. (1996) 'Managing diversity: new opportunities for women?', Warwick Papers in Industrial Relations No. 57. Coventry: IRU, Warwick University.

Liff, S. (1997) 'Two routes to managing diversity: individual differences or social group characteristics?', Employee Relations, Vol. 19, No. 1, pp. 11–26.

Liff, S. (1999) 'Diversity and Equal Opportunities: room for a constructive compromise?', Human Resource Management Journal, Vol. 9, No. 1, pp. 65–75.

Macpherson of Clung, Sir William (1999) The Stephen Lawrence Inquiry. A Report by Sir William Macpherson of Clung. London: HMSO.

Masreliez-Steen, G. (1989) Male and Female Management. Sweden: Kontura Group.

Miller, D. (1996) 'Equality management – towards a materialist approach', Gender, Work and Organisation, Vol. 3, No. 4, pp. 202–14.

Phillips, T. (2007a) Fairness and Freedom: Final Report of the Equalities Review. London: HMSO.

Phillips, L. (2007b) 'Take action on equality, HR is urged', People Management, Vol. 13, No. 5, 8 March, p. 9.

Platman, K. (2002) 'Matured Assets', People Management, Vol. 8, No. 24, 5 December, pp. 40–2.

Ross, R. and Schneider, R. (1992) From Equality to Diversity – a business case for equal opportunities. London: Pitman.

Runnymede Trust (2000) Moving on up? Racial Equality and the Corporate Agenda, A Study of the FTSE 100 companies. London: Central Books.

Shapiro, G. and Austin, S. (1996) 'Equality drives total quality', *Occasional Paper*. Brighton: Brighton Business School.

Skills and Enterprise Network (2000) *Labour Market and Skills Trends*. Sheffield: Department for Education and Employment.

Smethurst, S. (2007) 'Fair Traders', *People Management*, Vol. 13, No. 24, 29 November, pp. 28–31.

Thomas, R.R. (1992) 'Managing diversity: a conceptual framework', in S. Jackson (ed.) *Diversity in the Workplace*. New York: Guildford Press.

Wolff, C. (2007) 'Arriva; dramatic results on diversity', *Equal Opportunities Review*, No. 160, January, pp. 5–11.

Woodhams, C. and Lupton, B. (2006) 'Gender-based equal opportunities policy and practice in small firms: the impact of HR professionals', *Human Resource Management Journal*, Vol. 16, No. 1, pp. 74–97.

CHAPTER 11

Human Resource strategy

The objectives of this chapter are to:

1 Introduce the nature of HR strategy and its relationship with business strategy

2 Evaluate three theoretical perspectives on the nature of HR strategy and show how each expresses a different view on how the contribution of people to the organisation might be understood and enhanced

3 Identify the current drivers for downsizing, its varied nature and its potential consequences

4 Debate the challenges that downsizing may create for people management and how managers might address these

5 Explore the role of the line manager as downsizing agent

'No one expected the Spanish Inquisition' (google Monty Python if this doesn't make you laugh!) No one expected the near collapse of Northern Rock, especially Northern Rock. Its business strategy was growth based primarily on borrowing money from the money markets and lending it out as mortgages at a profit. For a long time the strategy worked brilliantly and Northern Rock grew fast. When the money markets almost stopped lending Northern Rock was, whilst having good quality mortgages, unable to function without alternative funds being made available from elsewhere. Northern Rock has received significant state support but is now shrinking dramatically, and with that comes downsizing, a people management strategy that Northern Rock never apparently countenanced in the heady days of 2006.

So Northern Rock had a clear strategy but didn't apparently have any contingencies worked out in case the strategy no longer worked due to

▶

▶ environmental changes. You may ask if working out strategies, both for business and for HRM, is a waste of time, because they can be forced to change for reasons outside of the control of the organisation.

Mintzberg (1994) helps us here as he views strategy as a process, rather than a piece of paper on which is written the business plan: a process, which is not necessarily rational and top down, but political and evolutionary with strategies being 'formed' as time passes rather than 'formulated' in advance. He proposed that the realised strategy is different from the initial vision, and in effect, strategy can only be identified in retrospect. Certainly for Northern Rock the realised strategy of business reduction and people downsizing was not the original plan!

This is not to say that producing a strategy is an unhelpful act, and indeed research carried out by PriceWaterhouseCoopers indicated that those organisations with a written HR strategy generated 35 per cent greater revenues per employee than those without (Higginbottom 2002).

There is an increasingly commonly held view that human resources are *the* source of competitive advantage for the business, rather than, say, access to capital or use of technology. Therefore the strategic as well as operational management of this resource is critical in impacting on employee behaviour and performance and consequently the performance of the organisation. Whilst involvement in the development of HR strategy is most often limited to more senior managers and sometimes HR specialists, all managers have a key role to play in the implementation of chosen strategies. An understanding of the theories relating to HR strategy provides a context for managers in this implementation role.

Not every organisation will have an explicit HR strategy; however in the most recent Workplace Employment Relations (WER) Survey it was found that 87 per cent of workplaces with a strategic plan included some issues relating to employment relations, broadly defined (Kersley *et al.* 2006).

In this chapter we first discuss the link between HR and organisational strategy and then evaluate some theoretical perspectives on HR strategy. The final part of the chapter is devoted to a single HR strategic issue, downsizing, which remains a frequent news topic.

THE NATURE OF HR STRATEGY AND ITS LINK WITH ORGANISATIONAL STRATEGY

Our understanding of HR strategy has changed considerably and we have moved from viewing strategy as a physical document to seeing it as an incremental process, influenced by organisational politics and generating learning. HR strategies are sometimes issue based rather than complete; in other words they focus on a critical issue of the moment, such as downsizing, rather than covering all areas of HR such as development, selection, reward and so on. In defining HRM strategy Tyson's (1995) view is a useful starting point, although somewhat limited, as will be seen from our later discussion:

> the intentions of the corporation both explicit and covert, toward the management of its employees, expressed through philosophies, policies and practices. (Tyson 1995)

Implementation of HR strategy has been weak, yet the ability to turn strategy into action quickly is among the qualities of the most successful organisations according to Ulrich (1998). Whilst the HR function has a varied role in implementing HR strategy it is inevitably the responsibility of all managers in the organisation, but the existence of an HR strategy is often only a minor influence on the policies and procedures that are used.

Activity 11.1

Interview six people, three managers and three non-managers, who are currently employed and ask them:

- How HR strategy is communicated to them

- What their understanding is of the organisation's HR strategy based on the HR policies with which they are familiar

- The extent to which HR practice reflects HR strategy and HR policies, and, if there are any discrepancies, how they would account for these

If you are currently or have been previously employed you may of course wish to use your personal experiences in place of one of the interviews.

The nature, desirability and feasibility of the link between business strategy and HR strategy is a consistent theme which runs through the strategy literature; however, each of the three theoretical perspectives we go on to evaluate takes a different view on this. The universalist perspective is founded on the concept that there is 'one best way' of managing human resources in order to improve business performance, and therefore 'best practice' HRM is favoured at the expense of fit with business strategy. You may find it helpful to return to Chapter 1 and re-read the section on best practice versus best fit HRM. The second focuses on the need to align employment policies and practice with the requirements of business strategy in order that the latter will be achieved and the business will be successful. This second approach is based on the assumption that different types of HR strategies will be suitable for different types of business strategies. Thirdly, a more recent approach to strategic HRM is derived from the resource-based view of the firm, and the perceived value of human capital. This view focuses on the quality of the human resources available to the organisation and their ability to learn and adapt more quickly than their competitors. The resource-based view suggests that HR strategy should be integrated into business strategy rather than being purely a response to it and that HR issues have the potential to drive organisational strategy. The argument here is that if people are the key to competitive advantage, then we need to build on our people strengths, and as the potential of our employees will undoubtedly affect the achievement of any planned strategy, it would be sensible to take account of this in developing our strategic direction. This is in sympathy with the notion of 'human capital' where it is the collective nature and quality of the people in the organisation which provide the potential for future competitive advantage.

THEORETICAL PERSPECTIVES OF STRATEGIC HRM

Universalist approach

The universalist approach is derived from the conception of human resource management as 'best practice', as we discussed in Chapter 1. Best practice refers to a group of HR policies and practices, and examples of what might be included in best practice are high levels of training, job security and high levels of pay linked to the organisation's performance. Best practice is based on the premise that one model of managing employees – a high-commitment model – is related to high organisational performance in all contexts, irrespective of the particular competitive strategy of the organisation. The high-commitment model means that HR policies and practices should all aim to generate employee commitment or loyalty to the organisation with the expectation that this will result in better employee and organisational performance.

Activity 11.2
The management view

Using the three examples above, of high levels of training, job security and high levels of pay linked to organisational performance:

- How might each of these encourage loyalty or commitment to the organisation?

- How might each make the individual work harder?

This approach is prescriptive as it 'tells' any organisation that it *should* manage employees using this one approach, and it should include the whole group or bundle of HR practices that result in individual commitment to the organisation and high performance. In other words this model should be universally applied.

The universalist perspective has grown from a large number of statistical research studies aiming to identify exactly which bundle of HR policies and practices is associated with high company performance. Pfeffer (1994) and Becker and Gerhart (1996) are well-known exponents of this view. For example Pfeffer (1998) identified seven critical people-management policies: emphasising employment security; recruiting the 'right' people; extensive use of self-managed teams and decentralisation; high wages solidly linked to organisational performance; high spending on training; reducing status differentials; and sharing information; and he suggests that these policies will benefit *every* organisation. While there is some support for this perspective, there remains some debate as to which particular human resource practices will stimulate high commitment, and different researchers have come up with different lists of practices in their bundles, some of which contradict each other. The approach has also been criticised for neglecting the employee view and assuming that employee and management interests are the same and that employees will act rationally. In addition not every organisation has the money to carry out these policies.

Activity 11.3
The employee view

The following HR policies and practices are frequently said to be part of the bundle:

- high levels of training

- job security

- high pay linked to organisational performance

For each explain why it may fail to make an individual more committed or loyal to the organisation and why it might not have the effect of making the employee work harder and perform better.

Falling somewhere between the universalist approach and the fit approach is the Harvard model of HRM. This model, produced by Beer *et al.* (1984), is analytical rather than prescriptive and recognises the different stakeholder interests that impact on employee behaviour and performance, and also gives greater emphasis to factors in the business environment that will help to shape human resource strategic choices. Stakeholders are anyone who has an interest in what the organisation does, for example employees, shareholders and customers.

Fit or contingency approach

The fit or contingency approach is based on two critical forms of fit. The first is external fit, sometimes referred to as vertical integration. This means that HR strategy fits with the demands of business strategy and enables the business strategy to be achieved. This is very different from the universalist perspective as it is saying that there is no 'best' HR strategy as the HR strategy must be designed to meet the needs of the individual business.

WINDOW ON PRACTICE

An example of external/vertical fit of HR strategy with business strategy

Take the example of a small pharmaceuticals business which manufactures, packages and sells drugs aimed at coughs and colds. The company only manufactures and does not do any research and development. As demand for its products is high in autumn and winter it needs to take on many more staff to meet this demand, as the products only have a short shelf life and therefore cannot be made too far in advance. However, whilst 'best' HR strategy would require high levels of training and job security and high levels of pay related to organisational performance, this may be inappropriate for this company. It therefore has a different HR strategy which relies heavily on temporary seasonal labour, designs jobs so that any training is minimised and pays modestly.

One of the foundations of this approach is found in Fombrun *et al.* (1984), who proposed a basic framework for strategic human resource management. Figure 11.1 represents the location of human resource management in relation to organisational strategy, so demonstrating the external fit of HR strategy with business strategy and business structure. Note how this is all clearly influenced by the context in which the business operates.

The second type of fit is internal fit or horizontal integration which means that all HR policies and activities fit together so that they make a coherent whole, are mutually reinforcing and are applied consistently. Figure 11.2 shows how activities within human resource management can be unified and designed in order to support the organisation's strategy.

The strength of this model is that it provides a simple framework to show how selection, appraisal, development and reward can be mutually geared to produce the required type of employee performance. For example, if an organisation required cooperative team behaviour with mutual sharing of information and support, the broad implications would be:

- **Selection:** successful experience of teamwork and sociable, cooperative personality; rather than an independent thinker who likes working alone
- **Development:** teamworking skills, development of emotional intelligence, developing others' skills
- **Appraisal:** based on contribution to the team, and support of others, rather than outstanding individual performance
- **Reward:** based on team performance and contribution, rather than individual performance and individual effort

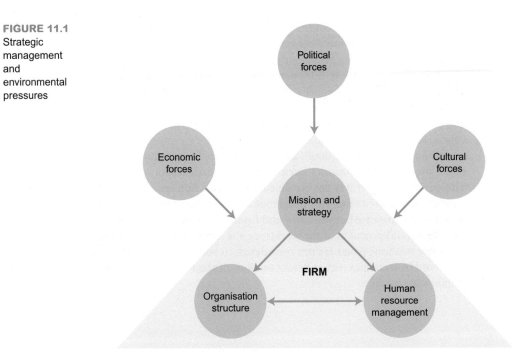

FIGURE 11.1
Strategic
management
and
environmental
pressures

(*Source*: C. Fombrun, N.M. Tichy and M.A. Devanna (1984) *Strategic Human Resource Management*, p. 35. New York: John Wiley and Sons, Inc. © John Wiley and Sons Inc., 1984. Reprinted by permission of John Wiley and Sons, Inc.)

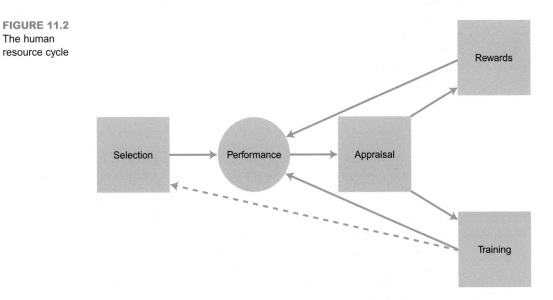

FIGURE 11.2
The human
resource cycle

(*Source*: C. Fumbrun, N.M. Tichy and M.A. Devanna (1984) *Strategic Human Resource Management*, p. 41. New York: John Wiley and Sons, Inc. © John Wiley and Sons Inc., 1984. Reprinted by permission of John Wiley and Sons, Inc.)

Focusing on both types of fit, human resource strategy has been conceived in terms of generating specific employee behaviours. In the ideal form of this there would be analysis of the types of employee behaviour required to fulfil a predetermined business strategy, and then an identification of human resource policies and practices which would bring about and reinforce this behaviour. A very good example of this is found in Schuler and Jackson (1987). They used the three generic business strategies defined by Porter (1980) and for each they identified employee role behaviour and HRM policies required. Their conclusions are shown in Table 11.1.

Although there is little doubt that both types of fit are valuable, questions have been raised over the fit/contingency perspective's simplistic response to organisation strategy. The question 'what if it is not possible to produce a human resource response that enables the required employee behaviour and performance?' is never addressed. So, for example, the distance between now and future performance requirements, the strengths, weaknesses and potential of the workforce, the motivation of the workforce and employee relations issues are not considered. In addition there is evidence that firms use different HR strategies with different sections of their workforce, as shown in the Window on practice.

WINDOW ON PRACTICE

Different HR strategies for different sections of the workforce?

We return to the small pharmaceuticals business introduced in the previous Window on practice: whilst production staff are employed on a temporary basis with little training and modest pay, the company may also employ full-time permanent marketing and sales staff who are offered job security, are highly trained and well paid, and are awarded bonuses according to organisational performance.

This perspective has been also criticised because of its dependence on a rational strategy formulation rather than on an emergent strategy formation approach. Rational strategy formulation is planning strategy clearly in advance and sticking to it whereas emergent strategy formation recognises that strategy changes as it is implemented and as unexpected opportunities arise or the original strategy hits an unexpected block. The fit/contingency approach has also been criticised because of the nature of the one-way relationship with organisational strategy, in other words that business strategy determines HR strategy, and also owing to its unitarist assumptions, as no recognition is made for employee interests and their choice of whether or not to change their behaviour to meet the demands of the HR strategy.

A further form of fit which we have not mentioned so far is cultural fit, and the next Window on practice demonstrates this aspect.

TABLE 11.1 Business strategies, and associated employee role behaviour and HRM policies

Strategy	Employee role behaviour	HRM policies
1 Innovation	A high degree of creative behaviour	Jobs that require close interaction and coordination among groups of individuals
	Longer-term focus	Performance appraisals that are more likely to reflect longer-term and group-based achievements
	A relatively high level of co-operative, interdependent behaviour	Jobs that allow employees to develop skills that can be used in other positions in the firm
		Compensation systems that emphasise internal equity rather than external or market-based equity
	A moderate degree of concern for quality	Pay rates that tend to be low, but that allow employees to be stockholders and have more freedom to choose the mix of components that make up their pay package
	A moderate concern for quantity; an equal degree of concern for process and results	Broad career paths to reinforce the development of a broad range of skills
	A greater degree of risk taking; a higher tolerance of ambiguity and unpredictability	
2 Quality enhancement	Relatively repetitive and predictable behaviours	Relatively fixed and explicit job descriptions
	A more long-term or intermediate focus	High levels of employee participation in decisions relevant to immediate work conditions and the job itself
	A moderate amount of co-operative, interdependent behaviour	A mix of individual and group criteria for performance appraisal that is mostly short term and results orientated
	A high concern for quality	A relatively egalitarian treatment of employees and some guarantees of employment security
	A modest concern for quantity of output	Extensive and continuous training and development of employees
	High concern for process: low risk-taking activity; commitment to the goals of the organisation	
3 Cost reduction	Relatively repetitive and predictable behaviour	Relatively fixed and explicit job descriptions that allow little room for ambiguity
	A rather short-term focus	Narrowly designed jobs and narrowly defined career paths that encourage specialisation, expertise and efficiency
	Primarily autonomous or individual activity	Short-term results-orientated performance appraisals
	Moderate concern for quality	Close monitoring of market pay levels for use in making compensation decisions
	High concern for quantity of output	Minimal levels of employee training and development
	Primary concern for results; low risk-taking activity; relatively high degree of comfort with stability	

Source: R.S. Schuler and S.E. Jackson (1987) 'Linking competitive strategies with human resource management practices', *Academy of Management Executive*, No. 3, August. Reproduced with permission of the Academy of Management.

WINDOW ON PRACTICE

The influence of national culture on human resource management strategies

Fields and his colleagues (2006) investigated whether, under similar conditions, organisations in different cultural contexts would strategically respond in a different manner. They compared US organisations with Hong Kong Chinese organisations and studied their strategic approach in conditions of uncertainty in the supply of qualified labour. They studied three aspects of HR relevant to this situation:

- training and development
- monitoring and assessment of employee performance, and
- staffing through an internal labour market

They found, as they expected, that in these conditions the Hong Kong Chinese companies increased their use of these three HRM strategies, but that the US companies decreased their use. They explain these different strategic approaches by reference to the cultural context.

You may wish to look ahead to the work of Hofstede, which we present in Chapter 14, before reading on.

Training and development (TD) Fields *et al.* (2006) suggest that more TD would be positively viewed by the more collective Chinese culture as a symbol that the organisation is fulfilling its moral obligation to employees, as a way to increase the value of each individual to the collective organisation, and as a reward. Each of these would be valued by Chinese employees, and encourage them to remain with the organisation. Alternatively in the more individualistic US culture managers would be reluctant to invest in TD when labour supply is scarce as employees may take advantage of this and use it to find a better job elsewhere.

Emphasis on performance assessment (PA)* Fields *et al.* (2006) suggest that in the Chinese culture, with greater power distance, greater PA may be viewed by employees as a positive symbol that managers are interested in them, and act as a reminder of the employees' moral association with the organisation – thus encouraging employees to stay. Alternatively in the US culture with lower power distance,** more PA would be viewed negatively. It may be seen as emphasising the difference between managers and employees, and as a way of tightening up the employment relationship, both of which may lead employees to seek employment elsewhere.

Internal labour market (IL) Greater use of the IL might be viewed in a collectivist culture by the Chinese employees as evidence that they are valued by the organisation and thus may encourage retention. Alternatively in an individualistic culture employees may view this unfavourably as evidence of a subjective rather than objective (based on merit) approach to promotion, and managers may view it as a means by which employees can barter for better reward in a tight labour market.

Source: Adapted from D. Fields, A. Chan, S. Aktar and T. Blum (2006) 'Human resource management strategies under uncertainty', *Cross Cultural Management: An International Journal*, Vol. 13, No. 2 pp. 171–86.

* Performance assessment is the same as performance appraisal which we explained in Chapter 5.

** Meaning the social distance between those with most and those with least power. For more details *see* Chapter 14 on Managing people internationally.

Resource-based approach

The resource-based view of the firm (Barney 1991) has stimulated attempts to create a resource-based model of strategic HRM. The resource-based view of the firm is concerned with the relationships between internal resources, of which human resources are one, strategy and firm performance. It focuses on the promotion of sustained competitive advantage through the development of human capital rather than merely aligning human resources to current strategic goals. Human resources can provide competitive advantage for the business, as long as they are unique and cannot be copied or substituted for by competing organisations. The focus is not just on the behaviour of the human resources (as with the fit approach), but on the skills, knowledge, attitudes and competencies which underpin this, and which have a more sustained impact on long-term survival than current behaviour, although this is still regarded as important. Briggs and Keogh (1999) suggest that business excellence is not just about 'best practice' or 'leapfrogging the competition', but about the intellectual capital and business intelligence to anticipate the future, today.

Barney states that in order for a resource to result in sustained competitive advantage it must meet four criteria, and Wright *et al.* (1994) demonstrate how human resources meet these. First, the resource must be *valuable*. Wright and his colleagues show how value is created by matching an individual's competencies with the requirements of the firm and/or the job.

The second criterion, *rarity*, is related to the first in that individuals with high levels of ability are rare and the talent pool is limited, with many employers currently experiencing difficulties in finding the talent that they require.

Thirdly, resources need to be *inimitable*. This quality applies to the human resource as competitors will find it difficult to identify the exact source of competitive advantage from within the firm's human resource pool, as behaviour is affected by the firm's history, and its norms and culture. If the source of competitive advantage is difficult to identify it is therefore difficult to copy.

Finally, resources need to be *non-substitutable*. Although in the short term it may be possible to substitute human resources with others, for example technological ones, in

measurement on from an ad hoc to a strategic and integrated approach. Kaplan and Norton widened the perspective on the measurement of business performance by measuring more than financial performance. Their premise is that other factors which lead to financial performance need to be measured to give a more rounded view of how well the organisation is performing. This means that measures of business performance are based on measures of strategy implementation in a range of areas. Kaplan and Norton identify three other areas for measurement in addition to financial measures: customer measures, internal business process measures and learning and growth measures. In each of these areas critical elements need to be identified and then measures devised to identify current levels and measure progress. Some organisations implementing this scorecard have developed the learning and growth area to include a wider range of HR measures.

The measures are designed to meet the needs of the individual organisation, but in an organisation desiring to develop and retain talent examples might be the annual rate of: days training per individual; qualifications achieved; rate of internal promotions; rate of secondments; employee turnover; and so on.

However, there are in-built barriers in the language of the resource-based view. One is the reference to people as 'human capital' which some consider unnecessarily instrumental. Another is the focus on 'firms' and 'competitive advantage' which makes it harder to see the relevance of this perspective for organisations in the public sector. There is also the issue of what is being measured and who decides this. The risk is that too much time is spent measuring and that not everything that is measured is of critical value to the organisation. So far, such measures appear very varied, although different firms will, of course, need to measure different things. Measures often appear to be taken without a coherent framework, as appears to be the case in the results documented by Scarborough and Elias (2002) for their ten case study organisations, and a version of the balanced scorecard appears to be a useful mechanism in this respect.

Why does the theory matter?

It is tempting to think of these theories of strategic HRM as competing with each other. In other words, one is right and the others are wrong. If this were the case, directors and board members would need only to work out which is the 'right' theory and apply that. This is, of course, a gross oversimplification, as each theory can be interpreted and applied in different ways, and each has advantages and disadvantages. It could be argued that different theories apply in different sectors or competitive contexts. For example Guest (2001) suggests that there is the possibility that a 'high performance/high commitment' approach might always be most appropriate in manufacturing, whereas strategic choice (which could be interpreted as choice to fit with business strategy) might be more realistic in the services sector. This could be taken one step further to suggest that different theories apply to different groups in the workforce, as we have shown with the pharmaceutical company example above.

Consequently, these three theories do not necessarily represent simple alternatives. It is also likely that some board directors and even HR managers are not familiar with any of these theories. In spite of that, organisations, through their culture, and individuals within organisations operate on the basis of a set of assumptions, and these assumptions are often implicit. Assumptions about the nature and role of human resource strategy, whether explicit or implicit, will have an influence on what organisations and managers actually do. Assumptions will limit what are seen as legitimate choices.

Understanding these theories enables managers, board members, consultants and the like to interpret the current position of HR strategy in the organisation, confront current assumptions and challenge current thinking and potentially open up a new range of possibilities.

So far we have taken a look at the assumptions behind different ways of approaching HR strategy. Now we move to more practical matters. HR strategy in an organisation may be nothing more than a not very precisely defined sense of direction, such as 'to be an employer of choice'; alternatively it may be detailed. It may be complete, covering all aspects of human resource management, or it may focus on a current critical issue such as downsizing, to which we now turn our attention.

KEY DEBATE: WHAT ARE THE PEOPLE MANAGEMENT IMPLICATIONS OF DOWNSIZING AND WHERE DOES THE LINE MANAGER FIT IN?

The prevalence and nature of downsizing

The last two decades have seen waves of downsizing in response to competitive pressures, often brought about by changing market demands and processes, increasing use of technology and the utilisation of cheap labour in emerging economies and Third World countries. Downsizing is often associated with restructuring, acquisitions and mergers, in addition to other measures to increase efficiency and minimise costs. Downsizing can be allied to efforts to change the skills base of the organisation and the use of outsourcing and offshoring. We explored in Chapter 1 the impact that downsizing may have in the psychological contract.

WINDOW ON PRACTICE

Prevalence of downsizing

As this chapter was being written in late June 2007 the media were awash with downsizing stories.

The first was Cadbury Schweppes which on 19 June reported that it was selling off the US beverages business and had adopted a four-year plan to

▶

▶ revitalise the confectionery business which involved cutting 7,500 of the 50,000 employees, with a projected profit increase of 50 per cent. The media identified both Cadbury and Schweppes as strong brands which were struggling, and referred to problems earlier in the year such as the salmonella outbreak which took some time to come to light and involved the recall of products that had been sold. The share price was performing poorly at the time in the context of a stock market in a period of bids fever where private equity companies have been buying out companies and making them leaner and fitter. Some reporters spoke of Cadbury taking actions that a private equity company would have taken if it had taken over. Employees who were interviewed spoke of 'being kept in the dark' and 'being the last to know', but recognised that in our global economy the company had to make itself more efficient.

Almost the next day, we heard about Jessops, the photographic specialist, which announced that it was cutting 550 jobs and closing 81 of its 315 stores. This action followed a series of three profit warnings and a major slump in its share price. The company was being squeezed by competition from the Internet and supermarkets and the slowdown in the growth of digital camera sales.

Within a couple of days we heard about the merger of the AA and Saga. Whilst no job cuts were announced the relevant unions feared the worst as one of the reasons for the merger was the advantage of sharing the customer base as both companies were heavily involved in insurance. The AA has recent experience of being in trouble and has to some extent been turned around after its acquisition three years ago which was accompanied by significant job cuts.

On the same day there was an announcement from Thomas Cook that 150 stores were to go and that between 2,500 and 2,800 jobs would be cut. This was as a result of the merger between Thomas Cook and MyTravel which was completed the week before and which was involved in an integration programme. The unions were concerned both about job losses which were greater than expected and about future lack of customer choice. Bland (2007) reported the Joint Chief Executive of Thomas Cook (Manny Fontenla-Novoa) as saying:

> As many as possible of those whose roles are potentially affected by today's news will be offered the opportunity for redeployment, as we are absolutely committed to retaining the skills and experience of all our workforce . . . [and those not taking this option would be provided with] appropriate redundancy packages and support.

On Friday 29 June we heard about the Royal Mail strike which focused on pay and conditions. Commentators reviewing the state of Royal Mail suggested its lack of competitiveness and loss of corporate business was due to the fact that competitors were:

> more efficient and operate on a cost base 25pc lower than the one represented by the Royal Mail's outdated machinery and enormous workforce. (Reece 2007)

and that:

> Competition against the Royal Mail is going to grow, not reduce. The organisation needs to start work immediately to stop this crippling rate of attrition by investing in modern machinery and axing jobs. (Reece 2007)

Sources: varied media sources and

B. Bland (2007) 'Thomas Cook to close 150 stores', **www.telegraph.co.uk**, 26.06 07 updated 5.14pm BST and

D. Reece (2007) 'Billy hasn't learned the lessons from Arthur's failures', **www.telegraph.co.uk**, 30.06.07 updated 2.15am BST.

A particular pressure at the moment is the activities of private equity companies which buy out companies, selling off the unprofitable parts and restructuring and downsizing the remainder to increase efficiency and profit. Whilst media attention to downsizing tends to focus on large well-known companies, the public sector is not immune to this activity; for example, Scarborough and North East Yorkshire NHS Trust announced staff losses of 600 staff (one-third of the workforce) in July 2007. In the university sector funding, the nature of the university experience, courses and the way they are delivered are all changing. The result of this is that universities often need to focus on becoming more efficient and developing a different skills base, and downsizing is used as a tool in pursuit of this.

Line managers are absolutely key to the implementation of any HR strategy, plan and practice, and this has been shown very clearly in the work of Purcell and colleagues (2003). In their research into people and performance they found that whilst a range of HR policies and practices did have a positive impact on employee performance, a poorly implemented policy was worse in terms of the impact on staff performance than having no policy at all. Implementation is particularly relevant for downsizing as this is inevitably a very sensitive issue, and line managers themselves play a complex role in managing employees whose jobs may be at risk as well as potentially feeling at risk themselves. In addition the overall impact of downsizing may make the organisation and its employees very vulnerable in a more general way, and there is considerable evidence of both short- and long-term damage caused by downsizing (*see*, for example, Gandolfi 2007).

There are strategic implications for all areas of the management of human resources in the organisation and for line managers as well as senior management. In the following part of this chapter we focus on implications and challenges and how these may be addressed. We then turn specifically to the role of the line manager as downsizing agent.

Whilst the word downsizing is often used as a catch-all phrase to indicate a deliberate plan to reduce staff numbers, there are many ways in which this can be achieved, and the approach taken will be dependent on the situation in which the organisation finds itself. At one end of the spectrum when a company is facing financial crisis and possibly bankruptcy, downsizing may be announced and actioned overnight. Kwiksave, for example, in a bid for survival closed stores as a matter of urgency, and some of the retained staff worked without payment whilst the company tried to find a buyer to rescue it financially. On the other hand some companies have the financial freedom to allow them to take a more strategic approach to downsizing so that it takes place in a gradual manner over a longer period, often a couple of years. Defensive approaches generally produce a much harsher approach to downsizing with little consultation or employee choice and with a heavy reliance on enforced redundancy. More proactive and strategic approaches can provide more opportunities for communication, management consultation and employee choice and enable more supportive approaches to people management to be taken in the areas of resourcing, employee relations, performance and training and development, all of which may limit the negative consequences of downsizing. We cover this whole spectrum in our discussion (following, for example, Bailey and colleagues, 1996) although there is an alternative view that the word 'downsizing' only reflects the more proactive situation.

Gandolfi (2006) in a broad conceptual framework of downsizing identifies three stages: pre-downsizing, while-downsizing and post-downsizing periods. There will be less time for the pre-downsizing and the while-downsizing periods where downsizing is a reactive and defensive measure. A model of the varied nature of downsizing is shown in Table 11.2.

TABLE 11.2 A model of the varied nature of downsizing

Approach	Defensive and reactive				Strategic and proactive. Systematic and planned
Likely causes	Financial difficulties and crises				General improvements in efficiency and implementation of longer-term business strategy
Likely methods	Immediate enforced redundancy	Longer-term enforced redundancy	Voluntary redundancy. Early retirements	Re-deployment	Natural attrition
Change method	Revolutionary				Evolutionary
Opportunities for management consultation	Less				More
Opportunities for employee choice	Less				More
Downsizing harshness	High				Low

Downsizing implications for people management

Resourcing implications and challenges

If a scheme of voluntary redundancy is adopted there is the issue of maintaining an appropriate skills base, and retaining talent and high performers. Highly skilled high performers are in a strong position to find alternative and maybe improved employment elsewhere, and there is always a danger that the organisation may be left with those employees who realise that they are not the most attractive proposition in the employment market. Also future recruitment for new skills may be damaged as the best talent may avoid applying to organisations that have recently cut back on their human resources, and the way this is done will affect the reputation of the employer, the importance of which we identified in Chapter 1.

The challenge is to carry out downsizing in a way that creates the best chance to retain the highest performers who have skills critical to the future development of the organisation, and Cross and Travaglione (2004) provide some evidence to suggest that the benefits of downsizing are dependent on retaining those employees most valuable to the organisation. In terms of staff losses, some form of enforced redundancy may be appropriate, subject to legal constraints (further details of which are in Chapter 9). Whilst offering early retirement has generally been seen as a 1980s and 1990s phenomenon, there are still employees being offered early retirement packages, usually in large organisations with some remnants of a final salary pension scheme still in place. Voluntary redundancy as well as natural attrition may also have a role to play, both of which are identified in Table 11.2.

However, also important are methods of reassuring employees with potential that they have an exciting future in the organisation, even if historical promotion routes have been blown away. Providing such reassurance can often be overlooked in the speedy execution of an employee reduction policy, but demands considerable general and one-to-one communication with key employees. In addition the support offered to employees who are leaving, and the way that downsizing is handled, will be key in maintaining the reputation of the organisation, attracting future talent and becoming an employer of choice. We have all heard of employees who have been informed they were redundant by email or text message.

When downsizing is allied to restructuring other issues come into play, for example those related to new job descriptions, new duties and new skills, and these raise implications of learning and development, change management and performance.

Activity Box 11.5

What specific actions can managers take that will minimise the damage to the reputation of their employer:

- in the pre-downsizing period
- in the while-downsizing period, and
- in the post-downsizing period?

Explain the anticipated impact of each of your suggested actions.

Performance implications and challenges

Maintaining performance levels when downsizing is in the air, when a programme has begun and after downsizing presents a series of slightly different challenges.

Rumours of downsizing can raise employee dissatisfaction significantly. Employees can become very distracted worrying about job security and applying for other jobs and this may detract from focusing on current job performance. Management actions stand the risk of easily being misinterpreted and allied to imagined plans to 'get rid of my job/get rid of me'. Worrying about what might happen can be more damaging that worrying about what will happen, as the lack of knowledge means that steps cannot easily be put in place to address the problem – if there is one.

Rumours of downsizing are a clear way to invoke negative feelings and damage well-being, potentially reducing employee effort and performance. Recent research demonstrates the importance of employee well-being (including positive feelings, general happiness and job satisfaction) to performance. For example in the National Health Service research has shown that feeling positive is significantly correlated with work performance and patient satisfaction (West 2005). More generally Bayliss (2005) suggests that 'happiness is not only a result of things going well, it is also a cause of them' and 'high spirits help us function better . . . all of which can tangibly benefit the bottom line of any work environment'. It has been suggested that employee satisfaction and well-being are key in explaining the link between people management practices and organisational performance, and that positive feelings at work stimulate extra effort on behalf of the organisation (*see*, for example, Peccei 2004). Positive feelings can promote higher performance in a range of ways: for example, they enable us to think in a more flexible, open-minded way, considering a much wider range of possibilities in accomplishing tasks and encouraging us to cooperate with and help other employees (West 2005).

All this suggests that rumours need to be addressed immediately, and line managers may find themselves in the difficult position of knowing some of what may be happening, but be unable to share this with their employees until a certain date for reasons to do with commercial sensitivity. However, as soon as possible employers need to be clear about what the downsizing plans are and ensure that all employees hear some accurate and hopefully detailed information. Opportunities for employees to ask questions about their concerns, and receive meaningful replies are equally important.

Whilst a downsizing programme is in progress workload often increases as changes are put in place and this may result in a very high workload for a temporary period. High levels of understanding and support are required from managers, who are themselves likely to be experiencing a period of particularly high pressure.

After a downsizing programme there may be discontent about the way communication and the programme were handled and this may have detrimental effects on performance, for example, some employees being concerned about another wave of downsizing. Another problem affecting performance may be the survivor syndrome where, following a harsh programme, the remaining employees may feel guilty that their colleagues have been removed but they are the lucky ones who have retained their jobs. In many cases downsizing appears to leave a smaller number of employees to cope with the existing, unchanged total workload. There are potentially severe mental and physical health consequences if this continues for longer than a transitional period.

If restructuring has resulted in a raft of new jobs performance may dip whilst expectations become clearer, new skills are developed and new areas of knowledge are built up. The role of training and development has a key role to play in this.

Training and development implications and challenges

As well as the need for training and development identified above there are many other ways in which training and development can minimise the negative consequences of downsizing. Preparing existing employees with job search and application skills, building confidence, enabling career change support, and providing ongoing guidance and feedback will all be important. On the other hand managers who will be involved in implementing the downsizing will need some training and development for this role.

WINDOW ON PRACTICE

The impact of training and development in a downsizing situation

Tzafrir and colleagues measured employee responses in a large metalwork factory in Israel which was undergoing a significant downsizing due to a major crisis. The training was voluntary and for all employees and comprised three parts:

— General knowledge input about the Israeli economy and issues such as employment relations, first aid, safety, management by objectives and time management.
— A skills-based approach to dealing with conflict. This included working on self-image, the influence of the group on the individual, interpersonal communication, conflict resolution, personal decision making and job search skills.
— Focused enrichment topics – e.g. in languages or maths.

They found that of those who were eventually dismissed in the downsizing, the ones who had attended the training had more positive reactions than the ones who had not, and this difference was significant. For those who remained in the company attending the training appeared to have no impact on their reactions.

Source: S. Tzafrir, R. Man-Negrin, G. Harel and D. Rom-Nagy (2006) 'Downsizing and the impact of job counselling and retraining on effective employee responses', *Career Development International*, Vol. 11, No. 2, pp. 125–44.

Development might also focus on knowledge management where skills and knowledge are being lost along with employees, and mechanisms need to be developed to capture that knowledge before key individuals leave. In addition support for survivors needs to be provided, addressing the feelings and insecurities they may have as a result of the downsizing.

Employee relations implications and challenges

Preparing the whole organisation for what will happen and how it will happen and explaining the reasons behind this is important, where time allows. Constant communication and information is critical at this time. There is evidence that employees will experience a breach of trust in the psychological contract, and handling the downsizing in the most humane and procedurally fair manner is important in minimising this. Survivors, in addition to those who leave, are likely to experience this. One of the authors investigated a company where a previously relational psychological contract was transformed into a transactional contract as a result of downsizing.

The line manager as downsizing agent

Those directly involved in putting a downsizing programme into action include the CEO, HR specialists and potentially all levels of managers. In some very large organisations there may be dedicated downsizing agents but in this section we focus on the role of the line/senior manager who will sometimes be supported by an HR specialist. Molinsky and Margolis (2006) suggest that until recently little attention has been paid to the impact on those individuals who carried out the downsizing. Those who take an active part in a downsizing programme may experience emotional distress, physical pain and fatigue, and Clair and colleagues (2006) suggest that this results in their reduced effectiveness both during and after the programme. It is therefore important to address this issue as it creates concerns both for the managers' well-being and for the performance of the organisation.

WINDOW ON PRACTICE

Molinsky and Margolis (2006) describe the case of Apparel Incorporated (a US Fortune 500 company although the name has been changed to preserve anonymity) which carried out a downsizing programme. The company made a real effort to make sure its processes were procedurally fair and offered generous severance pay and outplacement support. They briefed managers on the reasons for the programme so that they could explain these coherently to all employees, and trained them in how to carry out a termination interview in a respectful and compassionate manner using a common script. Managers were given role play opportunities to practise termination interviews. However, in spite of sound policies and procedures both line managers and HR specialists had great difficulty handling the termination interviews and were often unable to carry these out as planned. The authors argued that this was because the emotions of the managers carrying out these interviews were neglected and not prepared for. The managers experienced anxiety, fear, sympathy, guilt and shame, which they had not expected, when required to deliver the message to friends and colleagues.

Source: A. Molinsky and J. Margolis (2006) 'The emotional tightrope of downsizing: Hidden Challenges for Leaders and their Organizations', *Organizational Dynamics*, Vol. 35, No. 2, pp. 145–59.

Activity Box 11.6

Consider your own experiences of downsizing (or those of someone you know who has experienced this) and:

1 Describe the role that you (or they) played: include your involvement in implementing and/or being a victim or survivor of downsizing.

2 Identify the emotions that you (or they) experienced: it may help to think of incidents that happened to access your emotions, or you could ask friends and family about how you explained things to them.

3 Suggest what could have been done differently and why.

Clair and colleagues (2006) identified seven factors which make managers implementing downsizing more at risk of stress and burnout. Their data suggested that managers were more at risk if they lacked buy-in to the downsizing, for example if they thought it unjustified or that the wrong employees had been chosen. A second risk factor was if managers felt they had conflicting obligations, for example a professional obligation to be open and honest when asked about rumours of downsizing, but organisational pressures to maintain confidentiality about what was going to happen. Thirdly, some managers felt stigmatised for their role in downsizing and blamed by employees. Fourthly, personal ties could create problems when managers had close relationships with the employees who were laid off. Fifthly, fear for personal safety also concerned some managers who felt they might be targeted by angry employees who had lost their jobs. Sixth was fear about whether they would personally be laid off at the end of their downsizing task. Lastly, the researchers found that managers who had previous experience of downsizing were less emotionally engaged, but that this was often a warning sign of emotional trauma and burnout.

Feelings of emotional distress inevitably mean that managers are unable to play their required role in the downsizing process. Molinsky and Margolis (2006) found that in the termination meeting itself managers would go astray in a variety of different ways, for example in allowing the conversation to develop into bargaining for special allowances; in trying to cushion employees by not being forthright about what would have to happen; in allowing their own emotion to be released during the conversation; in arguing back; or in delivering the message mechanically and lacking in sensitivity.

In order to support managers in the best possible way the organisation needs to acknowledge the role of emotions, and prepare managers thoroughly for this by, for example, very realistic role plays with actors or individuals who have experienced redundancy. More general support can be provided by assessing stress levels in the organisation and providing stress management techniques and support. In particular, a forum where managers can talk about their feelings, perhaps with others in the same situation, may help.

Human Resource Management, Vol. 12, No. 7, pp. 1092–1106.

Higginbottom, K. (2002) 'Profits rise with a written HR strategy', *People Management*, Vol. 8, No. 25, 26 December, p. 9.

Kaplan, R. and Norton, D. (1992) 'The balanced scorecard – measures that drive performance', *Harvard Business Review*, January–February, pp. 71–9.

Kersley, B., Alpin, C., Forth, J., Bryson, A., Bewley, H., Dix, G. and Oxenbridge, S. (2006) *Inside the Workplace: Findings from the 2004 Workplace Employment Relations Survey*. London: Routledge.

Mintzberg, H. (1994) 'The fall and rise of strategic planning', *Harvard Business Review*, February.

Molinsky, A. and Margolis, J. (2006) 'The emotional tightrope of downsizing: Hidden Challenges for Leaders and their Organizations', *Organisational Dynamics*, Vol. 35, No. 2, pp. 145–59.

Peccei, R. (2004) 'Human Resource Management and the search for the Happy Workplace', Inaugural Address to the Erasmus Research Institute of Management, Erasmus University, Rotterdam, 15 January.

People Management (2002) 'Human Capital Review', *People Management*, Vol. 8, No. 15, 25 July, p. 9.

Pfeffer, J. (1998) *Competitive Advantage through People*. Boston: Harvard Business School Press.

Porter, M. (1980) *Competitive Strategy*. New York: Free Press.

Purcell, J., Kinnie, N., Hutchinson, S., Rayton, B. and Swart, J. (2003) *Understanding the People Performance Link: Unlocking the black box*, Research report. London: Chartered Institute of Personnel and Development.

Reece, D. (2007) 'Billy hasn't learned the lessons from Arthur's failures', **www.telegraph.co.uk**, 30.06.07 updated 2.15 am BST.

Roberts, Z. (2002) 'CIPD task force to create new framework for external reporting of human capital', *People Management*, Vol. 8, No. 23, 21 November, p. 7.

Scarborough, H. (2003) *Human Capital – External Reporting Framework*. London: Chartered Institute of Personnel and Development.

Scarborough, H. and Elias, J. (2002) *Evaluating Human Capital – Research Report*. London: Chartered Institute of Personnel and Development.

Schuler, R.S. and Jackson, S.E. (1987) 'Linking competitive strategies with human resource management practices', *Academy of Management Executive*, No. 3, August.

Tyson, S. (1995) *Human Resource Strategy*. London: Pitman.

Tzafrir, S., Man-Negrin, R., Harel, G. and Rom-Nagy, D. (2006) 'Downsizing and the impact of job counselling and retraining on effective employee responses', *Career Development International*, Vol. 11, No. 2, pp. 125–44.

Ulrich, D. (1998) 'A new mandate for human resources', *Harvard Business Review*, Jan.– Feb., pp. 125–34.

West, M. (2005) 'Hope Springs', *People Management*, Vol. 11, No. 20, pp. 38–9.

Wright, P., McMahon, G. and McWilliams, A. (1994) 'Human resources and sustained competitive advantage: a resource-based perspective', *International Journal of Human Resource Management*, Vol. 5, No. 2, May, pp. 301–26.

Chapter 12

Leading people

The objectives of this chapter are to:

1   Introduce a working definition which reflects the general nature of leadership

2   Examine the trait approach to leadership

3   Examine the style (behavioural) and contingency approach to leadership

4   Discuss the ways that leadership can be developed

5   Debate the nature and value of heroic and post-heroic leadership

Good leadership is generally seen as an essential ingredient of a successful organisation and critical to driving change and improvement. But what do we mean by 'good leadership'? Individual managers are often seduced by concepts of leadership that show them to be knights in shining armour with superhuman qualities and (this is the really dangerous bit) adoring followers. The followers rarely have that view of their managers. A different view of leadership is expressed in the work of Baxter and Macleod (2007) who investigated the implementation of improvement programmes in twenty large organisations. Each organisation understood the importance of continuous improvement, which was a business strategy they were all working on, and the specific techniques and tools they were using. However, the researchers report that:

'Yet, despite their knowledge of the methods, these organisations found it hard to turn their strategies into success on the ground. So what went wrong? In most cases problems included poor leadership – particularly where egotistical managers wanted to use these initiatives to further their

▶

▶ careers rather than focusing on the organisation – and a lack of empathy with employees' feelings of insecurity and anger' (Baxter and Mcleod 2007, p. 39).

This suggests that good leaders put the organisation first, rather than themselves, and seek to understand and involve their employees. Easily said, but not so easily done. This alternative perspective reflects leaders as empowering and supporting of others whilst humbly serving the organisation, rather than being the charismatic hero.

Whilst few would argue with the importance of the above characteristics, what is seen as good leadership does appear to change according to time and place. Sometimes heroes are needed but in today's climate in the UK there is an increasing emphasis on an empowering leadership style and the importance of leadership in a wide variety of roles in the organisation which call on different and more modest leadership skills, which can be learned and which are equally important.

In this chapter we first define leadership and investigate fundamental theories of what makes for effective leadership, exploring traits, behaviours and context, and then consider how leadership qualities and skills can be developed. The key issue we debate in the second part of this chapter is the value and different impacts of heroic versus empowering leaders.

SOME DEFINITIONS: LEADERSHIP AND MANAGEMENT

Northouse (2006) suggests that there are four components that characterise leadership: that leadership is a process; it involves influence; it occurs within a group context; and it involves goal attainment. This corresponds with Shackleton's (1995) definition, which we shall use as a working definition for the remainder of the chapter:

Leadership is the process in which an individual influences other group members towards the attainment of group or organizational goals. (Shackleton 1995, p. 2)

This definition is useful as it leaves open the question of whether leadership is exercised in a commanding or a facilitative manner, that is whether leaders direct people in what to do or provide support to them, making it easier for them to work out for themselves what is best for them to do. It does suggest, however, that the leader in some way motivates others to act in such a way as to achieve group goals.

The definition also makes no assumptions about who is the leader; it may or may not be the nominal head of the group. Managers, therefore, may or may not be leaders, and leaders may or may not be managers. Some authors distinguish very clearly between the nature of management and the nature of leadership but this draws on a particular perspective, that of the transformational leader, who initiates change and improvement as opposed to the manager who keeps the organisation ticking over efficiently. We will discuss the value and impact of transformational leaders, who are generally portrayed as heroes, in the key debate towards the end of the chapter. For now let us say that it is a school of thought that concentrates on the one leader at the top of the organisation, which is very different from organisations and individuals who use the terms manager and leader interchangeably with nothing more than a vague notion that managers should be leaders. Indeed, any individual may act as a manager one day and a leader the next, depending on the situation. In addition we should not assume that leadership is always a downwards process. Sometimes employees and managers lead upwards (Hollington 2006), that is, influencing the managers above them to pursue a certain course of action, and sometimes they lead sideways, influencing peers and colleagues.

The flow of articles on leadership continues unabated, but it would be a mistake to think that there is an ultimate truth to be discovered; rather, there is a range of perspectives from which we can try to make sense of leadership. Grint (1997) puts it well when he comments that

> **What counts as leadership appears to change quite radically across time and space. (p. 3)**

In the following three sections we will look at three questions which underlie virtually all the work on leadership. First, what are the traits of a leader, or an effective leader? Secondly, what is the 'best' leadership style or behaviour? Thirdly, if different styles are appropriate at different times, what factors influence the desired style? Answering these questions provides the foundation for debating the difference between heroic and empowering leaders.

WHAT ARE THE TRAITS OF LEADERS AND EFFECTIVE LEADERS?

Trait approaches, which were the earliest to be employed, seek to identify the traits of leaders – in other words what characterises leaders as opposed to those who are not leaders, the emphasis being on personality characteristics. These approaches rest on the assumption that some people were born to lead due to their personal qualities, while others are not. It suggests that leadership is only available to the chosen few and not accessible to all. These approaches have been discredited for this very reason and because there has been little consistency in the lists of traits that research has uncovered. In addition the focus has sometimes been on leaders generally, not distinguishing between effective and ineffective leaders. However, this perspective is frequently resurrected.

Kilpatrick and Locke (1991), in a meta-analysis, which is an overall analysis combining the results of a number of separate research studies on leadership, did seem to find some consistency around the following traits: drive to achieve; the motivation to lead; honesty and integrity; self-confidence, including the ability to withstand setbacks, standing firm and being emotionally resilient; cognitive ability; and knowledge of the business. They also note the importance of managing the perceptions of others in relation to these characteristics. Northouse (2006) provides a useful historical comparison of the lists of traits uncovered in other studies. Perhaps the most well-known expression of the trait approach is the work relating to charismatic leadership. House (1976), for example, describes charismatic leaders as being dominant, having a strong desire to influence, being self-confident and having a strong sense of their own moral values. We will pick up on this concept of leadership in the later debate on leaders portrayed as heroes who are identified as having charismatic personalities.

In a slightly different vein Goleman (1998) carried out a meta-analysis of leadership competency frameworks in 188 different companies. We discuss competency frameworks in more detail in Chapter 6 but for now it is sufficient to think of them as a combination of skills, abilities and traits with the emphasis on describing what people do rather than what they are in terms of their personality. These frameworks represented the competencies related to outstanding leadership performance. Goleman analysed the competencies into three groups: technical, cognitive and emotional, and found that, in terms of the ratios between the groups, emotional competencies 'proved to be twice as important as the others'. Goleman goes on to describe five components of emotional intelligence:

- **Self-awareness:** this he defines as a deep understanding of one's strengths, weaknesses, needs, values and goals. Self-aware managers are aware of their own limitations.
- **Self-regulation:** the control of feelings, the ability to channel them in constructive ways. The ability to feel comfortable with ambiguity and not panic.
- **Motivation:** the desire to achieve beyond expectations, being driven by internal rather than external factors, and to be involved in a continuous striving for improvement.
- **Empathy:** considering employees' feelings alongside other factors when decision making.
- **Social skill:** friendliness with a purpose, being good at finding common ground and building rapport. Individuals with this competency are good persuaders, collaborative managers and natural networkers.

Activity 12.1

Most of us get opportunities to lead people. This may be in a work situation but also it may be in an educational context, with our family or friends, in a volunteering context, in a sports environment or within other interests that we have.

1 Write down all of the occasions when you have led other people, or might be called upon to do so.

2 Assess your strengths and weaknesses on the five components of emotional intelligence identified by Goleman, in any context, leading people or otherwise.

3 How have these strengths and weaknesses affected the way you have led people in the past, or how might they affect the way you lead people in the future?

4 Which weaknesses do you want to improve as a priority?

5 How might you do this?

Goleman's research is slightly different from previous work on the trait approach, as here we are considering what makes an effective leader rather than what makes a leader irrespective of whether or not they are effective. It is also different in that Goleman refers to competencies rather than traits, which as we have said can include a combination of skills, abilities and traits, amongst other things. There is some debate over which competencies can be developed in people, the general feeling being that some can and some cannot. Goleman maintains that the five aspects of emotional intelligence can be learned and provides an example in his article of one such individual. In spite of his argument we feel that it is still a matter for debate, and as many of the terms used by Goleman are similar to those of the previous trait models of leadership, we categorise this model as an extension of the trait perspective. To some extent his work sits between the trait approach and the style approach which follows and which focuses very heavily on leadership abilities and behaviours. It is interesting that a number of researchers and writers are recognising that there is some value in considering a mix of personality characteristics and behaviours, and in particular Higgs (2003) links this approach to emotional intelligence. Rajan and van Eupen (1997) also consider that leaders are strong on emotional intelligence, and that this involves the traits of self-awareness, zeal, resilience and the ability to read emotions in others. They argue that these traits are particularly important in the development and deployment of people skills. Heifetz and Laurie (1997) similarly identify that in order for leaders to regulate emotional distress in the organisation, which is inevitable in change situations, the leader has to have 'the emotional capacity to tolerate uncertainty, frustration and pain' (p. 128). Along the same lines Goffe (2002) identifies that inspirational leaders need to understand and admit their own weaknesses (within reason); sense the needs of situations; have empathy and self-awareness.

We suggest that the qualitites/behaviours of emotional intelligence are fundamental to leading people effectively and that they have enduring value. It is worth noting that there are many different models of emotional intelligence with the emphasis on traits or abilities or both. For more details on this a good start is to read the Study Notes from Nicholas Clarke (2007) in *People Management*.

Activity 12.2

Think of different leaders you have encountered in a wide range of contexts including school, university, employment, family life, voluntary work, leisure activities and sports, or who are in public life. In particular think of those leaders (who *may* not have been called leaders) that were especially effective or ineffective:

1 What differences can you identify in terms of their traits (personal characteristics)?

2 What differences can you identify in terms of their behaviour?

3 Are the trait and behaviour lists connected in any way? If so how?

4 Which of these two approaches – trait or behaviour – do you find more useful in helping you to understand the nature of effective leadership?

DO LEADERS NEED DIFFERENT STYLES FOR DIFFERENT SITUATIONS?

WINDOW ON PRACTICE

Goffee and Jones (2006) highlight the situational nature of leadership by using examples of key figures. They identify how Winston Churchill was an inspirational wartime leader but when this time and place was gone his 'bulldog' style was not well suited to leading the reconstruction of post-war Britain. As an alternative they name Nelson Mandela who is someone who could offer leadership across a wide range of contexts, adjusting from leading whilst in a prison cell on Robin Island to leading from Union House in Pretoria when he was released and became President of South Africa.

Source: R. Goffe and G. Jones (2006) 'The Lizard Kings', *People Management*, Vol. 12, No. 2, 26 January, pp. 32–4.

A variety of models, sometimes termed contingency models, have been developed to address the importance of context in terms of the leadership process, and as a consequence these models become more complex. Many, however, retain the concepts of production-centred and people-centred behaviour as ways of describing leadership behaviour, but use them in a different way. Hersey and Blanchard (1988) developed a model which identified that the appropriate leadership style in a situation should be dependent on their diagnosis of the 'readiness', that is, developmental level or maturity, of their followers. The model is sometimes referred to as 'situational leadership', and works on the premise that leaders can 'adapt their leadership style to meet the demands of their environment' (Hersey and Blanchard 1988, p. 169). Readiness of followers is defined in terms of ability and willingness. Level of ability includes the experience, knowledge and skills that an individual possesses in relation to the particular task at hand; and level of willingness encompasses the extent to which the individual has the motivation and commitment, or the self-confidence, to carry out the task. Having diagnosed the developmental level of the followers, Hersey and Blanchard suggest that the leader then adapts their behaviour to fit. They identify two dimensions of leader behaviour: task behaviour, which is sometimes termed 'directive'; and relationship behaviour, which is sometimes termed 'supportive'. Task behaviour refers to the extent to which leaders spell out what has to be done. This includes 'telling people what to do, how to do it, when to do it, where to do it, and who is to do it' (Hersey 1985, p. 19). On the other hand, relationship behaviour is defined as 'the extent to which the leader engages in two-way or multi-way communication. The behaviours include listening, facilitating and supporting behaviours' (ibid.). The extent to which the leader emphasises each of these two types of behaviour results in the usual two-by-two matrix. The four resulting styles are identified, as shown in Table 12.2.

TABLE 12.2 Hersey and Blanchard's four styles of leadership

High relationship behaviour	High relationship behaviour
Low task behaviour	High task behaviour
Followers are able, but unwilling or insecure	Followers are unable, but willing or confident
Supportive (participating) style (3)	**Coaching (selling) style (2)**
Low relationship behaviour	Low relationship behaviour
Low task behaviour	High task behaviour
Followers are both able and willing or confident	Followers are unable and unwilling or insecure
Delegation style (4)	**Directing (telling) style (1)**

Source: Adapted from P. Hersey and K.H. Blanchard (1988) *Management of Organizational Behavior: Utilizing Human Resources*, 5th edn. Englewood Cliffs, NJ: Prentice-Hall International. © Copyright material, adapted and reprinted with the permission of Center for Leadership Studies, Escondido, CA92025.

There is an assumption that the development path for any individual and required behaviour for the leader is to work through boxes 1, 2, 3 and then 4 in the matrix. Hersey and Blanchard produced questionnaires to help managers diagnose the readiness of their followers.

WINDOW ON PRACTICE

Hilary Walmsley (1999) reports some of her work as a consultant with BUPA. One of the aims of the exercise she was involved in was to:

> raise individuals' awareness of their own management styles and encourage them to stop and think about which approach to adopt rather than automatically respond to every challenge in a similar way. (p. 48)

She recounts the experiences of Brian Atkins, General Manager of BUPA's Gatwick Park and Redwood Hospitals, as an illustration of this learning process. On joining the hospital group, which was undergoing a critical phase of change, in 1990, Atkins consciously used an authoritative leadership style, at the directive and controlling end of the spectrum. Once the hospital was soundly on course for recovery he began to use a more empowering and facilitative style. Atkins describes modern managers as 'style travellers', and suggests that they need to be skilled at using different styles, even though they may naturally prefer one approach. Walmsley notes that managers are tempted to use the same styles out of habit, and are often unaware of alternative styles they could use.

Source: H. Walmsley (1999) 'A suitable play', *People Management*, 8 April, pp. 48–50.

TABLE 12.3 Six leadership styles reported by Goleman

Coercive style	Leader demands immediate compliance
Authoritative style	Leader mobilises people towards a vision
Affiliative style	Leader creates emotional bonds and harmony
Democratic style	Leaders use participation to build consensus
Pacesetting style	Leader expects excellence and self-direction from followers
Coaching style	Leader develops people for the future

Source: Reprinted by permission of *Harvard Business Review*. Adapted from 'Leadership that gets results', by D. Goleman, March–April, pp. 80 and 82–3. Copyright © 2000 by the Harvard Business School Publishing Corporation; all rights reserved.

Goleman (2000) reports the results of some research carried out by Hay/McBer who sampled almost 20 per cent of a database of 20,000 executives. The results were analysed to identify six different leadership styles, which are shown in Table 12.3, but most importantly Goleman reports that 'leaders with the best results do not rely on only one leadership style' (p. 78).

Goleman goes on to consider the appropriate context and impact of each style, and argues that the more styles the leader uses the better. We have already reported Goleman's work on emotional intelligence, and he links this with the six styles by suggesting that leaders need to understand how the styles relate back to the different competencies of emotional intelligence so that they can identify where they need to focus their leadership development.

Activity 12.3

For each of Goleman's six styles think of a leader you have worked with, or know of. Think of leadership which has occurred in a wide variety of situations including school, university, employment, family life, voluntary work, leisure activities and sports, and where the leader may even have been a peer. For each of these individuals write a list of the behaviours that they use. Then consider the impact that these behaviours have on followers.

Do the behaviours have the same impact on all followers? If not, why not?

In a less mechanistic vein Goffee and Jones (2006) suggest that what works for one leader will not necessarily work for another. Whilst adaptability of styles to suit different contexts is key, aspiring leaders need to discover what it is about themselves that they can mobilise in a leadership situation. Given this perspective leadership appears very personal, and what might be most important is to understand your own leadership strengths and playing to these. This idea underpins the inspirational leadership model

managers organise things); leaders motivate and inspire (whereas managers control and solve problems); and leaders encourage change (whereas managers encourage order and predictability). There is a wide research base to support the value of transformational leadership and in particular transformational leaders have been associated with satisfaction, trust and commitment of subordinates, leader effectiveness, and to some extent firm performance in terms of profit.

The approach does have a great strength in taking followers' needs into account and seeking to promote their self-confidence and potential, and the idea of the knight in shining armour is very attractive and potentially exciting. However, in spite of the emphasis on process there is also an emphasis on leadership characteristics which harks back to the trait approach to leadership, which has been characterised as elitist. There is also the ethical concern of one person wielding such power over others. In addition whilst such leaders have often presided successfully over major changes and corporate turnarounds they have often subsequently been removed, or have removed themselves, from office when the organisation began to experience further problems. Transformational leaders may not be the most appropriate in all contexts and the transactional/transformational debate has often overshadowed the importance of 'management' activity. Transformational leaders may be more appropriate for major change and transactional leaders, being management focused, may be more appropriate for complex situations, for example working through the implications of a merger.

Maybe we should ask whether organisations really require such leaders. A very different conception of leadership is now offered as an alternative, partly a reaction to the previous approach, and partly a response to a changing environment. This is termed empowering or post-heroic leadership, and could be described as the currently favoured ideal way to lead. Whilst empowering leadership is often described as a new approach it is perhaps most similar to Goleman's (2000) 'democratic' and 'coaching' style.

WINDOW ON PRACTICE

Goffee and Jones (2006) provide an excellent example of leadership by someone lower down in the organisation. They met Marcia, who was a cleaning supervisor in a large New York office block. She had the ability to read people from different cultures, and although often brash was able to use humour to great effect, not tolerating slovenly cleaning. She managed in unpromising circumstances to forge a high-performing team as members knew she demanded that the job be done well but at the same time she cared about them.

Source: R. Goffe and G. Jones (2006) 'The Lizard Kings', *People Management*, Vol. 12, No. 2, 26 January, pp. 32–4.

Fulop and colleagues (1999) identify factors in a rapidly changing turbulent environment which by the 1990s had diluted the appropriateness of concentrating on the one leader at the top of the organisation. These factors include: globalisation making centralisation more difficult; technology enabling better sharing of information; and change being seen as a responsibility of all levels of the organisation – not just the top. They also note a dissatisfaction with corporate failures, identify few transformational leaders as positive role models, suggest that such a model of male authoritarian leadership is less relevant, and in particular that the macho leader with all the answers does not necessarily fit well with the encouragement of creativity and innovation. In addition they suggest that increasing teamwork and an increasing emphasis on knowledge workers mean that employees will be less responsive now to a transformational leader. The emphasis has therefore moved away from understanding the traits and style of the one leader at the top of the organisation who knows how to solve all the organisation's problems, to how empowering or post-heroic leaders can facilitate many members of the organisation in taking on leadership roles. In this context it has been suggested that female leadership styles, involving a more people-centred democratic approach, are more effective in today's team-based consensually driven organisations. Many commentators speak of leaders with integrity and humility, the ability to select good people and to remove barriers so they can fulfil their potential and perform (*see*, for example, Collins 2003; Alimo-Metcalfe and Alban-Metcalfe 2002).

The leader becomes a developer who can help others identify problems as opportunities for learning, showing trust in members of the organisation and coaching and encouraging them, giving them the freedom to grow via solving organisational problems. Such a leader is also one who can harness the collective intelligence of the organisation, and Fulop and colleagues (1999) note that this means in practice that they encourage the development of a learning organisation (which has been defined by Pedler, Boydell and Burgoyne (1989) as 'an organisation which facilitates the learning of all its members and continually transforms itself').

Senge (1990), who is a protagonist of the learning organisation, sees the leader's new roles in encouraging a learning organisation as designer, teacher and steward, rather than as traditional charismatic decision maker. He suggests that leaders should *design* the organisation in terms of vision, purpose, core values and the structures by which these ideas can be translated into business decisions. However, he also suggests that the leader should involve people at all levels in this design task. It is the role of the leader not to identify the right strategy, but to encourage strategic thinking in the organisation, and to design effective learning processes to make this happen. The leader's role as a *teacher* is not to teach people the correct view of reality, but to help employees gain more insight into the current reality. The leader therefore coaches, guides and facilitates. As a *steward* the leader acts as a servant in that they override their own self-interest by personal commitment to the organisation's larger mission. To play this role effectively Senge suggests that the leader will need many new skills, in particular vision-making skills – a never-ending sharing of ideas and asking for feedback. Skills that will encourage employees to express and test their views of the world are also key. These involve actively seeking others' views, experimenting, encouraging enquiry and distinguishing 'the way things are done' from 'the way we think things are done'.

WINDOW ON PRACTICE

The role that leaders play in the organisation in the twenty-first century is seen by some as very different from the hero roles of the past, and leaders are no longer expected always to know the solutions to problems.

Williams (2000), who talks about enabling and empowering leadership, suggests that 'twenty first century leaders are not expected to be all-knowing gurus and peddlers of panaceas' (p. 113). However, they are expected to know the right questions to ask, as Heifetz and Laurie (1997) suggest: 'leaders do not need to know all the answers. They do need to know the right questions' (p. 124).

Building on this a speaker from Henley Management College (Radio 4, 25 February 2001) argued that leaders need to be able to admit that they do not know all the answers, and that there was a paradox in leadership, as leaders need to display both boldness and humility.

Taking this one step further Anne Atkinson (Radio 4, 29 November 2000), speaking in relation to the tussle over who won the American presidential election, described the leader as a servant, arguing that the best leaders are unwilling leaders and do not seek power, but instead have a desire to benefit the people they lead.

These ideas take us some way from the charismatic and transformational view of the leader.

This changing perspective on leadership is well demonstrated by a survey on leadership skills reported by Rajan and van Eupen (1997). The research is based on interviews with 49 top business leaders, 50 HR directors and a postal questionnaire of 375 companies in the service sector. They asked what were the most important leadership skills during the period 1995–7 and compared the results with those of a similar survey conducted in the late 1980s. They found that the key skill was seen to be inspiring trust and motivation followed by visioning skills and ability, willingness and self-discipline to listen in 1995–7 compared with strategic thinking followed by entrepreneurial skills and originality in the late 1980s. The change in skills base reflects very well the change in the idealised leadership role and the increasing importance of facilitative people-related skills. They also note the prediction that the future will require an equal balance of traditionally masculine and feminine personality traits. For examples *see* Chapter 10 on managing diversity.

Higgs (2003) argues that leaders need a combination of skills and personality: envisioning, engaging, enabling, enquiring and developing skills are needed, together with authenticity, integrity, will, self-belief and self-awareness. These align with more recent developments where leadership is viewed in terms of ethical, authentic, spiritual and servant characteristics (Den Hartog *et al.* 2007), all of which reflect emerging values in our society.

From a slightly different perspective Heifetz and Laurie (1997) propose six guiding principles of post-heroic leadership, and they conclude that leadership is about learning and that the idea of having a vision and aligning people to this is bankrupt. The idea of one leader at the top creating major changes in order to solve a one-off challenge is no longer appropriate, as organisations now face a constant stream of adaptive challenges, and leadership is required of many in the organisation, not just one person at the top. They argue that employees should be allowed to identify and solve problems themselves and learn to take responsibility. The role of the leader is to develop collective self-confidence. As Grint (1997) puts it, 'the apparent devolvement (or desertion – depending on your perspective) of responsibility has become the new standard in contemporary models of leadership' (p. 13).

Activity 12.6

Different leadership styles may be appropriate to different situations, and we all as individuals react to the style being used.

Which style are you, as a follower, personally most comfortable with, and which style are you least comfortable with? Explain why that is the case.

These visions of leadership are very attractive but they do require a dramatic change in thinking for both leaders and followers. For leaders there is the risk of giving away power, learning to trust employees, developing new skills, developing a different perspective of their role and overriding self-interest. For followers there is the challenge of taking responsibility – which some may welcome, but others shun. Yet, if sustained competitive advantage is based on human capital and collective intelligence, it is difficult to relegate this perspective to 'just an ideal'.

We have contrasted two of the most recent trends in leadership, but of course they are not completely different. There are similarities for example in terms of visioning and developing followers. However, there are significant changes and we could say that whilst heroic leaders lead from the front, empowering leaders lead from behind.

WINDOW ON PRACTICE

Effective leadership

Hope (2006) explains how Lady Marie Stubbs turned round the inner London school after its previous Head, Philip Lawrence, was murdered. Stubbs set out to make the children feel valued, first, by physically transforming the building and secondly, by welcoming them back to the school individually. Another way she approached this was to break down the divide between teachers and pupils, for example, instead of locking the pupils out and the staff in at break times, she opened the school and created an atrium that students could use, with staff presence, and played music the pupils would relate to. In the same vein she secured the part-time use of games pitches at Harrow Public School. She consulted pupils on changes and gave them responsibility, such as handling reception for school visitors, focused on their aspirations and believed in them.

Edwards (2006) explains how Greg Dyke led the BBC. Whilst having a vision for the corporation Dyke constantly asked staff how he could improve, and really listened to them. He worked on the basis that he wanted to demonstrate to staff that he cared about them, as people work better if they are valued than if they are afraid. He was not afraid to be himself, and to admit mistakes and say sorry where this was appropriate. He made an effort to look at things from the point of view of the staff, and considered their interests, persuading them that the changes were in their best interests rather than just telling people what to do. He made a great effort to be accessible to staff and when he left thousands of staff across the country staged protests.

Source: K. Hope (2006) 'Lessons Learnt', *People Management*, Vol. 12, No. 6, 23 March, pp. 30–1; C. Edwards (2006) 'On being Gregarious', *People Management*, Vol. 12, No. 8, 20 April, pp. 32–4.

Activity 12.7

Identify the similarities and differences in the approaches of Stubbs and Dyke.

To what extent are they transformational leaders and to what extent are they empowering leaders?

While empowering leaders have been shown to fit with the current climate we may sometimes need heroic leaders. Kets de Vries (2003) makes the point that heroic leadership will never die as change makes people anxious and we need heroic leaders to calm them down, but since no one can live up to the expectations of heroic leaders, they will eventually become a disappointment. We reinforce our earlier conclusion that there is no one best way – different leaders and different leader behaviours are needed at different times.

Summary propositions

12.1 Leadership is a process where one person influences a group of others to achieve group or organisational goals – leadership is thus about motivation.

12.2 The trait model of leadership, although often discredited, continues to play a part in our understanding of leadership.

12.3 Behavioural models are more helpful than earlier models as they concentrate on what leaders do rather than on what they are.

12.4 Some behavioural models offer a 'one best way' of leadership, but more sophisticated models take account of contingency factors such as maturity of followers and the nature of the task.

12.5 Organisations approach leadership development very differently from each other and key differences are who is included in leadership development, the personal depth of development experiences and the mix of methods used.

12.6 Models of transformational leadership treat the leader as a hero who can (singlehandedly) turn the organisation around and deliver it from a crisis.

GENERAL DISCUSSION TOPICS

1   Do we need leaders at all? Discuss what alternatives there might be.

2   'Leadership development should be about learning the business and learning leadership skills. It should not be about personal exploration and understanding emotion as these should be kept personal.' Discuss your views using evidence to support them.

FURTHER READING

IDS (2003) 'Leadership Development', IDS Studies No. 753. London: Incomes Data Services.
A useful book outlining the work of five case study organisations, in terms of their conception of leadership, what prompted their leadership development programmes and an outline of the programmes themselves. The case organisations are the Dixons group, the Inland Revenue, Novartis

Pharmaceuticals, Portsmouth City Council and Skipton Building Society.

Goffee, R. and Jones, G. (2006) *Why Should Anyone be led by you?*, Harvard: Harvard Business School Press; and Goffee, R. and Jones, G. (2006) 'This time it's personal', *People Management*, Vol. 12, No. 21, 26 October, pp. 28–33.
Goffee and Jones combine sound concepts and practical advice on leadership, in the thought-promoting book and article. They identify the context where hierarchy is long enough to get things done,

and that the challenge facing many leaders is to enable highly talented followers to perform to their best. They recognise that leadership, as well as being non-hierarchical, is situational and relational. They suggest that, in meeting the leadership challenge, leaders need to know themselves and show who they are to a sufficient extent; they need to be prepared to take personal risks; they need to be sensitive to context and rewrite this; they need to be authentic, but to conform sufficiently; and they need to manage the social distance between themselves and their followers.

WEB LINK

www.inspiredleadership.org.uk

REFERENCES

Alimo-Metcalfe, B. and Alban-Metcalfe, J. (2002) 'The great and the good', *People Management*, Vol. 8, No. 1, 10 January, pp. 32–4.

Arkin, A. (1997) 'The secret of his success', *People Management*, 23 October, pp. 27–8.

Bass, B.M. (1985) 'Leadership: Good, Better, Best', *Organisational Dynamics*, Winter, pp. 26–40.

Baxter, L. and Macleod, A. (2007) 'Unhappy Mendings', *People Management*, Vol. 13, No. 7, 5 April, pp. 38–40.

Bennis, W.G. and Nanus, B. (1985) *Leaders: the strategies for taking charge*. New York: Harper and Row.

Blake, R.R. and Mouton, J.S. (1964) *The Managerial Grid*. Houston, Texas: Gulf Publishing.

Brockett J (2007) 'Coca-Cola's simulation centre finds top talent', *People Management*, Vol. 13, No. 20, 4 October, p. 16.

Clarke, N. (2007) 'Research Forum: Be selective when choosing emotional intelligence training', *People Management*, Vol. 13, No. 9, 3 May, p. 48.

Collins, J. (2003) 'From good to great', presentation to the CIPD National Conference, Harrogate, 22–24 November 2003.

Den Hartog, D., Caley, A. and Dewe, P. (2007) 'Recruiting Leaders: An analysis of leadership adverts', *Human Resource Management Journal*, Vol. 17, No. 1, pp. 58–75.

Edwards, C. (2006) 'On being Gregarious', *People Management*, Vol. 12, No. 8, 20 April, pp. 32–4.

Fulop, L., Linstead, S. and Dunford, R. (1999) 'Leading and managing', in L. Fulop and S. Linstead, *Management. A Critical Text*. South Yarra: Macmillan Business.

Goffe, R. (2002) 'Send out the right signals', *People Management*, Vol. 8, No. 21, 24 October, pp. 32–8.

Goffe, R. and Jones, G. (2006) 'The Lizard Kings', *People Management*, Vol. 12, No. 2, 26 January, pp. 32–4.

Goleman, D. (1998) 'What makes . . . a leader?', *Harvard Business Review*, Nov.–Dec., pp. 93–102.

Goleman, D. (2000) 'Leadership that gets results', *Harvard Business Review*, March–April, pp. 78–90.

Grint, K. (1997) 'Introduction', in K. Grint (ed.) *Leadership*. Oxford: Oxford University Press.

Heifetz, R. and Laurie, D. (1997) 'The work of leadership', *Harvard Business Review*, Jan.–Feb., pp. 124–34.

Heil, G., Bennis, W. and Stephens, D.C. (2000) *Douglas McGregor, revisited: managing the human side of the enterprise*. New York: Wiley.

Hersey, P. (1985) *Situational Selling*. Escondido, California: Centre for Leadership Studies.

Hersey, P. and Blanchard, K.H. (1988) *Management of Organizational Behavior: Utilizing Human Resources*, 5th edn. Englewood Cliffs, NJ: Prentice-Hall International.

Higgs, M. (2003) 'How can we make sense of leadership in the 21st century?' *Leadership and Organisation Development Journal*, Vol. 24, No. 5, pp. 273–84.

Hollington, S. (2006) 'How to lead your boss', *People Management*, Vol. 12, No. 24, 7 December, pp. 44–5.

Hope, K. (2006) 'Lessons Learnt', *People Management*, Vol. 12, No. 6, 23 March, pp. 30–1.

House, R. (1976) 'A 1976 theory of charismatic leadership', in J. Hunt and L. Larson (eds) *Leadership: the Cutting Edge*. Carbondale, Ill.: Southern Illinois University Press.

Kets de Vries, M. (2003) 'The dark side of leadership', *Business Strategy Review*, Vol. 14, No. 3, pp. 25–8.

Kilpatrick, S. and Locke, E. (1991) 'Leadership: Do Traits Matter?', *Academy of Management Executive*, Vol. 5, No. 2, pp. 48–60.

Kotter, J. (1990) *A Force for change: How leadership differs from management*. New York: Free Press.

McGregor, D. (1960) *The Human Side of Enterprise*. New York: McGraw-Hill.

Mitchell, S. (2007) 'Leaders in transition need organizational support to succeed in their new role', *People Management*, Vol. 13, No. 11, 31 May, p. 46.

Northouse, P. (2006) *Leadership – Theory and Practice*, 4th edn. California: Sage.

Pedler, M., Boydell, T. and Burgoyne, J. (1989) 'Towards the learning company', *Management Education and Development*, Vol. 20, Pt 1.

Rajan, A. and van Eupen, P. (1997) 'Take it from the top', *People Management*, 23 October, pp. 26–9.

Senge, P. (1990) *The Fifth Discipline: The art and practice of the learning organisation*. London: Century Business, Random House.

Shackleton, V. (1995) *Business Leadership*. London: Routledge.

Smedley, T. (2007) 'In at the deep end', *People Management*, Vol. 13, No. 5, 8 March, pp. 32–34.

Walmsley, H. (1999) 'A suitable ploy', *People Management*, 8 April, pp. 48–50.

Williams, M. (2000) *The war for talent: Getting the best from the best*. London: Chartered Institute of Personnel and Development.

CHAPTER 13

The HR contribution

The objectives of this chapter are to:

1 Explore the role of line managers in HRM

2 Explain a current model of HR roles and structure and how these impact on the line manager

3 Examine the extent of HR outsourcing and the benefits and drawbacks of this approach to the organisation

4 Debate the value for line managers and employees of HR shared services and e-HR

'There's a lot of mumbo-jumbo out there. HR isn't responsible for the people in the company. Managers are the ones who are responsible' (Smedley 2007, quoting Allan Leighton, Chairman of Royal Mail). Smedley goes on to report that Leighton rejected the idea that HR should push ahead on leading-edge practices such as flexible working and diversity; instead he firmly placed this with line managers. 'I don't think that's anything to do with HR. It's all to do with managing and line managers. In retail, store managers are responsible for all their people – they're often a thousand miles away from the HR department', Leighton stated. However, he did see a role for HR in helping to develop people policies, monitor progress and acquire needed training.

So line managers are responsible for HR, with some background support from the specialist HR function, but a line manager's role is not easy these days and as one senior executive said, 'We have to do our own finance and now we're doing HR's job as well!' (Dalziel and Strange 2007). You can almost hear the exasperated sigh!

Activity 13.1

Some organisations have specialist HR departments/functions, which may be structured in a variety of different ways, whilst others have no specialist HR function at all.

Based on your understanding of people management tasks and activities outlined in this book:

1 What might be the advantages of not having a specialist HR department?

2 What might be the disadvantages?

3 How might these disadvantages be overcome?

Herein lies the dilemma. Managers need to be free to manage their people as they are the ones in the front line and understand the business priorities. However, people management responsibilities require time, expertise and commitment (to people management) and busy line managers are not always blessed with all three of these. The key is how people management activities are shared between the line manager and the HR specialist so that each can contribute according to their skills. So, for example, if an employee has a grievance both the line manager and the HR specialist have different but complementary roles in resolving this. In this case the HR specialist would normally design appropriate procedures to comply with the law and provide ongoing guidance to the line manager, whilst the manager would initially listen to the grievance, investigate it and resolve it if possible. If the grievance remains unsolved the HR specialist may be involved in further meetings with the complainant.

If HR tasks are greatly devolved to line managers without the appropriate support then managers may flounder, feel 'dumped on', be overworked, and HR decisions may lack consistency throughout the organisation. This lack of consistency is likely to mean that employees receive inconsistent messages about what is expected from them, leading them to lose confidence in the organisation and to question whether it is really concerned about their well-being or just about their performance. Inconsistency may also promote complaints to the union about unfair or unequal treatment.

WINDOW ON PRACTICE

The authors have conducted research in a particular Health Trust where there was an emphasis on empowering managers to take on people management responsibilities. This Trust was also trying to encourage flexible working and made it clear that line managers were to support this and make immediate and local decisions when staff requested flexible working arrangements. Some departments allowed all staff to rearrange their hours in order, for example, to go to the hairdressers during normal working hours; some favoured women with children in agreeing to ad hoc or more permanent flexible arrangements; some only allowed flexible working if there was an emergency at home.

As staff became aware of what other departments did there was some disgruntlement from those in departments where a more restrictive view was taken. Also line managers, who were generally trying to do their very best to implement the Trust's policy and be fair to the employees in their department, were often concerned about whether what they were doing was compatible with what other departments were doing and often felt unsure about the limits of their empowerment.

However, if HR tasks are too dominated by HR specialists there are concerns that business priorities may suffer as HR in their ivory tower are disconnected from business realities, while line managers may avoid some of their people management responsibilities, so weakening their relationship with employees and missing opportunities for real performance improvement.

The sharing of tasks between the line manager and the HR specialist is also affected by the way that the specialist function is structured and where people specialists are located in the organisation. Historically HR departments have been highly centralised but there is currently a trend to decentralise HR staff so that they are located at lower levels in the organisation, say, within departments or at separate locations so that HR expertise is more accessible and HR specialists closer to business realities. Alongside this development, however, in some organisations line managers and employees now need to contact remote service centres and electronic HR systems for basic HR support and only access HR specialists in centres of HR expertise for more complex issues. A complex issue may be, for example, a grievance about lack of equal pay which may require considerable research, with any decision having potential consequences for other employees.

So the sharing of HR tasks between line manager and HR specialist is key. In this chapter we look at how such tasks may be shared, the varied nature of HR roles and structures in an organisation, what line managers can expect from the ever-changing HR function, and how to get the best out of such arrangements. The key debate focuses on the value of shared services for the delivery of HR.

THE ROLE OF LINE MANAGERS IN HR

There has been an emphasis for some time on line managers taking more ownership of HR activities, enabling HR specialists to act as a consultant, coach, facilitator and strategic partner. The advantages of this approach to restructuring HR activities have been identified as allowing HR specialists to focus on strategic (such as leading the design of a new performance management system to match changing business priorities and which aims to influence the organisational culture) rather than operational concerns, and a strengthening of the relationship between the employee and their manager resulting in a more positive management approach to employee performance. The importance of the role of the line manager in delivering HR is well documented, especially by Hutchinson and Purcell (2004), as in their research they found that first line manager behaviour is:

> the most important factor explaining the variation in both job satisfaction and job discretion, or the choice that people have over how they do their jobs. It is also one of the most important factors in developing organizational commitment. (p. ix)

Hutchinson and Purcell suggest that line managers bring HR policies to life, and in the passage quoted show how line managers have a direct impact on employee performance. The authors relate the example of four Tesco stores. Using a variety of measures they found that employee performance and related attitudes were similar in three of the stores but much weaker in the fourth. Each store was governed by the same HR policies and procedures but the difference lay in the store managers and the way that they implemented these. So line managers have a critical role in the success or otherwise of HR policies and procedures.

The CIPD conduced a survey in 2007 focusing on the role of line managers in HR and asked about who had the responsibility, either line managers or the HR function, for some major areas of HR activity. The results are shown in Table 13.1.

Table 13.1 shows only one activity where line managers are more likely to be solely or mainly responsible, and that is work organisation. On the other hand the HR function is more likely to have sole or major responsibility for pay and benefits, employee relations and implementing redundancies. Whilst recruitment and selection and training and development are most likely to be shared, when this does not happen line managers are more likely to take a greater role in recruitment and selection and HR more likely to take a greater role in training and development.

TABLE 13.1 Line manager and HR responsibility for some key HR activities: Comparison between 2007 and 2003

Work area	Line/mainly line has responsibility in 2007 (2003 figure in brackets)	Shared responsibility between line and HR in 2007 (2003 figure in brackets)	HR/mainly HR has responsibility in 2007 (2003 figure in brackets)
Recruitment/selection	29 (31)	55 (52)	16 (17)
Pay and benefits	7 (8)	28 (29)	65 (62)
Employee relations	6 (8)	40 (40)	54 (52)
Training and development	10 (12)	49 (44)	42 (43)
Implementing redundancies	4 (6)	34 (34)	62 (59)
Work organisation*	54	37	9

The figures are percentages.

*Work organisation was not asked about in 2003.

Source: This table is taken from Survey Report: The changing HR function (2007) with the permission of the publisher, the Chartered Institutue of Personnel and Development, London (www.cipd.co.uk).

However the table also importantly shows that in spite of the increased pressure to devolve HR activities there has been little change since 2003, and the difficulties of devolving HR activities to first-line managers have been consistently highlighted. In our research, we found that implementation was difficult, sometimes being described as a game of tennis where although there was a deliberate policy to devolve HR activities, and managers were encouraged to take them on, these often bounced straight back to HR specialists, as line managers did not feel they had the skill, interest or time for this. Hope-Hailey and colleagues (2005), for example, on the basis of their research found that line managers neither were motivated nor had the ability to take on people management responsibilities. However, McConville (2006) in the context of the NHS, the Armed Forces and the Fire Services, found that middle managers wanted to be proactive in HR and were committed to it, and exceeded their job requirements to carry out HR activities, but their already substantial workload created the greatest barrier. Caldwell (2004) found that managers resisted taking full ownership of HR and conversely HR professionals wanted to retain control over HR policy. His interviewees who were HR specialists were generally reluctant to take devolution 'too far', as ultimately too much devolution may result in the HR role itself being devalued. Our evidence supports this, that HR specialists were keen to hand over the responsibility for day-to-day HR activities, but were less keen to hand over authority for them and the associated budgets. Problematic aspects of line manager involvement in HR activities have also been identified as the lack of consistency of HR decisions, lack of integration (for example making sure decisions about reward are aligned with decisions about learning and development) and more difficulties, therefore, in implementing HR strategy.

WINDOW ON PRACTICE

Maxwell and Watson (2007), on the basis of their investigation into line manager and HR manager perspectives of line management involvement in HR in Hilton Hotels, propose three types of line manager buy-in which are key to their active involvement in HR activities. These are:

- a conceptual understanding of the reasons for their involvement
- the ability to implement these activities effectively through clarity of the HR role and having sufficient capability and
- an effective commitment in believing that their involvement in HR is valuable

Interestingly the authors also found a general lack of shared understanding between line managers and HR specialists relating to the role of line managers in HR, and some indications that similar perceptions on the part of HR and line managers appeared to be related to better hotel performance while more disparate perceptions were related to weaker hotel performance.

Source: G. Maxwell and S. Watson (2007) 'Perspectives on line managers in human resource management: Hilton International's UK Hotels', *International Journal of Human Resource Management*, Vol. 17, No. 6, pp. 1152–70.

ANALYSIS OF HR ROLES AND STRUCTURES

We have so far looked at HR activities and how these may be shared between the line manager and the HR function. There is another way to look at the HR contribution and that is to look at overall HR roles or purposes (which we list below) and the impact that each of these has on the line manager.

Early HR specialist roles (then termed 'personnel') focused on staff welfare and representing staff to management, but increasingly HR managers have become identified with management and to a lesser extent as the champion of the employees.

Activity 13.2

'HR specialists are there to support the employee. This means they can't be part of the management team, as you can't be on both sides at the same time.'

'HR specialists need to be part of the management team. They are not there to provide tea and sympathy for employees. It is up to managers to look after the well-being of their staff.'

Debate these two positions.

The most influential recent work has been carried out by Ulrich and Brockbank (2005) on the basis of research in leading-edge organisations in the USA. They identified five HR roles: employee advocate; human capital developer; strategic partner; functional expert; and the compound role of leader. Whilst Ulrich and Brockbank use these roles to focus on what an HR professional has to do to create value (that is make a valuable and identifiable contribution to organisational competitiveness), it is also extremely useful for the line manager to understand them as:

- line managers play a major part in some of these roles
- the roles make explicit what expertise may be available in the HR function that line managers can then draw upon
- if line managers understand the priorities and aspirations of the HR specialists they are in a better position to work more effectively with them and get the best out of this relationship

Table 13.2 Summarises the nature of these roles and their implications for line managers.

The model suggests that HR must deliver on all roles which means that there is a paradox as HR specialists act as employee advocate and part of management at the same time. As line managers take on more HR activities they inherit this paradox and potential conflict.

TABLE 13.2 Implications of the five Ulrich and Brockbank HR roles for the line manager

Roles from Ulrich and Brockbank (2005)	Explanation of role	Implications for the line manager
Employee advocate	Caring for, listening to, understanding and responding to employee needs. Covering issues such as grievances, the impact of strategy on employees, equality, diversity, health and safety, discipline and so on. All these are played out in the context of the realities of the firm and the performance standards required of individuals. This role has previously been termed 'employee champion'.	A large part of this role is increasingly devolved to the line manager with background support from HR specialists.
Human capital developer	Based on the premise that people are a critical asset of the organisation and need to be developed proactively with a focus on maximising their potential and contribution in the future.	Much of the day-to-day development activity is often devolved to line managers, for example assessing development needs, coaching employees, feedback and so on, as we discussed in Chapter 6. HR specialists in this area are likely to be more remote and more centralised, perhaps working in centres of HR expertise where varieties of higher-level coaching and facilitation and major development programmes and initiatives are organised, such as development centres, graduate programmes, development for succession planning.
Strategic partner	This role has multiple dimensions, including consultant, change agent, knowledge manager and business expert.	This is the role to which most HR specialists aspire, but it may only exist in part. In large organisations especially, the HR specialist may provide consultancy services for all levels of manager, may operate as a change agent at all levels of the business and be a resource in developing knowledge management strategies and practices. It is the challenge of becoming an expert in the business and being close to the business that is receiving considerable attention at the moment.

WINDOW ON PRACTICE

HR outsourcing at the BBC

Pickard (2006) provides details of the HR outsourcing deal between the BBC and Capita. The deal is worth £100m and involves the transfer of around 260 staff from the BBC to Capita, and is expected to save the BBC £50m. The contract is part of a wider transformation of HR at the BBC involving more than 200 redundancies, and focused on making the function more strategic and provide better value for money. The deal is Capita's first end-to-end HR outsourcing project, but the firm has already held contracts for single functions such as payroll. The services to be outsourced are:

- recruitment
- pay and benefits, but not pensions
- assessment, outplacement and some training and development
- HR administration
- relocation
- occupational health
- disability access services

HR remaining in the BBC has been centralised and includes pensions and training and development and a Business Partner model has been introduced in the divisions.

Source: J. Pickard (2006) 'Conflicting Schedule', *People Management*, Vol. 12, No. 5, 9 March, pp. 14–15.

In the BBC example in the Window on practice box above employees will notice a difference in situations such as: when they have a pay query as they will need to contact Capita; if they are off sick and called in for an occupational health interview they will meet an occupational health nurse from Capita; when a line manager needs to recruit it will be a Capita employee who works with them over placing the advertisement and administering the procedure. Both Unilever and BT have similar deals with Accenture.

Outsourcing the whole of HR (sometimes called end-to-end outsourcing) is also a very different proposition from outsourcing differentiated activities, which has been happening in an ad hoc manner for a much longer time. Blackburn and Darwen Borough Council, for example, has outsourced all its HR to Capita, including strategic HR, which is the one part that most organisations retain in-house.

Some organisations have clearly experienced advantages from outsourcing, although many of these are based in the USA. There is a question as to the extent to which such an approach should be applied in the same way in the UK, which has a different national culture, and there is evidence that firms in the UK are resisting outsourcing. BP experienced only limited success when it outsourced to Exault and John Hofmeister, director of HR at the Royal Dutch/Shell group, attacks outsourcing as leading to the corrosion of HR departments, and he claims that only high levels of internal HR staffing can lead to and maintain high levels of HR practices (*People Management* 2002). Outsourcing combined with other trends such as devolution fragments the HR function, and there is a challenge in pulling together the efforts of different providers (outsourcing agencies, line managers and remaining specialists in the HR function).

Such outsourcing has been dogged with many problems, to the extent that some organisations have brought HR back in-house, and others, for example BT, have acknowledged problems with the clarification of responsibilities and with communication. In terms of possible adverse consequences Cooke *et al.* (2005) identify potential skill, knowledge and capacity loss, reduction in quality of services, loss of employee morale, short-term disruption and discontinuity, and damage to long-term competitiveness. Outsourcing HR therefore has the potential to create a major negative impact on both line managers and employees.

KEY DEBATE: HR SHARED SERVICES – WHAT'S BEST FOR LINE MANAGERS AND EMPLOYEES?

Some organisations think that a better alternative to outsourcing is to use an HR service centre or shared service centre. Line managers and employees are likely to feel the impact of such centres, especially as they are often associated with restructuring of the HR function and the introduction of e-HR encompassing self-service online systems for line managers and employees. On such a system, the line manager may be able to update employee records and the employee may be able to log holiday bookings. Shared service centres are sometimes referred to as partnership service centres or insourcing, depending on the circumstances. For example the next Window on Practice shows how Rotherham Borough Council has entered into a strategic partnership with BT.

WINDOW ON PRACTICE

Rotherham Brought Together (RBT)

Incomes Data Services (IDS) (2003) reports how Rotherham Borough Council and BT created RBT. RBT is responsible for HR administration and payroll, the management of IT functions, procurement, customer contact and revenues and budgets.

Five hundred council staff have been seconded to RBT on their existing terms and conditions, and new appointees will be on the same conditions. For their part BT has invested heavily in RBT, and will take the profit from the operation. However, after a certain level of profit has been achieved the profit will be shared with Rotherham BC.

RBT includes an integrated HR/payroll system, self-service HR through an intranet, and an HR service centre to deal with transactional and operational HR issues. The first port of call is intended to be the intranet and then the service centre, but for some issues such as discipline and grievance a specialist adviser will be made available.

Alongside the creation of RBT line managers have been given more responsibility for HR, and HR staff have been centralised, although some senior HR staff remain in Rotherham BC with a remit which includes strategy, policy, organisational development and culture change, among other issues.

There is a plan to take on work from other clients in the future.

Source: Summarised from IDS (2003) 'Outsourcing HR administration', IDS Study Plus, Spring.

London bodies plan shared services

The Greater London Authority (GLA) and the Metropolitan Police (Met) are both planning shared service centres.

The Met plans to open its first centre in 2008 and it is designed to deal with font-line queries and provide self-updating access and HR services for both managers and employees. Such centres would be backed up by Centres of Excellence.

In the GLA the service centres are intended to group transactional functions such as payroll, pensions, absence management and occupational health, an approach already used by Transport for London. A framework is being developed for greater integration across the GLA group.

Source: J. Brockett (2006a) 'London Bodies Plan shared services', *People Management*, Vol. 12, No. 11, 1 June, p. 10.

MoD shares HR operations

The Ministry of Defence (MoD) has set up a dedicated in-house agency called the People, Pay and Pensions Agency (PPPA) to act as a shared services operation dealing with transactional HR issues. There will be two shared service centres, in Manchester and Bath, and they will cover payroll, absence management, discipline services, health and welfare. This covers 80,000 non-military staff and it is expected to save £283m over the next ten years.

The move is intended to support attempts to devolve more HR responsibility to line managers, and enable the professional HR function to concentrate more on strategic issues. The strategic HR team is made up of Business Partners and a core strategic team focusing on such areas as talent management. In parallel with these changes the overall HR function is being reduced from 3,000 HR managers at the end of 2004 to 1,700 by 2008.

Source: R. Manocha (2006) 'MoD Shares HR operations', *People Management*, Vol. 12, No. 5, 9 March, p. 10.

Shared services save RBS £11m

In 2004 the Royal Bank of Scotland (RBS) launched a shared services HR system to support 130,000 employees in eight divisions. The system is designed to allow managers and employees access to HR services online, and the bank claims to have saved £11m in each year of its operation. The online system was designed to replace paper and telephone transactions, but was introduced with a 'soft launch' where other methods of contact were allowed alongside the online self-service method. The next step is to introduce compulsory self service by agreeing dates when other transaction channels are cut off.

Source: *People Management* (2006b) 'Shared services save RBS £11m', Vol. 12, No. 5, 9 March, p. 13.

HR service centres often result from a company's drive to achieve a more efficient form of HR delivery, and this is primarily achieved by streamlining and centralising routine HR processes and transactions. Also you will note in the above Window on practice examples that there is a strong emphasis on devolution of HR tasks to line managers in conjunction with the introduction of service centres. In addition such a service centre is usually the primary point of reference for line managers with HR queries. The benefits they identify are savings from lower transaction costs, the removal of unneeded duplication, a more consistent HR approach across the whole of a company and an HR service which is more customer focused and more responsive to business needs.

Service centres may be HR centres or may be part of a shared centre with other functions, such as IT or finance. Other terms used are HR call centre or client centre. In terms of operation many centres will have staff based in the 'back office' dealing with administration and transactions, and different staffing for the 'front office' where enquiries from line managers are handled. Alternatively staff may be organised in teams by specialist function or client group (IDS 2003). Staff at the service centre would have electronic access to personal employee details and HR policies and so on.

One of the advantages of such centres is the metrics that can be derived to assess their performance. Examples are call waiting time, call count, call length, time taken to resolve queries, accuracy and satisfaction measures from users. There is usually a system of escalation where queries can be fed up to the next level if the original call centre operator cannot resolve them, so for example there would be access to a functional specialist for non-routine or complex queries. An example would be if an individual asked for a year of unpaid leave and there is no policy in place covering this request, and if the request is agreed to, it may set a precedent.

One form of shared services is to have an online or e-HR self-service system, as in the RBS example in the last Window on practice. Such systems may offer cost saving advantages, but can pose special problems of their own, inducing feelings of remoteness, dehumanisation and lack of customer friendliness. *People Management* (2006a) reports on a study by Roffey Park Institute which investigated line manager perceptions of e-HR. The two negative aspects most frequently reported were that line managers felt they had insufficient training on the system, and that employees were penalised when they did not keep their records up to date. Managers felt that they spent too much time on HR administration and that the online help available was of poor quality.

WINDOW ON PRACTICE

HR service centres: task limits

Recruitment administration is a task that a service centre would be likely to take on, and IDS (2001) provides an example of how this would work in practice. IDS (2001) suggests that:

- Service centre staff would:
  - place advertisements
  - issue application forms
  - receive application forms
  - deal with candidate management
  - provide information for shortlisting and interviewing
  - arrange interviews and assessment dates
  - prepare and send offer and reject letters
  - draw up and send out contracts
  - request references
  - send out starter packs
  - enter new starters on records system
  - monitor equal opportunities

- Line managers, perhaps supported by a local HR adviser, would:
  - determine the need for the vacancy
  - confirm/draw up job and person specifications
  - define selection and assessment processes
  - shortlist
  - carry out interviews
  - make the final selection decision
  - co-determine salary package

Source: Summarised from IDS (2001) 'HR Service Centres', IDS Study No. 707, April.

The problems with the service centre structure are that local knowledge and business solutions may be lost in the changeover, many low-level administrative roles are created with little potential for career development and there may be an obsession with measurement at the expense of service delivery. Service centres and e-HR often result in there being no HR specialist at a local level and there is evidence that the employee as well as the line manager experience may suffer as a result. For example an employee with a query or a problem cannot walk down the corridor or to the adjacent building to get advice from an HR specialist they are familiar with. Instead they will need to ring a number and speak to an anonymous person who does not know them as an individual.

Activity 13.5

There is evidence that line managers have experienced problems with HR service centres and e-HR.

1 What actions could be taken to enhance line manager experiences of this approach?

2 What actions could be taken to enhance employee experience of this approach?

Consequently employees may be less likely to see HR as form of support and advice and research suggests they are more likely to approach a union or use legal redress, making the employment relationship more adversarial. The unions are already picking up on this and Harry Donaldson (Regional Secretary of GMB Scotland) commented that unions were worried about HR shifting its focus away from the workforce and away from 'traditional HR' which was associated with welfare and trust. Given that line managers do not always have the skills, he suggested that the chasm thus created between HR and the workforce would be filled by the unions (CIPD 2005).

SUMMARY PROPOSITIONS

13.1 HR activities are a shared responsibility between line managers and HR specialists.

13.2 There is currently an emphasis on empowering line managers to take on more and more HR activities, but line managers do not always have the motivation, skill or time to take these on.

13.3 Ulrich and Brockbank identify five HR roles: employee advocate; human capital developer; strategic partner; functional expert; with leader being the summary role. There is an inbuilt conflict in the HR function being an employee advocate as well as part of the management structure, and as line managers take on more HR tasks they inherit this conflict.

13.4 The HR function is undergoing major restructuring. In some organsations a three-legged HR department structure appears to be evolving: a strategic/business partner group; administrative/transactional group usually comprising shared services, e-HR and/or outsourcing; a centre of functional expertise group. All of these have an impact on line managers and employees.

13.5 Whilst there have been some early problems with HR outsourcing, this route continues to be pursued by many organisations.

13.6 The use of HR service centres may result in difficulties for the line manager, and HR being distanced from employees, although there may be cost and consistency advantages.

GENERAL DISCUSSION TOPICS

1   'It is in a line manager's interest that HR specialists are recruited internally from line managers and then developed to become HR specialists, rather than recruit HR specialists who already have HR expertise but no line manager experience.' Discuss the advantages and disadvantages of this point of view.

2   'Line managers have enough to do without trying to offload someone else's job on to them. The line manager's job is to get the job done; the HR specialist is there to do the people part.' Discuss

3   'If HR expertise is to be outsourced then it should be a team of line managers who decide who it should be outsourced to and how, as they are the users of the service.' Discuss

FURTHER READING

Scott, A. (2007) 'The line's share', *People Management*, Vol. 13, No. 20, 4 October, pp. 34–5.

A good example of how line managers have become more involved in HR in Surrey County Council.

WEB LINK

www.cipd.co.uk

REFERENCES

Beckett, H. (2005) 'Perfect Partners', *People Management*, Vol. 11, 1 April, pp. 16–23.

Brewster, C. and Less, S. (2006) 'The success of NGOs hinges on their people – but HR is neglected in the sector', *People Management*, Vol. 12, No. 6, 23 March, p. 44.

Brockett, J. (2006a) 'London Bodies Plan shared services', *People Management*, Vol. 12, No. 11, 1 June, p. 10.

Brockett, J. (2006b) 'Outsourcing "endangers HR"', *People Management*, Vol. 12, No. 21, 26 October, p. 10.

Caldwell, R. (2003) 'The Changing Roles of Personnel Managers: Old Ambiguities, New Uncertainties', *Journal of Management Studies*, Vol. 40, No. 4, pp. 983–1004.

Caldwell, R. (2004) 'Rhetoric, facts and self-fulfilling prophecies: exploring practitioners' perceptions of progress in implementing HRM', *Journal of Management Studies*, Vol. 35, No. 3, pp. 196–215.

CIPD (2003) *HR Survey: Where we are, where we're heading.* London: Chartered Institute of Personnel and Development.

CIPD (2005) 'Address people needs, not just business needs, advises GMB', *People Management*, Vol. 11, No. 6, 24 March, p. 10.

CIPD (2006) *The HR Function: A report on an event to discuss the changing shape of the HR function.* London: Chartered Institute of Personnel and Development.

CIPD (2007) *The Changing HR Function: Survey Report 2007.* London: Chartered Institute of Personnel and Development.

Cooke, F., Shen, J. and McBride, A. (2005) 'Outsourcing HR as a competitive strategy? A Literature review and an assessment of implications', *Human Resource Management*, Vol. 44, No. 4, Winter, pp. 413–32.

Dalziel, S. and Strange, J. (2007) 'How to engage line managers in people management', *People Management*, Vol. 13, No. 19, 20 September, pp. 56–57.

Griffiths, J. (2004) Thorntons scraps HR Director post', *People Management*, Vol. 10, No. 14, 15 July, p. 9.

Griffiths, J. (2005) 'Local Heroes?', *People Management*, Vol. 11, No. 5, 10 March, pp. 12–13.

Hoe-Hailey, V., Farndale, E. and Truss, C. (2005) 'The HR department's role in organizational performance', *Human Resource Management Journal*, Vol. 15, No. 3, pp. 49–66.

Hutchinson, S. and Purcell, J. (2004) *Bringing Policies to Life: The vital role of front line managers in people management.* London: Chartered Institute of Personnel and Development.

IDS (2001) 'HR Service Centres', IDS Study No. 707, April. London: Incomes Data Services.

IDS (2003) 'Outsourcing HR Administration', IDS Study Plus, Spring. London: Incomes Data Services.

IRS (2001) 'HR in 2001: the HR audit', *IRS Employment Trends*, No. 728, May, pp. 4–10.

McConville, T. (2006) 'Devolved RM responsibilities, middle-managers and role dissonance', *Personnel Review*, Vol. 35, No. 6, pp. 637–53.

Manocha, R. (2006) 'MoD Shares HR operations', *People Management*, Vol. 12, No. 5, 9 March, p. 10.

Maxwell, G. and Watson, S. (2007) 'Perspectives on line managers in human resource management: Hilton International's UK Hotels', *International Journal of Human Resource Management*, Vol. 17, No. 6, pp. 1152–70.

People Management (2002) 'HR departments are corroded by the extent of outsourcing', Vol. 8, No. 20, 10 October, p. 10.

People Management (2004) 'Thorntons scraps HR Director post', Vol. 10, No. 14, 15 July, p. 9.

People Management (2006a) 'E-HR can alienate managers', Vol. 12, No. 4, 23 February, p. 16.

People Management (2006b) 'Shared services save RBS £11m', Vol. 12, No. 5, 9 March, p. 13.

People Management (2006c) 'Arcadia strips HR of its place on the board', Vol. 12, No. 9, 4 May, p. 10.

Pickard, J. (2004) 'One step beyond', *People Management*, Vol. 10, No. 13, 30 June, pp. 26–31.

Pickard, J. (2006) 'Conflicting Schedule', *People Management*, Vol. 12, No. 5, 9 March, pp. 14–15.

Smedley, T. (2007) 'Leighton: 'HR is not responsible for people', *People Management*, Vol. 13, No. 18, 6 September, p. 9.

Ulrich, D. and Brockbank, W. (2005) *The HR Value Proposition*. Boston: Harvard Business School Publishing.

CHAPTER 14

Managing people internationally

The objectives of this chapter are to:

1 Describe different international jobs

2 Consider some of the HR dimensions to international business

3 Explain the globalisation difference

4 Review different ways of working overseas

5 Consider how the international workforce will evolve

"'Toyota's recent and embarrassing surge in vehicle recalls was partly a failure by Toyota to spread its obsession for craftsmanship among its growing ranks of overseas factory workers and managers. If Toyota can't infuse its philosophy into its workers, these quality problems will keep happening," said Hirofumi Yokoi, a former Toyota accountant . . . Toyota is afraid of growing too fast and losing control.' (Fackler 2007)

The quotation above illustrates one of the main issues addressed in this chapter, variations in national and regional cultures and their management in the business. The other main topic is to examine the sort of roles held by 'international workers'.

The three men and one woman who got into conversation in the executive lounge of Frankfurt airport represented the four types of international employee found most often in contemporary companies. Elsewhere in the airport a fifth traveller waited in slightly less comfortable surroundings.

Willem is the genuine **international manager**. He speaks fluent English and German as well as his native Dutch and moves regularly throughout Europe and the United States, doing deals and opening up opportunities for his company. His mind travels easily across

Local action is informed by global thinking, but carried out quite separately as all action is local and has to be decided by referring to aspects of employment in one locality only. HRM deals with people who are employed within only one set of legal, cultural, demographic and physical conditions. A debug technician may be employed in Italy to do exactly the same job on exactly the same range of products as another employee of the same company in Ireland or Indonesia, but the terms and conditions of employment, the social conventions and the accepted management practices will be totally different.

Globalisation

In terms of the management of international businesses, the more recent concept of globalisation seeks to reduce the significance of national interests and emphasise attachment to the whole business, which is not a French, Japanese, Russian or Australian, but a global business, not identified with a particular nation. When British Airways became BA – a global business – the livery on the tail fin of BA's planes was replaced by a range of abstract designs that could be identified with different parts of the world. This initiative was not especially popular and when the British Prime Minister of the day, Margaret Thatcher, toured an exhibition which included model aircraft sporting the new design, she was so appalled that she covered one up with her handkerchief. This aspect of globalisation is not universal, as some businesses use their nationality of origin as a unique selling point. Scotch whisky is produced only in Scotland and Belgian chocolates only in Belgium, and the promotion of both products trades heavily on their nationality. Microsoft is a global business par excellence, being as near to universal in its usage as it is possible to be, yet it is indisputably American in its origins, ownership and culture. The Rolls Royce car business is now German owned, yet the cars are still manufactured in Britain, with an image that is carefully maintained. Edwards and Rees (2006, p. 26) suggest that the key features of a global business that impact on the management of people are first global *production*, with goods and services that are produced, distributed and sold worldwide; and secondly global *organisation*, so that the whole operation requires not only the integration of systems but also the management of social and cultural differences to produce effectiveness.

Helen Deresky (2008, p. 5) reproduces a whimsical description of globalisation 'from an unknown source', relating to the death of Princess Diana in Paris:

> **Princess Diana was an English princess**
> **With an Egyptian boyfriend**
> **Who crashed in a French tunnel,**
> **Driving in a German car with a Dutch engine,**
> **Driven by a Belgian who was drunk on Scotch whisky,**
> **Followed closely by Italian paparazzi,**
> **On Japanese motorcycles.**
> **She was treated by an American doctor,**
> **Using Brazilian medicines.**
> **This is sent to you by an American Indian,**
> **Using Bill Gates's technology.**
> **You are probably reading this on your computer**

That uses Taiwanese chips
And a Korean monitor,
Assembled by Bangladeshi workers in a Singapore plant,
Transported by Indian lorry drivers,
Unloaded by Sicilian longshoremen
And trucked to you by Mexican immigrants.

Activity 14.1

1 Think of where you work, where you have worked or where you hope to work in the future, and identify three activities where global thinking needs to influence local action. What are the local people management implications of this?

2 In the same situation what aspects of local action influence, or should influence, global thinking?

WINDOW ON PRACTICE

An expression that is often repeated in the French workplace is, 'Pourquoi le faire simple si l'on peut le faire compliqué?' (why make something simple if one can make it complicated?). This slightly ironic comment encapsulates the French practice of opting for elaborate and time-consuming work systems rather than less complicated alternatives.

A similar coment is made by Ann Moran, who was involved in a merger between a British company and a French one. She describes some of the cultural differences and their impact:

the effort needed to communicate has doubled. The French expect a response from the person to whom a communication was sent and not from a delegated person. To reply otherwise is taken as a slight.

. . .

More upward and more complicated communications are needed whilst keeping [within] the formal hierarchical framework that is normal in French companies. Open questioning of superiors by the French is not common.

. . .

In meetings French colleagues do not feel constrained to follow the agenda and sometimes walk out of the meeting for private discussion. (Moran 1994, pp. 112–13)

Culture

Culture is a word of diverse meanings in the twenty-first century, although four hundred years ago it was almost entirely used to describe the growing of crops. This use now survives in agriculture and horticulture. Once it was applied to human organisation in the eighteenth century, its meaning expanded to become much more varied and it is now used to describe civilisations, artistic expression and national character. More recently it has been widely used to describe the distinctive character of organisations, which have both the explicit quality of structure and the implicit and much more difficult to discern quality of culture. Here we are concerned with the impact on business and organisational affairs of different national and regional cultural patterns, which are the shared beliefs, values and resultant behaviours and attitudes in different nations and regions. Wherever they stand managers have to appreciate the important effect on human behaviour of the national culture from which groups of humans derive their identity.

Some things that initially appear specific to a particular national culture turn out to be understood and welcomed in almost all cultures. Italian pizza has been adopted in most countries of the world, and the expansion has been largely brought about by Pizza Hut, which is owned by Pepsi-Cola, an American company known for a drink that has also gone to every corner of the globe. Who would have expected that Muscovites would daily queue up outside the largest McDonald's in the world until it was overtaken by the branch in Beijing? Few brands are more obviously global than Microsoft. The wide international acceptability of these things could suggest that we are all members of the global village with converging tastes and values. Yet certain facets of national culture remain deeply rooted and have a way of undermining that argument.

Cultural diversity is very difficult for anyone to grasp. For example, to the European, Israel is in the Middle East and its ruling body is a government. To the Malaysian, Israel is in West Asia and ruled by a regime.

WINDOW ON PRACTICE

Richard Mead explains why hotel managers in South East Asia will say 'Yes' in reply to a question such as, 'Can the refrigerator in my room be repaired today?' even if it cannot be done so quickly:

> His cultural priorities tell him to give a pleasing answer and to satisfy immediate needs; the long-term problem can be resolved at a later date or may disappear. The guest may decide not to use the refrigerator; or will change his travel plans and move out that day; or can be accommodated in another room. (Mead 1990, p. 47)

Hofstede

The best known and most persuasive approach to understanding the maze of cultural diversity is the classic study by Geert Hofstede, first published in 1980 and revisited several times since. Hofstede (1991) analysed 116,000 questionnaires administered to employees of IBM in seventy different countries and concluded that national cultures could be explained by four key factors.

1 **Individualism** is the extent to which people expect to look after themselves and their family only. The opposite is collectivism which has a tight social framework and in which people expect to have a wider social responsibility to discharge because others in the group will support them. Those of a collectivist persuasion believe they owe absolute loyalty to their group.

2 **Power distance** measures the extent to which the less powerful members of the society accept the unequal distribution of power. In organisations this is the degree of centralisation of authority and the exercise of autocratic leadership.

3 **Uncertainty avoidance** The future is always unknown, but some societies socialise their members to accept this and take risks, while members of other societies have been socialised to be made anxious about this and seek to compensate through the security of law, religion or technology.

4 **Masculinity** The division of roles between the sexes varies from one society to another. Where men are assertive and have dominant roles these values permeate the whole of society and the organisations that make them up, so there is an emphasis on showing off, performing, making money and achieving something visible. Where there is a larger role for women, who are more service oriented with caring roles, the values move towards concern for the environment and the quality of life, putting the quality of relationships before the making of money.

Hofstede found some clear cultural differences between nationalities and compared his findings with the large-scale British study of organisations carried out in the 1970s (Pugh and Hickson 1976). From this he concluded that countries emphasising large power distance and strong uncertainty avoidance were likely to produce forms of organisation that relied heavily on hierarchy and clear orders from superiors: *a pyramid of people*. In countries where there is small power distance and strong uncertainty avoidance there would be an implicit form of organisation that relied on rules, procedures and clear structure: *a well-oiled machine*. The implicit model of organisation in countries with small power distance and weak uncertainty avoidance was a reliance on ad hoc solutions to problems as they arose, as many of the problems could be boiled down to human relations difficulties: *a village market*. The picture is completed by the fourth group of countries where there is large power distance and weak uncertainty avoidance, where problems are resolved by constantly referring to the boss who is like a father to an extended family, so there is concentration of authority without structuring of activities. The implicit model of organisation here is: *the family*. Table 14.1 shows which countries are in the different segments.

The implicit form of organisation for Britain is a village market, for France it is a pyramid of people, for Germany it is a well-oiled machine and for Hong Kong it is a family. If we can understand the organisational realities and detail in those four countries, then this can provide clues about how to cope in Denmark, Ecuador, Austria or Indonesia because they each share the implicit organisational form and implicit organisational culture of one of the original four.

TABLE 14.1 Country clusters

Pyramid of people	Well-oiled machine	Village market	Family
Arab-speaking	Austria	Australia	East Africa
Argentina	Costa Rica	Britain	Hong Kong
Belgium	Finland	Canada	Indonesia
Brazil	Germany	Denmark	India
Chile	Israel	Ireland	Jamaica
Colombia	Switzerland	Netherlands	Malaysia
Ecuador		New Zealand	Philippines
France		Norway	Singapore
Greece		South Africa	West Africa
Guatemala		Sweden	
Iran		United States	
Italy			
Japan			
Korea			
Mexico			
Pakistan			
Panama			
Peru			
Portugal			
Salvador			
Spain			
Taiwan			
Thailand			
Turkey			
Uruguay			
Venezuela			
Yugoslavia			

Activity 14.2

Identify your country and its type from those shown in Table 14.1. If it is not there, pick one with which you are familiar.

1 Do you agree with Hofstede's description of the type of organisation that is implicit?

2 Think of examples of how that implicit type of organisation affects HR activities.

It is not quite as easy as that statement suggests, however, because the clusters show only relative similarities and, inevitably, other studies do not entirely agree with Hofstede (for example, Ronen and Shenkar 1985), but there is sufficient agreement for us to regard the four-way classification as useful, if not completely reliable, although all the research material was gathered in the 1970s: there may have been radical changes since then.

Hofstede later produced a refinement of the uncertainty avoidance dimension, using the term 'time orientation' instead. Management researchers are typically from Western Europe or the United States, with all the cultural bias that such an orientation involves. Working with the Canadian Michael Bond, Hofstede used a Chinese value survey technique in a fresh study and uncovered the cultural variable of *long-term orientation* that none of the original, western, questions had reached. The highest scores on this dimension were from China, Hong Kong, Taiwan, Japan and South Korea. Singapore was placed ninth. Hofstede argues that countries in the West have derived their culture largely from the three religions of Judaism, Christianity or Islam, all of which are centred on the assertion of a truth that is accessible to true believers, whereas none of the religions of the East are based on the assertion that there is a truth that a human community can embrace. The 'Confucian' values found attached to this long-term orientation include perseverance, clearly maintained status differentials, thrift and having a sense of shame. In many ways these values are valuable for business growth, as they place a social value on entrepreneurial initiative, support the entrepreneur through the willing compliance of others who are seeking a place in the system, encourage saving and investment and put pressure on those who do not meet obligations.

Hofstede's work ignores all the countries of Russia and Eastern Europe, as well as the People's Republic of China. Roughly contemporary with Hofstede was the work of Trompenaars and Hampden-Turner (1997), who also investigated the value dimensions among 15,000 managers representing 47 different national cultures. This is not described further here, but the appropriate text is listed in the References at the end of this chapter.

The globalisation of management is now more real than at any time previously, but our understanding of how different cultures alter the HRM process is still slight. From a strategic perspective cultural diversity has many implications for human resource management. Hodgetts and Luthans 2000, p. 36 selected some of these where the culture of a society can directly affect management approaches.

1 **The centralisation of decision making** In some societies (especially the pyramid of people type) all important decisions are taken by a small number of managers in senior positions. In other societies (like the village markets) decision making is more decentralised. In a joint venture between two dissimilar societies, not only will these differences of approach need to be recognised, but management systems will have to enable members of the two cultures to understand each other and work together.

2 **Rewards and competition** The different levels of financial reward in different countries can be a problem, when those in country A appear to receive much more money than those in country B for doing the same job, but a more subtle difference is the way in which rewards are disbursed. In some instances there is a culture favouring individual recognition, whilst elsewhere there is a convention of group rewards. Similarly some societies encourage competition rather than cooperation, and in others the reverse applies.

3 **Risk** As Hofstede demonstrated in his first study, attitudes towards taking risks are a clear discriminator between cultures, with marked variations of uncertainty avoidance.

4 **Formality** The well-oiled machine cultures place great emphasis on clear procedures and strict rules, while pyramid of people cultures emphasise clear hierarchies and observance of rank. This cultural characteristic contrasts strongly with those of the village market type societies where relationships are more informal and ad hoc action more likely.

5 **Organisational loyalty** In Japan there tends to be a strong sense of loyalty to one's employer, while in Britain and the United States there is a growing sense of identification with one's occupational group, rather than with a particular employer. The long-standing importance of professional bodies and the decline in corporations' long-term commitment to looking after their employees' career development have increased this loyalty to one's occupation rather than to one's employer.

6 **Short- or long-term orientation** Hofstede's identification of an eastern predilection to the long term is beginning to influence strategic decisions on where to locate those organisational activities for which long-term thinking is particularly appropriate.

Understanding these cultural variations helps to shape HR decisions and helps shape the HR dimension in other areas of management decision making when there is a significant international element.

DIFFERENT WAYS OF WORKING OVERSEAS

The HR requirements of people working in the categories we described at the beginning of the chapter are similar to those working in any part of the business, but they have different dimensions. The stereotype of the male senior manager with a compliant wife, who willingly sacrifices her career to his ambitions is not as widely valid as it perhaps once was and the security of the corporate management career has lessened. Thus fewer managers are prepared to entrust their futures to a benign employer to the extent of willingly accepting a relocation that is domestically or socially unattractive, believing that 'they will look after you'. Being asked to take on an expatriate assignment has to be considered very carefully, weighing the undoubted attractions with associated risks:

> Personal achievement and life satisfaction are probably less likely to be solely equated with promotion within organizational structures; instead, career advancement is seen as a means of enhancing personal lifestyles which are separated from, rather than subordinated to, work roles . . . in the context of increased competition for a diminishing number of opportunities at senior managerial levels, they are less prepared to sacrifice their 'selves' or make the kind of open-ended commitments that might harm their domestic lifestyles. (Scase and Goffee 1989, pp. 82–3)

Although people frequently say they are not prepared to accept less attractive relocations, this claim is less often reflected in their executive lifestyles. It is easy to be sucked into a way of life and then to feel better about saying how intolerable it is.

The international manager

There is a small, elite group of genuinely international managers in the world of global business, people who not only are familiar with different countries and regions, but who operate internationally with other managers occupying similar roles in other companies. This world is similar to that of the diplomatic corps in the world's embassies, who have their own conventions and who develop their own culture and ways of working together. By becoming international in their thinking and working, these managers and deal-makers acquire the ability to work and negotiate with each other in a separate cultural world, inhabiting identical international hotels instead of embassies.

For a German to 'think Arab' one day and 'think Korean' the next is simply too demanding at all but the most superficial level. What is necessary is a mode of working where all 'think international' all the time, so that they move out of national culture-boundedness in order to operate in an international culture (Everett *et al.* 1986).

Michael Pinder quoted from a survey by an executive search agency seeking to identify the Euro-Executive, at a time when many Europeans regarded 'international' as meaning 'pan-European'. The profile sounds almost unattainable:

> **Fluent in at least one other [European] Community language, of greater importance is exposure to a diversity of cultures stemming both from family background – he or she is likely to have a mixed education, multi-cultural marriage and parents of different nationalities – and working experience . . . graduated from an internationally-oriented business school . . . line management experience in a foreign culture company . . . experience through various career moves of different skills, roles and environments. (Pinder 1990, p. 78)**

It seems unlikely that HR people seeking to fill overseas managerial posts set off looking exclusively among candidates with a multicultural marriage and parents of different nationalities, to say nothing of the legal problems were such discrimination to be practised. Appointment at this level, however, is only for the few, who think globally and act globally. In businesses we have contacted even the largest had barely 200 people who came into this category. As one manager put it, 'the number is as numerically insignificant as it is qualitatively vital'. The contractual and reporting arrangements for such people are so specialised that they fall outside the purview of a single chapter like this. Most people will have to think globally, but act locally; they will require international awareness for action within a national context.

The expatriates

International managers pass through foreign countries; expatriates go and live in them. This requires thorough management of the process, before they go, while they are away and – crucially – when they come back. Preparing people for expatriation and developing appropriate support for expatriates while overseas are generally well done. Repatriation is not always adequate.

Of the five examples at the beginning of the chapter, the stereotype of the expatriate is altering. Fewer people spend their whole career overseas unless they emigrate to the new country, and more include one or two spells of up to three years on overseas assignments as part of the process of acquiring the necessary breadth of experience and vision to operate at senior level in an international organisation.

The great majority of expatriates are men, usually married men, leading to the 'army wife' syndrome. Whether male or female the expatriate's spouse is nearly always placed in a position of total or partial dependency by corporate expatriation: one career is subordinated to another. This dependency is not only economic. Charles will have all the preoccupations and social networks of his job to absorb him, as well as a position and social status that is likely to be attractive. Caroline may well have a pleasant house and plenty of money, and may be lucky enough to enjoy an agreeable climate, but her social position will be that of wife and mother and her social activities may well be limited to coffee mornings with other expatriate wives. For the increasing proportion of expatriate wives with a professional career in suspension, this can require considerable ingenuity to adapt.

WINDOW ON PRACTICE

Susan Harris was an expatriate wife and mother in Malaysia, who had readily suspended a career in management consultancy so that her husband could take the career opportunity that three years in Miri on the island of Borneo offered. Provided with a house and servants on the shores of the South China Sea under perpetual sunshine, she improved her qualifications through distance learning.

Helga Nordstrom finished her executive career in the same company with a posting in Singapore, accompanied by her recently retired husband, who improved his golf handicap, became stage manager of a local amateur dramatic society and wrote a book about the Swedish history of neutrality.

Because of the demands that expatriation makes on both individuals and families, it has to be managed carefully and thoroughly.

Selection for expatriation

The possibility of an extended overseas assignment can come as a shock, which may or may not be welcome, presenting all the problems of considering the potential career handicap of turning down the opportunity and the potential domestic problems of accepting it. Employers seldom have the luxury of a large number of appropriately qualified people readily available to fill any vacancy, but the most satisfactory general approach to selection for expatriation is through the combination of performance management and career planning.

A feature of annual appraisal can be a discussion of whether people are interested in working overseas at all, the degree of technical expertise and managerial experience they possess and the domestic/social constraints that would affect the timing of such a move. That discussion can then be developed by identifying timings that would be appropriate for such a move, preferred locations and even some language training. As with all career management initiatives, this sort of programme sets up expectations of the future that the management may not be able to deliver because of changes in business activity, but it provides a cadre of people who would welcome an overseas move.

The particular location is the next most important determinant in matching the person to the job. Among the most important issues are:

- **Culture** How different from home is the culture of the country – in terms of religion, the social position of women, the degree of political stability/instability, the degree of personal security and petty crime, the quality of the local press and television, the availability of cable television and foreign newspapers, the nature of any health hazards?
- **Economic development** How well developed is the economy of the country – in terms of the standard/cost of living, the availability of familiar foods and domestic equipment, transport, postal and telephone services, the extent of local poverty, health and education facilities, the availability of international schools?
- **Geographical location** How far away is it and where is it – what is its climate, is it in a cosmopolitan city or more remote, what is the importance/unimportance of language proficiency, what is the size of the local expatriate community, what are the employment prospects of spouse?
- **The job** What has to be done and what is the situation, the nature of the organisation, the proportion of expatriates in the workforce, the technical, commercial and managerial demands of the job, the staffing and support available, and the extent to which the post involves managing local nationals?

The most important aspect of considering expatriation is making sure that the potential appointee and members of the family have a full understanding of what will be involved. There is no profile of the ideal expatriate, but here are some selection issues arranged under the four headings used already:

- **Culture** How well prepared is the expatriate family for an unfamiliar culture? In many ways the developed countries of Western Europe present fewer problems than those of further afield, but English is spoken more widely in Singapore than, for instance, in France. Malaysia is a multi-ethnic society, but with a Muslim majority in the population. The Muslim dominance of life in most Middle East countries has profound implications for expatriates, requiring a degree of puritanism that will be unfamiliar and a social role for women that is quite unlike that which western women experience. In the developing countries of the East there may be superb hotels, but little else to do in the evening. Manila and Bangkok have plenty of after-dark facilities for men on their own, but little for couples and even less for women on their own. Whatever the culture is, open-mindedness and tolerance are essential qualities for the expatriates to develop.
- **Economic development** Some eastern countries now enjoy a standard of living and material convenience that matches or surpasses that of fortunate people in the West, so that the expatriate will find excellent systems of transportation, postal and telephone services that will be similar to those of the home country. Elsewhere the situation will be very different and everyday life will require a great deal more

adjustment once one is outside the air-conditioned cocoon of the multinational company's offices. Medical and dental facilities may be sparse and few expatriate families can avoid being affected by the conditions of those among whom they live. Not only may they be distressed by the living conditions they see in most parts of the Indian subcontinent and South America, for instance, they will also have to contend with very high urban crime rates in some places.

- **Geographical location** This is a further twist to the economic development question. The heat and humidity of tropical climates is supportable when moving from air-conditioned home, via air-conditioned car to air-conditioned office or shopping mall. Those moving to more remote areas have greater problems in coping with the climate and the relative isolation, so they need to be emotionally self-sufficient and not too dependent on outside stimulation. The distance from home is another determinant of personal suitability to the posting. The Parisian working in Brussels could easily contemplate weekly commuting: the native of Brussels working in Madagascar could not. There will be a smaller expatriate community in most Italian cities than in Hong Kong, so that the expatriate family may have to work harder at establishing social contacts, and will therefore require considerable social skill and self-confidence. The geographical location will also determine the importance of local language proficiency for all members of the expatriate family.

- **The job** In a global business questions about the job may initially seem unproblematic. Many expatriates are simply moving to exercise their well-developed company expertise in a different location. The situation will, however, always be different no matter how similar the conventions and procedures. The various demands of the job need to be thoroughly considered, especially what may be involved in managing local nationals, where the subtleties of response to leadership and expectations of authority will probably still baffle the expatriate when finally on the way home from the tour of duty.

Preparing for expatriation

While 89 per cent of companies formally assess a candidate's job skills prior to a foreign posting, less than half go through the same process for cultural suitability. Even fewer gauge whether the family will cope. (*Financial Times*, 5 March 2001)

HR specialists have much to do in making arrangements for expatriation, but much has to be done by the expatriate family as well. If there is the relative luxury of a twelve-month period of preparation, language training can make real progress. This comes to life most effectively when there is a strong flavour of cultural orientation and familiarisation as well, so that two of the basic requirements of preparation are dealt with simultaneously. The nature of the language training provided is usually slightly different for the expatriate employee and for the expatriate spouse. The employee will concentrate on technical and business terms, while the spouse concentrates on what will be useful in everyday matters like shopping and trying to get the washing machine repaired, or in local social contacts.

An example of an interesting combination of linguistic expertise is that of an expatriate couple in Japan, where he speaks Japanese and she reads it, so he deals with waiters and taxi drivers, while she navigates and copes with restaurant menus.

More general aspects of cultural familiarisation can be achieved by various means, often depending on the individual. Some will read avariciously, both travel books and the range of novels that have been written about most parts of the world. Others prefer film and video. Can there be any better preparation for Australian suburban life than watching several episodes of *Neighbours*?

Some companies ask returned expatriates to write and present case histories about the country, with the obvious advantages that a potential expatriate can discuss with someone face to face their personal experiences in a situation which they are about to encounter. It should also be automatic for the potential expatriate to meet socially with any nationals from the country of expatriation who may be visiting the host company during the pre-departure stage.

The success of an overseas assignment will be enhanced by some previous experience overseas and some experience of the location, but brief business trips scarcely qualify as previous experience. A holiday could be better, as people on holiday usually go at least partly to see the country and the people. Much better is a visit before the move, which is made to prepare for the move. By this method it is possible to deal with such crucial issues as housing. Nothing reassures one about impending relocation so much as knowing where one is going to live. If there are children, arrangements for their schooling can also be made.

Continuing back-home arrangements while abroad can be extensive. There may be children remaining in boarding schools, or elderly relatives to be catered for and pets to worry about, as well as renting the family home and many more. There may be a need for some company help, especially with financial and similar arrangements.

Travel arrangements themselves are relatively straightforward, but still have to be organised. There may be a need for family visas and one or more work permits, removal of household effects as well as personal baggage, health checks and whatever range of immunisations and medication is required.

Repatriation

Coming back from an overseas assignment seldom receives the attention it needs. It is not expected to be problematic and therefore receives little attention: all the problems are expected to be associated with getting out and getting settled. Why should there be problems about coming home?

> **The long-term implications of ineffective repatriation practices are clear: few good managers will be willing to take international assignments because they see what happened to their colleagues . . . the only people willing to take on foreign assignments in the future will be those who have not been able to succeed on the home front.** (Deresky 2008, p. 370)

The first potential problem is the nature of the overseas experience. If it has been thoroughly satisfactory for all members of the family, with an enhanced lifestyle, plenty of career development and scope for the employee, plenty of money and exciting experiences for the family in an agreeable climate, then there may not be much initial enthusiasm for returning, so that it will be like coming back from an extended holiday, with all the reluctance that involves about leaving good friends and stimulating experiences to return to dreary old Barnstaple, or Dusseldorf or Des Moines.

On the other hand if the overseas experience has been difficult, with a loss of social life, a disagreeable climate, frustrations and disappointment at work and all sorts of petty inconveniences, then the prospect of returning home can become an obsession, with the days ticked off on the calendar and a great build-up of anticipation. When the day of return to hearth and home at last comes, Barnstaple (or Dusseldorf or Des Moines) may soon seem just a little ordinary compared with the wonderful picture that had been built up in expectation.

The second major problem is the career situation of the returning expatriate. Virtually all repatriated personnel experience some personal difficulty in reintegrating on return. There may be loss of status, loss of autonomy, lack of career direction and lack of recognition of the value of overseas experience. It may not be considered a management responsibility to fuss over a manager's personal readjustment, but an American study (Adler 1991, p. 238) showed that the effectiveness of expatriates took between six and twelve months to return to an acceptable level on repatriation, so there are some hard-headed reasons for taking this issue seriously.

The engineer

The term 'engineer' is used here broadly to cover all those technical specialists who spend spells of a few weeks or months at a time in an overseas location to carry out a particular job. Most often it is commissioning new plant and training local personnel in its use. The period overseas is not as long and the role is much more specific than that of the expatriate, so that the level of preparation is less. The experience is similar to that of seafarers, airline crew, travel couriers and the increasing number of western academics who spend a few weeks or months abroad. They are not living abroad: they are simply away from home for a spell, but with all the frustrations of air travel.

The selection criteria need to be strict, as the engineer needs complete technical expertise and the ability to cope with unforeseen technical problems without recourse to colleagues or specialised equipment, as both are probably not available. There will also be a need for personal resourcefulness and the ability to handle a wide variety of social situations, for which some cultural awareness training will probably be needed.

Compared with international managers and expatriates, engineers are more likely to be assigned to remote locations, with all the accompanying social isolation and possible climatic problems, even though they are usually accommodated in an international hotel. It can be a monotonous life, with little scope for social activity apart from enjoying the hotel bar and pool. Some extrovert and gregarious engineers cope successfully with people in different countries, striking up friendships and taking a keen interest in their surroundings, but most simply settle down to getting the job done through long working days followed by a couple of drinks in the bar after a shower and a relaxed meal.

Regular health checks are essential, as are efficient administrative arrangements for travel, accommodation and contact with base during assignment. Some engineers find it very difficult to settle back into the more routine tasks that often await them when the days of travelling are over.

The occasional parachutist

Occasional parachutists also need efficient administrative arrangements for travel and accommodation, which need to be made by, or in conjunction with HR. Like the engineer, they are representatives of the company and will be able to act as an invaluable communication link in both a formal and informal way during and after the visit. Large numbers of employees move between countries only in this mode and the exchanges can be very important in developing mutual understanding between the nationalities and in improving the compatibility of the systems and procedures of the two organisations.

The potential for doing harm should not be underestimated. Someone visiting for only a few days has little incentive to take the trouble to learn about the country and the people, and may therefore carry stereotypical assumptions that could be very damaging to relationships within the company. It can be helpful if novices travel together with an experienced person and before travelling talk with an expatriate or someone else familiar with the culture.

WINDOW ON PRACTICE

At the Irish manufacturing subsidiary of a French company there are problems if managers in the subsidiary are not competent in the native language of the parent company.

Only three of the five local senior managers speak French, with varying degrees of proficiency. As many of the managers in France speak English, everyday contact between the two countries is reasonable for even the non-French speakers in Ireland. However, all the documentation, from technical forms to invoices, is in French so it is exceptionally difficult and often impossible for those who do not speak French to extract the full meaning and nuances of any written communication.

The biggest problem is at meetings in France, which are conducted entirely in French. All five senior managers have to travel frequently to these meetings but most of what is said is lost on the two who do not speak French and their input is minimal. The effect of this is that the two managers lose the respect of their colleagues and their authority and confidence are undermined, leading to some serious errors and to stress in situations where clear thinking and constant dialogue between the two countries are required.

The mobile worker

All of the four types of overseas worker we have considered so far have been company employees and there has been the assumption that they have considerable support and facilitation from their company. It has also been indicated, particularly in the section about expatriates, that the level of support may be considerable. Benedicte is an example

larger and more varied in its ethnic make-up. It was also based on the assumption that these people were immigrating to settle, rather than just coming to work for a limited time.

By the twenty-first century the situation had changed for all the economies of the western world. Those from other countries did not necessarily subdue their national origins in order to 'fit in'. For years young Australians in London had spoken of the 'cultural desert' that was Australia when compared to Britain. By 2000 they were much more secure in their national cultural identity, their international icons in Hollywood and in the world of popular music to go alongside their infuriating superiority in almost every type of sport, especially those that had been nurtured in the public schools of England. Young Muslims became more assertive about their faith and their ethnicity, determined to maintain those values and to resist 'assimilation'. From mainland Europe the French, Germans and Spanish who came regularly for a short spell to hone their English language skills were joined by those from new EU countries with ready access and arriving with useful practical skills, economic need and a willingness to accept levels of both payment and working conditions that Britons were keen to avoid. Another characteristic of the changing workforce in all western countries, of which Britain is a convenient example, is that the new workers are less likely to settle and more likely to come for a limited period.

The discussions around this situation are predominantly political and social, with all the associated problems of sensationalism in newspaper coverage, but the management of the workplace is inescapably a practical concern for managers day by day, yet little academic examination is so far available.

Whatever the pattern in the future, the labour market seems set to become internationally more fluid and the United States less economically dominant, with the development of India and China and the further economic advances in Russia. It is not quite so certain that the Anglo-American cultural significance will wane, with global interest in the English language as a lingua franca that appears still to be relatively easy for others to learn, the widespread enthusiasm for association football and athletic spectaculars like the Olympic Games, the pervasiveness of Hollywood's output, Boeing aircraft and Microsoft. It remains to be seen how effectively the peoples of the world will deal with environmental challenges, which appear to be unresolvable without some sort of supranational initiative that has so far failed to emerge. All of these issues will profoundly affect the way in which people are employed, deployed, led and remunerated: the solid core of people management.

Managing a workforce with an overseas mobile element

Managing the mobile worker remains a problem, as labour mobility can interfere with government policies. There is a long history of emigration and asylum seeking from countries where people fear persecution or find poor levels of career opportunity and living standards to those countries where living conditions and career opportunities seem better. In the twenty-first century destination countries, like the United States, Scandinavia and Britain, have felt unable to cope with such large numbers and have tried to stem the flow, whilst reluctant to deny sanctuary to those in need and quite willing to accommodate those able to fill skill shortages.

WINDOW ON PRACTICE

For many years Britain had a shortage of plumbers, but by the year 2000 this deficiency had been largely made up by large-scale immigration of plumbers from Poland, which had become a member of the European Union. Polish plumbers were generally applauded for their hard work and skill level, their families quickly joined them and the Roman Catholic Church could scarcely cope with the large increase in the numbers attending Mass. By 2008 job prospects in Britain were not quite so good and conditions in Poland had improved, so slightly more Poles returned to Poland than came from Poland.

The example of the Polish plumber is repeated in many other areas, nurses from the Caribbean in most European countries, Filipina maids and domestic servants in Hong Kong, Pakistani engineers in the Middle East, Turkish workers in German factories and so on.

Returning to the practical question of managing a workforce which includes a significant number of people who are from a different cultural background and who may not be committed to remaining in the country where they are employed, there are management problems that may be much influenced by political and social considerations, so all employment practices have to be set in the current environment in which the business is set. Some of the general considerations are the following.

Informal recruitment systems

Informal systems of recruitment have long been used to recruit people and may be of particular relevance for those with limited knowledge of the host country language and its social conventions. Existing employees introduce friends and relations to the company using no particular selection criteria apart from physical ability to do the job. New recruits have contacts within the organisation to help them settle and there will be informal methods of controlling the workforce that the management may find convenient without inquiring too closely about how they are enforced. An account of a situation from the 1970s shows how things can get out of hand. In this case a company had had a steady stream of Pakistani recruits for some years:

> Mohammed I. joined the company as a machine operator . . . feeling that Pakistanis were getting poor treatment he started union recruitment to the engineering union. The workforce polarised racially, with Pakistanis joining the union and the white employees did not, fearing that their interests would not be adequately represented. One of them commented, 'Pakistani mafia ran this place; if you were not Pakistani, you did not get a job here'. (Torrington *et al.* 1982, p. 70)

Since then this type of practice has become even more self-contained. In the late evening of February 2004 a gang of Chinese workers were collecting cockles in

Morecambe Bay in the north west of England when many of them were cut off by the incoming tide; 23 of them died. They were all illegal immigrants from China, untrained and inexperienced, who had been 'imported' by a gangmaster to work in appalling working and living conditions. This is an extreme case, but there are similar examples where a workforce with no English language is employed en bloc by a contractor to carry out a defined task, with an intermediary gangmaster being the sole manager, interpreter and employer.

CIPD provides general guidance in its factsheet:

> **Managers should be trained so that they can communicate effectively with people from other cultures and to be sensitive to different communication styles and attitudes to work. It is particularly important to recognise that ideas about team working vary from one culture to another. For example, some place greater emphasis on consensus and collaboration whereas others value clear direction from strong leadership in a strict hierarchy. Again, some encourage honesty, even open criticism, whereas others would prefer more diplomacy and conciliation, with no show of strong feelings. It is possible to build effective teams by having a clear framework that does not ignore cultural differences but encourages communication and ensures that everyone understands the common goals.** (CIPD 2007, p. 5)

The most recent research in this area has been by French and Mohrke (2006), who considered the situation of recent migrants from new members of the European Community after the number of members increased. They confirmed the general opinion that such employees were often recruited into low-pay, low-status jobs because of their reliability, a willingness to take 'low-status' jobs and then to work long, flexible hours. They also confirmed that there was some disadvantage to indigenous job seekers due to employers' preference for the new arrivals.

The 'ghetto' department

The 'ghetto' department is a problem already referred to. If a core group of people from a single country are recruited for a particular job, others from the same country will be attracted to the same department and gradually their native tongue becomes the main method of communication. Informal working practices evolve that may not meet general health and safety requirements, efficiency standards and so forth. The extreme is where the working group is separated in some way from the main workforce, either geographically as in some aspects of agriculture or temporally as in a permanent night shift. This means that the working group is not only introspective in the way it carries out its duties, it is also completely out of touch with the rest of the workforce in terms of matters such as access to the medical centre, the personnel department and training opportunities, promotion prospects and awareness of the general culture and ethos of the business and its organisation.

Additional facilities

Mobile workers from other countries will expect some additional facilities. It may be that mobile workers require facilities for religious observance, for example so that they are able either to pray briefly at the workplace, or to have time off for religious festivals. In some western countries the practice of observing Good Friday as a day of holiday has changed with the holiday being moved to Easter Tuesday, but practising Christians who need a holiday on Good Friday are always accommodated. The beginning of the university year usually sees some Jewish students absent for Jewish New Year celebrations, and other religions are gradually finding more flexibility. Common to almost all mobile workers is a wish for extended leave to visit friends and family, and they may request four to six weeks in order to justify the considerable cost of intercontinental travel. Such requests can be accommodated either by transferring leave entitlement from one year to another or by allowing some unpaid leave to be attached to annual leave. One manager's reaction to this was, 'But suppose one of our "own" people wants an extra month to trail a caravan round Europe?' The answer may well be, 'Well, why not?'

Foreign language skills

Foreign language facility can be a valuable skill of the mobile worker. As trade becomes increasingly international in its ramifications, businesses can find language skills among its employees useful, not only to interpret for newcomers with limited facility in the host country language, but also to translate written material or to interpret in meetings or videoconferencing with foreign nationals. Clearly undertaking this sort of role requires not only a facility in both languages, but also a familiarity with the employing organisation and its products and an ability to deal with such social situations that interpreting produces.

Employment security

Security of employment may not be an objective for mobile workers, who adopt a short-term attitude to the job they take for a few months or longer. They are essentially opportunistic in their approach, with their career interests lying elsewhere. This has both advantages and disadvantages for the employer.

Summary propositions

14.1 Employees work in foreign countries in quite varied ways, all of which require different management approaches.

14.2 Taking an international management perspective requires businesses to have a clear national identity, with decision making and organisation centralised.

14.3 Adopting a globalisation perspective requires a business to seek to reduce the significance of a host nation at the centre and emphasises attachment to the whole business, regardless of nationality.

▶

▶ **14.4** Understanding of cultural contexts is crucial to understanding why attitudes and behaviour vary so markedly in different countries. So far the most widely adopted approach to understanding this diversity is in the work of Hofstede (*see* Further reading below).

14.5 With the increasing international mobility of workers seeking employment, managers need to adopt some new methods if they are to manage successfully a workforce in their own country with a significant element of foreign employees, many of whom may be seeking temporary work rather than a settled connection.

GENERAL DISCUSSION TOPICS

1 At the beginning of the chapter different examples of international employees were suggested. In terms of the employment and management of such people do you think that distinguishing between the 'engineer' and the 'occasional parachutist' is helpful, or are the practices needed basically the same?

2 Which do you find personally attractive as your next career move, to be an 'international manager' or an 'expatriate' or neither? What changes in your personal circumstances would make you change your mind?

3 In the first part of the Skills Package we have this definition:

'The **stereotype** is the standardised expectation we have of those who have certain dominant characteristics: typical stereotypes are that politicians are not to be trusted, women are more caring than men, and that men are more aggressive than women. The behaviour of some people in a category makes us expect all in that category to behave in the same way. This is obviously invalid, but is a tendency to which we are prone.'

What racial, ethnic or national stereotypes are you aware of that could impair collective or individual management effectiveness?

FURTHER READING

Hofstede is so important that two different books are recommended. The first is the most useful summary and explanation of his work, and includes the topic of the long-term orientation. The second is a reflective revisiting of the whole issue of culture:

Hofstede, G. (1991, reprinted 2004) *Cultures and Organizations: Software of the Mind*. New York: McGraw Hill.

Hofstede, G. (2001, reprinted 2003) *Culture's Consequences: Comparing Values, Behaviours, Institutions and Organizations Across Nations*. New York: Sage.

Also useful is:

Trompenaars, F. and Hampden-Turner, C.A. (1997) *Riding the Waves of Culture: Understanding Cultural Diversity in Business,* 2nd edn). London: Nicholas Brealey Publishing Ltd.

A useful single-author text is Tayeb, M. (2003) *International Management: Theories and Practices*. Harlow, England: Prentice Hall.

An up-to-date review of the field by a range of experts is Lucas, R., Lupton, B. and Mathieson, H. (2007) *Human Resource Management in an International Context*. London: Chartered Institute of Personnel and Development.

For thorough treatment of the expatriation issue Brewster, C.J. (1988) *The Management of Expatriates*, Cranfield School of Management Monograph is the best available.

For a study of the migration experience in a field where it is a worldwide phenomenon, *see*: Winkelman-Gleed, A. (2006) *Migrant Nurses: Motivation, Integration, Contribution*. Oxford: Radcliffe Publishing.

Web links

www.eca-international.com
is the website for Employment Conditions Abroad, which is an international consultancy able to provide detailed practical guidance on contractual and other conditions in different countries, as well as advice on terms and conditions for expatriates in those countries.

www.roffeypark.com
has links to an international programme of surveys, research and publications, enabling survey participants to receive copies of the reports of the research to which they contribute.

www.managementcentre.co.uk
The Management Centre is a training consultancy working exclusively in the not for profit sector. Working internationally is a significant part of its portfolio.

www.ind.homeoffice.gov.uk
For British readers there is regular information from the Home Office, including: *The code of practice for all employers on the avoidance of race discrimination in recruitment practice while seeking to prevent illegal working*.

REFERENCES

Adler, N.J. (1991) *International Dimensions of Organizational Behavior*. Boston, Mass: PWS-Kent.

Braham, J., Pearn, M.A. and Rhodes, E. (1982) *Discrimination and Disadvantage in Employment*. London: Harper & Row.

CIPD (2007) *Employing Overseas Workers*. London: Chartered Institute of Personnel and Development.

Deresky, H. (2008) *International Management*, 6th edn. Upper Saddle River, NJ: Pearson Education.

Edwards, T. and Rees, C. (2006) *International Human Resource Management*. Harlow: FT/Prentice Hall.

Everett, J.E., Stening, B.W. and Longton, P.A. (1982) 'Some Evidence for an International Managerial Culture', *Journal of Management Studies*, April, pp. 153–62.

Fackler, M. (2007) *New York Times*, 17 February, 'The "Toyota Way" is Translated for a New Generation of Foreign Managers', **www.nytimes.com**.

French, S. and Mohrke, J. (2006) *Impact of New Arrivals on the North Staffordshire Labour Market*. London: Low Pay Commission.

Gurria, A. (2008) *A Profile of Immigrant Populations in the 21st Century*. Paris: Speech by Secretary General of OECD, 20 February.

Hitner, T.J., Knights, D., Green, A.E. and Torrington, D.P. (1982) *Racial Minority Employment* Research Paper No. 35. London: Department of Employment.

Hodgetts, R.M. and Luthans, F. (2000) *International Management*. New York: McGraw-Hill.

Hofstede, G. (1991, reprinted 2004)) *Cultures and Organizations: Software of the Mind*. New York: McGraw Hill.

Hofstede, G. (2001, reprinted 2003) *Culture's Consequences: Comparing Values, Behaviours, Institutions and Organizations Across Nations*. New York: Sage.

Maitland, A. (2006) 'Top Companies Value Overseas Experience', *Financial Times*, 3 July.

Mead. R. (1990) *Cross-cultural Management Communication*. Chichester: Wiley.

Moran, A. (1994) 'Ferranti-Thomson Sonar Systems: An Anglo-French Venture in High Tech. Collaboration', in D.P. Torrington (1994) *International Human Resource Management,* Hemel Hempstead: Prentice Hall International.

Pinder, M. (1990) *Personnel Management for the Single Market*. London: Pitman.

Pugh, D.S. and Hickson, D.J. (1976) *Organisational Structure in its Context*. Farnborough: Saxon House.

Ronen, S. and Shenkar, O. (1985) 'Clustering Countries on Attitudinal Dimensions: A Review and Synthesis', *Academy of Management Review*, Vol. 10, No. 3, pp. 435–54.

Scase, R. and Goffee, R. (1989) *Reluctant Managers: Their Work and Lifestyles*. London: Unwin Hyman.

Smith, D.J. (1977) *Racial Disadvantage in Britain*. London: Penguin.

Torrington, D.P., Hitner, T.J. and Knights, D. (1982) *Managing the Multi-racial Work Force*. Aldershot: Gower Press.

Trompenaars, F. and Hampden-Turner, C.A. (1997) *Riding the Waves of Culture: Understanding Cultural Diversity in Business*, 2nd edn. London: Nicholas Brealey Publishing Ltd.

Schneider , S.C. and Barsoux, J-L. (2003) *Managing Across Cultures*, 2nd edn. Harlow: Pearson Education.

CHAPTER 15

The future of HRM

The objectives of this chapter are to:

1 Reach a judgement about which issues are likely to move to the top of the HRM agenda during the coming twenty years

2 Explain the significance of demographic trends for future labour market conditions and the extent of diversity among the working population

3 Discuss the sources of increased competitive intensity in industries and the organisational consequences from an HRM perspective

4 Explore likely shifts in the emphasis of employment regulation away from labour markets and towards the achievement of a range of wider government objectives

5 Debate the merits of the argument that traditional employment practices will change radically in the future in response to environmental trends

In the summer of 2007 the international business services firm PricewaterhouseCoopers (PwC) conducted a survey among 2,739 recent graduate recruits from the USA, the UK and China. All had recently been offered jobs with the firm, but had yet to start their contracts. The survey concerned the expectations of the recruits about the nature of the working lives they will have in the future, particularly focusing on the ways in which they perceive that their 'world of work' will differ from that of their parents.

▶

> ▶   Some of the findings were unsurprising. There was, for example,
> widespread agreement among all the graduates that they would work
> 'across geographic borders' to a greater extent than their parents did, and
> general agreement that they would work partly from home and partly from
> offices. In other respects, however, the findings were contrary to what might
> be described as 'received wisdom' about contemporary trends in working
> life. Three-quarters of the international sample, and 82.5 per cent of the UK
> graduate recruits, expected to work 'regular office hours' in the future,
> similar numbers expecting to have only 2–5 employers during their careers.
> On these issues, therefore, the expectation was that their experiences would
> not differ greatly from those of their parents.
>
>   Perhaps the most interesting feature of this survey was the answers
> given to the question, 'Will you deliberately seek to work for employers whose
> corporate responsibility behaviour reflects your own values?' of UK
> graduates 71.2 per cent, of the Chinese recruits 87.2 per cent and of the
> US sample 90.2 per cent agreed with this statement. This strongly suggests
> that employers who want to recruit and retain the brightest and the best in
> the future are going to have to pay a great deal more attention to the ethics
> of their activities than was the case in the past.
>
> *Source:* PwC (2007).

Over the past twenty years the world of work in countries such as the UK has changed
in important ways. In some industries and professions profound changes have occurred
leading many commentators to argue that we have experienced a second industrial
revolution, every bit as significant in its long-term impact as the first one was in the late
eighteenth and nineteenth centuries. Elsewhere significant changes have occurred, but of
a less profound nature and over a longer time scale. As far as the workplace is concerned,
it is thus fair to conclude that the British workplace has experienced a mixture of
evolution and revolution. The question that now needs to be addressed is, what will
happen in the next twenty years? In the future, will the trends we have witnessed
consolidate, reverse, continue or accelerate, or will new trends emerge to take us in
entirely new directions?

Mark Twain famously wrote that 'prediction is difficult, especially when predictions
relate to the future'. Reaching conclusions about the future world of work is particularly
difficult because of the wide range of influences that need to be taken into account and
because so many people with such different ideas have actively joined the debate.
Moreover, of course, as plenty have found to their cost, it is never long before the future
becomes the present and past predictions are revealed to have been of limited accuracy.
Nonetheless, in this chapter we are going to try to look forward by drawing attention to
the major trends in the business environment which, assuming they continue, are going
to have the most important long-term impact on employment and the management of

people in UK organisations. We start by focusing on demographic trends and their likely long-term impact on labour markets in the UK. We go on to address the future effects of continued increases in the competitive intensity faced by organisations. Our third discussion concerns the future regulatory agenda for HR management and its likely development beyond employment law to encompass the achievement of a wider set of government objectives. Finally, our key debate in this chapter concerns the very different claims that are made by commentators about the future of the job and of traditional employment contracts.

THE LABOUR MARKET

In Chapter 3 we established that demand for workers in the UK has been on an upward trajectory for several decades. There have been relatively short periods in the past during times of recession when the increase has temporarily slowed or even reversed, but over the long term the total number of people who are employed has grown significantly. In 2008, according to government statistics, 29.3 million people in the UK were in employment (ONS 2008, p. 20). This compares with a figure of just 24.7 million in 1986. By 2020, according to the most authoritative recent projections, the number is expected to rise to at least 30.1 million (Beavan *et al.* 2005, p. 37) and will continue to increase thereafter. At the same time, however, the number of people of working age is projected to decline somewhat. This is a result of the structure of the UK's population which is illustrated clearly in Figure 15.1. In the middle of the diagram you see a bulge, representing the generation born between 1945 and 1964. This cohort is often referred to as 'baby boomers' because of the high birth rates that occurred at that time. It is largely because of the size of this generation, as well as the increased propensity of women to work for longer periods of their lifetimes, that the supply of labour has been able to keep pace with the growing demand for labour in the economy over recent decades. This situation, however, has already begun to change as the big baby boom generation has started to retire. The cohort of people coming up behind the baby-boomers (born between 1965 and 1985), as you can see from Figure 15.1, is considerably smaller in number, meaning that there are hundreds of thousands fewer people aged between 25 and 45 than there are between 45 and 65. After 2010, when the first baby-boomers reach 65, there will be a steady growth in the mismatch between the supply of labour, which will decrease, and the demand for labour, which we expect will continue to increase.

Activity 15.1

Why do you think that people, on average, choose to have fewer children than they did a generation ago? Can anything be done to reverse the trend? To what extent should governments see it as their role to encourage more births?

TABLE 15.1 Population trends, UK, 2006–2031

thousands

	2006	2011	2016	2021	2026	2031
United Kingdom	60587	62761	64975	67191	69260	71100
England	50763	52706	54724	56757	58682	60432
Wales	2966	3038	3113	3186	3248	3296
Scotland	5117	5206	5270	5326	5363	5374
Northern Ireland	1742	1812	1868	1922	1966	1999

Source: Office for National Statistics (2008) *Labour Market Statistics*, January 2008. London: Office for National Statistics.

If current patterns of immigration and emigration continue in the future the UK's population will increase dramatically, meaning that many concerns about an inadequate supply of labour can cease. This is the case, not least because the average age of people coming into the UK from overseas to settle is much lower than that of existing UK residents who leave to settle abroad. Table 15.1 shows population projections assuming a continuation of current trends. But it is reasonable to question the extent to which the absorption of such a vast number of people would ever be politically possible given the implications there would be for demands on housing, roads and public services. Moreover, the government has announced new immigration rules (to be introduced in stages from 2008) which aim to reduce the numbers of immigrants substantially. It is also reasonable to question for how long the current interest in migrating to the UK from overseas can continue.

In conclusion, it is difficult to reach definitive judgements about how much changing demographic patterns will influence labour market conditions in future decades. Population ageing suggests that labour markets will tighten considerably, while immigration statistics suggest they need not. Only time will tell for sure. What is very likely, however, is a substantial tightening of some labour markets as a result of specific skills shortages. In Chapter 3 (*see* pp. 70 to 71) we quoted key statistics from the Leitch Report looking at skills in England. Here it was concluded that irrespective of changes in the overall size of the population, we remain seriously underqualified and underskilled. Too few of us are educated to degree level and far too many of us lack sufficient basic numeracy and literacy skills to meet the anticipated acceleration in demand for people to fill more highly skilled and specialised roles. The most likely scenario is thus one in which there are sufficient people available to fill a decreasing number of low-skilled jobs, but too few people with the skills and experience necessary to fill a fast-growing number of higher-level, professional, technical and managerial positions.

Looking forward, two major practical implications arise as a result of these demographic trends which are likely to become increasingly significant as far as the management of people is concerned. First, organisations are going to find it increasingly difficult to fill more highly skilled and specialised roles, at least from traditional sources. These labour markets are likely to tighten considerably, leading to a need to source more skills overseas. Secondly, we can be certain that we are therefore going to see much greater ethnic and cultural diversity in the make-up of our workforces. Managing these issues is likely to dominate the HRM agenda in most organisations in coming years.

WINDOW ON PRACTICE

In 2006 the Confederation of British Industry (CBI) published a survey of employers which revealed a lack of basic educational skills among new recruits. According to respondents the big problem in the UK is a lack of basic numerical skills among school leavers, but good reading and writing skills are also in short supply. The problem extends to graduate recruits too. The survey suggests that 23 per cent of employers are unhappy with levels of literacy among their graduates and that 13 per cent are concerned about numeracy levels. The response, according to the CBI, is for one in three employers to provide remedial tuition in reading, writing and arithmetic.

Source: Green (2006).

Tighter labour markets

Labour markets are already much tighter in the UK than they were ten or twenty years ago. According to successive annual surveys carried out by the Chartered Institute of Personnel and Development (CIPD 2002–7), a good majority of employers are now regularly experiencing difficulties recruiting the people they need:

2002:	77%	2005:	85%
2003:	93%	2006:	82%
2004:	85%	2007:	84%

The key reasons for recruitment difficulties according to the survey respondents are a lack of specialist skills in the labour market, a tendency for qualified job applicants to ask for more money than can be afforded and a lack of sufficient experience on the part of people applying for jobs.

A recent snapshot survey by the Learning and Skills Council (2006) shows that the problem extends to small and medium-sized businesses too:

- 17 per cent of organisations in their sample had vacancies at the time the survey was conducted – a total of 571,000
- 7 per cent of organisations had vacancies at that time which they classed as 'hard'
- 25 per cent of vacancies are considered by employers to be in areas where there are skills shortages (i.e. around 150,000 at any one time)
- 16 per cent of organisations claim that there are 'skills gaps' among their existing staff
- 6 per cent of all staff are described by employers as not being proficient in their jobs due to skills gaps (that is 1.3 million employees in England)

Long-term demographic trends suggest strongly that the current situation is not temporary, but is here to stay. Moreover, where skills are already in short supply in the UK, the problem is likely to worsen considerably.

From a human resource management point of view the likely outcome over the coming decades is one in which the art of recruiting and retaining people in a tight labour market stays right at the top of the agenda. Competence in this area, more than any other, will make the difference between an HRM function which is successful and one that is not. It will be necessary for organisations to work hard at developing and retaining positive reputations as employers, to differentiate their offerings as employers from those of their competitors through employer branding exercises and to take a flexible approach to staffing their organisations. Where wage budgets are under pressure, it will be necessary for all managers to develop strong interpersonal skills, to demonstrate emotional intelligence and to see themselves as team leaders more than as supervisors. Effective management development programmes will thus be more necessary than is currently the case, while employee development more generally will assume greater significance as a key method of attracting and retaining people. Another area of HR activity that is likely to assume particular importance is the capacity to design organisations and to allocate activities across teams in such a way as to minimise the reliance on the hard-to-recruit groups.

Managing a diverse team

Over the course of the past decade we have seen an increase of 70 per cent in the number of people working in the UK who originate elsewhere (Caldwell 2007). While the pace of growth may well decline, there is no question that the numbers will further increase in the years to come, not least because employers will increasingly seek comparatively rare skills overseas. In London and in some other urban centres many organisations already operate with a workforce which is highly diverse in terms of its national origin. The extent to which this happens is likely to increase much further in the coming decades. It means that gaining an understanding of cultural differences in terms of workplace expectations will need to widen beyond the ranks of expatriate workers to encompass a far wider group of managers and employees. Organisations which are able to achieve this most successfully stand to benefit greatly from the development of a good reputation in overseas labour markets and among communities of people who have migrated to the UK from the same countries and regions. Moreover, they stand to gain from enhanced performance on the part of their overseas recruits.

It is partly a question of being culturally sensitive in a general sense. Not only do organisations which are serious about diversity need to eliminate unfairness or discrimination, they need to be seen to be doing so and hence perceived by their employees, all the time, as acting entirely equitably. The other requirement is the development on the part of managers and colleagues who originate in the UK of a full understanding of the way in which workplaces are culturally different in many overseas countries and hence that recruits coming to the UK from abroad have different expectations and different behavioural norms that need to be respected and taken into account. Laroche and Rutherford (2007) give many good examples in their book. Examples are as follows:

- In the UK when we select people for jobs we focus primarily on the skills and experience that are necessary to do the particular job well. The better matched the skills and the more relevant the experience, the better the chances that a candidate will be offered the job. For candidates from elsewhere in the world, particularly for people from Southern Asia and the Middle East, such an approach is alien. They are used to a business culture in which educational qualifications are far more significant, the most successful job applicants being those with the highest degrees from the most prestigious institutions. Moreover, a broad range of experience is seen as being more important than experience that is focused narrowly in one area. As a result CVs sent by people from these countries are typically very different from those that UK-based applicants would draw up. They will also tend to stress different kinds of qualities when interviewed.

● Interpersonal behaviour in UK workplaces appears cold and unfriendly to people from other parts of the world. We tend to like to maintain a substantial 'personal space' around us which, when it is 'invaded' by someone else, makes us feel uncomfortable. Touching extends just to formal handshaking and, occasionally, perhaps a brief congratulatory pat on the back or upper arm. We rarely display emotion at work, and tend to regard such displays with suspicion, regarding the person concerned as lacking in the capacity to make cool, detached judgements. The situation in many overseas countries is very different. Personal space is much smaller, handshakes last for longer, touching is common, even senior managers display plenty of emotion and people regularly kiss and hug one another at work.

● Business cultures in UK workplaces are a great deal less hierarchical than is the case in most other countries. Managers are not, on the whole, autocratic in their approach. They consult widely before making decisions, tend to have reasonably open and genuine relationships with those they manage and will often actively encourage critical scrutiny of their thinking. Delegation of authority for decision making is the norm, senior managers often not expecting to be informed about everything that is going on in their divisions. The situation in many other countries, including European countries, is wholly different. Hierarchy is more important, questioning the boss unacceptable and consultation far rarer. Managers expect to be informed about what is happening and delegate decision making to a far lesser extent.

Activity 15.2

According to the demographers at the United Nations several European countries are going to see substantial falls in their populations over the next forty years due to low fertility rates. It is estimated that the German population will fall from 83 million to 79 million by 2050, and the Italian population from 58 million to 51 million. In Russia the projected fall is from 143 million to 112 million. By contrast the British and French populations are projected to increase modestly during this period, while in Turkey the population will increase hugely from 77 million today to 101 million in 2050.

1 What do you think are the main long-term implications for organisations in these different European countries?

2 What will the effect be on the labour market?

3 What will be the effect on the capacity of public sector organisations to deliver vital public services?

COMPETITIVE PRESSURES

The future size and make-up of the working population over the coming twenty years can be predicted with reasonable confidence. This is not the case when it comes to making judgements about likely future developments in the market for goods and services. Here much more is uncertain because there are so many influences which could have a major impact. We cannot be at all certain whether or not the world economy will continue to grow, let alone at the very impressive rates that have been achieved over the past twenty years. So much rests on volatile variables such as oil prices, diplomatic relations between countries, terrorist activity, possible technological breakthroughs and levels of economic confidence in major economies. A major international recession is always a possibility, the results of which would be to throw into reverse many of the global economic trends we have witnessed having so great a transformative approach over recent decades.

However, while accepting the problems associated with predicting future trends in these areas, it is fair to claim that the most likely future scenario is one in which most organisations in countries such as the UK will continue to face greater levels of competition than is currently the case. Competitive intensity is not at all easy to measure in any kind of clear and objective way. There are no internationally recognised indices or generally recognised methods for tracking the growth of competitive pressures in a particular industry over time. Instead economists tend to rely on a range of diverse proxy measures, none of which by themselves proves that we are experiencing considerably greater competitive intensity, but which taken together strongly suggest that we are. Hence over time there have been strong trends towards greater concentration of market power in the hands of larger organisations (Mahajan 2006), much greater levels of import penetration into UK markets from overseas producers (Wadhwani 1999) and a reduction in the amount of time that any one organisation is able to achieve and maintain market dominance in an industry (Thomas and D'Aveni 2004). In some industries competition has become so intense that they are characterised by economists as being 'hyper-competitive' in nature (Sparrow 2003).

The trend towards greater levels of competition has three principal causes, although the extent to which each has a significance in particular industries varies. Across much of the manufacturing sector, agriculture and the extractive industries, globalisation is the key source of additional competition. National markets are increasingly being subsumed into single international markets with many more players and far less predictability. Hence, for example, the UK steel industry has been transformed over thirty years from one which mainly produced steel for consumption in the UK to one which sells its products all over the world and competes fiercely with overseas providers. In 1970 only 5 per cent of steel used in the UK was imported, by 2006 over half came from overseas. In other industries technology is the main driver of increased competition. Technological advances both create greater opportunities, but also drive competitive intensity by requiring organisations to keep ahead of their rivals all the time. This is the case across the IT, telecommunications, pharmaceuticals, science-based industries and hi-tech manufacturing sectors, a result being a progressive lowering of prices for consumers. A good example is broadcasting, where thanks to technological developments, the number of TV channels widely available to UK consumers increased from 1 in 1950 to 5 in 2000 and now there are hundreds. The final major cause of additional competition is government policy, which has increasingly favoured the creation of competitive markets in sectors which were previously regulated or even nationalised. Governments see the promotion of competition as a means of improving efficiency and quality of services, at the same time driving wealth creation and innovation in the economy. A good example here is the very great growth in the extent of competition in the airline industry over recent years as international agreements restricting the number of airlines which could operate each major route have been removed, allowing very considerable increases in competition.

There is no reason looking forward to expect anything but a continuation of these established trends. Technology continues to advance at a fast rate, itself helping to make global economic activity easier and cheaper. Meanwhile governments show no sign of reversing their preference for deregulation, privatisation and marketisation.

What are the implications for employment practices and for the HRM agenda? There are a number, none of which is new, but which we can say with some confidence will grow in importance in the future.

Flexibility

Competition leads to increased volatility and unpredictability in an organisation's trading environment. The greater the degree of competitive intensity the more fleet of foot an organisation is required to be. Changes have to be made more quickly and more regularly, resources being switched from one activity to another in order that opportunities may be seized when they occur. Established sources of competitive advantage may cease to add value, while new potential sources must be exploited. This means that once valued skills can quickly become obsolete, leading to redundancies and to a requirement for staff to develop new skills. It also requires organisations to be in a position to deploy people opportunistically so that there are sufficient people with the right qualifications in a position to provide a new service, develop a new product or meet increased demand for new lines.

Flexibility is thus likely to move further up the HRM agenda in the decades ahead. There will be a greater level of 'churn' as people leave and join organisations with somewhat greater frequency, a great deal more multiskilling on the part of non-specialists and greater investment in employee development so that an organisation is able both to recruit and retain good people, and also maximise its capacity for flexibility.

Cost control

Another inevitable consequence of increased competitive intensity, particularly for UK organisations which are obliged to compete with rivals in developing countries with much lower cost bases, is a continual need to reduce expenditure and to keep a lid on costs. From an HR perspective this inevitably means that less money is available for pay rises or enhanced benefit packages. This poses a major problem in an era of tightening labour markets because it means that an organisation's capacity to buy its way out of a skills shortage is severely limited. A premium will therefore be placed on the capacity to recruit and retain effectively at relatively low cost. In practice this will require a shift in traditional approaches to rewarding employees, making much more use of the approaches associated with 'total reward' thinking we outlined in Chapter 7. In particular, we are likely to see greater focus being placed on relational rewards, creating jobs which are as 'rewarding' as possible in the widest sense of the word, but which are less costly. This is a great deal more difficult to achieve in practice than giving people pay rises, requiring more sophisticated interpersonal skills, the possession on the part of managers of a good deal of emotional intelligence and creative thinking about the management of the employment relationship. Methods will have to be found and introduced which have the effect of making people feel more valued, just as positively motivated and generally highly satisfied with their work, but which do not involve paying them more money.

Evaluating the HR contribution

The third major implication of increased competition from an HRM point of view will be increased pressure for the function itself to demonstrate its own worth in terms of valued added and costs controlled. We can thus expect to see more examples of HR accounting measures being developed and used, more quantative targets being set for HR specialists to meet, more benchmarking of HR performance against that of competitors and pressure to organise the HR function in such a way as to secure greater value for money. It is likely that this will involve greater use of IT as activities that can be automated and/or transferred online to organisational intranets are treated in this way. In many cases this will reduce the requirement for people to undertake HR roles which are essentially administrative in nature (e.g. payroll officers) or which can be carried out by IT applications (e.g. many training roles). Outsourcing of HR activity to specialist providers will also increase as organisations find that they can buy in services that are of higher quality than those provided in-house, but less expensive too.

Activity 15.3

Aside from the need to become more flexible, the pressure to reduce costs and a need for the HR function in organisations to justify its existence, what other people management consequences might flow from increasing competitive intensity in organisations?

REGULATION

The third major long-term trend which has had a major impact on the way organisations manage people in recent decades has been the very substantial increase in the extent of employment legislation. Over thirty years, as was explained in Chapter 9, the UK has moved from having some of the most lightly regulated labour markets in the world to sharing, along with the other EU member states, a very highly regulated system. It is reasonable to characterise this change as comprising a regulatory revolution, so great has been the transformation in the amount of regulation to which the employment relationship has become subject and its day-to-day impact on management practice. However, it is also reasonable to assert that the revolution has now nearly run its course and that we are unlikely to witness in future years a continuation in this field of the established pace of change. There is no question that the existing body of employment law will be further adjusted from time to time to improve the extent to which it meets the legislators' aims. For example, we can anticipate reform of equal pay law and greater clarity being established over which groups of atypical workers are and are not covered by different areas of employment law. Some groups who do not currently enjoy as much protection from employment law as they might, such as agency workers, will in all likelihood be given greater rights. There are also good reasons for anticipating a greater degree of pan-EU harmonisation of employment regulation in the future, involving perhaps dismissal law, as further attempts are made to 'level the playing field' in a bid to enhance free, fair and open competition across the Union. However, measures of this kind will on the whole amount to fine-tuning of existing employment rights rather than major extensions along the lines we have witnessed since the 1970s.

However, this does not mean that the impact of regulation on organisations will lessen, nor that HR managers will have to pay less attention to developments in the regulatory sphere. Instead, there are good grounds for arguing that future years will see a shift away from direct regulation of the labour market towards other forms of regulation which have the capacity to have just as significant an impact.

This process has already begun, as government ministers are increasingly looking to employers to assist them in meeting objectives across a wide range of policy areas. We can expect to see this increasing because many of the changes governments are seeking to affect can only realistically be achieved with the active cooperation of employers. Moreover, in some cases, policy objectives require quite major changes in our accustomed behaviour, making them something of a hard sell at the ballot box. Because employers do not have votes, there is reason to expect that the lion's share of the changes will be obtained from *forcing* them to adjust their methods, governments being happy merely to *persuade* the populace as a whole of the need to change. There are numerous examples regularly reported including a potential role for employers in helping the government reach its targets for reducing obesity, encouraging employers to sponsor academy schools and the achievement of the ambitious pension-savings agenda we discussed in Chapter 7. Other major examples are discussed below.

Skills

The government has set itself a demanding set of targets for the coming decades years as far as raising skills levels is concerned. These were set out in a major White Paper (DIUS 2007) and include the following (to be achieved by 2020):

- 95 per cent of adults to be functionally literate and numerate (currently 85 per cent and 79 per cent respectively)
- over 90 per cent of adults to have gained a level 2 qualification (currently 69 per cent)
- two million more people with level 3 qualifications

- 500,000 people to be in apprenticeships
- 40 per cent of adults to have degree-level qualifications (now 29 per cent)

Much of the policy is focused on schools and colleges. It includes, for example, the aim to make full-time education until the age of 18 universal. However, many of the proposals are focused on adult learners and on the role to be played by employers.

Employers are being given incentives to make a 'Skills Pledge'. This amounts to a public declaration that they will take responsibility for helping their staff to gain basic levels of educational attainment (i.e. literacy, numeracy and level 2 qualifications in areas of value to the employer). In return for making the pledge, the employer will get access to the services of a government-funded 'skills brokerage service' and other support to help source appropriate training providers. Public funding will be made available for much of this training.

At present the government is not proposing any compulsion in this area, for example by introducing a continental-style training levy system whereby employers who do not participate are effectively forced to do so by paying an additional tax which is then used to fund training. However, significantly, the White Paper raises the possibility of this happening following a 'review' in 2011. One way or another therefore, be it on a voluntary or compulsory basis, employers are going to be required to cooperate in order to bring the government's skills agenda to realisation.

Welfare to work

Another recent government White Paper (DWP 2007) sets objectives for reducing the proportion of people of working age who live off state benefits of one kind or another and encouraging them into employment. It is primarily concerned with welfare reform and with ways of reducing the number of economically inactive people. It starts by setting out the scale of the problem:

- there are over three million people in the UK of working age who have been on benefit for over a year
- there are three million households, with 1.7 million children, in which no one is working
- in total, a quarter of adults of working age are not currently working

The White Paper goes on to propose the use of a combination of new incentives and disincentives aimed at increasing the participation rate to 80 per cent, although no definite target date is set. The title given to the new initiative is 'Pathways to Work'. More specific aims include a reduction of a million in the number of people claiming incapacity benefit, a reduction of 300,000 in the number of single parents who are working and an increase of a million in the number of over-fifties who are working.

These aims are to be met partly by providing new state-funded programmes aimed at preparing people for work which are more personalised and responsive to individual needs and preferences than at present. Another initiative involves extending assistance to people once they have started work in order to facilitate retention and career progression. People will, for example, continue to see job centre advisers after they have started working. We are also going to see the establishment of the principle that people who can work and are offered work must take it. Moreover, there will be a requirement for job seekers to undertake a period of unpaid work experience once they have been claiming benefits for a year, the prospect of benefit withdrawal being implied for those who do not cooperate.

All of these initiatives will require active support from employers, as will a further proposal to set up clearly defined partnerships between government agencies and organisations which will involve long-term benefit claimants taking jobs and getting training for a year, partly paid for by government and supported by the Learning and Skills Councils.

Activity 15.4

1 To what extent do you think the government will be successful in persuading employers to devote time and resources to helping to increase skills and attainment levels among the UK population?

2 What grounds are there for anticipating a degree of resistance on the part of employers?

Carbon emissions

The need to reduce carbon emissions in order to stem global warming is now firmly established as a government priority, challenging new targets having been set early in 2008 by the European Union. In 2005 Sir Nicholas Stern was commissioned by the UK government to undertake a major review into the economics of climate change. His report was published in the autumn of 2006 and subsequently in book form in 2007. It has been hugely influential internationally as well as in the UK, its power lying in its conclusion. Here Stern argues that tackling climate change and promoting continued economic growth are not alternatives. Instead, it is in our economic interests, as well as our environmental interests, to reduce the amount of greenhouse gas emissions and hence stabilise global warming:

> The world does not need to choose between averting climate change and promoting growth and development. Changes in energy technologies and in the structure of economies have created opportunities to decouple growth from greenhouse gas emissions. Indeed, ignoring climate change will eventually damage economic growth. (Stern 2007)

Using economic models Stern argues that world GDP will decline by 5 per cent a year as a result of damage done to the economy by climate change, but that temperature rises can be limited and many of the costs of dealing with climate-induced disruption avoided if just 1 per cent of current annual world GDP each year was to be invested in reducing greenhouse gas emissions. Stern argues for a 'strong and deliberate' public policy response to climate change, accepting that the lion's share of the burden should fall on the wealthiest, developed countries. He suggests that there are three areas where action must be taken:

1 Carbon pricing. By this Stern means tax, fines for those who do not comply with stricter regulations and expanded 'carbon trading schemes'
2 Public funding of research aimed at the development and deployment of low carbon technologies
3 Public investment in measures which educate the public about ways of greening their lifestyles and which remove barriers that prevent people from living in a more energy-efficient way

From an organisational perspective the result is likely to be very considerable pressure to reduce energy use, car usage and the number of business flights that employees take. The thorniest practical issue concerns car usage by employees commuting in and out of work. The government is keen to 'encourage' as many people as possible out of cars and on to public transport, and is providing incentives to organisations which help them achieve this. This has major implications for the recruitment and retention of staff, where staff are located and their day-to-day efficiency. It should also serve to push flexible working patterns and homeworking schemes higher up the organisational agenda.

Getting people out of their cars is going to require huge shifts in attitudes and accustomed behaviours which will not be at all easy to achieve. At present across the UK, according to the British Social Attitudes Survey (2004 and 2006), 48 per cent of us commute to work each day driving our own cars, a further 11 per cent being driven to work as passengers in cars. Only 7 per cent commute by bus and just 3 per cent by train. Moreover, when asked, people largely refuse to accept that traffic congestion is a major problem. Generally people are prepared to accept, in theory, that car usage should be reduced, but only if public transport is substantially improved first. Big majorities are firmly against measures such as 'doubling the cost of petrol', 'charging £2 to enter towns at peak times', charging '£1 per 50 miles on motorways', increasing parking costs and taxing parking spaces. We can thus conclude that 'the commuting issue' is likely to become established as a major one of significance to HR agendas in the future. This will be the case whether or not the government finds ways of compelling employers to encourage people to alter their accustomed methods of commuting.

Waste

Aside from the global warming issue, the other major environmental debate of our time concerns waste. We are a very wasteful society, man's treatment of the planet being likened by some commentators to a bird which fouls its own nest. In the industrialised countries we throw away into our dustbins around 500 kg of waste per person per year – a figure that is increasing all the time due to the proliferation of packaging surrounding consumer goods, the marketing of disposable items and of products that are cheaper to throw away than to repair when they are faulty. Our industrial processes are also hugely wasteful. For every car that is manufactured, 15 tonnes of solid waste are produced. In fact, household waste only comprises a small proportion of the solid waste that OECD countries produce, the vast majority emanating from industrial processes.

There are three ways in which waste is disposed of: landfill, incineration and recycling. In the UK, despite major recent increases in the amount of recycling we carry out, recycling still only accounts for a small minority of the total. The problem is that our landfill sites are now nearing capacity. The government has therefore set itself targets to achieve in switching to incineration and recycling, both of which are a good deal more environmentally friendly, but also costly. The aim is for a third of all waste to be incinerated by 2015 and a third to be recycled. Achieving this without hugely increasing spending is proving difficult. It requires the following:

- encouraging households to sort items for recycling before throwing rubbish away
- reducing the amount of waste produced in the first place and
- efficiency savings in the methods/processes used to collect and dispose of waste

The result is a public policy agenda which is controversial because it aims to use incentives as well as disincentives to try to change our customary behaviour and that of organisations. As there are rarely votes in pushing private households into doing things they do not want to do or in charging them more for a service they have hitherto received cheaply or even free, it is likely that businesses will be targeted more often and rather harder. This will inevitably mean that more resources have to be devoted to waste management and that reducing the amount of waste produced quite dramatically will become an organisational priority. We may well see waste-trading schemes introduced, along the lines of the emissions-trading schemes identified above. The significance for the HR function arises because ultimately delivering on this agenda requires changes in people's perceptions, attitudes and behaviours. Communicating the agenda and providing the necessary training will thus become HR priorities.

WINDOW ON PRACTICE

In recent years the Honda formula 1 racing team has taken a number of steps aimed at improving its 'green credentials'. These have led to the organisation being awarded ISO 14001 accreditation which rewards environmental initiatives. Not all the steps taken are directly related to HRM, but many are and those that are not nonetheless help to enhance the attractiveness of the Honda brand in its key labour markets. The major initiatives are as follows:

- replacing sponsors' logos on the cars with pictures of the earth taken from space
- introducing an environmental awareness training programme for staff
- encouraging staff to monitor their use of energy at home
- actively seeking feedback and ideas for new initiatives from staff
- removing personal waste bins next to desks and installing recycling bins for collective use in their place
- encouraging staff to switch to environmentally friendly cars
- encouraging homeworking to reduce commuting

Source: Cotton 2008.

KEY DEBATE: FUTURE CONTRACTUAL ARRANGEMENTS

While there is general agreement among commentators about the nature of the work we will be carrying out in the coming decades and the profile of the workforce that will be employed to carry it out, there is considerable disagreement about the types of contract (both legal and psychological) that will be prevalent. For some years now a diverse group of futurologists have gained considerable influence by predicting substantial changes in this area. The most prominent figure in the UK is Charles Handy, who has published a series of books in which he argues that radical change is in store (*see* Handy 1984, 1989, 1994 and 2001). A broadly similar analysis has been developed by Davidson and Rees Mogg (1997), Rifkin (1995) and Bridges (1995), and more recently by Susan Greenfield (2003a and 2003b). While each of these writers, and others who have advocated the evolution of a similar future for the world of work, justify their conclusion somewhat differently, all predict a switch in the dominant form of work from employment to various forms of self-employment. Moreover, where employment continues, people will be far more likely to work from home (connected to others electronically) and to work for small, highly specialised companies and will neither have nor expect long-term job security.

For Handy the future is one in which portfolio careers will dominate. People will move from employer to employer regularly, often working for two concerns at the same time. There will be periods of self-employment and periods of employment, the conventional working life being likened to that of an actor auditioning for work and moving from production to production on stage, screen and TV. There will be periods in between assignments when we will be underemployed, and other periods when we have more than enough work on our plates. Davidson and Rees-Mogg (1997, p. 237) prefer the example of film production companies which assemble a group of talented specialists to work on a project, but when it is over 'the lighting technicians, cameramen, sound engineers and wardrobe specialists will go their separate ways'.

Others, including Greenfield (2003a, p. 92), go further in arguing that 'the concept of the "job" as we know it may disappear altogether' and that 'firms will perhaps bid for employee time almost on a day-to-day basis'. Insecurity of employment, according to this view, will soon become the norm.

The analysis on which these writers base their predictions is thoughtful and logical and can be persuasive. At root they all argue that greater volatility in the world of employment is inevitable as organisations experience increasing volatility in their product markets. Because employers will no longer operate in markets which are at all stable and predictable, it follows that they will be unable to guarantee any kind of stable employment. In such a world, it is argued, no organisation can be viable if it burdens itself with large numbers of dependent employees expecting to enjoy lengthy, stable careers. Instead organisations will continually be expanding and contracting, forming and dissolving, and hiring different people, with different skill sets on an 'as needs' basis. Greenfield's conclusion is the same, but for her the change will arise not as a result of increased competition. She predicts greater cooperation and less competition, but nonetheless argues that increased technical specialisation will mean that the most efficient and effective enterprises will be those which are small and highly flexible. Rifkin argues that traditional jobs will disappear because technological advances will create a world in which machines do many of the jobs currently performed by people. His future is a world of underemployment in which there are not enough jobs to go round, forcing a large proportion of the workforce either into self-employment or into a working life of short-term employment as and when opportunities arise.

A number of arguments have been advanced in opposition to this radical vision of an employment-free future world of work. Nolan (2004) has led the assault in the UK, drawing on empirical data to show that in most respects, despite evidence of increased volatility in product markets, traditional, long-term, full-time employment is showing no sign whatever of withering away. Indeed, in some respects the trend is towards greater security, albeit in smaller enterprises. He is contemptuous in his criticisms of those who continue to peddle what he sees as misleading myths:

> **Scarcely a week passes without a well-paid visionary heralding the demise of paid work and employment or the growing salience in the new economy of the 'free-worker'. Attention to detail is invariably slight. The great variance in the patterns of work and the consequences of past upheavals in employment are routinely ignored. (Nolan 2004, p. 7)**

He goes on to make reference to the real trends that are observable in both the UK and the USA, many of which we have referred to in this and earlier chapters:

- employment levels (i.e. the number of traditional jobs) are rising and not falling
- the vast majority of workers continue to be employed in permanent jobs
- job tenure rates have remained broadly stable for decades
- around a third of the workforce has been employed (already) for ten years or more by their current employer
- self-employment has not grown appreciably over the past decade
- the number of temporary workers has fallen substantially over the past ten years

While this evidence is very convincing, it is too early to condemn Handy, Rifkin and Greenfield as having been hopelessly wrong in their predictions. It is possible that over the coming few decades they will be proved right. But it is fair to point out that, at least in the case of Handy, the same claims were being made twenty-five years ago about what the world of work would be like today, and in many respects the opposite has turned out to be the case.

One possible reason that the predictions of these futurologists may prove to be inaccurate is their over-reliance on an analysis of what is likely to happen to product markets, ignoring in the process other determinants of employment arrangements discussed above such as labour market pressures and the regulatory environment. The evidence suggests that they are right about increasing competition and the need for organisations to become more specialised, flexible and productive, but that they are wrong to ignore other factors in the evolving business environment which serve to push organisations in an opposite direction to that which they would prefer given a free hand. For example, it is very often claimed that in the future, because employers will be unable to guarantee long-term employment, they will instead provide their workers with a capacity for greater 'employability'. People will be recruited and motivated, not with the promise of job security, but with skills development and work experience which will help

GENERAL DISCUSSION TOPICS

1 What are the major trends in your own organisation's future demand for skills? To what extent do you foresee these being harder to source in the future and why?

2 What purpose does a study of current demographic trends serve from the point of view of the HR function in organisations?

3 Why do you think management writers continue to predict a revolution in the way work is organised in industrialised countries, despite the presence of evidence suggesting a continuation of the approaches that are currently prevalent?

FURTHER READING

Robert Taylor, formerly labour affairs editor of the *Financial Times*, has published five excellent papers over the past few years focusing on different aspects of the future of work. These draw on the large range of academic research that has been contributed to the Economic and Social Research Council's Future of Work programme. You can download these papers without charge at **www.leeds.ac.uk/esrcfutureofwork/**.

A special edition of *The British Journal of Industrial Relations* (Vol. 41, No. 2) published in June 2003 was devoted to research on and debates about the future

of work. Many leading writers in the field contributed articles which set out the first findings from the ESRC's Future of Work programme.

The government's Office for National Statistics also has an excellent website which can be used to gain access to a large range of authoritative articles and statistics concerning demographic trends and the demand for and supply of skills in the UK. You will find summaries of the most recent trends in their annual publications *Social Trends* and *Labour Market Review*.

REFERENCES

Beavan, R., Bosworth, D., Lewney, R. and Wilson, R. (2005) *Alternative Skills Scenarios to 2020 for the UK Economy*. Cambridge: Cambridge Econometrics.

Bridges, W (1995) *Jobshift: how to prosper in a workplace without jobs*. London: Nicholas Brealey.

British Social Attitudes Survey (2004) *British Social Attitudes: The Twentieth Report, 2003–4 edition*. London: National Centre for Social Research, Chapter 3.

British Social Attitudes Survey (2006) *British Social Attitudes: The Twenty-Second Report, 2005–6 edition*. London, National Centre for Social Research, Chapter 6.

Caldwell, C. (2007) 'No easy answers on immigration', *Financial Times*, 19 October.

CIPD (annual) *Annual Recruitment and Retention Survey*. London, Chartered Institute of Personnel and Development.

Cotton, C. (2008) 'Go the Green Mile', *People Management Guide to the Reward and Benefits Market*, January, pp. 8–9.

Davidson, J.D. and Rees-Mogg, W. (1997) *The Sovereign Individual: The coming economic revolution. How to survive and prosper in it*. Basingstoke: Macmillan.

Department for Innovation, Universities and Skills (DIUS) (2007) *World Class Skills: Implementing the Leitch Review of Skills in England*. White Paper, July 2007. London: HMSO.

Department for Work and Pensions (DWP) (2007) *In Work, Better Off*. White Paper, July 2007. London: HMSO.

European Commission (2000) *The Future of Work*. London: Kogan Page.

Green, M. (2006) 'Employers alarmed at skills shortage', *Financial Times*, 21 August.

Greenfield, S. (2003a) *Tomorrow's People*. London: Penguin/Allen Lane.

Greenfield, S. (2003b) 'Flexible Futures', *People Management*, 23 October, pp. 52–3.

Handy, C. (1984) *The Future of Work*. Oxford: Blackwell.

Handy, C. (1989) *The Age of Unreason*. London: Business Books.

Handy, C. (1994) *The Empty Raincoat: making sense of the future*. London: Hutchinson.

Handy, C. (2001) *The Elephant and the Flea: Looking Backwards to the Future*. London: Hutchinson.

Kaletsky, A. (2006) 'Why the sun is rising over Britain, not Japan', *The Times*, 10 November, p. 21.

Laroche, L. and Rutherford, D. (2007) *Recruiting, Retaining and Promoting Culturally Different Employees*. New York: Butterworth Heinemann.

Learning and Skills Council (2006) *National Employers Skills Survey 2005: Key Findings*. London: LSC (available online).

Mahajan, S. (2006) 'Concentration ratios for business by industry in 2004', *Economic Trends*, No. 635, October. London: Office for National Statistics.

Nolan, P. (2001) 'Shaping things to come', *People Management*, 27 December.

Nolan, P. (2004) *Back to the Future of Work* (**www.leeds.ac.uk/esrcfutureofwork/downloads/ events/colloquium_2004/nolan_paper_0904.pdf**).

ONS (2008) *Labour Market Statistics, January 2008*. London: Office for National Statistics.

PwC (2007) *Managing Tomorrow's People: The Future of Work to 2020*. London: PricewaterhouseCoopers. (This report can be downloaded at **www.pwc.com**.)

Rifkin, J. (1995) *The End of Work: The decline of the global labour force and the dawn of the post-market era*. New York: Puttnam.

Sparrow, P.L. (2003) 'The Future of Work?', in D. Holman, T. Wall, C. Clegg, P. Sparrow and A. Howard (eds) *The New Workplace: a guide to the human impact of modern working practices*. Chichester: Wiley.

Stern, N. (2007) *The Economics of Climate Change*. Cambridge: Cambridge University Press.

Taylor, A. (2007) 'UK immigration may be close to peak', *Financial Times*, 24 July.

Thomas, L.G. and D'Aveni, R.A. (2004) 'The Rise of Hypercompetition from 1950 to 2002: Evidence of increasing industry destabliization and temporary competitive advantage', Working Paper. Copenhagen: Copenhagen Business School.

Wadhawani, S. (1999) 'Is Inflation Dead?', lecture delivered at the National Council of Applied Research, New Delhi, India, 17 December.

Managing people: fundamental skills

Face-to-face skills in management

The objectives of this introduction to Fundamental skills are to:

1 Explain why developing skill in face-to-face situations is important for all managers

2 Explain what makes for effectiveness in interaction

3 Review the fundamental skills of (a) setting the tone, (b) listening, (c) questioning and (d) feedback

4 Provide some practical exercises to develop your skills and some web links.

Why managers need to develop skills in various face-to-face situations

Managers spend more of their time talking to other people than anything else they do: that is their job. They have responsibilities, they have a defined role, they probably have targets to meet, a group of staff to worry about and to energise, they have customers to understand and to satisfy, products to conceive and produce, but what they actually *do*, above all else, is talk to people. Furthermore the face-to-face meeting is the crucial and decisive stage in most management initiatives.

International agreements between nations or between businesses may be weeks or months in the making and involve extensive, detailed work by hundreds of people, but the agreement will not be made until the signatories actually meet, shake hands and sign. Also there will be at least some aspects of the agreement that are not shaped until that meeting produces a mutually acceptable shape. Recruiting an employee almost always requires the parties to meet before the employment begins and it is at that meeting that the parties finally agree to work together. Performance management often requires the completion of detailed forms, but any change in actual performance will follow an interview to review progress and prepare future action. Learning may be self-directed and computer based but much still requires the direct interaction between someone who knows and someone trying to find out. Discipline needs someone to explain where someone else is failing and what will happen if there is not improvement. There are many other examples: selling, buying, opinion surveys, mediation, negotiation, case conferences, committees and so on. Some of these are areas of specialised HR expertise that other managers need to understand and use and we have a small number of the most obvious in this skills package. The idea that managers need to learn how to talk to people may sound strange to some, who say things like:

> 'I've been talking to people all my life. It's natural. We don't need to learn how to do it, any more than we have to learn how to walk.'

> 'Well, I never think of myself as a people person. I rely on HR for that.'

> 'I say what I think, but sometimes people don't listen.'

Yet that is precisely where our natural skill that we learned as children really needs honing and focusing for the managerial job. Working out what to do may be easy or difficult, but getting people to share that understanding and then making things happen in the way they should is a high art. The core expertise of HR specialists is skill in interaction and handling of face-to-face situations effectively, so you expect them to be more effective in many situations, such as training, selection interviewing and negotiating with union representatives, but managers in other specialisms require face-to-face skills as well, and these can be improved or focused more effectively.

Effectiveness in interaction

The mysteries of non-verbal behaviour

To be effective we need to understand non-verbal behaviour, or body language. We all reveal our feelings by what we do as well as in what we say. A person blushing is obviously embarrassed and someone crying is clearly distressed, but there are a host of other signs or *tells* that indicate what a person is feeling. The person who is able to read these signals has a great advantage in interactions. The term 'tell' comes from the study of poker players, who are as anxious to conceal their own hand as they are to guess what is in someone else's. It is an interesting feature of human behaviour that we all lie when we think it will help us socially. Some of you will be outraged by that comment because of your personal honesty and integrity, but remember the word 'socially' in the above sentence. However morally upright and truthful you may be in most things, you will occasionally withhold or distort the truth in a social context, or your life would be impossible. Consider the following examples:

Meeting an old acquaintance at a party, 'Oh, how nice to see you'. (This may conceal your true feelings, 'If I'd known you were coming, I'd have stayed away'.)

Responding to a friend's enquiry, 'How are you?' with 'I'm fine, thank you' (when you have had a worrying pain in the chest for a few days and your teenage daughter is giving you hell).

At the end of a presentation by the representative of an office equipment company, 'That was most interesting. If you just give me a few days, I'll come back to you, and I'm sure it will be a "yes"' (when you really mean, 'I've seen three others and they're all better in every way, but it's easier to fob you off with a possibility than prolong the agony now').

When your two-year old son wakes up with stomach ache, 'Just go back to sleep, darling, and it will be better in the morning' (when you really haven't a clue what the problem is, but it doesn't seem too serious, and you must try to get some sleep yourself).

Most of the time these little white lies don't matter, after all you are not really interested in the health of your friend but merely chatting, and reassuring your son may be all he needs to ease his ache. In other situations it may be helpful to read *correctly* the non-verbal signals that you are receiving and to be aware of the signals you are inadvertently sending yourself. Doing this correctly can be quite difficult, although there has recently been a great deal of self-help literature dealing with body language, mostly giving bewildering suggestions about how to understand the reactions of someone from the opposite sex. The main reservation must be that such books are always limited to a particular cultural context, usually Anglo-American, and those from different backgrounds can find them at least confusing and sometimes unhelpful. In Chapter 15 about the future of people management we refer to some of the unfamiliarity felt by people in other countries taking up work in the UK. Inter-personal behaviour in UK workplaces appears cold and unfriendly to people from other parts of the world. Personal space is interpreted quite differently and physical contact is very limited. Displays of emotion at work are regarded with suspicion, and managerial practices usually involve a degree of consultation with subordinates that many other nationalities find puzzling.

WINDOW ON PRACTICE

Some of the more obvious non-verbal signals are:

1 We tend to move closer to those we trust or in whom we have confidence and further away from those we fear or distrust (so it may not just be your bad breath).
2 We tend to emphasise or underplay our height according to the situation. A need to be assertive is accompanied by pulling the head back in order to 'look down' at the other person. A concern to maintain the goodwill of the other person may be accompanied by ducking the head or bowing slightly.
3 Men tend to scratch their heads when baffled and touch their nose when afraid.
4 Women's first reaction to a crisis will be clutch their forehead (Whatever will I do?) and then put a hand to their mouth (Oh God. Is it my fault?)
5 Job applicants at interview improve their chances by more smiling, eye contact, head nodding and head shaking than average.

Are some people more effective than others?

Effective face-to-face people are likely to have some basic qualities. *Poise* enables a person to be at ease in a wide variety of social situations, often enjoying them, and able to talk with different types of people in a relaxed and self-confident way. This self-confidence comes partly from the feedback of willing responses constantly provided by other people so it may help to 'feed' lines that will produce a good response.

Another element of poise is knowing what you are talking about, as we demonstrate our poise more in familiar situations than in strange circumstances. Questions, and even criticism, are easier to deal with and are often wanted, so stimulating the interchange.

A necessary part of poise is being *responsive* to the needs, feelings and level of understanding in other people. This prevents poise from becoming too egocentric. The teacher, for instance, will be looking for signs of misunderstanding in the student so that the message can be restated or clarified, and the market research interviewer will be looking for signals that the question has been accurately construed, or that it needs elaboration. Responsiveness can include offering rewards, like friendliness, warmth, sympathy and helpfulness to the other person. These not only sustain and strengthen the relationship, but may also be held back as a means of trying to get one's own way.

Skills activity 1.1

Think of a recent face-to-face situation in which you were involved, such as an interview, a discussion, a seminar, an argument or a tribunal. Identify three ways in which the other person, or some of the other people, were especially effective in the exchanges, and analyse why. Then think of ways in which your own participation did not seem satisfactory to you. What were these and what were the reasons?

Some things get in the way

Certain general problems impair effectiveness. They are mostly ways in which people tend to hear what they expect to hear rather than what they are being told, in three particular ways.

The *frame of reference* is the standpoint from which a person views an issue, and understanding of the issue will be shaped by that perspective rather than any abstract 'reality'. It is a set of basic assumptions or standards that frame our behaviour. These are developed through childhood conditioning, through social background, education and our affiliations. Differences in the frames of reference held by different people present inescapable problems. Can Israelis and Arabs ever really understand each other? How can those who manage and direct ever appreciate the point of view of those who are managed and directed?

The frame of reference on any particular matter is largely determined by opinions developed within a group with which we identify, as few of us alter our opinions alone. This begins in childhood, when we adopt the views and opinions of our parents. As we grow older, we become much more independent in setting our values, but also join other groups, whose values we begin to adopt: school, scouts, youth groups, sports teams, gangs, work and so on. We both follow and help to shape opinion in our group, and most of us are in a number of such reference groups. This produces complexities: some people can be vociferously anti-union as citizens and voters in general elections, yet support a union of which they are members at their workplace.

The *stereotype* is the standardised expectation we have of those who have certain dominant characteristics: typical stereotypes are that politicians are not to be trusted, women are more caring than men and that men are more aggressive than women. The behaviour of some people in a category makes us expect all in that category to behave in the same way. This is obviously invalid, but is a tendency to which we are prone. We must always listen to what people are actually saying to us rather than hearing what we think a person of that type *would say*.

Stereotypes are necessary at the start of working relationships. We cannot deal with every individual we meet as being a void until we have collected enough information to know how to treat them, so we always try to find a pigeonhole in which to put someone. We begin conversations with a working stereotype, so that, for example, we stop someone in the street to ask directions only after we have selected a person who looks intelligent and sympathetic. If we are giving directions to a stranger we begin our explanation having made an assessment of their ability to understand quickly, or their need for a more detailed, painstaking explanation. The stereotype becomes a handicap only when we remain insensitive to new information enabling us to develop a fuller and more rational appraisal of the individual with whom we are interacting.

Being aware of the dangers of stereotyping others, and trying to exercise self-discipline, can reduce the degree to which you misunderstand other people, but you still have the problem that your respondents will put *you* into a stereotype and hear what you say in accordance with whatever their predetermined notion may be.

Cognitive dissonance is the difficulty we all have in coping with behaviour that is not consistent with our beliefs. Such behaviour will make us uncomfortable and we will try to cope with the dissonance in various ways in order to reduce the discomfort. Either we persuade ourselves that we believe in what we are doing, or we avoid the necessary behaviour. We all interpret or decode words that we hear in order to make sense of them. If we decode the words we hear in a way that does not agree with what we believe, then we tend to reinterpret them in a way that we can believe.

WINDOW ON PRACTICE

When electronic files were first introduced in Edgar's office at the insurance company, he took all the training and acquired good skill at manipulating files, storing and retrieving data. The introduction of the new system went very smoothly and Edgar was a most effective user. Three weeks later the office manager came back very late from a meeting, long after everyone else had gone home: everyone except Edgar, who had stayed late in order to update his old manual files 'because he thought that was still the best way, and he didn't mind doing it in his own time'.

SKILLS TABLE 1.1 Four categories of interaction

Enquiry	**Exposition**
Selection	Presentation
Attitude survey	Lecture
Health screening	Briefing
Joint problem solving	**Conflict resolution**
Appraisal	Negotiation
Counselling	Arbitration
Brainstorming	Discipline

Different types of interaction

It is helpful to group interactions into four broad types: enquiry, exposition, joint problem solving and conflict resolution, as indicated in Skills table 1.1.

- Enquiry is that group of situations where the manager needs to find things out from someone else, with the selection interview being the classic example. Others are a doctor diagnosing the cause of your headache, a police officer interrogating a suspect or a waiter clarifying exactly what you would like for breakfast. What needs to be found out may be factual information, attitudes, feelings, levels of understanding or misunderstanding. The main skill is in types of questioning.
- Exposition is almost the direct opposite. Instead of finding things out, you are trying to convey information, to develop in the other person a level of knowledge and understanding, acceptance of an argument or agreement with a proposition. Although some questioning is often an integral part of exposition, the main skill is in clear articulation, fluency, good organisation of material and effective illustration.
- Joint problem solving involves developing an exchange in which both parties work together to unravel a problem or understand a situation which neither fully understands beforehand. It is not one person transferring an 'answer' to another, but both trying to understand together something which they can only partly understand alone. The skills involve some questioning and explanation, but also careful listening and feedback. Joint problem solving assumes that both parties trust each other and see a common interest in helping the other.
- Conflict resolution begins without that mutual confidence, as the parties have interests that inevitably conflict and they are not likely fully to trust each other. The skills here are first those of presentation and then listening, questioning and feedback.

Fundamental skills in setting the tone

Any interaction begins by someone setting the tone of what is to follow. A shop assistant who says, 'Can I help you?' is trying to set a tone of knowledgeable helpfulness to a customer that might eventually result in a sale. Someone running a selection interview will begin by explaining what is to happen and providing other contextual information that will enable the candidate to engage in the process constructively. There will also be a process of conveying more subtle messages to say, 'I'm in charge; I know what I'm doing; you can trust me'. In other interactions the way of setting the tone is different, but some features are common:

- Speak first
- Smile, looking confident and relaxed (much easier said than done)
- Have brief, harmless exchanges that enable the parties to speak to each other without the answers mattering (weather, travel problems, etc.), but always react appropriately to answers
- Explain your understanding of what is to happen
- Check that that is understood and accepted

Fundamental skills in listening

Giving attention

- Posture is important. Inclining the body towards the other person is a signal of attentiveness, so our posture should be inclined forward and facing the other squarely with an open posture: folded arms can be inhibiting.
- Eye contact is crucial to good listening, but is a subtle art. It is one of the most intimate ways of relating to a person and many managers fear that the relationship may become too close.
- We also show physical responses in our attentiveness or inattentiveness. First we have to avoid distracting the other person by doing things that are unrelated to what is being said; fiddling with a pen, playing with car keys, scrutinising our fingernails, wringing our hands, brushing specks of dust off our sleeves are a few typical behaviours that indicate inattention. Skilled listeners not only suppress these, they also develop minor gestures and posture variants that are directly responsive to what the other is saying.
- Being silent helps you to listen by providing space for the other person to speak, but it also gives you the chance to observe the other person and to think about what is being said. Most people are uncomfortable with silence and try to fill it with inconsequential chat, but this interferes with listening. Silence still has to be attentive and the longer the silence, the harder it is to be attentive: think of the last lecture you attended and how hard it was to maintain attentiveness.

Skills activity 1.2

Over the next week, experiment with the following, in this order:

1 At the supermarket practise eye contact and other signs of attentiveness during exchanges with the check-out operator, especially the way you smile when leaving. What reaction have you evoked?

2 Do the same thing with someone at home, or with a close friend, including the physical responses and give more thought to being silent in exchanges. How do you feel afterwards?

3 Now try the same things in a conversation at work or some other social situation with someone you do not know too well, perhaps someone you do not like very much. How do you feel about them afterwards? How do you think they feel about you?

Fundamental skills in questioning

- Closed questions seek precise, terse information and are useful when you want clear, straightforward data. Most encounters feature closed questioning at some point.
- Open-ended questions avoid terse replies by inviting respondents to develop their opinions without the interviewer prescribing what the answer should be. The question does little more than introduce a topic to talk about. The main purpose is to obtain the type of deeper information that the closed question misses, as the shape of the answer is not predetermined by the questioner. You are informed not simply by the content of the answers, but by what is selected and emphasised.
- Indirect questions take an oblique approach on a difficult matter. A blunt 'Did you like that job?' almost suggests you didn't, or at least raises the suspicion that the interviewer thinks you didn't. Put indirectly as 'What gave you the most satisfaction in that job?' it has the merit of concentrating on the work rather than the person.
- The probe is a form of questioning to obtain information that the respondent is trying to conceal. When the questioner realises that the respondent is doing this he or she has to make an important, and perhaps difficult, decision. Do I respect the other person's unwillingness and let the matter rest, or do I persist with the enquiry? Reluctance is quite common in selection interviews where a candidate may wish to gloss over an aspect of the recent employment history. The most common sequence for the probe takes the following form: (a) direct questions, replacing the more comfortable open-ended approach ('What were you doing in the first six months of 2008?'). Careful phrasing may avoid a defensive reply, but those skilled at avoiding unwelcome enquiries may still deflect the question, which leads you to (b) supplementaries, which reiterate the first question with different phrasing ('Yes, I understand about that period. It's the first part of 2008 that I'm trying to get clear:

after you came back from Belgium and before you started with Amalgamated Industries'). Eventually this should produce the information the questioner needs. (c) Closing. If the information has been wrenched out like a bad tooth and the interviewer looks horrified or sits in stunned silence, then the candidate will feel badly put down. The interviewer needs to make the divulged secret less awful than the candidate had feared, so that the interview can proceed with reasonable confidence ('Yes, well you must be glad to have that behind you'). It may be that the interviewer will feel able to develop the probe by developing the answer by a further question such as 'And how did that make you feel?' or 'And how did you react to that? It must have been a terrible blow'. It is only reasonable to do this if the resultant exchange adds something useful to the questioner's understanding of the client: simple nosiness is not appropriate.

WINDOW ON (MAL)PRACTICE

One rather dubious version of the probe is to offer an exaggerated explanation for something being avoided. In the imaginary situation described above the selector might do this:

Selector: 'Yes, I understand about that period. It's the first part of 2008 that I'm trying to get clear: after you came back from Belgium and before you started with Amalgamated Industries. You weren't in prison or anything, were you?'

Candidate: 'Oh no. I had a nervous breakdown'

The explanation suggested by the selector is so appalling that the candidate rushes to offer a less appalling explanation. This is not recommended, but it is interesting to know about. It might happen to you one day.

Some common lines of questioning should be avoided because they can produce an effect that is different from what is intended.

- Leading questions ('Would you agree with me that . . . ?') will not necessarily produce an answer that is informative, but an answer in line with the lead that has been given.
- Multiple questions give the candidate too many inputs at one time ('Could you tell me something of what you did at university, not just the degree, but the social and sporting side as well, and why you chose to backpack your way round the world? You didn't travel on your own, did you?'). This sort of questioning is sometimes adopted by interviewers who are trying very hard to efface themselves and let the respondent get on with the talking. However helpful the interviewer intends to be, the effect is that the candidate will usually forget the later parts of the question, feel disconcerted and ask, 'What was the last part of the question?' By this time the interviewer has also forgotten, so they are both embarrassed.
- Taboo questions are those that invade the reasonable personal privacy of the other person. Some questions have to be avoided, especially in selection interviews, as they

could be interpreted as biased. It is at least potentially discriminatory, for instance, to ask women how many children they have and what their husbands do for a living. Questions about religion or place of birth should also be avoided. Some questions may do no more than satisfy the idle curiosity of the questioner. If there is no point in asking them, they should not be put.

Skills activity 1.3

Tomorrow at work make a note of incidents where someone else does not fully understand what you have said, or who interpreted you incorrectly. In the evening review the list to work out what went wrong and how you could have avoided the problem.

Fundamental skills in feedback

As well as listening, it is necessary to provide feedback to demonstrate that you have received and understood what you are being told.

In *reflection*, the listener picks up and restates the content of what has just been said. In a difficult situation the listener picks out the emotional overtones of a statement and 'reflects' them back to the respondent without any attempt to evaluate them. The interviewer expresses neither approval nor disapproval, neither sympathy nor condemnation. This is sometimes known as 'empathic feedback'. An example is from a discussion with a staff member who is grumbling about career prospects:

Staff member: 'Seniority doesn't count for as much as it should in this company.'

Manager: 'You feel there is not enough acknowledgement of loyalty and long service?'

This elicits further comment which will either endorse or modify the interpretation of the statement that the manager is asking for. A less productive response would have been:

'Oh, I don't know about that.'

The staff member is immediately put on the defensive, having to justify the initial comment against manifest disagreement or even disapproval from the manager. The further response may be cautious and not useful.

At a more prosaic level, there is *summary and re-run* to show you are listening and providing the opportunity for any misunderstandings to be pointed out. In appraisal, for instance, the respondent will produce lots of information in an interview and you will be selecting that which is to be retained and fully understood. From time to time you interject a summary sentence or two with an interrogative inflection:

'So you feel that the difficulty in meeting sales targets has been more to do with production problems than with customer demand? We've got the product right but are not able to deliver quickly enough?'

EXERCISES

Both of these exercises require the cooperation of a friend or colleague

1 Asking open-ended/follow-up questions

   a You both prepare one or two open-ended questions about a similar topic, such as your experience of computer usage at work, what you did over Christmas, or what sort of house you would ideally like to own.

   b You put an open-ended question to your partner and develop the reply with follow-up questions.

   c Change roles and repeat the exercise.

   d Discuss and evaluate the experience.

2 Listening, summary and re-run

   a You both spend two minutes preparing a brief statement on different controversial topics.

   b Make your statement to your partner.

   c Your partner restates what you have said, reflecting and summarising it as accurately as possible.

   d You make whatever corrections are necessary until you are satisfied that your partner has understood your point of view accurately.

   e Change roles and repeat the exercise.

   f Discuss and evaluate the experience.

The selection interview

> The objectives of this part of Fundamental skills are to:
>
> 1 Review the varieties of selection interview and its purpose
>
> 2 Explain interview strategy and consider the number of interviews and interviewers
>
> 3 Explain interview structure and the five key aspects of method

Martin was on his way to the office and was already worrying about how he would get on with the interview. It was his first time and it was such an important job that it must be right. Would his nervousness show, and would that make him look stupid in front of those key people? Was he properly prepared, with his notes in the right order? Would he be able to put his points across properly, or would he be misunderstood? And all the time there was that real worry: would the decision go the right way?

The selection interview is one of the most familiar and forbidding encounters of working life. Most people have had at least one experience of being interviewed as a preliminary to employment and few people enjoy it. Martin was apprehensive about how he would perform, yet he wasn't the candidate: he was a member of the panel!

Varieties of selection interview

Selection interviews come in all sorts of forms as they have to fit with the conventions of the employing organisation and the nature of the position which has to be filled. Auditions for singers and dancers in a musical consist of one or more subjective on-the-spot assessments from people with experience in the field. The judgements are partly based on technical competence in singing, dancing, deportment or speaking lines, but endorsed by assessments of such intangibles as personal appearance and personality.

There is no HR involvement in the selection, although there may have been some preliminary check on such matters as work permits and union membership. The crucial decisions are made by the choreographer, the musical director and director, the 'line managers' in our terminology. In the completely different field of social work, selection interviews of candidates for work in child protection will involve careful assessments of personal potential for this most taxing and sensitive of roles, following earlier background checks and references, but much of the interview itself by practising social workers will focus on the candidate's understanding of the current law relating to child protection.

Apart from those specialised situations, line managers are closely involved in all face-to-face selection situations, often as the sole management decision maker alone with a candidate. Although the interviewer may be the sole *management* decision maker, this is not the only decision-making role. Managers have to do their best to make the right decisions in the management interest, but the candidate is also making a decision, and may well decide that they do not want the job after meeting the manager at the interview.

The purpose of the selection interview

The interview is a controlled conversation with a purpose:

- to collect information from candidates in order to predict how well they would perform in the job for which they have applied, by measuring them against predetermined criteria
- to provide candidates with full details of the job and organisation to help them decide if the job is right for them
- to conduct the interview in a way that complies with legal requirements and that leaves candidates feeling that they have been given a fair hearing

Exchanging information

The interview is a flexible and speedy means of exchanging information, over a broad range of topics. The employer has the opportunity to sell the company and explain job details in depth. Applicants have the chance to ask questions about the job and the company in order to collect the information they need for their own selection decision. The interview is also the logical culmination of the employment process, as information from a variety of sources, such as application forms, tests and references, can be discussed together.

Selection interviewing has important ritual elements, as the applicant is seeking either to enter, or to rise within, a social system. Applicants are sure that they should display moderately deferential behaviour and arrive in their best clothes. At least at the beginning they will wait for the interviewer both to start the conversation and then to lead its development according to a structure that the interviewer wishes to follow. The interviewer, in turn, will accept the right and need to be in charge and will tend to emphasise a degree of social superiority *in that particular situation*.

Those who are already inside and above display their superiority and security, even unconsciously, in contrast with the behaviour of someone so obviously anxious to share the same privileged position. Reason tells us that this is inappropriate at the beginning of the twenty-first century as the books are full of advice to interviewers not to brandish their social superiority, but to put applicants at their ease and to reduce the status differentials. This, however, still acknowledges their superiority as they are the ones who take the initiative; applicants are not expected to help the interviewer relax and feel less apprehensive. Also the reality of the situation is usually that of applicant anxious to get in and selector choosing among several. Status differentials cannot simply be set aside. The selection interview is at least partly an initiation rite, a process of going through hoops and being found worthy in a process where other people make all the rules.

The interviewer and the candidate are both aware of fundamental aspects of ritual that apply, and observing these enables both of them to feel secure. Our opening story about Martin is not untypical of interviewers who are not familiar with interviewing.

WINDOW ON PRACTICE

Elizabeth tells the story of her first interview of a potential graduate recruit to her company. It was a preliminary interview that she was conducting alone. 'I was all ready, but feeling apprehensive. Five minutes before the interview was due to begin I was actually outside looking for him! He duly arrived and I sat him down and started asking him questions far too quickly. Soon I noticed he was steaming slightly and was horrified to realise that he had come by motorbike and was still wearing his oilskins, which I had been far too nervous to notice. What made it worse was that he had assumed from my behaviour that I was the receptionist, about to offer him a cup of coffee, when I suddenly started quizzing him about thermodynamics!'

Although ritual is stylised, its rigidity is to be tempered with the process of setting up rapport, a slightly old-fashioned word of French origin, which describes a feeling of mutual understanding and reasonable trust between people who are to communicate easily. We referred to this in the section of the Fundamental skills introduction on setting the tone as being a necessary feature of many different types of interview.

Skills activity 2.1

For a selection interview in which you recently participated, either as selector or as applicant, consider the following:

1　What were the ritual features?

2　Were any useful ritual features missing?

3　Could ritual have been, in any way, *helpfully* reduced?

Interview strategy

The approach to selection interviewing varies considerably from the amiable chat in a bar to the highly organised, multiperson panel.

Frank and friendly strategy

By far the most common is the approach which has been described as frank and friendly. Here the interviewer first aims to establish and maintain rapport. This is done in the belief that if interviewees do not feel threatened, and are as relaxed as possible, they will be more forthcoming in the information that they offer. It is straightforward for both interviewer and interviewee and has the potential advantage that interviewees will leave with a favourable impression of the business.

Problem-solving strategy

A variation of the frank and friendly strategy is the problem-solving approach. It is the method of presenting the candidate with a hypothetical problem and evaluating the answer.

These are sometimes called situational interviews. The questions asked are derived from the job description and candidates are required to imagine themselves as the job holder and describe what they would do in a variety of hypothetical situations. This method is most applicable to testing elementary knowledge, such as the colour coding of wires in electric cables or maximum dosages of specified drugs. It is less effective to test understanding and ability.

There is no guarantee that the candidate would actually behave in the way suggested. The quick thinker will score at the expense of those who can take action more effectively than they can answer riddles.

Biographical strategy

Similar to the problem-solving strategy is the biographical method. The focus is on the candidate's past behaviour and performance, which is a more reliable way of predicting future performance than asking interviewees what they would do in a certain situation. Candidates are requested to describe the background to a situation and explain what they did and why; what their options were; how they decided what to do; and the anticipated and real results of their action. The success of this method depends on in-depth job analysis, and preferably competency analysis, in order to frame the best questions. Bearing in mind the importance of structure in selection interviewing, the biographical approach is an excellent method.

Stress strategy

In the stress approach the interviewer becomes aggressive, disparages the candidates, puts them on the defensive or disconcerts them by strange behaviour. The advantage of the method is that it may demonstrate a necessary strength or a disqualifying weakness that would not be apparent through other methods. The disadvantages are that evaluating the behaviour under stress is problematic, and those who are not selected will think badly of the employer. The likely value of stress interviewing is so limited that it is hardly worth mentioning, except that it has spurious appeal to many managers, who are attracted by the idea of injecting at least some stress into the interview 'to see what they are made of', or 'to put them on their mettle'. Most candidates feel that the procedures are stressful enough, without adding to them.

These three alternatives are different approaches to conducting the interview and are primarily directed at getting to understand the interviewee as a whole person. In any interview some of the questions will be more focused than others on what the candidate knows about the job to be done and what skills and knowledge the candidate has that are essential to doing the job properly. These are known as technical questions, where the answers are mainly factual. Reverting to what we said about questioning in the introduction to the Skills package, these questions are more likely to be closed rather than open and direct rather than indirect, but they will still be put, heard and answered within the situation that one of the above strategies has set up.

WINDOW ON (MAL)PRACTICE

Following a panel interview to select a senior manager for a public corporation, the HR manager was tidying up the papers in the room and found a scrap of paper on which a member of the panel had scribbled, 'looks like a good screw'. The HR manager decided that this was not a case of a panel member relieving boredom by examining the structure of the table round which the members had been sitting.

The selection interview sequence

Preparation

We assume that the preliminaries of job analysis, recruitment and shortlisting are complete and the interview is now to take place. The first step in preparation is for the interviewers to brief themselves. They will collect and study a job description or similar details of the post to be filled, a candidate specification or statement of required competencies and the application forms or curricula vitae of the candidates. They will also evaluate any other evidence about the candidate that may be available from other forms of assessment that have been made, such as test results and group activities.

If there are several people to be interviewed the interview timetable needs greater planning than it usually receives. The time required for each interview can be determined beforehand only approximately. A rigid timetable will weigh heavily on both parties, who will feel frustrated if the interview is closed arbitrarily at a predetermined time and uncomfortable if an interview that has 'finished' is drawn out to complete its allotted timespan. However, the disadvantages of keeping people waiting are considerable and underrated.

Some selectors regard candidates as supplicants waiting on interviewers' pleasure, and who have no competing calls on their time, and some selectors may think a short period of waiting demonstrates who is in charge. There are flaws in this reasoning. Most candidates will have competing calls on their time, as they will have taken time off to attend and will have earmarked the anticipated interview time to fit into a busy schedule. Some may have other interviews to go to. An open-ended waiting period can be worrying, enervating and a poor preliminary to an interview. If the dentist keeps you waiting you may get distressed, but when the waiting is over you are simply a passive participant and the dentist does not have the success of the operation jeopardised. The interview candidate has, in a real sense, to perform when the period of waiting is over and the success of the interaction could well be jeopardised.

The most satisfactory timetable is the one that guarantees a break after all but the most voluble candidates. If candidates are asked to attend at hourly intervals, for example, this would be consistent with interviews lasting between 40 and 60 minutes. This would mean that each interview began at the scheduled time and that the interviewers had the opportunity to review and update their notes in the intervals. The whole plan can still go wrong if one or more candidates fail to turn up.

Setting

The appropriate setting for an interview has to be right for the ritual and right from the point of view of enabling a full and frank exchange of information. It is difficult to combine the two. Many of the interview horror stories relate to the setting in which it took place. A candidate for a post as Deputy Clerk of Works was interviewed on a stage while the panel of 17 sat in the front row of the stalls, and a candidate for a Headteacher post came in to meet the interview panel and actually moved the chair on which he was to sit. He only moved it two or three inches because the sun was in his eyes, but there was an audible frisson and sharp intake of breath from the members of the panel.

Remaining with our model of the individual interviewer, here are some simple suggestions about the setting:

- The room should be suitable for a private conversation
- If the interview takes place across a desk, as is common, the interviewer may wish to reduce the extent to which the desk acts as a barrier, inhibiting free flow of communication
- All visitors and telephone calls should be avoided, as they do not simply interrupt: they intrude and impede the likelihood of frankness
- It should be clear to the candidates where they are to sit

Interview structure

There are several important reasons why the employment interview should be structured, making use of the application or CV:

- The candidate expects the proceedings to be decided and controlled by the interviewer and will anticipate a structure within which to operate
- It helps the interviewer to make sure that they cover all relevant areas and avoid irrelevancies
- It looks professional
- Structure can be used to guide the interview and ensure that it makes sense
- It assists the interviewer in using the time available in the most effective way
- The application form can be used as a memory aid by the interviewer when making notes directly after the interview or during it
- It makes it easier to compare candidates

The interview

There are several different ways to structure the interview. We recommend the form set out in Skills table 2.1. This divides activities and objectives into three interview stages: opening, middle and closing. While there are few, if any, satisfactory alternative ways for conducting the beginning and the end of the interview, the middle can be approached from a number of different angles, depending on the circumstances.

The interviewer needs to work systematically through the structure that has been planned, but not too rigidly. Interviewers should abandon their own route whenever the candidate chooses one that seems to the interviewer to be more promising.

The opening of the interview is the time for mutual preliminary assessment and tuning in to each other. A useful feature of this phase is for the interviewer to sketch out the plan or procedure for the interview and how it fits in the total employment decision process. It is also likely that the application form will provide an easy, non-controversial topic for these opening behaviours.

SKILLS TABLE 2.1 Interview structure: a recommended pattern

Stage	Objectives	Activities
Opening	To put the candidate at ease, develop rapport and set the scene	Greet candidate by name
		Introduce yourself
		Explain interview purpose
		Outline how purpose will be achieved
		Obtain candidate's assent to outline
Middle	To collect and provide information	Asking questions within a structure that makes sense to the candidate, such as biographical, areas of the application form, or competencies identified for the job
		Listening
		Answering questions
		Summarise interview
Closing	To close the interview and confirm future action	Check candidate has no more questions
		Indicate what happens next and when

One objective is for the two parties to exchange words so that they can adjust their receiving mechanism to be mutually intelligible. It also provides an opportunity for both to feel comfortable in the presence of the other. Interviewers able to achieve these two objectives may then succeed in developing a relationship in which candidates trust the interviewer's ability and motives so that they will speak openly and fully. The interviewer's effectiveness will greatly depend on their being skilled at this process.

For the middle of the interview the biographical approach is the simplest. It works on the basis that candidates at the time of the interview are the product of everything in their lives that has gone before. To understand the candidate the interviewer must understand the past and will talk to the candidate about the episodes of his or her earlier life, education and previous employment. The advantage of this is that the objectives are clear to both interviewer and interviewee, there is no deviousness or 'magic'. Furthermore, the development can be logical and so aid the candidate's recall of events. Candidates who reply to enquiries about their choice of A level subjects will be subconsciously triggering their recollection of contemporaneous events, such as the university course they took, which are likely to come next in the interview. The biographical approach is the simplest for the inexperienced interviewer to use as discussion can develop from the information provided by the candidate on the application form. Some version of sequential categories, such as employment, education and training, seems the most generally useful, but it will need the addition of at least two other categories: the work offered and the organisational context in which it is to be done. The middle of the interview can be structured by systematically working through items of the job description or the person specification. Increasingly, where competencies have been identified for the job, these are used as the basis of the structure. The middle of the interview is the logical place for the technical questions that we have already mentioned, probably before or after the more general questioning, rather than being mixed in with this.

In the preparatory stage of briefing, the interviewer will also prepare notes on two elements to incorporate in their plan: key issues and checkpoints.

Key issues will be the two or three main issues that stand out from the application form for clarification or elaboration. This might be the nature of the responsibilities carried in a particular earlier post, the content of a training course, the reaction to a period of employment in a significant industry or whatever else strikes the interviewer as being productive of useful additional evidence.

Checkpoints are matters of detail that require further information: grades in an examination, dates of an appointment, rates of pay, and so forth, including at least some of the technical questions.

At the close of the interview the explanation of the next step needs especial attention. The result of the interview is of great importance to the candidates and they will await the outcome with anxiety. Even if they do not want the position they will probably hope to have it offered. This may strengthen their hand in dealings with another prospective employer, or with their present employer, and will certainly be a boost to their morale. The great merit of the convention in the public sector is that the chosen candidate is told before the contenders disperse: the great demerit is that they are asked to say yes or no to the offer at once.

In the private sector it is unusual for an employment offer to be made at the time of the interview, so there is a delay during which the candidates will chafe. Their frustration will be greater if the delay is longer than expected and they may start to tell themselves that they are not going to receive an offer, in which case they will also start convincing themselves that they did not want the job either! It is important for the interviewer to say as precisely as possible when the offer will be made, but ensuring that the candidates hear earlier rather than later than they expect, if there is to be any deviation.

The interviewer will need to call into play certain other aspects of method.

1 Some data can be collected by simple observation of the candidate. Notes can be made about dress, appearance, voice, height and weight, if these are going to be relevant, and the interviewer can also gauge the candidate's mood and the appropriate response to it by the non-verbal cues that are provided. The remainder of the evidence will come from listening to what is said, so the interviewer has to be very attentive throughout; not only listening to the answers to questions, but also listening for changes in inflection and pace, nuances and overtones that provide clues on what to pursue further. The relative amount of time the two spend talking is important, as an imbalance in one direction or the other will mean that either the candidate or the interviewer is not having enough opportunity to hear information. Being silent and deliberately leaving verbal lulls in face-to-face situations provides the opportunity for the other person to say more, perhaps more than was initially intended. Silence still has to be attentive and the longer the silence, the harder it is to be attentive.

2 In order to have something to hear, the interviewer will have to direct the candidate. This, of course, is done by questioning, encouraging and enabling the candidate to talk, so that the interviewer can learn. The art of doing this depends on the personality and style of the interviewer who will develop a personal technique through a sensitive awareness of what is taking place in the interviews. The selection interviewer needs to distinguish between different types of question, as described in the introduction to the Fundamental skills.

3 The best place for the interviewer to make notes is on the application form or CV. In this way they can be joined to information that the candidate has already provided and the peculiar shorthand that interviewers use when making notes during interviews can be deciphered by reference to the form and the data that the note is embellishing. It also means that the review of evidence after the interview has as much information as possible available on one piece of paper. An alternative is to record notes on the interview plan where the structure is based on job description, person specification or competencies. Interviewers are strangely inhibited about note taking, feeling that it in some way impairs the smoothness of the interaction. This apprehension seems ill founded as candidates are looking for a serious, businesslike discussion, no matter how informal, and note taking offers no barrier, provided that it is done carefully in the form of jottings during the discussion, rather than pointedly writing down particular comments by the candidate which make the interviewer seem like a police officer taking a statement.

4 Data exchange marks a change of gear in the interview. Rapport is necessarily rather rambling and aimless, but data exchange is purposeful and the interviewer needs to

Tan, K.H. (1995) *Planning, Recruiting and Selecting Human Resources*. Shah Alam, Malaysia: Federal Publications.

Selection interviewing varies considerably across different cultures. Most of the available literature is rooted in Anglo-American practice. Some insights into practice in other situations can be found in the three works given above.

WEB LINKS

Apart from material on the companion website for this book, **www.pearsoned.co.uk/torrington** plenty of material from consultants can be accessed.

www.thedevco.com (the Development Company)

www.bps.org.uk (British Psychological Society)

www.opp.co.uk (Oxford Psychologists Press)

www.shl.com/shl/uk (Saville and Holdsworth, test developer/supplier)

www.kenexa.com (test developer)

www.intest.com is the website of the International Test Commission which provides guidelines on computer-based and Internet-delivered testing

PRACTICAL EXERCISE IN SELECTION INTERVIEWING

For this exercise you need a cooperative, interested relative, or a very close friend, who would welcome interview practice.

1 Follow the sequence suggested in Skills Table 2.1 to give your partner practice in being interviewed for a job, and giving yourself practice in interviewing and note taking.

2 After the interview, discuss your mutual feelings about the process around questions such as:

Selector	'Did you ever feel you were being misled? When? Why?'
	'Did you feel the interview got out of your control? When? Why?'
	'How could you have avoided the problem?'
	'How was your note taking?'
	'What, if anything, made you bored or cross?'
	'What did you find most difficult?'
	'How comprehensive is the data you have collected?'
Candidate	'Were you put at your ease?'
	'Were you at any time inhibited by the selector?'
	'Did you ever mislead the selector? When? How?'
	'Did the selector ever fail to follow up important points? When? Which?'
	'Were you in any way disconcerted by the note taking?'
	'Has the selector got a comprehensive set of data about you, so that you could feel any decision made about you would be soundly based?'
	'What did you think of the interview experience?'

3 Now swap roles

The appraisal interview

The objectives of this part of Fundamental skills are to:

1   Explain the purpose and nature of the appraisal interview

2   Suggest a model sequence for conducting appraisal interviews

The website of an American management consultancy has the following opening:

> For many managers the formal performance appraisal interview is one of the most dreaded activities of the role. Of course, managers often have no problem evaluating the outstanding performer. The problem is with everyone else. We are put in the position of providing information to a subordinate that often runs contrary to the subordinate's own self-evaluation or self-image. This can lead to a number of outcomes that many managers would prefer avoiding.
>
> 'Nevertheless, for many of us, we are forced to carry out the interview and realize that this is indeed one of the most important parts of our jobs'.

A novelist, a textbook writer, a popular singer, a newspaper editor, an athlete or an owner of a corner shop all share the common factor that their performance is measurable by a clear, unambiguous set of facts. When Paula Radcliffe runs a race the effectiveness of that performance is measured in the time taken. The measure of both performances can then be compared with that of competitors. There are no mitigating circumstances. The writer may feel that the publisher should have done a better job or that the reviewers were incompetent, but that has no weight compared with the inescapable fact of the number sold. The shop owner may grumble about local authority planners or about unfair competition from the local hypermarket, but that explanation will not stop customers from drifting away.

Very few working people have that same absolute measure of their own personal performance, which is all part of a more general, corporate activity. Individual effectiveness is not measured by an indicator of customer appreciation, as so many other members of the corporate body contribute to the effectiveness or ineffectiveness of any individual's activity. The inexorable logic of the marketplace or other external arena has to be mediated by internal measures, especially by managerial judgement. This is tricky.

Appraising performance does not involve a precise measurement, it requires a subjective assessment. It is rarely done well but is still anxiously – although apprehensively – sought by people wanting to know how they are doing. It is difficult to do, it is frequently done badly because appraisers know that the person they are appraising is someone with whom they need to maintain a good working relationship, so they are reluctant to risk alienating the appraisee with blunt criticism, especially if it is difficult to explain and justify. If, however, a problem of performance is not confronted in the interview it will still be there, with the possibility that disciplinary action may be needed, the inevitable reaction to which is, 'Why didn't anyone tell me earlier?' On the rare occasions when appraisal is done well it can be invaluable for the business, and literally life transforming for the appraisee. Along with the disciplinary interview it is probably the most demanding and skilful activity for any manager to undertake and is dreaded by both appraisers and appraisees. Recent research about capability among British schoolteachers produced the following conclusion:

> headteachers link capability to personal qualities such as 'open-minded and prepared to adapt and take on new skills' or 'attitude' or where generalised descriptions such as 'unable to do the job properly' or 'not meeting standards' are offered. Measurement is also inevitably imprecise when it is subjective, making the judgement difficult to substantiate and prone to challenge. This leads to the risk that the yardsticks of acceptable performance chosen are those that can best be justified rather than those that are most important. (Torrington *et al.* 2003)

It is this tendency for qualitative appraisal to be unstructured, avoiding awkwardness and being unsuitable for comparison that we have to try and reduce. It is not easy and requires a high level of *mutual trust* between appraiser and appraisee: a tall order for any manager.

Appraisal problems

There are many problems in carrying out an appraisal interview. For example:

- **Prejudice** You may be prejudiced against the appraisee, or you may be anxious not to be prejudiced; either could distort your judgement.
- **Insufficient** knowledge of the appraisee You may have to interview someone because of your position in the hierarchy rather than because you have a good understanding of what the appraisee is doing: this is a particular problem for people newly promoted.

- **The 'halo effect'** If the appraisee is generally likeable (or the opposite) this can influence your assessment of the work that they are doing.
- **The problem of context** It is always difficult to distinguish the work the appraisee is doing from the context in which the work is being done, especially when there is an element of comparison with other appraisees. The sales executive with a 'hard' territory may appear less effective than a colleague with an easier territory.

Skills activity 3.1

Think of jobs where it is difficult to disentangle the performance of the individual from the context of the work. How would you focus on the individual's performance in these situations?

- **The formality** Although the appraiser probably tries to avoid stiff formality, both participants in the interview realise that the encounter is relatively formal, with much hanging on it.
- **Outcomes are ignored** Follow-up action for management to take, especially if it was agreed in the interview, *must* take place.
- **Appraising the wrong features** Sometimes behaviours other than real work are evaluated, such as time-keeping, looking busy and being pleasant, because they are easier to see. Is this the important aspect of the appraisee's work, or are they merely useful?
- **Everyone is 'just above average'** Most appraisees are looking for reassurance that all is well, and the easiest way for appraisers to deal with this is (and the appraiser probably likes an easy life) to state or infer that the appraisee is doing at least as well as most others, and better than a good many. It is much harder to deal with the situation of presenting someone with the opinion that they are average; who wants to be average?

WINDOW ON PRACTICE

In 1997 the Secretary of State for Education issued guidance to schools and local education authorities about capability procedures to deal with the problem of schoolteachers who did not perform satisfactorily. This degree of formality for dealing with performance is very rare outside schools and produced major problems. Teachers who were 'put on procedure' found that so humiliating that they rarely improved and usually spent long periods of absence from school suffering from stress. Throughout the education system there was a preference for informal arrangements to deal with this very difficult issue.

The appraisal interview style

The different styles of appraisal interview were succinctly described fifty years ago as being either *problem solving, tell and sell or tell and listen*. This remains the most widely adopted means of identifying the way to tackle the interview.

The *problem-solving* style is where the appraiser encourages the appraisee to start reviewing the performance, identifying any problems and how they could be overcome. This means that the appraiser is determining how the interview is going to start, with fuller evaluation emerging from discussion with the appraiser. At least initially the problems are those that the appraisee recognises and is able to acknowledge; this is a vital step towards the problems being solved. This is certainly a most effective style provided that both the appraiser and appraisee have the skill and ability to handle it. Our suggestions later in this package are based on this style, but it is not the only style.

In *tell and sell*, the appraiser acts as judge, using the interview to tell the appraisee the result of the appraisal and how to improve. This 'ski instructor' approach can be appropriate when appraisees have little experience and have not developed enough self-confidence to analyse their own performance.

Tell and listen still casts the appraiser in the role of judge, passing on the outcome of an appraisal that has already been completed and listening to reactions. Both of these approaches could sometimes change the assessment, as well as enabling the two people to have a reasonably frank exchange. They can be appropriate where the appraisee has relatively little experience and cannot therefore set the agenda effectively.

It is tempting to identify the problem-solving approach as the best, because it appears to be the most civilised and searching, but not all appraisal situations call for this style, not all appraisees are ready for it and not all appraisers normally behave in this way.

The appraisal interview sequence

Certain aspects of the appraisal interview are the same as those of the selection interview discussed in Fundamental skills 2. The appraiser determines the framework of the interview, there is the same need to open in a way that develops mutual confidence as far as possible and there is the use of closed and open-ended questions, reflection and summarising. It is also a difficult meeting for the two parties to handle. The appraiser has to have a degree of confidence and personal authority that few managers have in their relationship with all those whom they have to appraise. For the appraisee there are concerns about career progress, job security, the ongoing working relationship with the appraiser and basic anxieties relating to self-esteem and dealing with criticism.

The fundamental difference between selection and appraisal is that the objective is to reach a *mutual* understanding that will have some impact on the future performance of the appraisee: it is not simply to formulate a judgement by collecting information, as in selection. A medical metaphor may help. A surgeon carrying out hip replacements will select patients for surgery on the basis of enquiring about their symptoms and careful consideration of the evidence. The surgeon asks the questions, makes the decision and implements that decision. A physician examining a patient who is overweight and short of breath may rapidly make the decision that the patient needs to lose weight and take more exercise. It is, however, not the physician but the patient who has to implement that decision. The physician can help with diet sheets, regular check-ups and terrifying advice; the real challenge is how to get the patient to respond.

The easy part of appraisal is sorting out the facts. The difficult bit is actually bringing about a change in performance. The interview, like the discussion in the physician's consulting rooms, is crucial in bringing about a change of attitude, fresh understanding and commitment to action.

Preparation

The appraiser should brief the appraisee on the form of the interview, possibly asking for a self-appraisal form to be completed in advance. This will only be appropriate if the scheme requires it. As we have seen, self-appraisal gives the appraisee some initiative, ensures that the discussion will be about matters which the appraisee can handle and on 'real stuff'.

The appraiser has to review all the available evidence on the appraisee's performance, including reports, records or other material regarding the period under review. Most important will be the previous appraisal and its outcomes.

Most of the points made earlier about preparing for the selection interview apply to appraisal as well, especially the setting. Taking time and trouble to ensure that the setting and supportive nature of the discussion is considerate of the appraisee's needs really pays off in getting a positive response from the appraisee.

Interview structure

A recommended structure for a performance appraisal interview is shown in Skills table 3.1.

Rapport is unusual because it attempts to smooth the interaction between two people who probably have an easy social relationship, but now find themselves ill at ease. This is

SKILLS TABLE 3.1

Purpose and rapport	Agree purpose with appraisee Agree structure for meeting Check that preparation is complete
Factual review	Review of known facts about performance in previous period: appraiser reinforcement
Appraisee views	Appraisee asked to comment on period under review. What has gone well and what less well; what could be improved; what was liked and what disliked; possible new objectives
Appraiser views	Appraiser adds own perspective, asks questions and disagrees, as appropriate, with what appraisee has said
Problem solving	Discussion of any differences and how they can be resolved
Objective setting	Agreeing on what action should be taken, and by whom, with targets and review dates

not the sort of conversation they are used to having together, so they have to find new ground rules. The appraisal interview itself may be easier to introduce and handle if, as generally recommended, there are mini-reviews throughout the year. This should ensure that there are no surprises, and the two people concerned get used to having performance-focused meetings, however informal. This type of review happens in some companies, but some appraisers find it difficult. There is still the problem of appraisee reaction to the tentative presentation of aspects of their performance that they are not doing properly. A minority will misconstrue adverse comments to focus on the good at the expense of the not so good, while a different minority will do the exact opposite: demoralised collapse at facing a suspended sentence. The majority will obviously react sensibly and most appraisees will have the simple guts to face up to issues that are problematic.

The opening of the interview itself still needs care. The mood needs to be light, but not trivial, as the appraisee has to be encouraged towards candour rather than gamesmanship.

Skills activity 3. 2

What do you think of the following openings to appraisal interviews heard recently?

a 'Well, here we are again. I'm sure you don't like this business any more than I do, so let's get on with it.'

b 'Now, there's nothing to worry about. It's quite painless and could be useful. So just relax and let me put a few questions to you.'

c 'I'm really not too sure about what we should be doing. What should we talk about?'

d 'Right. Let battle commence!'

Factual review is reviewing aspects of the previous year's work that are unproblematic. The appraiser should begin by reviewing the main facts about the performance, without expressing opinions about them but merely summarising them as a mutual reminder, perhaps reviewing previous objectives set and including the outcome of the previous appraisal. This will help to key in any later discussion by confirming such matters as how long the appraisee has been in the job, any personnel changes in the period, turnover figures, training undertaken and so forth.

The appraiser does most, but not all, of the talking, and can isolate those aspects of performance that are clearly satisfactory, mention them and comment favourably. This will consolidate rapport and provide the basic reassurance the appraisee needs in order to avoid being defensive. The favourable aspects of performance will to some extent be *discovered* by the factual review process. It is important that 'the facts speak for themselves' rather than appraiser judgement being offered, for example:

'Those figures look very good. How do they compare with . . . ? That's X per cent up on the quarter and Y per cent on the year . . . That's one of the best results in the group. You must be pleased with that . . . How on earth did you do it?'

The evidence, including that collected throughout the year as we suggested earlier, is there before the eyes of both parties, with the appraiser pointing out and emphasising. It is also specific rather than general, precise rather than vague. This type of approach invariably raises the question from appraisers about what to do in a situation of poor performance. Appraising stars is easy; what about the duds? The answer is that all appraisees have some aspects of their performance on which favourable comment can be made, and the appraisal process actually identifies strengths that might have been previously obscured by the general impression of someone who is not very good. The appraiser may discover something on which to build, having previously thought the case was hopeless. If there is not some feature of the performance that can be isolated in this way, then the appraiser probably has a management or disciplinary problem that should have been tackled earlier.

The appraiser then asks for the *appraisee's views* on things that are not as good as they might be in the performance, areas of possible improvement and how these might be addressed. These will only be offered by the appraisee if there has been effective positive reinforcement in the previous stages of the interview. People can only acknowledge shortcomings about performance when they are reasonably sure of their ground. Now the appraisee is examining areas of dissatisfaction by the process of discussing them with the appraiser, with whom it is worth having the discussion, because of the appraiser's expertise, information and 'helicopter view'. The likely result of debating these matters is either that they will be shown to be less worrying than they seemed when viewed only from the single perspective of the appraisee, and that ways of dealing with them become apparent, or that they are confirmed as matters needing attention.

This stage in the interview is fraught with difficulties for the manager, and is one of the reasons why an alternative style is sometimes preferred. Some appraisees do not want to discuss the matter, but simply to be told by the manager, whose job it is. In this situation tell-and-sell or tell-and-listen styles are more appropriate.

Appraiser views can now be used in adding to the list of areas for improvement. In many instances there will be no additions to make, but usually there are some needs that the appraisee cannot, or will not, see. If they are put at this point in the interview, there is the best chance that they will be understood, accepted and acted upon. It is not possible to guarantee success. Demoralised collapse or bitter resentment is always a possibility, but this is the time to try, as the appraisee has developed a basis of reassurance and has come to terms with some shortcomings that he or she had already recognised.

The appraiser has to judge whether any further issues can be raised and if so, how many. The process of feedback is one that needs care and thought because it is precisely what it describes. The term derives from the process in telecommunications whereby the strength and quality of the message from the sender is improved by the positive feedback from the receiver. In appraisal the views on performance from the appraisee provide the basis on which the appraiser views have to be built because what the appraisee has said and acknowledged is what the appraisee can 'live with'. That self-awareness now needs to be enlarged in a way that the appraisee can continue to understand and acknowledge.

Some of the problems already acknowledged will be dealt with simply by the appraiser putting them in a different light; others will be dealt with by an offer of specific help; some may need to be added. None of us can cope with confronting all our shortcomings, all at the same time, and the appraiser's underlying management responsibility is to ensure that the appraisee is not made less competent by the appraisal interview. Appraisers do not use the interview to justify their criticisms; they use it to enhance the appraisee's performance.

Problem solving is the process of talking out the areas for improvement that have been identified, so that the appraisee can cope with them. Underlying causes are uncovered through further discussion. Gradually huge problems come into clearer and less forbidding perspective, perhaps through being analysed and broken up into different components. Possibilities for action, by both appraiser and appraisee, become clear.

These central stages of the interview, factual exchange, appraisee views, appraiser views and problem solving, need to move in that sequence. Some may be brief, but none should be omitted and the sequence should not alter.

The final stage of the encounter is to agree what is to be done: **objective setting**. Actions need to be agreed and nailed down, so that they actually take place. One of the biggest causes of appraisal failure is with action not being taken, so the objectives set must be not only mutually acceptable, but also deliverable. It is likely that some action will be needed from the appraiser as well as some from the appraisee.

Making appraisal work

The criteria for appraisal must be genuinely related to success or failure in the job, rather than vaguely defined personal qualities. They should also be amenable to objective, rather than subjective judgement, and they should appear fair and relevant to the appraisee. An excellent performance appraisal system is of no use at all if managers do not know how to use the system to best effect. Appraisal interviews need to be supported by follow-up action. Work plans agreed by appraiser and appraisee need to be monitored to ensure that they actually take place, or that they are modified in accordance with changed circumstances or priorities. Training needs should be identified and plans made to meet them.

SUMMARY PROPOSITIONS

Skills 3.1 Performance appraisal is not always well done, but it has considerable potential, when done well.

Skills 3.2 Among the problems of appraisal are prejudice, insufficient knowledge by the appraiser of the appraisee, the halo effect, the problem of context, ignoring the outcomes, appraising the wrong features and the tendency for everyone to be just above average.

Skills 3.3 Three approaches to the appraisal interview are problem solving, tell and sell, and tell and listen.

Skills 3.4 Features of the interview itself are rapport; factual review; appraisee views on performance; appraiser views; problem solving; and objective setting.

Skills 3.5 Appraisers must follow up on interviews, making sure that all agreed action (especially that by the management) takes place.

GENERAL DISCUSSION TOPICS

1 'What right does he have to ask me questions about my motivation and objectives? I come here to do a job of work and then go home. What I want to do with my life is my business.'

How would you react to that comment by someone who had just emerged from an appraisal interview?

2 In what situations have you seen outstanding individuals depress the performance of a team where the other people were demoralised by the dominance of that individual? How do you cope with this?

FURTHER READING

Cook, J. and Crossman, A. (2004) 'Satisfaction with Performance Appraisal Systems: A study of role perceptions', *Journal of Managerial Psychology*, Vol. 19, No. 5, pp. 526–41.
One of the more recent detailed studies of an aspect of performance appraisal deals first with the proposition that people are more satisfied with the process if they are both an appraiser and an appraisee, and secondly with the need for process to be perceived to be fair. The fieldwork was carried out in a British government laboratory.

Fletcher, C. (1999) *Appraisal: routes to improved performance*. London: Chartered Institute of Personnel and Development.

Lowry, D. (2002) 'Performance management', in J. Leopold (ed.) *Human Resources in Organisations*. London: Prentice Hall.
The appraisal interview has not been the subject of much research in recent years, but the above reviews provide practical suggestions.

Redman, T., Snape, E., Thompson, D. and Kaching Yan, F. (2000) 'Performance appraisal in the National Health Service', *Human Resource Management Journal*, Vol. 10, No. 1, pp. 1–16.

Torrington, D.P., Earnshaw, J.M., Marchington, L. and Ritchie, M.D. (2003) *Tackling Underperformance in Teachers*. London: Routledge Falmer.
Recent studies of appraisal in specific professional contexts include the above.

WEB LINKS

General information about aspects of performance can be found at:

www.hrmguide.co.uk/hrm/chap10
www.som.cranfield.ac.uk (the Performance Management Association)
www.learningmatters.com
Trade unions, some employers and most public bodies provide information about the performance management arrangement on their websites. One example of general interest is at:

www.governyourschool.co.uk
Consultancy firms provide information about their particular approach. A selection of interesting sites (without any assessment of the value of their products) is:

www.hrwigwam.co.uk
www.openview.hp.com/solutions
www.hse.gov.uk (the Health and Safety Executive)
www.managingabsence.org.uk (a site supported by government and industry partners)
www.statistics.gov.uk (the Office for National Statistics site)
www.cbi.org.uk (the Confederation of British Industry)
www.leadersdirect.com (an American site of the Self Renewal Group)
www.audit-commission.gov.uk (Best Value Performance Plan Toolkit from the Audit Commission)
www.apse.org.uk (Association for Public Service Excellence)
www.performance-appraisals.org (an American business site)
www.berr.gov.uk (Department for Business, Enterprise and Regulatory Reform – the former DTI)
www.employment-studies.co.uk (the Institute of Employment Studies site)
www.acas.org.uk (Advisory, Conciliation and Arbitration Service)

EXERCISE

You again need the cooperation of a friend or colleague who has a job or background similar to your own, so that you can relate to the work experience of each other without being in a directly related role. It is better *not to use* a spouse, sibling or parent. One of you is A, the other is B.

1 Preparation by A

   Write down your response to the following questions on separate cards:

   a What activity do you perform in your job that is very important? (This should begin with a verb; e.g. 'carrying out appraisal interviews'. It should not be a role or responsibility.

   b What is an activity you do frequently that is not necessarily important, but which takes up a good deal of time?

   c What activity which, although important, is not likely to appear in your diary?

   d What activity, not mentioned so far, is the most important?

2 Discussion led by B

   a How are **a** and **b** similar and how different?

   b What makes them easier, or harder, to do than **c**?

   c Which is it more important that you do well, **b** or **c**?

   d On what criteria did you select **d**?

   e Which gives you most satisfaction, and why, **a**, **b**, **c** or **d**?

3 Now swap roles

   This gets both of you examining the job you do in conversation with someone else and with the perspective in the questions, which you may not have seen before. This should give you a slightly better understanding of what you do and practice at understanding someone else's work.

   This is carried further in an exercise on the book's companion website **www.pearsoned.co.uk/torrington**.

Coaching

The objectives of this part of Fundamental skills are to:

1 Review the scope and potential of coaching

2 Explain the concept of the career anchor and its importance to the coach

3 Consider the qualities of the coach

Coaching is enabling people to learn by a process that goes beyond simple instruction. Protégés frequently have to discover for themselves, as this is the only way in which they will understand, and they frequently need the help of a coach to be a sounding board for their uncertainties, to point out things about their performance which they try to ignore and to be a wise counsellor in times of difficulty or lack of confidence. The role of the manager in coaching has already been covered in Chapter 6 on people development, and face-to-face coaching skills are similar to those of appraisal, so this part of the Skills package concentrates on the coaching relationship and its management.

The scope and potential of coaching

Coaching is as important for the person who is proficient or expert as it is for the beginner, even though they are still acquiring the basics. The more expert a person becomes, the more important a coach becomes to hone performance, to take a broad view of the context in which the protégé's career is developing and how it may proceed. Coaching is a part of the job of every manager and it is being used increasingly in business circles to bring on the effectiveness of people at all levels.

WINDOW ON PRACTICE

In 2005 the British sporting public was hungry for success in tennis. Wimbledon annually stages the world's greatest tennis tournament and winning is the greatest achievement in a player's career, yet it was over seventy years since a British man had won the title. A young Scot, Andy Murray, suddenly emerged as the great hope of British tennis. He was young, skilled and with a great competitive temperament, who had been coached by his mother, but he needed a different coach to take him forward to international success. He needed someone with international experience as well as personal authority, who could take the already acquired skill of this fiery young man and develop it, and him, to greater international achievement. Brad Gilbert was an experienced coach. He took on the coaching of Andy Murray, whose accomplishments soon began to increase. Brad Gilbert was not as good a player as Andy Murray, but had a breadth of international experience and expertise that provided exactly the right complement to Andy's youth, talent and temperament.

The story of Andy Murray illustrates an interesting aspect of the coaching relationship: coaching is still valuable when the protégé can do the job better than the coach. By 2007 Andy Murray had decided to move on beyond Brad Gilbert, whose expertise and style were no longer what he felt he needed. Currently there is great enthusiasm for coaching to be seen as a central feature of the managerial role so that every manager is expected to act as a coach to those for whom the manager has direct line responsibility. Coaching takes the place of supervision and instruction to the extent that the manager concentrates on developing the skills and capacities of the individual members of their team, enabling them to perform rather than directing their performance. This is a nice distinction that takes account of changes in the types of jobs that people have and the moves towards flexible rather than hierarchical organisation structures. The reality is rarely so clear-cut, as managers have to combine coaching with direction. Other members of the business may be involved in coaching on particular aspects of the protégé's work, regardless of the hierarchical working relationship between them.

WINDOW ON PRACTICE

Sheila was having great problems at work, unable (or unwilling) to adopt new working practices, and especially frightened of the computer. Her manager and the HR department had tried training courses, counselling and warnings, but with

▶

▶ little success. She was depressed, lacking sleep and fearful for her future. Kathryn was about to return from maternity leave and was hoping for a job-share, working only half the week. The manager agreed, provided that she would work alongside Sheila, who would continue working full-time. Kathryn accepted reluctantly, as Sheila's 'problems' were well known, but she was a generous-spirited young woman and worked cheerfully, making most of the decisions and doing more than half the work. Before long the working relationship changed so that Sheila was more than pulling her weight, as well as sleeping better and free of depression; the manager was delighted.

A few months later Kathryn left, and moved to a job nearer home, and when she left she received a card from Sheila, in which she had written:

'Thank you for sharing your time, your patience and your cheerful confidence with me. My life has changed and I feel a new woman. You have given me my life back.'

Kathryn did not see herself as a coach, but she filled the coaching role perfectly, in spite of having no 'authority over' Sheila of a hierarchical nature.

The career anchor

The important concept of the career anchor was identified by Edgar H. Schein, one of the founding fathers of organisational psychology during his thirty years as Sloan Fellows Professor of Management at MIT. The career anchor is something that is so important to a person's self-image that it will be abandoned only reluctantly, and then only if it can be replaced by something else equally rewarding. Schein described career anchors as much broader than motivation, and including the following:

- self-perceived talents and abilities
- self-perceived motives and needs
- self-perceived attitudes and values

Our perception of ourselves in these areas comes from direct experiences of work, from successes, from self-diagnosis and feedback. The conclusions that we draw both drive and constrain future career development. Career anchors can identify a source of personal stability in the person which has determined past choices and will probably determine future choices. They are, of course, personal and infinitely variable from one person to another, but they are a crucial area of understanding needed by coaches. What are this person's anchors? What will they cling to and abandon only with the greatest reluctance? Sheila's main anchors were, first, a conviction (misplaced) that her well-used skills were all that she needed in her current job and, secondly, that she could not afford to lose her job. This combination led her to a sort of paralysis in which she clung on to her first. Kathryn had never heard of career anchors but was stuck with having to work with Sheila and simply modelled for her the process of doing the job in a new way.

Any coach who can spot a protégé's anchors correctly has a very good chance of establishing trust, especially if the protégé has never really worked out what their anchors are, nor heard of the concept. If the coach guesses the anchors wrongly, or has fixed views on what they should be, then coaching becomes very difficult. Personal career anchors certainly change over time. The person who is technically anchored at 30, because at that time personal technical expertise is seen as the main source of confidence and self-worth, may have become managerially anchored at 40 and security/stability anchored at 50. However, that is a stereotypical assumption only; personal career anchors vary considerably, depending on the individual personality, ambition, domestic situation and career progress. Coaches have to work out the anchors for each individual at the time when the coaching conversation takes place, not yesterday or last year.

The qualities of the coach

Coaching is usually a one-to-one activity, for which the coach needs various qualities:

Trust

As the coach will often need to deal with what are usually very private aspects of someone's life, it is first necessary that the learner has absolute trust in the coach's integrity and commitment to the coaching. They will probably argue, may have flaming rows and not speak to each other for days. Protégés will, for instance, usually be highly skilled performers having a shrewd knowledge of their job and a fair understanding of what they can and cannot do. A coach may need to challenge some part of that self-confidence, which the learner will then be anxious about, because that seems to be removing one of the things that the learner has previously relied on – a career anchor – and there will be a disagreement. Something that has previously been an anchor will probably not be abandoned unless there is a grounded belief in the coach's trustworthiness.

Respect

Closely allied to trust and the next requirement of expertise is *mutual* respect. The protégé needs to feel that the coach is worthy of respect because of being trustworthy, being expert in the job of the protégé, being proficient at the job of coaching, having a great deal of broader experience, being good at explaining things and explaining the right things. These proficiencies have to be strong enough to dispel the protégé's possible other thoughts about the coach, such as 'has-been', 'past-it', 'couldn't hack it at the sharp end', 'the job is not like it was in his day'. Coaches are often older than protégés, so ambitious learners may be tempted to think in this way. Equally the coach must have respect for the learner: there must be no condescension or patronising behaviour, but a real respect for the protégé's skill, accomplishments and ambitions.

Job expertise

The coach needs to *know how* to do the job at least as well as the protégé; this is not the same as *being able to do* the job as well as the protégé. The person training the novice usually has to be expert at actually doing the job of the learner; the coach enhancing the skill of someone who is proficient does not need that particular level of ability, as long as there is the understanding. It is often important that the coach is *not* as practically skilled; otherwise coaching may become 'watch me; do this', instead of 'listen to what I say and then work out how to do better'.

WINDOW ON PRACTICE

England won the Rugby World Cup in 2004 and much of the credit for this victory went to Clive Woodward (who soon became Sir Clive). Subsequently he left his job as Rugby coach, saying that he would like to try his approach in another sport, perhaps Soccer. Despite one or two opportunities he never succeeded in this area. Notwithstanding his apparent effectiveness in motivating sportsmen, he appeared not able to succeed when outside his own job expertise. Similarly someone who has considerable expertise and success in acting as a coach for research staff in a laboratory may be much less effective with a sales team.

Listening

Coaches have to be very sensitive and conscientious listeners. The coaching relationship has many similarities with performance appraisal, in that the coach can only work to improve what the learner is able to acknowledge and understand. There will be a great deal of explanation and even simple instruction, but the starting point will usually be in the protégé's head, who will ask questions, express frustrations or describe a problem that the coach may believe to be the wrong problem. All the time the coach listens with close attention and works on understanding the questions, what lies behind the frustrations and why the wrong problem has been identified – and what makes the coach so sure it is the wrong problem anyway?

Schoolteachers sometimes say that gifted teachers are able to develop children's understanding almost entirely by getting them to ask the right questions. Coaches who can do this with adults are on the way to being outstanding, although the method has to be rather more subtle and not manipulative. The introduction to our Skills package had some advice on this, especially reflection and reflecting and summarising.

Evaluating

The coach listens to the protégé, listens to what other people say and can probably study aspects of the protégé's performance, so that there is a collection of information to process. The coach needs to be able to evaluate all of this data dispassionately but effectively, having the advantage of a degree of objectivity, and assembling it in a way that will make a constructive contribution to the coaching process.

Challenging

However true it may be that talking a problem through should enable a learner to solve whatever the career block may be, it is also true that few of us can do this with everything. We always tend to construe a situation in a way that puts us in the right. There will be times when the coach simply has to confront the protégé with a different interpretation of what is going on and challenge them to accept the validity of criticism. Some coaches who are not the direct line manager say that it is not their role to do that, and that challenging should be left to the manager, but that is just shirking the responsibility. A coach cannot just do the nice, 'agreeing' things, giving lots of understanding smiles and sympathetic nods of support. The coach is in a privileged position, being trusted to provide help, including guidance on what is wrong, however reluctant the protégé may be to hear it.

Practical help

A part of the coaching relationship will be to provide straightforward practical suggestions: 'Have you thought of . . .?', 'Have you spoken to . . .?', 'Would it help if I went through it with you . . .?', 'No, that simply won't work'.

It might well be thought that all of these great qualities are to be found in any competent manager, so that the learner automatically has the line manager as coach. However, not all managers have all these qualities particularly well developed, and there are advantages in the coach being outside the line. A 'supportive outsider' can be a help to managers in unravelling and evaluating the mixed messages they are hearing in the workplace, where custom and practice are lagging behind policy, which – in turn – appears to be out of line with organisational culture. However, a line manager may well be suspicious of supportive outsiders who appear to be giving messages that contradict what the manager is saying. After all, coaching is not quite the same as counselling, where an outsider has a better justification.

The solution to this dilemma seems to be to acknowledge that all managers need to adopt a coaching mode of working with individual members of their department, but that other supportive *insiders* could be called upon to act as individual mentors, where there is a good working relationship or prior familiarity between prospective coach and prospective learner.

SUMMARY PROPOSITIONS

Skills 4.1 Coaching is a way in which one person (the coach) enhances the working performance of another (the protégé) regardless of the level of job skill that the two have and regardless of the hierarchical relationship between them.

Skills 4.2 The career anchor is a concept of what is absolutely essential for the protégé to maintain if he or she is able to keep self-confidence and the ability to develop. These vary greatly between individuals and a coach has to understand what anchors each protégé.

Skills 4.3 Requisite qualities in a coaching relationship are for there to be mutual trust and respect between the parties.

Skills 4.4 Required qualities of a coach are: expertise in the job of the protégé, skilled listening, skill in evaluating information, an ability to challenge and a willingness to provide practical help.

GENERAL DISCUSSION TOPICS

1 How important is it for the coach to be (a) expert in the protégé's job, (b) older than the protégé and (c) the direct line manager?

2 What are the sort of career anchors held by members of the group? What career anchors have changed since members started with their present employer?

3 What are the problems for (a) the direct line manager and (b) the employing organisation if the coach is a supportive insider or a supportive outsider?

FURTHER READING

Caplan, J. (2003) *Coaching for the Future.* London: Chartered Institute of Personnel and Development.

Clutterbuck, D. and Gover, S. (2004) *The Effective Coach Manual.* Burnham: Clutterbuck Associates.

Clutterbuck, D. and Megginson, D. (2005) *Making Coaching Work*. London: Chartered Institute of Personnel and Development.

Clutterbuck, D. and Wynne, B. (1994) 'Mentoring and Coaching', in A. Mumford *Handbook of Management Development*, 4th edn. Epping, Essex: Gower Press.

Hawkins, P. and Schwenk, G. (2006) *Coaching Supervision – Maximising the potential of Coaching, A Change Agenda*. London: Chartered Institute of Personnel and Development.

Jarvis, J. and Lane, D. (2006) *The Case for Coaching: Making evidence based decisions on coaching*. London: Chartered Institute of Personnel and Development.
All the above publications include solid research evidence to produce a thorough assessment of current practice, including examples of good practice and guidelines for managers.

Schein, E.H. (1990) *Career Anchors*. San Diego, Calif.: University Associates.

Schein, E.H. (2004) *Organizational Culture and Leadership*, 3rd edn. New York: Wiley Publishers.
The 1990 book by Ed Schein is now not easy to obtain, although it contains the most thorough explanation of the career anchor concept. The 2004 third edition of his classic text contains a perfectly adequate treatment of the topic.

WEB LINKS

On the book's companion website, **www.pearsoned.co.uk/torrington**, there is supplementary material on handling group discussion as a form of learning. This is the usual method for social skills training and attitude development.

Another useful website is the site for the European Mentoring and Coaching Council which has recently launched a kitemarking scheme for mentoring and coaching qualifications:

www.emccouncil.org

EXERCISE

Coaches can only be effective if they listen, which is more than allowing people to talk and more than hearing what they say. Look back on the comments about listening at the beginning of this Skills Package and bear in mind this little SWAT homily about coaching:

- Find **Space** to listen by ensuring the meeting is private and free from interruption.
- Be **Willing** to listen, believe the protégé has something to say; make sure you understand; don't make any assumptions until the story is complete.
- Pay **Attention** to what is being said, with strong focus on the protégé.
- Indicate that there is plenty of **TIME**, showing no impatience.

Try this out in any one-to-one conversation with anyone and see how effective you can become at using listening to understand the other person.

The disciplinary interviews

The objectives of this part of Fundamental skills are to:

1 Review the concept of discipline

2 Examine the nature of interviewing in discipline

3 Outline an approach to disciplinary interviewing by suggesting a model sequence

In January 2008 a world-wide recession was nearly triggered by a massive banking fraud. Jerome Kerviel was a relatively lowly employee of the French Bank Société Générale in Paris who built up a series of financial manipulations which lost five billion euros of his employer's money. That is such a huge amount that it is more than the GDP of dozens of nations. When his employers eventually uncovered this catastrophe during 'an all-night interview' on 19 January their attempts to repair the damage and prevent any further catastrophe caused such turbulence in international money markets that the US Federal Reserve Bank reduced interest rates by no less than 0.75 per cent.

We do not know exactly what was said in the all-night interview, but it would have been in one way uncomplicated: no doubt about guilt, demonstrated by solid evidence, leading inevitably to heavy punishment. This part of our Skills package does not deal with such open-and-shut situations, but with those cases where someone is not doing what they should and the purpose of the interview is to correct the behaviour, if possible.

The least popular of all management activities is talking to people when things have gone wrong. Reading most books on management you might think that things never go wrong. The writing has such an upbeat tone that it is *entirely* positive, enthusiastic, visionary, forward looking and all the other qualities that are so important. Sometimes, however, things really do go wrong and have to be sorted out. The sorting out involves at some point a meeting between a dissatisfied manager and an employee who is seen as the cause of that dissatisfaction. Procedures, as required by law, can do no more than force meetings to take place: it is the meetings themselves that produce answers.

Many present-day views of discipline are connected with the idea of punishment: a disciplinarian is one seen as an enforcer of rules, a hard taskmaster or martinet. To discipline schoolchildren is usually to punish them by keeping them in after school or chastising them. Disciplinary procedures in employment are usually drawn up to provide a preliminary to dismissal, so that any eventual dismissal will not be viewed as unfair by a tribunal. This background makes a problem-solving approach to discipline difficult for a manager, as there is always the sanction in the background making it unlikely that the employee will see the manager's behaviour as being authentic. There will always be a feeling somewhere between outright conviction and lingering uncertainty that a manager in a disciplinary interview is looking for a justification to punish rather than looking for a more constructive solution. Our approach in the following pages is based on the more accurate notion of discipline as attempting to modify the working behaviour of a subordinate, with the modification not necessarily involving punishment.

Despite the difficulties, our aim here is to formulate an approach to the interview that achieves an adjustment in attitude, with the changed attitude being confirmed by subsequent experience. The manager believes that the employee's subsequent working behaviour will be satisfactory, the conflict of interest between the parties is resolved and the interview only succeeds when there is that confirmation.

Skills activity 5.1

What disciplinary incidents can you recall where the situation was not clear-cut and where an interview with a manager produced a resolution to the problem that was effective, although quite different from what had been anticipated by the manager at the beginning of the interview?

The nature of disciplinary interviewing

A problem-solving approach to a disciplinary interview is analytical and constructive, not only for the interviews that are built into the discipline procedure, but also for interviews that avoid recourse to the rigid formality of procedure.

In disciplinary problems there will be underlying reasons for the unsatisfactory behaviour and these need to be discovered before solutions to the problems can be attempted.

The discipline sequence

Preparation

The first requirement is to check the procedural position and to ensure that the impending interview is appropriate. In disciplinary matters care is needed about the procedural step, as the likelihood of penalties may already have been set up by warnings, thus reducing the scope for doing anything else in the impending interview apart from imposing a further penalty. The best interviews are where the manager pre-empts procedure, so the parties to the interview are less constrained by procedural rules. The manager will be at pains to explain that the interview is informal and without procedural implications.

What are the facts that the interviewer needs to know? Disciplinary interviews always start at the behest of the management so the manager will again need to collect evidence and consider how it may have been interpreted by intermediaries. This evidence will include some basic details about the interviewee, but mainly it will be information about the aspects of the working performance that are unsatisfactory and why. Too often this information exists only in opinions that have been offered and prejudices that are held. This provides a poor basis for a constructive interview, so the manager needs to ferret out details, with as much factual corroboration as possible, and should try to make a shrewd guess about the interviewee's perspective on the situation.

It is almost inevitable that the interviewee will start the interview defensively, expecting to be blamed for something and therefore will be ready to refute any allegations, probably deflecting blame elsewhere. The manager needs to anticipate the respondent's initial reaction and be prepared to deal with the reaction as well as with facts that have been collected. Unless the interview is at a very early, informal stage, the manager also needs to know about earlier warnings, cautions or penalties that have been invoked. More general information will also be required, not just the facts of the particular disciplinary situation under consideration, but knowledge to give a general understanding of the working arrangements and relationships. Other relevant data may be the employee's length of service, type of training, previous experience and so forth.

Most managers will benefit from advice before starting. It is particularly important for anyone who is 'in procedure' to check the position with someone such as an HR manager, as the management's ability to sustain any action will largely depend on maintaining consistency with what the management has done with other employees previously. The manager may also have certain ideas of what could be done in terms of retraining, transfer or assistance with a domestic problem. The feasibility of such actions needs to be verified before they are broached with an employee whose work is not satisfactory.

Where is the interview to take place? However trivial this question may seem it is included for two reasons. First, because we have seen a number of interviews go wrong because the parties arrived at different places; this mistake seems to happen more often with this type of encounter than with others. Secondly, because there may be an advantage in choosing an unusually informal situation, according to the manager's assessment. A discussion over a latte in the local coffee shop may be a more appropriate setting for some approaches to disciplinary problems, although they are seldom appropriate if the matter has reached procedure. Also employees frequently mistrust such settings, feeling that they are being manipulated or that the discussion 'does not count' because it is out of hours or off limits. If, however, one is trying to avoid procedural overtones, this can be a way of doing it.

> ### Skills activity 5.2
>
> **What incidents have you experienced or heard about where the location of the interview was clearly unsuitable for the nature of the encounter?**

The disciplinary interview

Discipline arises from management dissatisfaction so the opening move is for a statement of why such dissatisfaction exists, dealing with the *facts* of the situation rather than managerial feelings of outrage about them. This shows that the manager sees the interview as a way of dealing with a problem of the working situation and not (at least not yet) as a way of dealing with a malicious or indolent employee. If an employee has been persistently late for a week, it would be unwise for a manager to open the disciplinary interview by saying, 'Your lateness this week has been deplorable', as the reason might turn out to be that the employee has a seriously ill child needing constant attendance through the night. Then the manager would be embarrassed and the potential for a constructive settlement of the matter would be jeopardised. An opening factual statement of the problem, 'You have been at least twenty minutes late each day this week . . .', does not prejudge the reasons and is reasonably precise about the scale of the problem. It also circumscribes management dissatisfaction by implying that there is no other cause for dissatisfaction: if there is, it should be mentioned.

Now the manager needs to know the explanation and asks the employee to say what the reasons for the problem are, perhaps also asking for comments on the seriousness of the problem itself, which the employee may regard as trivial but the manager regards as serious. If there is such dissonance it needs to be drawn out. Getting the employee's reaction is usually straightforward, but the manager needs to be prepared for one of two other types of reaction. Either there may be a need to probe because the employee is reluctant to open up, or there may be angry defiance. Disciplinary situations are at least disconcerting for employees and frequently very worrying, surrounded by feelings of hostility and mistrust, so that it is to be expected that some ill feeling will be pent up and waiting for the opportunity to be vented.

First possible move to closure

If the employee sees something of the management view of the problem and if the manager understands the reasons for it, the next step is to seek a solution. A disciplinary problem is as likely to be solved by management action as by employee action. If the problem is lateness, one solution would be for the employee to catch an earlier bus, but another might be for the management to alter the working shift to which the employee is assigned. If the employee is disobeying orders, one solution would be for them to start obeying them, but another might be for the employee to be moved to a different job where orders are received from someone else. Some managers regard such thinking as unreasonable, on the grounds that the contract of employment places obligations on individual employees that they should meet despite personal inconvenience. However, the point is not how people *should* behave, but *how* they behave. Can the contract of employment be enforced on an unwilling employee? Not if one is seeking such attitudes as enthusiasm and cooperation, or behaviour such as diligence and carefulness. The disenchanted employee can always meet the bare letter rather than the spirit of the contract.

The most realistic view is that many disciplinary problems require some action from both parties, some require action by the employee only and a small proportion require management action only. The problem-solving session may quickly produce the possibility for further action and open up the possibility of closing the interview.

This simple, logical approach outlined so far may not be enough, due to the unwillingness of employees to respond to disciplinary expectations. They may not want to be punctual or to do as they are instructed, or whatever the particular problem is. There is now a test of the power behind management authority. Three further steps can be taken, one after the other, although there will be occasions when it is necessary to move directly to the third.

Second possible move to closure: persuasion

A first strategy is to demonstrate to employees that they will not achieve what they want, if their behaviour does not change:

'You won't keep your earnings up if you don't meet targets.'

'It will be difficult to get your appointment confirmed when the probationary period is over if . . .'.

By such means employees may see the advantages of changing their attitude and behaviour. If they are convinced, there is a strong incentive for them to alter, because they believe it to be in their own interests.

Third possible move to closure: disapproval

Another strategy is to suggest that continuing the behaviour will displease those whose goodwill the employee wishes to keep:

'The Management Development Panel are rather disappointed . . .'.

'Some of the other people in the department feel that you are not pulling your weight.'

A manager using this method needs to be sure that what is said is both true and relevant. Also the manager may be seen by the employee as shirking the issue, so it may be appropriate to use a version of, 'I think this is just not good enough and expect you to do better'.

We asked for a restraint from judgement in the early stages of the interview, until the nature of the problem is clear. The time for judgement has now come, with the proper deployment of the rebuke or the caution.

Fourth possible move to closure: penalties

When all else fails or previously discussed strategies are clearly inappropriate, as with serious offences about which there is no doubt, penalties have to be invoked. In rare circumstances there may be the possibility of a fine, but usually the first penalty will be a formal warning as a preliminary to possible dismissal. In situations that are sufficiently grave summary dismissal is both appropriate and possible within the legal framework.

Closure

We have indicated possible moves to closure at four different points in the disciplinary interview. The manager now needs to think of the working situation that will follow. In closing the interview, the manager will aim for the flavour of closure to be as positive as possible so that all concerned put the disciplinary problem behind them. This is achieved by careful summarising of who is going to do what, always concentrating on solutions to the problem rather than the person who has the problem. Then it is helpful to close by a positive look forward, such as:

> 'I'm sure we can deal with this over the next few weeks (or months, be realistic as well as positive) and then we can forget all about it.'

> 'After our talk I think you can look forward to a very satisfactory career here with us, but we really must crack this problem first, and then put it to bed.'

Where the outcome of the interview is to impose or confirm a dismissal, then the manager will be exclusively concerned with the fairness and accuracy with which it is done, so that the possibility of tribunal hearings is reduced, if not prevented. It can never be appropriate to close an interview leaving the employee humbled and demoralised.

WINDOW ON PRACTICE

The American Eric Harvey has reduced what he calls 'positive discipline' to three simple steps:

1 Warn the employee orally
2 Warn the employee in writing
3 If steps 1 and 2 fail to resolve the problem, give the employee a day off, with pay (Harvey 1987)

A similar, very positive, approach was outlined in a seminal paper by Huberman in 1967.

SUMMARY PROPOSITIONS

Skills 5.1 Disciplinary interviews are central to the process of sorting things out when there is a management/employee problem, but most managers dislike such interviews intensely.

Skills 5.2 Disciplinary interviews are one of the means whereby people at work achieve self-discipline and autonomy, reducing the need for supervision and reducing the need for recourse to the formality of procedure.

Skills 5.3 The disciplinary interview starts with an explanation of the management position, then ensuring understanding of the employee's position and focusing on the problem. If that does not produce a satisfactory result, the manager may have to move through three more steps: persuasion, showing disapproval or invoking penalties.

GENERAL DISCUSSION TOPICS

1   'If employees breach the terms of their employment contract, they should automatically be dismissed.'

    Apart from legal considerations, how reasonable do you regard this attitude to be?

2   Some managers dislike disciplinary situations as they feel they lack the appropriate authority; an American, Scott Myers, even wrote a book with the title, *If I'm in charge, why is everybody laughing?*. How would you deal with this uncertainty?

FURTHER READING

Disciplinary interviewing is not a popular topic in management books, but the following are very sound treatments:

Edwards, P.K. (2000) 'Discipline: towards trust and self-discipline?', in S. Bach and K. Sisson (eds) *Personnel Management: A comprehensive guide to theory and practice*. Oxford: Blackwell, pp. 317–37.

Harvey, E.L. (1987) 'Discipline versus punishment', *Management Review*, March, pp. 25–9.

Hook, C.M., Rollinson, D.J., Foot, M. and Handley, J. (1996) 'Supervisor and manager styles in handling discipline and grievance', *Personnel Review*, Vol. 25, No. 3, pp. 20–34.

Huberman, J.C. (1967) 'Discipline without punishment', *Harvard Business Review*, May, pp. 62–8.
A comprehensive answer to the second of the questions raised in the general discussion topics above can be found in:

Milgram, S. (1974) *Obedience to Authority*. London: Tavistock.

Milgram, S. (1992) *The Individual in a Social World*, 2nd edn. New York: Harper & Row.

WEB LINKS

www.ncvo-vol.org/workarea
www.cipd.co.uk/subjects/emplaw/discipline

Notes on certain key terms

This is not really a glossary as we have selected certain key terms only, and they are not simply defined but briefly discussed. We hope that this might act as a reminder, to some extent add more perspective and act as a way back into the text during revision and coursework preparation.

360 degree appraisal is an approach to appraising the performance of an individual that incorporates judgements by people other than the hierarchical superiors of the person appraised: peers, subordinates and sometimes customers. The objective is to obtain a balanced and unbiased assessment. (Chapter 5)

Assessment/development centres are not buildings or departments. They are approaches to selection that deploy a range of selection techniques, especially group methods, with the objective of assessing a person's potential for a post as comprehensively and as objectively as possible. The method was first developed in the early 1940s by the British War Office Selection Boards to select appropriate candidates for training as officers in the armed forces. It was forty years later that the approach was adopted by business organisations.

Usually a group of applicants for broadly similar posts are brought together for a period varying from a half day to two or three days to undertake various forms of assessment: work simulation exercises such as in-tray exercises, psychological tests, interviews, group discussion and individual presentations. The evidence from these varied activities is combined to assess the suitability of candidates for appointment or promotion to a post on offer, using a set of competencies required for the post and a series of behavioural statements which indicate how these competencies are played out in practice. The activities for each assessment centre event require detailed design to select the appropriate components to assess suitability for the specific post so that every competency will be measured via more than one task. Although assessment centres provide one of the most

effective ways of selecting candidates – due to using multiple measures, multiple assessors and predetermined assessment criteria – they are not as widely used as most other methods because of the resources they require. A variant is the Development Centre where the method is the same but the objective is to asses the individual development needs and potential of a group of existing employees. (Chapter 4, Chapter 6).

Behavioural competencies are used to define the behaviour associated with high performance in a role, and as a way of identifying employee development needs. A framework of competencies is first defined and then a list of behaviours is specified. Someone who can demonstrate the appropriate behaviours is deemed to have the competency that is being used. Competencies are broader than skills, which are seen as much more specific and more likely to involve manipulation, physical dexterity, analysis of systems, visual perception and spatial judgement. (Chapter 6)

Benefits is a term covering a variety of features surrounding a particular job that have some cash value as well as other attractions. The significance of these in the balance sheet of the business has grown considerably, varying between a quarter and a half of the typical employment costs. Pension contributions are likely to be the largest slice, but others include car allowance, travel allowance, subsidised canteen, staff discounts and free parking. Some benefits may be greatly valued by some but not others: crèche facilities, private health insurance and fitness centre membership are some that vary in the importance to individual staff members.

Best practice/best fit. This contrast is between two approaches to HRM. One approach is that there is a best way of doing things. Certain HR practices and approaches will always lead to competitive advantage for the business, regardless of the particular product market strategy being pursued: more advanced selection methods, a serious commitment to employee involvement, substantial investment in training and development, the use of individualised reward systems and harmonised terms and conditions of employment between different groups of employees. Best fit advocates argue that there is no single best approach to all situations It depends on the particular circumstances of each organisation. HR policies and practices must be appropriate to the situation of individual employers. What is right for one will not necessarily be right for another. Key variables include the size of the establishment, the dominant product market strategy being pursued and the nature of the labour markets in which the organisation competes. (Chapter 1)

Career Anchor is a concept developed by Ed. Schein of MIT, who has identified eight themes, one of which will be the guiding force that influences a person's career choices, based on self-perception of their own skills, motivation, and values. He believed that people develop one underlying anchor, perhaps subconsciously, that they are unwilling to give up when faced with different pressures. The eight (all self-perceived) are: technical or functional competence, general managerial competence, autonomy, security, creativity, dedication to a cause, challenge and lifestyle.

The salience of any of these will almost certainly change over a career, but someone anchored on security will seek this rather than autonomy in a career. The debate at the end of Chapter 2 was on the topic of work life integration, which showed that some people have lifestyle as their career anchor. (Skills package 5)

Coach/protégé describes the roles in a coaching relationship. Coaching is an approach that has come into management from sport where the role is either to provide co-ordination and overall strategy for a team or it is to enhance the performance of an individual. In sport it is almost invariably off the field, in contrast to the captain who is on the field. It is

working with the whole person of the protégé, not just in technical competence, so that the role is different from that of teaching: 'he teaches chemistry and coaches rugby'. It has been taken up in business as an approach for line managers in some instances, but also for other respected figures in the business, who can take up a coaching relationship with a person without having the direct line relationship. Protégés are the other half of the relationship, seeking advice and guidance from the (usually) older and more experienced or influential coach (Chapter 6, Skills package 5).

Cognitive dissonance is where a person is coping with inconsistent thoughts, beliefs or attitudes that make attitude change or new behaviour difficult. Parents who have always adopted a particular approach in their parenting, like smacking naughty children, and are convinced that it is what children need, might find it very difficult to act on advice that warns against smacking children. (Skills package 1)

Culture/Organisational Culture. In management circles interest in culture was originally an attempt to grasp the realities of collective life in a department or organisation that can not be easily seen and described with such identifiers as job titles, departments and organisation charts. Organisational culture refers to the beliefs, conventions and general patterns of behaviour that characterise a particular business or organisation.

Recently it has been especially important in explaining the differences in management practice in various countries, when business is being done between countries with national cultures that are markedly different from each other. Managers have to appreciate the important effect on human behaviour of the national culture from which groups of humans derive their identity. Singapore Airlines, for instance, had a world-wide system of performance appraisal, but had to adapt the system for application in their Bangkok office because of local religious beliefs about reincarnation and a consequent refusal to write negative comments about colleagues. (Chapter 14)

Demography/Demographic Trends. Demography is the study of statistical data which illustrate the changing structure of a human population. HR people have to understand the implication of predictions made by extrapolating these data into the future: demographic trends. To some extent this can be very reliable, so that the size of the population in a country between the ages of 16 and 25 in five years time can be calculated on the simple basis of finding out the current population between the ages of 11 and 20 and making slight adjustments based on current mortality data for the age group. However, there are less predictable social factors that affect the validity of some predictions. As the twentieth century drew to its close there was great concern about 'the demographic time bomb', which described the anticipated drop in the number of adolescents joining the labour force because of a declining birth rate twelve years earlier. The carefully predicted explosion never quite happened because the shortages were made up by increasing female participation in the work force and some increase in immigration. At the same time technological advances in manufacturing and agriculture reduced the demand for personnel at that time. (Chapter 15)

'Devolving to the line' has become a hot topic among HR people as it becomes increasingly necessary for line managers to control the HR aspects of management within their own sphere of activity. The concept has a number of difficulties. HR people fear they are relinquishing not just duties but also an area of expertise and line managers worry about the implications of the word 'devolving' or the logical derivative, 'devolution' with the connotations of shifting things *down*, as a dictionary definition of devolution is delegating authority to a lower level. Does this mean that HR are dumping unwanted chores, and who says we are at a lower level anyway? One way to get beyond these hang-ups is to talk of partnerships, where working relationships share both duties and responsibilities, respecting and valuing the different areas of expertise. (Chapter 13)

Discipline is not punishment, although punishment may eventually be part of discipline. The two main parts of discipline are a set of rules and a code of behaviour. A subsidiary part is punishment to correct disobedience. Within all of that there is a human need for explanation, justification and persuasion, as well as sound judgement to decide on appropriate punishments, if necessary. (Skills package 6)

Discretionary effort is what most HR practices are intended to achieve, as it is what people put into their jobs over and above the strict requirements of their job description, encouraging initiative, collaboration and 'going the extra mile'. Most people at work want this sort of opportunity, but they need the right sort of job and situation for it to be feasible. Some jobs provide little scope and probably have to be done in a very specific way, with initiative being a problem. (Chapter 1)

Diversity has become the clarion call to replace the idea of equality of opportunity and it is promoted as a route to being a successful business. The successful management of diversity is claimed to have clear business benefits. Valuing all employees giving them all opportunities to develop their potential, enables them all to make their maximum contribution. Employee relations, workforce quality and performance are all improved in terms of diverse skills, creativity, problem-solving and flexibility. These assertions all make sound sense, but they are value judgements that are difficult to justify on any other basis than common sense and fair play. Whether they actually move towards greater equality is still to be seen. (Chapter 10)

Employer branding is a relatively recent approach to recruitment, developing an attractive brand image of the business as an employer, so that potential employees regard working there as highly desirable. This means that any particular job opportunity is set against a background of the business being one where working is worthwhile. Whatever management strategies are used to project the brand it is essential that the projected image is rooted in the actual lived experience of employees; otherwise those who are recruited are not subsequently retained, and resources are wasted recruiting people who resign quickly after starting. (Chapter 3)

Employee involvement means management involving employees in decisions that are conventionally management decisions. The belief is that this leads to objectives being more effectively set and more efficiently achieved if employees have some say in decision-making, especially as it affects their own areas of work. Managers do not have a monopoly of wisdom and decisions can be improved by enabling other stakeholders in the business to scrutinise and make constructive suggestions. If the involvement is genuine, rather than cosmetic, then the implementation of initiatives will be more effective because of the old management saying, 'People will support what they have helped to create.' Research suggests that other benefits include lower staff turnover, lower levels of absence, the ability to attract more recruits and higher levels of performance.

Involvement must be genuine and not cynical or inadequate. There are many examples of managers using a form of consultation that is then apparently ignored. In some cases this may be deliberate ('We had to go through the motions of asking people for their opinions, but we always knew what we had to do.') In other cases it may be thoughtless, ('Well some of the reaction showed that they clearly did not understand the complexities of the issue.'). So did you ask an inappropriate question? Do you need to explain why the reaction can not be acted upon?

Involvement is most sensible on matters where there is an issue that clearly affects the people involved: not all decisions should be referred to employees, as they will either be disinterested or will feel unable to make useful comment, ('Aren't managers paid to decide on these things?') Involving employees does not reduce managerial responsibility. Ultimately it is for managers to make decisions and to be held accountable for them. (Chapter 8)

Employment Tribunals were first established (as *Industrial* Tribunals) in 1964 by the Industrial Training Act of that year, but their remit was greatly extended after the Industrial Relations Act of 1971, which introduced the principle of unfair dismissal to British law, and tribunals were its first judges. Tribunals now deal with most disputes between employers and their employees, or ex employees. Hearings are before a bench of three, one broadly representing employers' interests, one representing employees' interests with a third member who is legally qualified and who chairs proceedings. Appeals from Employment Tribunals go to the Employment Appeal Tribunal,

chaired by a judge, usually with two lay members. (Chapter 9)

Emotional intelligence has become a fashionable concept in psychological research and more recently has been popular in management circles. It is an attempt to expand our understanding of intelligence beyond the cognitive aspects which have been traditionally been used as the criteria for measurement. Pinning down a broadly acceptable definition is proving elusive, but its roots are clear. There were signs in the early work of Charles Darwin, emphasising the importance of emotional expression for adaptation and survival but rather more specific was in 1920, when E.L. Thorndike used the term social intelligence to describe the skill of understanding and managing other people. By the 1990s one of many more attempts was, 'the ability to monitor one's own and others' feelings and emotions, to discriminate among them and to use this information to guide one's thinking and actions.' This makes no explicit reference to managing other people, so it was not until Goleman's work, described in chapter 13, that the concept became popular in management circles. (Chapter 13)

Expectancy Theory is the reasoning that underpins a belief in incentives. First developed in relation to behaviour at work by Victor Vroom in 1964, it can be roughly summarised by saying that a person's working performance will be enhanced by the expectation that the performance will be rewarded by outcomes *that the person desires*, so some people will be motivated more by the likelihood of, for instance, promotion than by the possibility of more money (Chapter 7).

The 'flexible firm' is here in inverted commas because we use the term in a specific way. Any business needs to be flexible to survive, let alone prosper. We use it specifically to refer to forms of employment and work organisation that enable managements to use employees in a flexible way and which enable employees to get beyond the rigidity of the standard working week to meet the demands of their personal lives and domestic arrangements. Some jobs have become less secure in their contractual arrangements and some have required a greater degree of interchangeability of tasks and variations in working hours as employers seek competitive advantage. Employees, and prospective employees, have seen opportunities to work for limited hours or at unusual times that help them fit work into non-work demands. The patterns of work organisation have become central to the whole employment relationship and to organisational performance. The term 'flexible firm' was first coined by Atkinson (1984). (Chapter 2)

Globalisation/internationalisation describe two slightly different aspects of modern business. Many companies work internationally, importing materials and resources and exporting products and services. If their business expands they may appoint agents in overseas countries to represent their interests, or they may establish overseas subsidiaries. The company remains with a distinctive national head office and branding. Globalisation represents a further step as the company operates major businesses in different countries and regions. Its national identity is submerged beneath its global identity and branding. As these businesses grow larger and therefore more powerful, some commentators and pressure groups grow very concerned that their commercial interests can de-stabilise and harm the economies of individual countries, especially smaller countries in the developing world. (Chapter 14)

Hierarchy is a term that can be misunderstood as meaning only 'the people who are up there above me and making my life difficult'. Although a dictionary will include a version of that as a subsidiary definition, the essence of hierarchy is that it is a way of organising people, things or groups one above another according to some criterion, such as authority, status or skill. It is widely used in science to understand the observed characteristics of the natural world: kingdoms, phyla, classes, orders, families, genera and species. Human organising principles are not so clear cut, but any organisation has a hierarchy or hierarchies within it as an essential way of getting things done. Practice varies markedly between countries. (Chapter 15)

Human Capital describes the combined knowledge and experience of an organisation's staff which is a significant source of competitive advantage because the unique combination is difficult for competitors to replicate. Failing to engage, reward, develop and retain people effectively causes accumulated human capital to leak away to competitors, reducing the effectiveness of commercial defences and making it harder to maintain competitive advantage (Chapter 1).

Induction is managing the process whereby a new recruit is absorbed into the business and able to feel comfortable, confident and ready to deliver expectations. It is one of the main ways to reduce early wastage and places emphasis not only on necessary preliminary training in procedures and practices, but also offers socialisation into the social structure and norms of the organisation. (Chapter 3)

Job evaluation is a way of setting up hierarchy of all the jobs in the organisation in terms of the skills and expertise required and the demands the job makes. This is then used to establish a set of pay grades reflecting the relative worth of jobs within an organisation based on objective assessment. Its use has extended greatly over the last twenty years as a method of harmonising the terms and conditions enjoyed by different groups of employees, following a merger or acquisition, or the signing of a single-status agreement with a trade union. Equal pay claims are determined largely on the basis of job evaluation. Job evaluation is not the sole determinant of how much a person should be paid; other factors are the going rate in the labour market, the impact of incentive schemes, overtime and the value of certain allowances, like travelling and subsistence. (Chapter 7)

Labour Markets. All people looking for employment and all employers aiming to recruit seek out opportunities in the appropriate labour market, as each has different conventions, so it is essential to select the right market and to follow the conventions. If you wish to recruit a bricklayer, you would not advertise in a national broadsheet newspaper. If you wish to recruit a chief executive officer you would not approach your local Job Centre. Final year undergraduates who send out eloquent letters along the lines of, 'I believe that I have the right qualities to transform your business . . . . .' will usually be disappointed. Any large organisation also has an internal labour market where existing employees seek transfers or promotion. This needs careful management to ensure that the conventions are understood and the practices are consistent. (Chapters 1 and 3)

Leadership is a term construed in different ways. In chapter 12 we use the definition, 'Leadership is the process in which an individual influences other group members towards the attainment of group or organizational goals'. (Shackleton 1995, p. 2) The tricky bits in practice are 'influences' and 'group or organizational goals'. Is influencing done by heroic personal endeavour leading the admiring troops into battle, or is it done by patient and quiet empowering of people, both individually and in groups? Are the goals those of the leader – 'what I want to achieve' – or on the needs and objectives of the business? Is the leader needed to command or to facilitate? In some cases the objectives of the leader and the organisation are the same. If, for instance, Sir Paul McCartney is recording a new song, all those involved in the process recognise that it is his unique skill, flair, voice and interpretation that has to be captured. Although many people make a contribution, his wishes prevail: he and the product are synonymous. In most cases the situation is quite different and the over-emphasis on 'what I want to achieve' risks either flawed decisions or meeting the objectives of the leader at the expense of the group. (Chapter 13)

Management or leadership style. One way of looking at leadership or management action is to consider the character traits that the leader needs to possess. A contrasted approach is to try and understand the style or behaviours that a manager needs to develop to deal with particular jobs and situations. This is not so attractive to some actual or potential leaders, whose ego demands that they have the right qualities which set them apart as special, but emphasis on management style as a way of developing leadership in managers has become the dominant mode of thinking in management development and training. (Chapter 13)

National Vocational Qualifications (NVQs) are a peculiarly British invention introduced in the early 1990s with two objectives, first to enable people with jobs for which there was no qualification to obtain recognition and secondly, to standardise a range of existing qualifications from professional bodies. NVQs are set out as a series of job standards that specify the job tasks that a person needs to be able to do competently in order to justify the award of the NVQ at the appropriate level. By 2001 over three million certificates had been issued. (Chapter 6)

Performance appraisal. Everyone wants effective performance. The individual wants the satisfaction of achievement and results, managers want individuals to be effectively co-ordinated and productive, customers want a good product and good service at the right price, government want efficient businesses in a growing economy. Achieving performance is complicated. It is not simply paying people lots of money, although not paying people enough money may well inhibit performance. It is not simply being nice to people and releasing them from supervision, as they may do the wrong things. But how does anyone know that their performance is satisfactory? Sometimes performance can be objectively measured. The authors of this book, for instance, will have the effectiveness of their performance as authors measured solely by the number of copies sold. It is no good us blaming poor sales on the failure of the publisher to market properly, nor on the unfair growth of the second hand market, nor on too many competing texts. Numbers sold are the sole criterion of success or failure. Few people in normal employment produce performance that can be measured in an acceptable way by such precise criteria because the work they do is embedded among the work of many others. Disentangling the performance of an individual so that it can be measured objectively by an unequivocal yardstick is rarely possible: the performance has to be judged or *assessed* and all assessment involves personal opinion, attitudes, values and bias. Performance appraisal is a management approach which seeks to make as consistent and objective as possible the performance judgements by a variety of people assessing a variety of other people holding a variety of jobs. (Chapter 5)

Psychological contract is a concept that has been evolving for forty years, although it has only emerged in its current wording towards the end of the twentieth century. It is basically an unwritten contract between the individual employee and the employing organisation that specifies the expectations that each has of the other from their working relationship. An early formulation was by Enid Mumford in 1972, but thinking at this stage was quite complex and tentative. The term 'psychological contract' is simpler and has entered into general usage to describe the relationship more broadly than in the administrative detail of the legal contract of employment. (Chapters 1 and 8)

Selection criteria have to be defined and appropriate if a selection decision is to avoid bias, eccentricity or randomness. Currently the most widely used criteria are either person-based or competency-based. The first are specified criteria relating to the person to be appointed: qualifications, experience and so forth. Competency-based criteria are related to the job to be done or the post to be filled: what does the job require that the occupant needs to be able to do? These are usually contained in a person specification. (Chapter 5)

Short/long term orientation is a term coined to describe the perspective typically adopted by citizens of different national cultures, with short term usually associated with countries in the west and long term with countries in the east.

Trade union density is a statistical measure of how strong trade union membership is in a group of employees. The group may be a country, a continent, an industry, in a geographical area or among an age range or in any other grouping. The measure is the percentage of employees from the group who are union members. In the last quarter of 2006 the figure was 28.4 per cent. for the U.K. working population. Density is higher for women than for men, and higher for older employees. More than a third of employees aged 35 and over were union members, compared with a quarter of those aged between 25 and 34. (Chapter 8)

Unfair Dismissal is the novel legal concept introduced in 1971. It is when someone is dismissed in circumstances where the employer does not have a valid reason for the dismissal or has acted unreasonably. A dismissal is potentially fair if it is because of misconduct, lack of capability or qualifications, redundancy, retirement, a legal reason that prevents the dismissed person from doing the job (for example, delivery drivers losing their driving licence), or some other substantial reason. Constructive dismissal is unfair if the employer's behaviour was so unreasonable that the employee had no choice but to resign – but you must resign first rather than claim constructive dismissal and then hope that the tribunal will agree with you! Wrongful dismissal is different, as it is a breach of contract by your employer in dismissing you, typically by dismissing you without notice or without following a procedure required by the contract. Some dismissals can be both wrongful and unfair. (Chapter 9)

Validity was of great interest to early behavioural theorists as they asserted that any experiment had to meet three criteria: it could be controlled, it could reliably be repeated and the outcomes should be valid, in that the outcomes actually supported what theorists claimed to demonstrate. In HR this interest in validity is now mainly directed at selection methods. How valid are the various methods used in predicting success in the post by the candidate selected by the methods adopted. Some research suggests that assessment centres and structured interviews are the most valid methods, and that unstructured interviews and references are the least valid. Despite this unstructured interviews are the most widely used method. (Chapter 4)

Vicarious liability is the liability which falls to one person as a result of the actions of another. Employers are therefore liable for the actions of their employees *in the course of their employment*. The act must either be authorised or connected with an authorised act in such a way that it can be regarded as a way of performing that act. A court could decide that it was merely a 'detour', making the employer liable. An employee acting in his or her own right rather than on the employer's business is engaging in what the law quaintly describes as a 'frolic' for which the employer will not be liable.

Work life integration is a recent concept that has become popular in some of the more economically sophisticated societies in Europe, in North America and in Japan. It is the result of a sustained period of relatively full employment at the end of the twentieth century and into the beginning of the twenty-first. For some people the salience of work in their lives is lessening and they look to move from a life of total commitment to work, and possible high rewards to less demanding, or part-time work or self-employment in order to achieve a more welcome work-life balance or integration. A widespread employer perception of skill shortages has led to employer willingness to consider a variety of employment contracts and general flexibility so that organisational need for efficiency matches individual aspirations for greater control over their working. That is the theory and it is not clear how widespread mutually acceptable practices are. (Chapter 2)

Index